Turbo C®
Developer's Library

MW00561405

HOWARD W. SAMS & COMPANY
HAYDEN BOOKS

Related Titles

The Waite Group's Advanced C Primer++
Stephen Prata

The Waite Group's C++ Programming (Version 2.0)
Edited by The Waite Group

The Waite Group's C Primer Plus, Revised Edition
Mitchell Waite, Stephen Prata, and Donald Martin

The Waite Group's Microsoft® C Bible
Naba Barkakati

The Waite Group's Microsoft® C Programming for the IBM®
Robert Lafore

The Waite Group's Turbo C® Bible
Naba Barkakati

The Waite Group's Turbo C® Programming for the IBM®
Robert Lafore

C Programmer's Guide to Serial Communications
Joe Campbell

QuickC™ Programming for the IBM®
Carl Townsend

Understanding C
Carl Townsend

C Programmer's Guide to Microsoft® Windows 2.0
Carl Townsend

Hayden Books C Library

Programming in C, Revised Edition
Stephen G. Kochan

Programming in ANSI C
Stephen G. Kochan

Advanced C: Tips and Techniques
Paul Anderson and Gail Anderson

Portability and the C Language
Rex Jaeschke

Hayden Books UNIX® System Library

Topics in C Programming
Stephen G. Kochan, Patrick H. Wood

For the retailer nearest you, or to order directly from the publisher, call 800-428-SAMS. In Indiana, Alaska, and Hawaii call 317-298-5699.

Turbo C®
Developer's Library

Edward R. Rought
Thomas D. Hoops

HOWARD W. SAMS & COMPANY
A Division of Macmillan, Inc.
4300 West 62nd Street
Indianapolis, Indiana 46268 USA

©1988 by Edward R. Rought and Thomas D. Hoops

FIRST EDITION
FIRST PRINTING—1988

All rights reserved. No part of this book shall be reproduced, stored in a retrieval system, or transmitted by any means, electronic, mechanical, photocopying, recording, or otherwise, without written permission from the publisher. No patent liability is assumed with respect to the use of the information contained herein. While every precaution has been taken in the preparation of this book, the publisher and author assume no responsibility for errors or omissions. Neither is any liability assumed for damages resulting from the use of the information contained herein.

International Standard Book Number: 0-672-22642-1
Library of Congress Catalog Card Number: 88-61756

Acquisitions Editor: *James S. Hill*
Development Editor: *Jennifer L. Ackley*
Editor: *Albright Communications, Incorporated*
Designer: *Glenn Santner*
Cover Illustrator: *Geoffrey Smith/Graphica Inc., Dayton, OH*
Indexer: *Gloria and Bill Bjerstedt*
Technical Reviewer: *Michael P. Maurice*
Compositor: *Impressions, Inc.*

Printed in the United States of America

Trademark Acknowledgments

All terms mentioned in this book that are known to be trademarks or service marks are listed below. In addition, terms suspected of being trademarks or service marks have been appropriately capitalized. Howard W. Sams & Co. cannot attest to the accuracy of this information. Use of a term in this book should not be regarded as affecting the validity of any trademark or service mark.

Btrieve, Xtrieve, XQL, NetWare, and Advanced NetWare are registered trademarks of Novell, Inc.

dBASE is a registered trademark of Ashton-Tate, Inc.

Hercules Graphics Adapters is a trademark of Hercules Computer Technology.

IBM, IBM PC, and IBM AT are registered trademarks and IBM XT and PC-DOS are trademarks of International Business Machines, Inc.

Lotus and Lotus 1-2-3 are registered trademarks of Lotus Development Corp.

MS-DOS, Microsoft Librarian, Microsoft C, and Microsoft Assembler are registered trademarks of Microsoft Corporation.

Turbo C, SideKick, and Turbo Pascal are registered trademarks of Borland International.

Contents

List of Routines

Main Library

▼

Btrieve File System

▼

Novell Networking

▼

Preface

If you create programs, you have probably been faced with having to create solutions that you know someone else has already perfected. Perhaps you have also faced the perplexities of how to create high-performance intelligent routines for developing professional software. This text and its software secrets were created to aid you in these and other areas that plague software developers daily, and to enhance your abilities as a Turbo C developer.

The *Developer's Library* provides a comprehensive set of functions written by application developers in a style that is easy to use, learn, and maintain. The *Developer's Library* includes routines for

- menu management
- database development
- data entry
- screen handling and windows
- file management
- entry screen design
- printing
- sound
- networking

and many other areas that are used daily in application development. The thorough descriptions and explanations provide not only practical instruction, but insight into the conceptual considerations behind the solutions.

In addition to the individual routines, we present several applications, including

- a complete customer information tracking system
- utilities for assisting in using the library
- a pop-up calculator

These applications are not scaled-down versions, but what we actually use for our commercial products and in-house needs.

For those developers, like ourselves, who don't enjoy manually typing programs from text listings, we have an optional diskette package containing all the source code from this text. The diskette package also contains updates, additional routines not included in the text, and ready-to-use libraries for Turbo C.

We are sure you will find these routines beneficial tools for your daily application development.

Acknowledgments

We would like to acknowledge Jim Hill and the excellent staff at Howard W. Sams & Company for their support in producing this text, and Nan Borreson and the superb technical staff at Borland International for their assistance to us and other users in the industry. Special thanks to Tom Reinertson and Madelyn Poarch of Novell, Inc. (formerly SoftCraft, Inc.) for their technical contribution on Btrieve and XQL. We also would like to add a special thanks to Richard McKellar and Joseph Hongbo He for their contributions to this text and to our wives, Diane and Janet, for their support.

Ed Rought and Tom Hoops

1 Introduction

Why Use a Library for Creating Applications?

The Scope of This Text

Concepts Used in Creating the Library

Using the Library

Conventions Used in the Library

Sections in the Library

Hardware and Software Configurations

Ordering the Library on Disk

Global Variable and Btrieve Variable Files

This text was designed for the application developers of today, those daring souls that enjoy taking a concept and creating a solution to a problem. Whether you are a novice or a professional, you deserve the chance to eliminate the dreary part of your task—creating all those background routines that make up a high-quality professional application. The routines in the *Developer's Library* allow you to eliminate most of those little nuisance functions: performing tasks for menuing, data entry, printer control, network solutions, and file management. This library was designed for creating top-notch solutions. The routines are integrated into a complete environment that can be used to create applications for business, science, engineering, and other fields that require professional computer solutions. They enable you to concentrate on how and what your application has to accomplish rather than the tools you need to build along the way to create your desired end product.

The *Developer's Library* is a comprehensive collection of high-performance routines created by application developers. You will find that the more you use the library the easier it becomes to create those solutions you have always wanted. This text was designed to provide a thorough introduction to how the routines function and to act as a comprehensive reference guide for your day-to-day use.

There are three chapters of routines. Chapter 2 contains the bulk of the library and is not geared toward any specific software packages. Chapters 3 and 4 contain routines designed for use with the Btrieve file management system and the Novell Networking environment, respectively. These chapters contain solutions to selected application problems that we have encountered. They do not provide all the possible routines that could be created for these environments, but do give you enough material to show how to create your solutions when operating in one of these areas.

This library of routines aids you in creating applications with a consistent feel and look, and also allows you to establish your own methods and means for performing basic tasks common to most applications. When we began creating applications, we didn't have a neatly integrated set of routines to perform all the nuisance operations necessary for professional, high-performance applications. We assume that is why you are reading this text, to acquire an environment of library routines to supplement the Turbo C programming environment and begin that new project you have in mind.

The following pages contain the necessary routines for you to begin developing almost any application. You will find routines for

- sound
- menus
- string manipulation
- screen handling
- printer handling
- file management
- entry screen design
- networking

and much more. The true test of these routines is in how they perform and interact. You will find that every routine has been optimized for performance and flexibility. We made numerous design decisions during the creation of these libraries. Many times we traded flexibility for performance and sometimes we traded performance for flexibility. Each routine has a section that discusses the limitations and potential modifications—ideas for enhancing the routine's flexibility or performance and information about some of the drawbacks to those changes.

Why Use a Library for Creating Applications?

When developing software applications, whether a single package or an integrated set of application modules, users appreciate consistency in the way the application deals with situations. Consistency is one of the prime benefits to the end user when you develop an application with a well-planned library of routines. For you, as the developer, consistency is a side benefit. Your primary benefit is the amount of time you save by not having to create a new routine every time an operation needs to be accomplished. The *Developer's Library* provides the routines you need to perform your background tasks, allowing you to concentrate on how your application is to be designed and the routines needed to accomplish the application.

We acknowledge that our library does not contain the graphics, mathematical, statistical, or other specialized routines contained in many other programmers' libraries. Our goal was to provide not another set of stand-alone routines for performing single operations, but an environment of tools for creating your own applications.

By properly applying the *Developer's Library*, you can develop applications in the same manner that you would if you were using a database management system such as dBASE. When you use environments like dBASE, you don't have to worry about acquiring data, converting dates, creating menus, detecting printer errors during reports, etc. These functions are built into the database environment. Unfortunately, those database environments typically perform very slowly and you must work within their rules. By implementing this library, you can be released from those worries, and if you don't like the exact way they operate, you have the source code to modify. Not only can you do things your way, you can do them with increased performance. An application created in C with these tools will outperform most database development packages on the market.

The Scope of This Text

Teaching C is not included in this text, but we do pass on some of the concepts of proper application design. There are several excellent texts available. We strongly recommend that you spend some time browsing through the bookstores for a text that covers the topics that interest you. A text that we found very suitable for new and experienced C programmers is *Turbo C Programming for the IBM* (Lafore 1986). You will find that no matter how well-written a reference manual from a software manufacturer is, there are always areas that aren't covered to the extent that you need.

Concepts Used in Creating the Library

Many of the routines in the *Developer's Library* arose from a need and almost all were hotly debated as to implementation. The prime directive for all the routines during their phase of design was that they had to perform to the utmost of the machine's ability without overtaxing the programmer's ability to use and maintain the function.

C offers a wide variety of methodology and syntax for implementing a solution. We felt that a straightforward, unencrypted easy-to-read-and-maintain format for our code was best. This philosophy may not please the C purist, but it does produce routines that are not only easier to maintain but also easy to train others to maintain and use. Although C code can be so compacted that numerous operations occur on a single line, the coding, debugging, and maintenance time required can be extensive. Therefore, our source code is expanded for easier reading with little or no significant loss in performance or gain in object code size. When performance was of the utmost importance (e.g., screen I/O, string manipulations), assembly or tight coding practice was implemented.

Additionally, C's ability to use macros and typedefs were restricted, because many current C programmers have their own set of standard defines and typedefs. A new set could burden the user with inconsistencies or conflicts in the conventions used in their current routines. We also believe macros have the detrimental side effect of cloaking the performance or meaning of the actual code used to perform an operation (e.g., fgetc vs. getc).

We kept the number of required parameters to a minimum, because it is almost impossible to remember how to call all the other routines, our library routines, and the application-specific routines. This is also why you will find the names of the routines generally provide descriptions of the routine's function. We found it much easier to remember a routine by its name than to try to remember how we abbreviated the name.

To facilitate performance and ease of use, many of the routines use a short list of parameters rather than complex lists or record definitions. For instance, we have encountered routines for quickly writing to video memory that look like the following:

```
FstScrn(int  X,
        int  Y,        /*Screen coordinates*/
        int  ForeG,
        int  BackG,    /*Fore & Background attr*/
        int  BMode,    /*Buffer mode*/
        char *StrPtr,  /*Pointer to string*/
        int  NumChars) /*Length of string*/
```

Using this routine for writing a simple message such as *Testing one two three* at column 1, row 1, in reverse video, looks like this:

```
FstScrn(1, 1, 0, 7, 1, "Testing one two three",
       strlen("Testing one two three"))
/*an intermediate string could replace the two literals*/
```

In contrast, performing the same display with this library's F_Write procedure looks like the following:

```
F_Write(1, 1, Reverse, "Testing one two three");
```

Most of the routines in the library were designed with the K.I.S.S. (Keep It Short and Simple) philosophy. This design aids in creating source code that is easier to read, debug, and maintain for programmers that aren't familiar with the code's style. When you multiply one to five parameters by the hundreds of times a routine may be used, you can see that keeping parameters to a minimum is essential. Several programmers' libraries encrypt the exact usage of the routine into several numeric parameters. We found this made the finished code very difficult to read and debug. We avoided this where possible, but, in a few cases, you may need to look up format parameters to determine exactly what will be returned.

Another design feature of the library is the use of strings for most information that is stored or output. The flexibility provided by having your data in strings provides for easier manipulation and performance in routines that perform functions such as printing and screen display. Having numerical data stored as strings can be a performance hindrance in some applications, so you should convert your data to a temporary numeric variable and then perform your calculations. For example, if you wanted to calculate compound interest at 12 percent annual for 48 months, you could create a program like the following:

```
strcpy(BalStr, "1700");
for (C = 1; C <= 48; C++)
{
  gcvt(atof(BalStr) * 1.12, 16, BalStr);
}
Pattern(BalStr, 9, 2);
```

An alternate method that has superior performance is

```
strcpy(BalStr, "1700");
TempFloat = atof(BalStr);
for (C = 1; C <= 48; C++)
{
  TempFloat = TempFloat * 1.12;
}
sprintf(BalStr, "%9.2f", TempFloat);
```

When you make your decision on which approach to use, consider the following:

- level of performance
- ease of maintenance
- ease of construction
- ease of use

These are the primary considerations when creating any computer application, but not the only ones. You should use them as a basis for developing your own style for creating professional applications.

Using the Library

These routines are meant to be used with the large code model of Turbo C. However, all screen I/O routines and many other routines are compatible with the small code model. A program shell with the proper initialization statements and inclusions is provided in Chapter 5. This shell should be the basis for all applications using these routines. Turbo C version 1.5 and greater provides a librarian facility (TLib.exe) for managing all your routines in one library file. Microsoft's Librarian, available with most Microsoft compilers, can provide similar facilities for Turbo C version 1.0.

The library has several routines that can take advantage of definable information at run-time. For example, the routine Get_Video_Mode can load parameters from a configuration file set up by the utility VIDEOCFG (provided in Chapter 5). This utility can be run by the user to create a video preference file for color systems. Other routines with similar capabilities are Help_File and Menu. Help_File uses a standard ASCII text file for its information source. Users can modify the file for their specific applications and your application isn't wasting code space by having to contain the help text in the program. Menu has a similar benefit in that it reads a menu definition from disk at the point the menu is required, in addition to being able to use a simple literal definition. This also saves on code space and provides the ability to use the utility MAKE MENU (provided in Chapter 5) to modify the menu definitions without having to recompile the application.

The Developer's Library Header File (Plib.h) is required to compile the library routines and any applications that use these routines.

Developer's Library Header File (Plib.h)

▼

```
/*** Sound-related prototypes ***********************************************/

void Beep_Bomb(void);

void Beep_Hi(void);

void Beep_Lo(void);

void No_Sound(void);

void Sound(int Freq);

/*** Screen-related prototypes **********************************************/

char Blend(char Atr);

void Bomb_Mess(char *Mess);

void Clear_Frame(char WinColor,
                 int XTL,
                 int YTL,
                 int WinWid,
                 int WinDep);

void Clr_Scr(void);

void Cnvg_Mess(char *Mess);

int Cursor_Off(void);

void Cursor_On(int Cursor);

void Draw_Frame(int TLCX,
                int TLCY,
                int Wide,
                int Len,
```

```
               int Lines,
               char *Atr,
               char *Title,
               char WinBack);

void F_Write(unsigned int X,
             unsigned int Y,
             char Attribute,
             char *St);

void F_WriteXY(int X,
               int Y,
               char Atr,
               char *St);

void Get_Video_Mode(char *FName);

void Goto_XY(int X,
             int Y);

void Hi_Mess(char *Mess);

void Lo_Mess(char *Mess);

void Message(char *Mess);

void Move_Scrn_Mem(char far *source,
                   char far *dest,
                   unsigned len);

void Restore_Screen(char *WinBuff);

void Save_Screen(char *WinBuff);

void Scroll_Mess(int XL,
                 int XR,
                 int Y,
                 char Atr,
                 char StopEOL,
                 char *Mess);

void Set_Window_Attr(char Atr,
                     int  X,
                     int  Y,
                     int  Wid,
                     int  Len);

int WhereX(void);
```

```
int WhereY(void);

/*** String-related prototypes ********************************************/

char *Cen(char *CStr,
          char *TStr,
          int FW);

int Common_Chars(char *Str1,
                 char *Str2);

char *Copy(char *Source,
           int Position,
           int NumChars,
           char *Destin);

void Delete(char *DlStr,
            int Start,
            int NumChars);

char *Erase_White(char *St);

char *Erase_White_Begin(char *St);

char *Erase_White_End(char *St);

void Insert(char *ObStr,
            char *TrgStr,
            int Position);

char Is_Text(char *Txt);

char *LJ(char *LStr,
         char *TStr,
         int FW);

int Num_Chars(char Ch,
              char *St);

int Num_Decs(char *Num);

int Num_Ints(char *Num);

char *Pattern(char *RlStr,
              int FldWdth,
              int NumDecs,
              char *Buffer);
```

```
int Pos(char Ch,
        char *St);

float Range_Max(char *Rng);

float Range_Min(char *Rng);

char *Replace(char *Src,
              char *Target,
              int Position);

char *RJ(char *RStr,
         char *TStr,
         int FW);

char *Rpt(char *Rpc,
          char *RStr,
          int Repts);

char Str_IsInt(char *PNum);

int Str_Pos(char *SearchStr,
            char *TargStr,
            char CaseFlag);


/*** Data entry-related prototypes *******************************************/

char Check_Date(char *Date);

char Ent_Control(int LastField,
                 char DataBase,
                 char PageMode,
                 int *Page);

void Ent_Scr(int FieldNo,
             int X,
             int Y,
             char *Prompt,
             char *RType,
             char *Value);

void Flush_KB_Buffer(void);

int Get_One_Char(void);

int Look_One_Char(void);
```

```
void Input_Alpha(int Size,
                 char *ValSet,
                 char *St);

void Input_Date(char *Date);

void Input_Num(char *Num,
               char *Pattern,
               float Min,
               float Max);

void Menu(char *Command,
          int *IPtr,
          char *STag,
          char CaseSense,
          int WinX,
          int WinY,
          int WinWid,
          int WinDep,
          char BkGrnd);

int Num_Pattern_Size(char *Pattern,
                     int *Ints,
                     int *Digs,
                     int *Decs);

void Prompt(int X,
            int Y,
            char Attr,
            char *Prompt,
            char *RType,
            char *Value);


/*** Printer-related prototypes ***********************************************/

void Print(char *Str,
           int LnfNo);

void Print_At(int X,
              int DY,
              char *Strng);

void Print_Char(char PrntCh);

void Print_Codes(char *Sequence);


/*** File-related prototypes **************************************************/
```

```
char Copy_File(char *OFName,
               char *DFName);

char Created(char *FName);

void Help_File(char *HFName,
               char *HTitle);

char Read_Line(FILE *RFile,
               char *Line,
               int MaxLineSize);

void Write_Line(FILE *RFile,
                char *Line);

void Write_String(FILE *RFile,
                  char *Line);


/*** Time-related prototypes **************************************************/

void Calibrate_Delay(void);

void Delay(int MilliSecs);

char *Get_Time(int TimeFormat,
               char *Buffer);

char *Time_Add(char *Time,
               float Hrs,
               char *Buffer);

float Time_Diff(char *Tim1,
                char *Tim2);

char *Time_Sub(char *Time,
               float Hrs,
               char *Buffer);


/*** Date-related prototypes **************************************************/

float Cal_Julian(char *DateVar);

char *Date_Add(char *Date,
               int NumDay,
               char *Buffer);
```

```
char *Date_Comp(char *Date,
                char *Buffer);

int Date_Diff(char *Date1,
              char *Date2);

char *Date_Sub(char *Date,
               int NumDay,
               char *Buffer);

char *Day_Of_Week(char *Date,
                  int DayCase,
                  char *Buffer);

char *Julian_Cal(float JDN,
                 char *Buffer);

char *Month_Of_Year(char *Date,
                    int MonthCase,
                    char *Buffer);

char *M_D_Y(char *Date,
            int MDYCase,
            char *Buffer);

char *Today(char *Buffer);

char *Undate_Comp(char *CDate,
                  char *Buffer);


/*** Misc prototypes ********************************************************/

void Calculator(void);

void Install_Crit_Error(void);

char *Num_To_Word(float Num,
                  char *NumStr);

char Show_Dir(char *FName);


/*** Novell-related prototypes **********************************************/

char Close_LST_Device(void);

char Get_NPrinter_Status(char PrinterNo);
```

```
char *Get_NTime(int TimeFormat,
                char *Buffer);

char *Get_Station_Number(char *Buffer);

char *Global_Broadcast_Message(char *SenMess,
                               char *Buffer);

char Modify_LST_Device(void);

void Set_Spool_Flags(char PrntNo);

char Set_File_Attributes(char *FileName,
                         int Attribute);


/*** Btrieve-related prototypes **********************************************/

int Add_Record(char FileNum,
               char *DataRec,
             int CurKeyNum);

int BTrv (int OP,
          char *POS_BLK,
          char *DATA_BUF,
          int *DATA_LEN,
          char *KEY_BUF,
          int KEY_NUM);

int Change_Record(int FileNum,
                  char *DataRec,
              int CurKeyNum);

int Close_File(int FileNum);

int Delete_Record(int FileNum,
                  int CurKeyNum);

int End_BTrieve(void);

int Get_Record(int FileNum,
               char *DataRec,
             int CurKeyNum,
             char *Key);

int Highest_Record(int FileNum,
                   char *DataRec,
                   int CurKeyNum);
```

```
int Lowest_Record(int FileNum,
                  char *DataRec,
                  int CurKeyNum);

int Make_File(char *BtrvVar,
              char *FileName,
            char *FileDefName);

void Mode_Select(int FileNum,
                 int *Mode,
                 char *Title);

void Mode_Update(int FileNum,
                 int Mode,
                 char *Title);

int Next_Record(int FileNum,
                char *DataRec,
            int CurKeyNum);

int Next_Key(int FileNum,
             char *Key,
           int CurKeyNum);

int Open_File(int FileNum,
              char *FileName,
            char *StandardRec,
            int Mode);

int Prev_Key(int FileNum,
             char *Key,
           int CurKeyNum);

int Prev_Record(int FileNum,
                char *DataRec,
            int CurKeyNum);

int Record_Entry_Control(char PassThru,
                         int CurKeyNum,
                         int FileNum,
                         int *Mode);

int RMake_File(char *BTrvVar,
               char *FileName,
               char *FileDef,
               int DefRecLen);

int Search_Record(int FileNum,
```

```
                char *DataRec,
            int CurKeyNum,
            char *Key);

float Used_Recs(char *BTrvVar);
```

Conventions Used in the Library

During the creation of the *Developer's Library*, we made several decisions about what conventions should be used for variable names, library routine names, and their representations in this text. Being a multilingual developer, we faced two problems. The first required a compatiblility with our existing application, which was not compatible with the common C case convention. Secondly, after trying the common C case convention, we found teaching new staff programmers how to differentiate our library from the libraries shipped with the compiler was difficult, especially when looking for documentation. Therefore, both case conventions are included on the optional diskette, but our convention is used in this text.

We maintained a consistent pattern to variable and routine names. Variables are comprised of a leading uppercase letter for each primary word in the name. For example, BaseOfScreen can be identified as a variable because Base, Of, and Screen are capitalized with no separation between the words. Routine names use an underscore to separate the words in the routine's name. For example, Read_Line can be identified as a routine because the two words are separated by an underscore. This distinction will help you to read the program code and distinguish routines from variables.

A standard indention of two spaces is used for different code blocks, because fewer make it hard to read and more make lines too long when several levels of nesting are required.

In the routine and variable list declarations, variables are lined up with one parameter to a line. This is useful in reading the routine declarations and eliminating the missed parameter when calling the operation. Immediately after the declaration, we include a general comment to describe the purpose and use of the routine.

Sections in the Library

Each routine listed in the library has several sections of information about that routine, designed to provide specific reference or background on how the routine is used. The following paragraphs describe each section.

Description

▼

The Description provides a brief overview of the routine's usage and any essential restrictions or specifications. We kept the description short to allow fast reference when using the text as a reference manual after you have become more familiar with the library and its operation.

Routine Declaration

▼

The Routine Declaration shows the format used in declaring the routine. The declaration will show all parameters required, the type for each parameter, and the type for any routine, if applicable. When using the text as a reference, these declarations provide quick reference to calling the routine.

Passed Variables

▼

The Passed Variables descriptions show the variable's name, type, and general description. If the variable has limitations or specific requirements, they will be discussed in this section.

Global Variables

▼

The Global Variables that are set by the particular routine will be discussed under this heading. Each section starts with the variable name and provides a discussion of each variable and its limitation or requirement.

Error Codes/ Messages

▼

Error Codes/Messages provides a description of any errors that can be generated by the routine or any messages that may be displayed.

Discussion

▼

The Discussion of the routine's usage is a detailed review, providing background on why and how the routine was developed, how it should be used, and an overview of how the code actually functions.

Limitations and Modifications

▼

Most routines created by any programmer can be improved. This section provides suggestions for modification and insight into the limitations inherent to the routine in its current design. The limitations are normally imposed to improve performance or increase functionality toward a particular purpose. Undoubtedly, you will find more potential modifications for the routines as you work with them in your particular applications. If you feel that you have found some significant modifications that you would like to pass on to others using the library, feel free to send them to us so we can evaluate their inclusion in future revisions of this text.

Routine Source Code

▼

The Routine Source Code for the routine is included in this section. Before you begin reading the Routine Source Code for any of the routines, we recommend that you review the section in this chapter titled "Conventions Used in the Library," which describes our format for variables, library routines, and documentation. Knowing these formats aids you in understanding the routine's flow.

Sample Usage Source Code

▼

The source code for the sample usage is included in this section. In most cases, these are simple examples of how the routine is called. The sample shown with each routine may include the use of other library routines, which can be a source of additional examples of many of the routines. In addition to the samples shown, you can also use the Cross-Reference Guides (Appendix A) to find other library routines that use this routine. The sample usage programs, in most cases, show the minimum Turbo C elements required for the execution of the particular routine.

Sample Usage Output

▼

This section shows the output from the sample usage programs. If there is more then one possible result from the sample usage, some of these may also be shown. Please note that, because several of the samples perform a moving, colorized, or audible demonstration, this section will show only the final visual result from the sample usage output.

Hardware and Software Configurations

The library was developed for use on IBM PC types of computers under Turbo C. To transport the library to another machine type or extension of C, routine substitutes may need to be created for the routines that use machine language portions, perform DOS or ROM BIOS calls, or are keycode-dependent. Some examples of machine-dependent routines are F_Write, Move_Scrn_Mem, Cursor_On, and Cursor_Off. Even though these routines are specific to the MS-DOS and Personal Computer environment they can be emulated for other environments.

The routines included for Novell and Btrieve are specific to those software packages. The Novell operations were designed and tested using Advanced NetWare 86 version 2.0a. At the time they were created, this was the latest version, but, by the time this text is printed, there may be a new version to the Advanced NetWare on the market. If you are using an older version of standard NetWare (not Advanced NetWare), you should be able to use most of the routines. The Btrieve routines were developed with the DOS 3.1 Network version 4.04 and single-user version 4.11 Btrieve package.

Ordering the Library on Disk

For most of us, entering thousands of program lines from a book is not one of the more pleasant aspects of programming. So we also provide the *Developer's Library* on diskette. The diskette includes all source code for the libraries, the sample usage programs, and the sample applications in both lowercase C convention and our case convention. The diskette also includes any new additions and examples to the library routines that have occurred since this text went to print. To order the source code diskette, see the order form in the back of the book.

Global Variable and Btrieve Variable Files

In developing these libraries there were several areas where it was more efficient to create global values that could be used throughout the routines. The following paragraphs cover the global variables required to use the libraries and a sample record structure for use with the Btrieve file management system.

The global variable definition file is separated into five sections:

- video variables
- operation variables
- keyboard variables
- time-related variables
- Btrieve variables

The Btrieve variables have been placed in a separate file so they can be excluded from programs which do not use Btrieve.

Video variables provide global names for video-related variables required by the library. This section starts with the three main video attributes used in the library (Normal, VidHigh, Reverse). Then the colors set and used by the library routines are defined: Black, Blue, Green, Cyan, Red, Magenta, Brown, White, and BWhite (Bright White). These are followed by the variable Background, used to hold the current background color used by the video display routines. The last two video variables, WaitForRetrace and BaseOfScreen, are set by the library to maintain information about the type of video adapter installed in the computer system.

WaitForRetrace is set true (1) if the adapter is a color adapter. This variable will force the video display routines to synchronize with the display adapter's horizontal and vertical retrace signals. The retrace is required to eliminate flicker and snow that can result on color systems. This synchronization is not required on monochrome systems. The second variable, BaseOfScreen, contains the memory address to the start of video memory for the type of video adapter installed. This is used by the display routines to determine where to write information displayed on the screen.

The operation variables section contains five variable definitions: AbortPrint,

Bookmark

HOWARD W. SAMS & COMPANY

DEAR VALUED CUSTOMER:

Howard W. Sams & Company is dedicated to bringing you timely and authoritative books for your personal and professional library. Our goal is to provide you with excellent technical books written by the most qualified authors. You can assist us in this endeavor by checking the box next to your particular areas of interest.

We appreciate your comments and will use the information to provide you with a more comprehensive selection of titles.

Thank you,

Vice President, Book Publishing
Howard W. Sams & Company

COMPUTER TITLES:

Hardware
- ☐ Apple 140
- ☐ Macintosh I01
- ☐ Commodore I10
- ☐ IBM & Compatibles I14

Business Applications
- ☐ Word Processing J01
- ☐ Data Base J04
- ☐ Spreadsheets J02

Operating Systems
- ☐ MS-DOS K05
- ☐ OS/2 K10
- ☐ CP/M K01
- ☐ UNIX K03

Programming Languages
- ☐ C L03
- ☐ Pascal L05
- ☐ Prolog L12
- ☐ Assembly L01
- ☐ BASIC L02
- ☐ HyperTalk L14

Troubleshooting & Repair
- ☐ Computers S05
- ☐ Peripherals S10

Other
- ☐ Communications/Networking M03
- ☐ AI/Expert Systems T18

ELECTRONICS TITLES:
- ☐ Amateur Radio T01
- ☐ Audio T03
- ☐ Basic Electronics T20
- ☐ Basic Electricity T21
- ☐ Electronics Design T12
- ☐ Electronics Projects T04
- ☐ Satellites T09
- ☐ Instrumentation T05
- ☐ Digital Electronics T11

Troubleshooting & Repair
- ☐ Audio S11
- ☐ Television S04
- ☐ VCR S01
- ☐ Compact Disc S02
- ☐ Automotive S06
- ☐ Microwave Oven S03

Other interests or comments: ______________________________

____

____

Name ______________________________

Title ______________________________

Company ______________________________

Address ______________________________

City ______________________________

State/Zip ______________________________

Daytime Telephone No. ______________________________

A Division of Macmillan, Inc.

4300 West 62nd Street Indianapolis, Indiana 46268

22642

Bookmark

HOWARD W. SAMS
& COMPANY

NO POSTAGE
NECESSARY
IF MAILED
IN THE
UNITED STATES

BUSINESS REPLY CARD

FIRST CLASS PERMIT NO. 1076 INDIANAPOLIS, IND.

POSTAGE WILL BE PAID BY ADDRESSEE

HOWARD W. SAMS & CO.
ATTN: Public Relations Department
P.O. BOX 7092
Indianapolis, IN 46209-9921

HOWARD W. SAMS & COMPANY
HAYDEN BOOKS

The Waite Group's Advanced C Primer++
Stephen Prata
ISBN: 0-672-22486-0, $24.95

The Waite Group's C++ Programming (Version 2.0)
Edited by The Waite Group
ISBN: 0-672-22619-7, $24.95

The Waite Group's C Primer Plus, Revised Edition
Mitchell Waite, Stephen Prata, and Donald Martin
ISBN: 0-672-22582-4, $23.95

The Waite Group's Microsoft® C Bible
Naba Barkakati
ISBN: 0-672-22620-0, $24.95

The Waite Group's Microsoft® C Programming for the IBM®
Robert Lafore
ISBN: 0-672-22515-8, $24.95

The Waite Group's Turbo C® Bible
Naba Barkakati
ISBN: 0-672-22631-6, $24.95

The Waite Group's Turbo C® Programming for the IBM®
Robert Lafore
ISBN: 0-672-22614-6, $22.95

Programming in C, Revised Edition
Stephen G. Kochan
ISBN: 0-672-48429-X, $24.95

Programming in ANSI C
Stephen G. Kochan
ISBN: 0-672-48408-0, $24.95

Advanced C: Tips and Techniques
Paul Anderson and Gail Anderson
ISBN: 0-672-48417-X, $24.95

Portability and the C Language
Rex Jaeschke
ISBN: 0-672-48428-5, $24.95

Topics in C Programming
Stephen G. Kochan, Patrick H. Wood
ISBN: 0-672-46290-7, $24.95

C Programmer's Guide to Serial Communications
Joe Campbell
ISBN: 0-672-22584-0, $26.95

QuickC™ Programming for the IBM®
Carl Townsend
ISBN: 0-672-22622-7, $22.95

Understanding C
Carl Townsend
ISBN: 0-672-27278-4, $17.95

C Programmer's Guide to Microsoft® Windows 2.0
Carl Townsend
ISBN: 0-672-22621-9, $24.95

To order, return the card below, or call 1-800-428-SAMS. In Indiana call (317) 298-5699.

Please send me the books listed below.

Title	Quantity	ISBN #	Price

☐ Please add my name to your mailing list to receive more information on related titles.

Subtotal ______
Standard Postage and Handling **$2.50**
All States Add Appropriate Sales Tax ______
TOTAL ______

Name (please print) ______
Company ______
City ______
State/Zip ______
Signature ______
(required for credit card purchase)
Telephone # ______

Enclosed is My Check or Money Order for $______
Charge my Credit Card: ☐ VISA ☐ MC ☐ AE
Account No. ☐☐☐☐ ☐☐☐☐ ☐☐☐☐ ☐☐☐☐ Expiration Date ______

22642

Place
Postage
Here

HOWARD W. SAMS & COMPANY

Dept. DM
4300 West 62nd Street
Indianapolis, IN 46268-2589

InputAbsolute, RecChanged, PrintAtX, FieldLineNum, CritOperation. AbortPrint is set by the Critical_Error_Handler when the user aborts a print operation due to an error. InputAbsolute is used to determine whether or not the data entry routines should remove trailing white space from user-generated alphanumeric input. RecChanged is used by the Btrieve management routines to determine if the current record has been changed by the user, thus requiring the routines to update the disk file. PrintAtX contains the current horizontal position for output printed through the library routine Print_At. FieldLineNum contains the current entry screen field number used by the library routines Ent_Control and Ent_Scr. The last operation variable, CritOperation, contains the number representing the user's menu selection generated by the Critical_Error_Handler installed by Install_Crit_Error.

The next section of variables, keyboard variables, contains only one item, CurKey. This variable contains the value of the last character retrieved from the keyboard buffer by the library routine Get_One_Char. The value returned will be the keyboard scan code for normal keystrokes, and the equivalent negative value of the second scan code for keystrokes generated by command or function keys. For example, when function key 1 (F1) is pressed, Get_One_Char will return −59 because the scan code returns the first byte as zero and the second byte as 59.

The fourth section, time-related variables, also only has one entry: CalDelay. CalDelay holds the calibration factor used by the library routine Delay to adjust time delays to the clock speed of the system running your application. CalDelay is set by calling the library routine Calibrate_Delay.

The last section is a separate file containing one variable, BTrvRecInfo, which is an array of 20 structures containing information about the files available to Btrieve. This array structure reduces the number of parameters required by the Btrieve record management routines. The array contains the pointer to the standard data structure for your application (*RecPtr), the Btrieve file position information buffer (BtrvVar[128]), and the length (RecLen) in bytes of the data structure pointed to by *RecPtr. You can expand or contract the number of elements as required by your application, even though the array is shown as containing only 20 elements. If you change the size of this structure in the global variables, you will also need to change the external definition in each of the Btrieve routines.

Here is the complete listing of global variables (Plib.glo):

```
/*  Video Variables */
char
  Normal,
  VidHigh,
  Reverse,
  Black,
  Blue,
  Green,
  Cyan,
  Red,
  Magenta,
```

```
  Brown,
  White,
  BWhite,
  Background,
  WaitForRetrace;

int
  BaseOfScreen;

/* Operation variables */
char
  AbortPrint,
  InputAbsolute,
  RecChanged;

int
  GloRptLine,
  PrintAtX,
  FieldLineNum,
  CritOperation;

/* Keyboard variables */
int
  CurKey;

/* Time variables */
unsigned int
  CalDelay;
```

The following is a complete listing of the Btrieve variables (Plib.Btv):

```
/* Btrieve variables */
struct
{ char
    *RecPtr,
    BTrvVar[128],
    CurInd[256];

  int
    RecLen;
} BTrvRecInfo[20];
```

2 Main Library Routines

Beep_Bomb Produces a distinctive sound used by library routines to indicate fatal errors.

Beep_Hi Produces a short high-pitch tone used to indicate general errors during the execution of library routines.

Beep_Lo Produces a short low-pitch tone used to indicate data or entry errors during the execution of library routines.

Blend Provides integration of the specified video attribute on a string written to the screen with the attributes set for the current window.

Bomb_Mess Used for fatal error handling, executes a Beep_Bomb with a message on the 25th line and then halts the program.

Cal_Julian Calculates the Julian number of days since year 0 of the date passed.

Calculator Produces a pop-up numeric and date calculator for use in applications.

Calibrate_Delay Determines the proper number of looping cycles to use to create an exact delay time value for the library routine Delay.

Cen Centers the passed string in a specified length of spaces.

Check_Date Verifies that the date passed is a valid calendar date.

Clear_Frame Clears all text in a portion of the display screen.

Clr_Scr Clears all text from the video display.

Cnvg_Mess Divides a string into two equal portions and converges the strings from the outer edges of the screen until they meet in the center of the screen.

Common_Chars Indicates

if all the characters in a specified string are in common with the second specified string.

Copy Copies a selected portion of a string into another string.

Copy_File Creates a duplicate copy of a disk file.

Created Determines if the specified disk file has been created.

Cursor_Off Disables the display of the video cursor block.

Cursor_On Enables the display of the video cursor block.

Date_Add Calculates the date resulting from the addition of a specified number of days to a specified date.

Date_Comp Returns a string date in the form YY/MM/DD from a string date passed in the form MM/DD/YY.

Date_Diff Calculates the number of days between two dates.

Date_Sub Calculates the date resulting from the subtraction of a specified number of days from a specified date.

Day_Of_Week Returns the textual name for the day of the week indicated by the specified date.

Delay Causes a delay in program processing for the number of milliseconds specified.

Delete Deletes a specified portion of the indicated string value.

Draw_Frame Displays a window of a specified size with the designated title and border format.

Ent_Control Manages the looping structure for data entry screens using Ent_Scr.

Ent_Scr Provides the capability for user defined data entry screens.

Erase_White Removes all spaces from the passed string.

Erase_White_Begin Removes all leading spaces from the passed string.

Erase_White_End Removes all ending spaces from the passed string.

F_Write Displays the passed string on the video screen using the specified attributes at the indicated column and row. This routine is written in machine language and displays text rapidly without flicker or snow.

F_WriteXY Displays the string in the same manner as F_Write, except the cursor is placed at the end of the displayed string.

Flush_KB_Buffer Removes all characters remaining in the keyboard buffer.

Get_One_Char Reads a character from the keyboard buffer, accommodates standard characters and command keys.

Get_Time Returns the current system time in one of several formats.

Get_Video_Mode Initializes the global video control variables for the library display routines.

Goto_XY Sets the current cursor position to the row and column positions passed.

Help_File Provides an interactive on-screen help system based on a specified text file.

Hi_Mess Displays the passed string message and produces a Beep_Hi.

Input_Alpha Allows formatted entry of alphanumeric data.

Input_Date Allows validated entry of calendar dates.

Input_Num Allows formatted entry for string representations of numeric values with specified minimum/maximum values and in a specified format.

Insert Inserts a substring into a specified string at a specific starting position.

Install_Crit_Error Installs the library error handling of DOS errors.

Is_Text Determines if the string passed contains characters in the ASCII range of 33 to 255.

Julian_Cal Calculates the calendar date for the Julian date passed.

LJ Left justifies the indicated string in the specified number of spaces.

Lo_Mess Displays the passed string message and produces a Beep_Lo.

Look_One_Char Reads the next key from the keyboard buffer without removing the character from the buffer.

M_D_Y Returns the textual representation in a specified format of the passed date.

Menu Allows multiple screen capacity for cursor selectable menus or option listings.

Message Displays the passed message on the 25th line of the video display.

Month_Of_Year Returns the month of the year in a specified format for the passed date.

Move_Scrn_Mem Copies a specified number of bytes to or from screen memory and a specified memory buffer.

No_Sound Turns off any sound being generated through the computer's speaker.

Num_Chars Returns the number of occurrences of a specified character in a string.

Num_Decs Returns the number of decimal digits in a floating point number.

Num_Ints Returns the number of integer digits in an integer or floating point number.

Num_Pattern_Size Returns the maximum field length for a data entry field based on the pattern string indicated.

Num_To_Word Converts a real number to its textual representation.

Pattern Formats the passed string number to the specified length and number of decimal places.

Pos Locates the position of the first occurrence of a character in a string.

Print Outputs the passed string to a printer followed by the specified number of line feeds.

Print_At Outputs the passed string to a printer at the specified column followed by the indicated number of line feeds.

Print_Char Outputs the passed character to the current printer.

Print_Codes Prints the ASCII value of a textual representation of numeric values.

Prompt Gets the user's response to a specified message with entry formatting.

RJ Right justifies the passed string in the specified number of spaces.

Range_Max Retrieves the maximum value of a number to be updated by Input_Num or Prompt.

Range_Min Retrieves the minimum value of a number to be updated by Input_Num or Prompt.

Read_Line Reads a line of text from a text file with a specified maximum line size.

Replace Overwrites a section of a specified string with a second string.

Restore_Screen Restores the contents of a buffer to the video display.

Rpt Repeats the specified string the indicated number of times.

Save_Screen Stores the current video display memory into a buffer.

Scroll_Mess Scrolls a line of text from right to left in a specified window.

Set_Window_Attr Changes the video attributes of a specified window.

Show_Dir Produces a sorted menu of filenames retrieved from a specified directory.

Sound Produces a tone on the computer's speaker at a specified frequency until a No_Sound operation is called.

Str_IsInt Checks to determine if a string is an integer value representation.

Str_Pos Locates the first occurrence of a string or character in another string.

Time_Add Adds a specified

number of hours to the indicated time.

Time_Diff Determines the number of hours between two specified times.

Time_Sub Subtracts a specified number of hours from the indicated time.

Today Returns the system date in the form MM/DD/YY.

Undate_Comp Returns a string date in the form MM/DD/YY from a string date in the form YY/MM/DD.

WhereX Returns the current column position of the video cursor.

WhereY Returns the current row position of the video cursor.

Write_Line Writes a line of text to a text file and appends a carriage return and line feed after the string.

Write_String Writes a line of text to a text file without appending a line terminator.

This chapter contains the bulk of the *Developer's Library*. The routines described here do not require any additional software packages. The operations in this chapter deal with a wide range of situations encountered during the creation of an application. The routines are listed alphabetically to provide easy reference to the library. The more you use the library, the more you will come to appreciate the flexibility and performance of the operations.

Each section provides an in-depth description of not only the actual workings, but the concepts behind the design of the code. You may want to pay particular attention to the section titled "Limitations and Modifications." These can provide insight into additional ways to use the routines by making your own adaptations and help you bypass some potential problems in making modifications.

When you first begin to use the library, you may want to use the Cross-Reference Guide (Appendix A), located at the end of the text. This list separates the routines into several categories to aid you in learning which routines perform different types of operations.

Beep_Bomb

Description

▼

Beep_Bomb creates a distinctive sound that gets the user's attention and informs the user of a fatal error condition. The routine produces a sound similar to that commonly used to indicate a bomb dropping from an aircraft and exploding on impact. The approximate duration of Beep_Bomb is 4.5 seconds.

Routine Declaration

▼

```
void Beep_Bomb(void)
```

Passed Variables

▼

None

Global Variables

▼

None

Error Codes/ Messages

▼

None

Discussion

▼

Beep_Bomb provides a distinctive sound when a fatal error has occurred within an application. We simulated the sound of a bomb being dropped from an aircraft, with a short explosion at the end. This routine uses the Sound, No_ Sound, and Delay routines included in the library to create the effect. Sound, No_Sound, and Delay are also available in the libraries provided with Turbo C version 1.5 and later.

Beep_Bomb uses a for loop with a decrementing count to control the falling sound. Then a second for loop creates the reverberating sound to simulate the impact.

Limitations and Modifications

▼

The exact tone and duration of Beep_Bomb may differ from machine to machine due to the wide variety of speakers and hardware drivers used in creating sounds on PCs. You may want to adjust the value used in the Sound command to suit your particular taste.

Routine Source Code

▼

```
#include <math.h>
#include <string.h>
```

```
#include <stdio.h>
#include <stdlib.h>
#include <ctype.h>
#include <plib.h>

void Beep_Bomb(void)
/*
  Produces a sound similar to a bomb dropping.
*/
{ /* Beep_Bomb */
  int
    C;

  for (C = 5000; C >= 200; C--)
  {
    Sound(C);
    Delay(1);
  } /* for */
  for (C = 1; C <= 100; C++)
  {
    Sound(50);
    Delay(1);
    Sound(1000);
    Delay(1);
  } /* for */
  No_Sound();
} /* Beep_Bomb */
```

Sample Usage Source Code

▼

```
/*
  This program will call Beep_Bomb.
*/
extern unsigned _stklen=16384; /* Minimum recommend stack size */
#include <stdio.h>
#include <math.h>
#include <dos.h>
#include <mem.h>
#include <alloc.h>
#include <ctype.h>
#include <string.h>
#include <stdlib.h>
#include <plib.h>
#include <plib.glo>


/*****************************************************************************/
main()
```

```
{
  Calibrate_Delay();           /* Calibrate delay factor */
  Get_Video_Mode("Video.CFG"); /* Get display adapter type */
  Install_Crit_Error();        /* Set up application critical error handler */
  InputAbsolute=AbortPrint=0;  /* Initialize global variables */

  /* Application code to follow */
  Clr_Scr();
  printf("Beep_Bomb will now sound\n");
  Beep_Bomb();
} /*main*/
```

Sample Usage Output

▼

```
Beep_Bomb will now sound
```

Beep_Hi

Description

▼

Beep_Hi informs the user of general operational errors. This routine produces a 2kHz tone for a duration of 0.05 second. Data entry errors are indicated by the routine Beep_Lo.

Routine Declaration

▼

```
void Beep_Hi(void)
```

Passed Variables

▼

None

Global Variables

▼

None

Error Codes/ Messages

▼

None

Discussion

▼

Beep_Hi provides a standard tone for nonfatal, general operational errors not related to data entry errors and handled by Beep_Lo. Beep_Hi uses the library routines Sound, Delay, and No_Sound to produce the effect. Sound, No_Sound, and Delay are also available in the libraries provided with Turbo C version 1.5 and later.

Limitations and Modifications

▼

The exact tone of Beep_Hi may differ from machine to machine due to the wide variety of speakers and hardware drivers used in creating sounds on PCs. You may want to adjust the value used in the sound command to suit your particular taste.

Routine Source Code

▼

```
#include <math.h>
#include <string.h>
#include <stdio.h>
#include <stdlib.h>
#include <ctype.h>
#include <plib.h>

void Beep_Hi(void)
/*
  Produces a 2kHz tone for .05 second.
*/
{ /* Beep_Hi */
  Sound(2000);
  Delay(50);
  No_Sound();
} /* Beep_Hi */
```

Sample Usage Source Code

▼

```
/*
  This program will call Beep_Hi ten times.
*/
extern unsigned _stklen=16384; /* Minimum recommend stack size */
#include <stdio.h>
#include <math.h>
#include <dos.h>
#include <mem.h>
#include <alloc.h>
#include <ctype.h>
#include <string.h>
#include <stdlib.h>
#include <plib.h>
#include <plib.glo>


/****************************************************************************/
```

```
main()
{
  int
    Temp;

  Calibrate_Delay();           /* Calibrate delay factor */
  Get_Video_Mode("Video.CFG"); /* Get display adapter type */
  Install_Crit_Error();        /* Set up application critical error handler */
  InputAbsolute=AbortPrint=0;  /* Initialize global variables */

  /* Application code to follow */
  Clr_Scr(); /* Clear Screen */
  printf("Beep_Hi will now sound 10 times with a pause between soundings.\n");
  for ( Temp = 1 ; Temp <= 10 ; Temp++ )
  {
    Beep_Hi();
    Delay(100);
  }
} /* main */
```

Sample Usage Output

▼

```
Beep_Hi will now sound 10 times with a pause between soundings.
```

Beep_Lo

Description

▼

Beep_Lo indicates an error in data entered by the user. These errors can be from invalid keystrokes or bad data entered for a field. The routine produces a 100Hz tone for a duration of 0.05 second.

Routine Declaration

▼

```
void Beep_Lo(void)
```

Passed Variables

▼

None

Global Variables

▼

None

Error Codes/ Messages

▼

None

Discussion

▼

Beep_Lo provides a standard tone when actual data entry errors are encountered during the execution of an application. For example, if an invalid date is entered in the routine Input_Date, a Beep_Lo sounds to indicate that although the numbers entered are valid numbers, the date is in error. The routine uses the Sound, No_Sound, and Delay routines included in the library to create the effect. Sound, No_Sound, and Delay are also available in the libraries provided with Turbo C version 1.5 and later. Beep_Bomb and Beep_Hi also indicate other conditions.

Limitations and Modifications

▼

The exact tone of Beep_Lo may differ from machine to machine due to the wide variety of speakers and hardware drivers used in creating sounds on PCs. You may want to adjust the value used in the sound command to suit your particular taste.

Routine Source Code

▼

```
#include <math.h>
#include <string.h>
#include <stdio.h>
#include <stdlib.h>
#include <ctype.h>
#include <plib.h>

void Beep_Lo(void)
/*
  Produces a 100Hz tone for .05 second.
*/
{ /* Beep_Lo */
  Sound(100);
  Delay(50);
  No_Sound();
} /* Beep_Lo */
```

Sample Usage Source Code

▼

```
/*
  This program will call Beep_Lo ten times.
*/
extern unsigned _stklen=16384; /* Minimum recommend stack size */
#include <stdio.h>
#include <math.h>
#include <dos.h>
#include <mem.h>
#include <alloc.h>
```

```
#include <ctype.h>
#include <string.h>
#include <stdlib.h>
#include <plib.h>
#include <plib.glo>


/****************************************************************************/
main()
{
  int
    Temp;

  Calibrate_Delay();            /* Calibrate delay factor */
  Get_Video_Mode("Video.CFG"); /* Get display adapter type */
  Install_Crit_Error();         /* Set up application critical error handler */
  InputAbsolute=AbortPrint=0;  /* Initialize global variables */

  /* Application code to follow */

  Clr_Scr();
  printf("Beep_Lo will now sound 10 times with a pause between soundings.");
  for ( Temp = 1 ; Temp <= 10 ; Temp++)
  {
    Beep_Lo();
    Delay(100);
  }
} /* main */
```

Sample Usage Output

▼

```
Beep_Lo will now sound 10 times with a pause between soundings.
```

Blend

Description

▼

Blend returns an attribute with the background portion of the passed attribute byte set to the color currently in the global variable Background. The foreground color of the passed attribute is not affected, and the routine has no effect on monochrome displays if the video color variables have not been changed since being established in Get_Video_Mode.

Routine Declaration

▼

```
char Blend(char Atr)
```

Passed Variables

▼

Atr char This field contains the video attribute to be used with the current setting of Background.

Global Variables

▼

None

Error Codes/ Messages

▼

None

Discussion

▼

Blend provides an easy method of adjusting text displayed on color video displays to match the background of the current window. The global variable Background is set by the library routines Clear_Frame, Draw_Frame, and Menu. Background can also be set directly.

When using Blend, do not combine default foreground colors with the same default background colors. For instance, the default foreground for the attribute VidHigh (see Get_Video_Mode) is Cyan. If a window is cleared by Clear_Frame to a background of Cyan and the text is output in the VidHigh attribute (e.g., F_Write(2, 7, Blend(VidHigh), "Hi there")), the text will be invisible because the foreground matches the background (Cyan on Cyan).

Blend masks out the high-order nibble of the passed attribute and copies the value of Background high-order nibble into it. Get_Video_Mode sets Background to blue for color video adapters and black for monochrome adapters. See the Global Variables for a complete list of the available colors and attributes.

Limitations and Modifications

▼

The primary limitation of Blend is that it does not intelligently mix colors. It can return an attribute such as Blue on Blue, which would make the text invisible.

Routine Source Code

▼

```
extern char
  Background;

char Blend(char Atr)
/*
  This function will return the attribute passed in (Atr) with its background
  nibble set to the global variable Background's nibble.
    i.e., Clear_Frame(1, 1, 10, 10, Red);
         F_Write(2, 2, Blend(Normal), "Hi there!");
         (Hi there would appear with Normal's foreground in Red's
```

```
        background)
*/
{ /* Blend */
  char
    I;

  I = (Atr & 0x0f) | Background;
  return(I);
} /* Blend */
```

Sample Usage Source Code

▼

```
/*
  This program needs to be executed on a color system to see its effects.
  It is intended to demonstrate a usage of Blend.
  It will use Clear_Frame() to set up the Green color background
  and then use F_Write() to display some lines with and without Blend
  for comparison.
*/

extern unsigned _stklen=16384; /* Minimum recommend stack size */
#include <stdio.h>
#include <math.h>
#include <dos.h>
#include <mem.h>
#include <alloc.h>
#include <ctype.h>
#include <string.h>
#include <stdlib.h>
#include <plib.h>
#include <plib.glo>


/****************************************************************************/
main()
{
  Calibrate_Delay();            /* Calibrate delay factor */
  Get_Video_Mode("Video.CFG"); /* Get display adapter type */
  Install_Crit_Error();         /* Set up application critical error handler */
  InputAbsolute=AbortPrint=0;  /* Initialize global variables */

  /* Application code to follow */

  Clear_Frame (Green, 1,1,80,25) ;
  F_Write (5, 5, Reverse, "Here we set up a green background color first. ");

  F_Write (12, 12, Normal, "This is Normal attribute.");
  F_Write (12, 13, Reverse, "This is Reverse attribute.");
```

```
  F_Write (12, 14, VidHigh, "This is VidHigh attribute.");

  F_Write (19, 19, Blend (Normal), "This is Blend (Normal) attribute.");
  F_Write (19, 20, Blend (Reverse), "This is Blend (Reverse) attribute.");
  F_Write (19, 21, Blend (VidHigh), "This is Blend (VidHigh) attribute.");

} /* main */
```

Sample Usage Output

▼

```
Here we set up a green background color  first.

           This is Normal attribute.
           This is Reverse attribute.
           This is VidHigh attribute.

                  This is Blend (Normal) attribute.
                  This is Blend (Reverse) attribute.
                  This is Blend (VidHigh) attribute.
```

Bomb_Mess

Description

▼

Bomb_Mess informs the user of a fatal error that has occurred in the application. A call to Message points out the error, a call to Beep_Bomb gets the user's attention, and a call to exit halts the application.

Routine Declaration

▼

```
void Bomb_Mess(char *Mess)
```

Passed Variables

▼

***Mess String Pointer** A pointer to the string value to be displayed by Bomb_Mess. The display of the string pointed to will be truncated if it exceeds 80 characters in length.

Global Variables

▼

None

Error Codes/ Messages

▼

Bomb_Mess displays the error message passed in the variable *Mess.

Discussion

Bomb_Mess is a very simple routine in its execution, but very essential in any major application. The routine displays the message passed in *Mess by calling Message(), calls Beep_Bomb to get the user's attention, and halts the program by executing Turbo C's exit routine. We primarily use Bomb_Mess when the user should be informed immediately of a major error, such as corrupted files or bad conversions.

Limitations and Modifications

Because Bomb_Mess is used for fatal conditions, its use is discretionary. Areas where you would want to use Bomb_Mess include run-time errors, I/O errors, conversion errors between text and numbers, or any error that creates a situation where the process cannot be continued if the results are undetermined.

You may want to expand on Bomb_Mess to perform a more selective scope of data handling by hard coding error messages into the procedure and then passing an error number. There are several possibilities for performing elegant error handling with this procedure.

Routine Source Code

```
#include <process.h>
#include <math.h>
#include <string.h>
#include <stdio.h>
#include <stdlib.h>
#include <ctype.h>
#include <plib.h>

void Bomb_Mess(char *Mess)
/*
  This function will write *Mess as Message would, then call Beep_Bomb
  and finally terminate execution of the program. This function is useful
  for notifying the user of fatal errors.
*/
{ /* Bomb_Mess */
  Message(Mess);
  Beep_Bomb();
  exit(0);
} /* Bomb_Mess */
```

Sample Usage Source Code

```
/*
  This program will make a call to Bomb_Mess.
*/
extern unsigned _stklen=16384; /* Minimum recommend stack size */
```

```
#include <stdio.h>
#include <math.h>
#include <dos.h>
#include <mem.h>
#include <alloc.h>
#include <ctype.h>
#include <string.h>
#include <stdlib.h>
#include <plib.h>
#include <plib.glo>


/*****************************************************************************/
main()
{
  Calibrate_Delay();            /* Calibrate delay factor */
  Get_Video_Mode("Video.CFG");  /* Get display adapter type */
  Install_Crit_Error();         /* Set up application critical error handler */
  InputAbsolute=AbortPrint=0;   /* Initialize global variables */

  /* Application code to follow */

  Clr_Scr();
  Bomb_Mess("A Beep_Bomb will sound, with this message on the 25th line");

} /*main*/
```

Sample Usage Output

▼

```
A Beep_Bomb will sound, with this message on the 25th line
```

Cal_Julian

Description

▼

Cal_Julian converts a calendar date in the form MM/DD/YY to its equivalent Julian Day Number. The Julian Day Number is based on the number of days since January 1, 4713 B.C. (Julian calendar) and is returned as a floating number with no decimal.

Routine Declaration

▼

```
float Cal_Julian(char *DateVar)
```

Passed Variables

***DateVar String Pointer** A pointer to the string date, in the form of MM/DD/YY, to be converted to Julian Day Number format.

Global Variables

None

Error Codes/Messages

None

Discussion

Cal_Julian converts standard calendar dates to Julian Day Numbers. Because Julian Day Numbers represent the number of days in floating number form, Cal_Julian makes mathematical calculations with dates much easier to perform by allowing you to mathematically manipulate the floating number. When you have completed your calculations on the Julian Day Number, you can convert the Julian Day Number back to calendar date format with the Julian_Cal function. Cal_Julian is used extensively by the other date-related routines in the library.

Cal_Julian converts the calendar date by first parsing out the month, day, and year from the date string passed. These string values are converted to numeric values used in the calculation performed in the last line of the routine. The year value (YearV) has 1900 added to it prior to calculating the final value to adjust for the 20th century.

Limitations and Modifications

The only real limitation to Cal_Julian is that you will need to adjust the value added to YearV when the year 2000 arrives to indicate the 21st century. The value of 1900 was added to provide the proper century for the calculation, leaving only two digits required for the year.

You may also want to change Cal_Julian to use the system date to retrieve the century and modify the routine's offset. If you do use the system date, set the century in a global variable at the beginning of your application so you don't have to get the system date each time Cal_Julian is called. If you do get the system date on each calling of Cal_Julian, you may see a decrease in performance.

Routine Source Code

```
#include <math.h>
#include <string.h>
#include <stdio.h>
#include <stdlib.h>
```

```
#include <ctype.h>
#include <plib.h>

extern char
  Normal,
  Reverse,
  VidHigh;

extern int
  CurKey;

float Cal_Julian(char *DateVar)
/*
  Returns the Julian number of days since year 4713 B.C., Jan. 1, noon, from
  the parameter DateVar which is a date in the standard form MM/DD/YY.
*/
{/* Cal_Julian */
  char
    TStr[81];

  float
    MonthV,              /* Month value */
    YearV,               /* Year value */
    DayV,                /* Day value */
    Yl;                  /* Temporary work variables */

  /* Parse out the month, day, and year */
  YearV = atof(Copy(DateVar, 7, 2, TStr));
  DayV = atof(Copy(DateVar, 4, 2, TStr));
  MonthV = atof(Copy(DateVar, 1, 2, TStr));
  /* Adjust for the 20th century */
  YearV = YearV + 1900;

  Yl = YearV + (MonthV - 2.85) / 12;
  return(floor( floor( floor(367.0 * Yl) - floor(Yl) - 0.75 * floor(Yl)
              + DayV) - 0.75 * 2.0) + 1721115.0);
}/* Cal_Julian */
```

Sample Usage Source Code

▼

```
/*
  This program will allow the user to enter a date then compute
  the number of days since 4713 B.C., Jan. 1, noon, using Cal_Julian.
*/

extern unsigned _stklen=16384; /* Minimum recommend stack size */
#include <stdio.h>
#include <math.h>
```

```
#include <dos.h>
#include <mem.h>
#include <alloc.h>
#include <ctype.h>
#include <string.h>
#include <stdlib.h>
#include <plib.h>
#include <plib.glo>


/*****************************************************************************/
main()
{
  char
    TempDate[9];

  Calibrate_Delay();            /* Calibrate delay factor */
  Get_Video_Mode("Video.CFG"); /* Get display adapter type */
  Install_Crit_Error();         /* Set up application critical error handler */
  InputAbsolute=AbortPrint=0;  /* Initialize global variables */

  /* Application code to follow */

  Clr_Scr();
  TempDate[0] = 0;
  printf("Enter a valid date in the form MM/DD/YY: ");
  scanf("%s", TempDate);
  printf("\nThis is the Julian equivalent of the date you entered: ");
  printf("%10.0f", Cal_Julian(TempDate));

} /*main*/
```

Sample Usage Output

▼

```
Enter a valid date in the form MM/DD/YY: 02/25/88

This is the Julian equivalent of the date you entered: 2447230
```

Calculator

Description

▼

Calculator provides a pop-up calculator in your application that can perform numeric and date calculations. The calculator also has incorporated memory functions and operates in the same manner as standard algebraic calculators.

Routine Declaration

▼

```
void Calculator(void)
```

Passed Variables

▼

None

Global Variables

▼

None

Error Codes/ Messages

▼

None

Discussion

▼

Calculator contains a pop-up calculator that can perform numeric and date calculations. The routine can be used in your applications and is received well by most end users as an attractive and functional feature of an application. When called from within your application, Calculator will save the current screen, pop-up a calculator, and restore the screen upon exiting.

Calculator operates like a normal algebraic calculator with addition, multiplication, subtraction, division, and square root, and includes memory functions. You can also set the number of decimal places of precision used in displaying your results.

For date calculations, you can add and subtract days from a specified date or determine the difference between two dates. The options D and N switch between the numeric mode and date mode and are entered as if they were operators like + or −. To complete an entry sequence, press = or <RETURN> and to clear the displayed register, use C to clear all values in the display and E to clear the value just entered. When entering a number or date, use <BACKSPACE> to edit the value just entered. The calculator does not provide full field editing. To exit from the calculator, press <ESC>.

Calculator begins by saving the screen display, cursor format, and cursor location for restoration at the end of the routine. The local variables are then initialized and the calculator is displayed on the screen. Next, a while loop continues acquiring and processing user commands until an Escape is pressed. The first section in the loop is governed by an if conditional based on what mode the calculator is in, Numeric or Date. If the mode is Numeric, Calculator displays the current calculator register values and waits for the user to press a key. Once a key is pressed, a switch statement evaluates the procedures required to fulfill the desired operation. If the mode is set for Date operation, a similar switch statement interprets the keystrokes. When the user presses Escape, Calculator restores the screen and the cursor format, and positions the cursor at its original location.

Limitations and Modifications

▼

Even though this calculator is versatile, there is still a lot of room for adding additional features and options. For example, you could change the data entry to use the library entry routines, add a simulated tape display, or add financial or programming calculation options. This routine provides a starter kit that you can modify to your taste for using in your applications.

Routine Source Code

▼

```
#include <math.h>
#include <stdio.h>
#include <stdlib.h>
#include <mem.h>
#include <dos.h>
#include <alloc.h>
#include <ctype.h>
#include <string.h>
#include <plib.h>

extern char
  Reverse,
  VidHigh,
  Normal;

extern int
  CurKey;

/*
  This is a routine used by Calculator to perform the actual calculations
  for numbers.
*/
void Perform_Chain(char *OpStr,
                   char *RegX,
                   double *Result)
/*
  This routine will perform the actual operation.
*/
{ /* Perform_Chain */
  if (Is_Text(OpStr))
  {
    switch (OpStr[0])
    {
      case '+':
        (*Result) += atof(RegX);
      break;
      case '-':
        (*Result) -= atof(RegX);
```

```
      break;
      case '*':
        (*Result) *= atof(RegX);
      break;
      case '/':
        if (atof(RegX) != 0.0)
          (*Result) /= atof(RegX);
        else
          Hi_Mess("Error - cannot divide by zero");
      break;
      case '=':
        OpStr[0] = 0;
      break;
    } /* switch */
  } /* if Is_Text(OpStr) */
  else
    (*Result) = atof(RegX);
}/* Perform_Chain */

void Calculator(void)
/*
  Pop-Up calculator procedure.
*/
{ /* Calculator */

  char
    Abort,
    Operation,
    CalcMode,
    ResultStr[31],
    RegX[31],
    XDate[31],
    XDay[31],
    YDate[31],
    OpStr[31],
    TStr[81],
    TStr1[81],
    OldScreen[4000];

  int
    Dummy,
    Precision,
    OldCursor,
    OldX,
    OldY;

  double
    Result,
```

```
  CalcMem;

/* Save the current screen, initialize variables and draw the calculator. */
Save_Screen(OldScreen);
OldX = WhereX();
OldY = WhereY();
OldCursor = Cursor_Off();
Precision = 2;
CalcMode = 'N';
OpStr[0] = 0;
Result = 0.0;
Operation = 1;
Abort = 0;
strcpy(RegX, "0");
Today(XDate);
XDay[0] = 0;
CalcMem = 0.0;
F_Write(40, 2, VidHigh, "╔══════════════════════════════╗");
F_Write(40, 3, VidHigh, "║║Result                      ║║");
F_Write(40, 4, VidHigh, "║║████████████████████████████║║");
F_Write(40, 5, VidHigh, "║╠════════════════════════════╣║");
F_Write(40, 6, VidHigh, "║║Entry              Operation║║");
F_Write(40, 7, VidHigh, "║║████████████████████ ███████║║");
F_Write(40, 8, VidHigh, "║╠════════════════════════════╣║");
F_Write(40, 9, VidHigh, "║║── Numeric ──┬── Memory ──║║");
F_Write(40, 10, VidHigh, "║║+ add         │press M then ║║");
F_Write(40, 11, VidHigh, "║║- subtract    │ +  -  *  /  ║║");
F_Write(40, 12, VidHigh, "║║* multiply    │Recall Clear ║║");
F_Write(40, 13, VidHigh, "║║/ divide      ├─────────────║║");
F_Write(40, 14, VidHigh, "║║= or <RETURN> │C  clear all ║║");
F_Write(40, 15, VidHigh, "║║              │E  clear ent ║║");
F_Write(40, 16, VidHigh, "║║─── Dates ────┼──── Misc ───║║");
F_Write(40, 17, VidHigh, "║║  MM/DD/YY    │N numeric    ║║");
F_Write(40, 18, VidHigh, "║║+ # of days   │D date       ║║");
F_Write(40, 19, VidHigh, "║║- # of days   │P Precision  ║║");
F_Write(40, 20, VidHigh, "║║F difference  │S square root║║");
F_Write(40, 21, VidHigh, "║║  between dates│<ESC> exit  ║║");
F_Write(40, 22, VidHigh, "╚══════════════════════════════╝");
while (!Abort)
{
  if (CalcMode == 'N')
  {
    strcpy(TStr, "%30.");
    itoa(Precision, TStr + 4, 10);
    strcat(TStr, "f");
    sprintf(ResultStr, TStr, Result);
    F_Write(42, 4, Reverse, RJ(ResultStr, TStr, 30));
    F_Write(42, 7, Reverse, RJ(RegX, TStr, 20));
```

```
F_Write(63, 7, Reverse, Cen(OpStr, TStr, 9));
F_Write(55, 3, Normal, Cen("Numeric", TStr, 10));
Get_One_Char();
Message("");
if (CurKey > 0)
{
  switch(CurKey)
  {
    case 48: /* 0...9 */
    case 49:
    case 50:
    case 51:
    case 52:
    case 53:
    case 54:
    case 55:
    case 56:
    case 57:
      if (Operation)
      {
        RegX[0] = 0;
        Operation = 0;
      }
      if (strcmp(OpStr, "=") == 0)
        OpStr[0] = 0;
      if (strlen(RegX)<18)
      {
        RegX[strlen(RegX)+1] = 0;
        RegX[strlen(RegX)] = CurKey;
      }
      else
        Lo_Mess("Too much input");
    break;

    case 46:  /* . */
      if (Operation)
        RegX[0] = 0;
      if (Pos('.', RegX) == 0)
        strcat(RegX, ".");
      else
        Lo_Mess("Decimal point already in field");
      Operation = 0;
    break;

    case 78:  /* N, n */
    case 110:
      Lo_Mess("Numeric mode already engaged");
    break;
```

```
case 68:  /* D, d */
case 100:
  CalcMode = 'D';
  F_Write(43, 4, Reverse, Rpt(" ", TStr, 29));
break;

case 80:  /* P, p */
case 112:
  do
  {
    F_WriteXY(42, 7, Reverse, LJ("Decimals 0...9 :", TStr, 20));
    Get_One_Char();
    Precision = CurKey-48;
    if ((Precision > 9) || (Precision < 0) && (CurKey != 27))
      Hi_Mess("Decimal specification must be between 0 and 9");
  } while (!(((Precision < 10) && (Precision >= 0)) ||
            (CurKey == 27)));
break;

case 45:  /* - */
  Perform_Chain(OpStr, RegX, &Result);
  strcpy(OpStr, "-");
  Operation = 1;
break;

case 43:  /* + */
  Perform_Chain(OpStr, RegX, &Result);
  strcpy(OpStr, "+");
  Operation = 1;
break;

case 47:  /* / */
  Perform_Chain(OpStr, RegX, &Result);
  strcpy(OpStr, "/");
  Operation = 1;
break;

case 42:  /* * */
  Perform_Chain(OpStr, RegX, &Result);
  strcpy(OpStr, "*");
  Operation = 1;
break;

case 8: /* Backspace */
  if (strlen(RegX) > 0)
    Delete(RegX, strlen(RegX), 1);
  else
    Lo_Mess("Nothing to delete");
```

```
break;

case 83:  /* S, s */
case 115:
  if (atof(RegX) >= 0.0)
    Result = sqrt(atof(RegX));
  else
    Hi_Mess("Error - cannot find root of a negative number");
  Operation = 1;
  OpStr[0] = 0;
break;

case 99: /* C, c */
case 67:
  strcpy(RegX, "0");
  Result = 0.0;
  Operation = 1;
  OpStr[0] = 0;
break;

case 69: /* E, e */
case 101:
  strcpy(RegX, "0");
  Operation = 1;
break;

case 77: /* M, m */
case 109:
  F_Write(1, 25, Reverse,
      Cen("Enter CalcMem operation (+, -, *, /, Clear, Recall)",
         TStr, 80));
  Get_One_Char();
  switch (CurKey)
  {
    case 43:  /* + */
      CalcMem += atof(RegX);
    break;
    case 45:  /* - */
      CalcMem -= atof(RegX);
    break;
    case 42:  /* * */
      CalcMem *= atof(RegX);
    break;
    case 47:  /* / */
      if (atof(RegX) == 0.0)
        Hi_Mess("Error - cannot divide by zero");
      else
        CalcMem /= atof(RegX);
```

```
          break;
          case 67: /* C, c */
          case 99:
            CalcMem = 0.0;
          break;
          case 82: /* R, r */
          case 114:
            strcpy(RegX, ecvt(CalcMem, Precision, &Dummy, &Dummy));
          break;
          case 27: /* Esc */
            Abort = 1;
          break;
          default:
            Lo_Mess("No such CalcMem function available");
          break;
        }
        if (CalcMem == 0.0)
          F_Write(67, 3, Normal, " ");
        else
          F_Write(67, 3, Normal, "M");
        Message("");
        Operation = 1;
      break;

      case 13: /* ENTER, = */
      case 61:
        if (OpStr[0])
        {
          switch (CalcMode)
          {
            case 'N':
              switch (OpStr[0])
              {
                case '*':
                  Result *= atof(RegX);
                break;
                case '/':
                  if (atof(RegX) != 0.0)
                    Result /= atof(RegX);
                  else
                    Hi_Mess("Error - cannot divide by zero");
                break;
                case '+':
                  Result += atof(RegX);
                break;
                case '-':
                  Result -= atof(RegX);
                break;
```

```
                } /* switch OpStr[0] */
                break;
                case 'D':;
                break;
              } /* switch CalcMode */
              strcpy(OpStr, "=");
              Operation = 1;
            } /* if OpStr[0] */
            else
              Lo_Mess("No operation specified");
          break;

          case 27: /* Esc*/
            Abort = 1;
          break;

          default:
            Hi_Mess("No such function");
          break;
        } /* switch */
      } /* if CurKey */
      else
        Lo_Mess("Bad key pressed");
    } /* if CalcMode */
    else  /* Dates */
    {
      F_Write(55, 3, Normal, Cen("DATES", TStr, 10));
      F_Write(1, 25, Reverse, Cen("Enter date and press <Return>", TStr,
              80));
      F_Write(63, 7, Reverse, Rpt(" ", TStr, 9));
      Cursor_On(OldCursor);
      Prompt(42, 7, Normal, "Date:         ", "C", XDate);
      Erase_White(XDate);
      if (!XDate[0])
        Today(XDate);
      Cursor_Off();
      F_Write(42, 4, Reverse, RJ(XDate, TStr, 30));
      if (CurKey != 27)
      {
        F_Write(1, 25, Reverse, Cen("Enter operation", TStr, 80));
        Get_One_Char();
        Cursor_On(OldCursor);
        switch (CurKey)
        {
          case 43: /* +, - */
          case 45:
            OpStr[0] = CurKey;
            OpStr[1] = 0;
```

```
        XDay[0] = 0;
        F_Write(1, 25, Reverse, Cen(
   "Enter the number of days to be added or subtracted and press <Return>",
            TStr, 80));
        F_Write(42, 4, Reverse, Cen(XDate, TStr, 30));
        F_Write(63, 7, Reverse, Cen(OpStr, TStr, 9));
        Prompt(42, 7, Reverse, "# Days:         ", "5I,0 20000", XDay);
        Erase_White(XDay);
        if (!XDay[0])
          strcpy(XDay, "0");
        if (CurKey != 27)
        {
          switch (OpStr[0])
          {
            case '+':
              strcpy(XDate, Date_Add(XDate, atoi(XDay), TStr));
            break;
            case '-':
              strcpy(XDate, Date_Sub(XDate, atoi(XDay), TStr));
            break;
          } /* switch OpStr[0] */
        } /* if CurKey */
        F_Write(42, 4, Reverse, Cen(XDate, TStr, 30));
      break;

      case 78: /* N, n */
      case 110:
        Message("");
        Cursor_Off();
        CalcMode = 'N';
      break;
      case 68:  /*D, d*/
      case 100:
        Lo_Mess("Date mode already engaged");
      break;
      case 70: /*F, f*/
      case 102:
        F_Write(1, 25, Reverse,
                Cen("Enter second date and press <Return>", TStr, 80));
        F_Write(63, 7, Reverse, Cen("F", TStr, 9));
        YDate[0] = 0;
        Prompt(42, 7, Normal, " - DATE:    ", "C", YDate);
        if (!YDate[0])
        {
          Today(YDate);
          F_WriteXY(WhereX(), WhereY(), Reverse, YDate);
        } /* if !YDate[0] */
        if (CurKey != 27)
```

```
          {
            sprintf(TStr1, "# Days difference = %d", Date_Diff(XDate,
                    YDate));
            F_Write(42, 4, Reverse, Cen(TStr1, TStr, 30));
          } /* if CurKey */
          strcpy(XDate, YDate);
        break;

        case 27:
          Abort = 1;
        break;

        default:
          Hi_Mess("No such operation");
        break;
      } /* switch CurKey */
    } /* if CurKey */
    else
      Abort = 1;
  }  /* if CalcMode else */
 }  /* while !Abort */
 Restore_Screen(OldScreen);
 Cursor_On(OldCursor);
 Goto_XY(OldX, OldY);
} /* Calculator */
```

Sample Usage Source Code

▼

```
/*
  This program will clear the screen and run the Calculator.
*/

extern unsigned _stklen=16384; /* Minimum recommend stack size */
#include <stdio.h>
#include <math.h>
#include <dos.h>
#include <mem.h>
#include <alloc.h>
#include <ctype.h>
#include <string.h>
#include <stdlib.h>
#include <plib.h>
#include <plib.glo>


/******************************************************************************/
main()
{
```

```
  Calibrate_Delay();            /* Calibrate delay factor */
  Get_Video_Mode("Video.CFG"); /* Get display adapter type */
  Install_Crit_Error();         /* Set up application critical error handler */
  InputAbsolute=AbortPrint=0;   /* Initialize global variables */

  /* Application code to follow */
  Clr_Scr () ;
  Calculator () ;

} /*  main  */
```

Sample Usage Output

▼

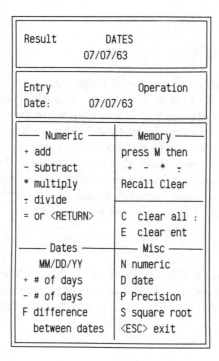

```
Result          DATES
            07/07/63

Entry              Operation
Date:        07/07/63

—— Numeric ——————— Memory ——
+ add              press M then
- subtract           +  -  *  ÷
* multiply         Recall Clear
÷ divide
= or <RETURN>      C  clear all :
                   E  clear ent
——— Dates ———————— Misc ———
   MM/DD/YY        N numeric
+ # of days        D date
- # of days        P Precision
F difference       S square root
  between dates    <ESC> exit
```

Calibrate_Delay

Description

▼

Calibrate_Delay sets the global variable CalDelay, used to determine the number of loop cycles that equal one millisecond on the host computer.

Routine Declaration

▼

```
void Calibrate_Delay(void)
```

Passed Variables

▼

None

Global Variables

▼

CalDelay This variable is set only in the library routine Calibrate_Delay and is used only by the library routine Delay. The variable contains the number of loop cycles required in Delay to equal one millisecond on the computer running the application.

Error Codes/Messages

▼

None

Discussion

▼

Calibrate_Delay sets a calibrated number of loops required in the routine Delay to achieve a one-millisecond delay. The routine is usually executed at the beginning of an application, allowing it to be self-adjusting to the current hardware.

Since the PC's hardware clock doesn't have millisecond resolution, Calibrate_Delay uses clock ticks from DOS' current time as limits for a loop that counts the number of repetitions that can be accomplished in five clock ticks. The number of loops completed is then divided to determine the number of loop cycles required to equal one millisecond. This value is then stored in the global variable CalDelay for use by the routine Delay.

Limitations and Modifications

▼

If the user's machine has the ability to change CPU clock speed during the execution of an application, the delay factor may be inaccurate after such a change. This is not a major problem, because simply restarting the application will readjust the delay.

Routine Source Code

▼

```
extern unsigned int
  CalDelay;

void Calibrate_Delay(void)
/*
  This procedure will calibrate the system variable CalDelay to
  the system at run-time so Delay will perform accurately.
*/
{ /* Calibrate_Delay */
  long far
    *TimePtr = {0x0040006c};
  unsigned long
```

```
    OldTime;

  CalDelay = 0;
  OldTime = *TimePtr;
  while (OldTime == *TimePtr);
  OldTime = *TimePtr + 5;
  while(*TimePtr <= OldTime)
    CalDelay++;
  CalDelay = CalDelay / 91;
} /* Calibrate_Delay */
```

Sample Usage Source Code

▼

For a sample usage of this routine, see the sample usage for the library routine Delay.

Cen

Description

▼

Cen returns the pointer to BufferStr containing the original text centered in a field of spaces FieldWidth wide. If the original string is longer than the width specified, the buffer string will contain a string truncated to the length specified in FieldWidth.

Routine Declaration

▼

```
char *Cen(char *TextStr,
          char *BufferStr,
          int FieldWidth)
```

Passed Variables

▼

***TextStr String Pointer** A pointer to the string to be centered in a string of spaces FieldWidth spaces wide.

***BufferStr String Pointer** A pointer to the string that will contain the centered string.

FieldWidth integer The width of the field in which the text string is to be centered.

Global Variables

▼

None

Error Codes/ Messages

▼

None

Discussion

▼

Cen is a useful function for creating formatted output for screen displays and printed reports. You can use Cen with screen writing routines such as F_Write or printing routines such as Print_At.

Cen first calculates the length of the text to be centered. If the text exceeds the field width, the truncated version of text string is copied to the buffer. If the string does not exceed the field width, the left and right space padding size is calculated and the buffer string is assembled using the paddings, the text string, and a null terminator. Finally, the pointer BufferStr is returned.

Limitations and Modifications

▼

If you are centering numeric data, you will need to convert the numbers to string values and format them to the length and number of decimal positions required before passing them to Cen. For more information on numeric to string conversions, see the Turbo C routines sprintf and printf.

Routine Source Code

▼

```
#include <string.h>

char *Cen(char *CStr,
          char *TStr,
          int FW)
/*
  This function will copy CStr into *TStr centered in a field
  FW wide with space character fills. If FW is smaller than the
  length of LStr, *TStr will contain the truncated version of
  CStr (from 0 to FW). Cen will return the pointer to *TStr.
*/
{ /* Cen */
  int
    T,
    T1,
    LS,
    LC,
    RC;

  LS = strlen(CStr);
  if (LS <= FW)
  {
    LC = (T1 = FW - LS) >> 1;
    RC = LC + (T1 & 0x0001);
```

```
    for (T = 0, LC--; T <= LC; T++)
      TStr[T] = ' ';
    for (T1 = 0, LS--; T1 <= LS; T++, T1++)
      TStr[T] = CStr[T1];
    for (RC += T; T < RC; T++)
      TStr[T] = s" ';
    TStr[T] = 0;
  } /* if LS */
  else
  {
    for (T = 0, FW--; T <= FW; T++)
      TStr[T] = CStr[T];
    TStr[T] = 0;
  } /* if LS else */
  return(TStr);
} /* Cen */
```

Sample Usage Source Code

▼

```
/*
  This program will output text centered in a field of 70 characters
  using the function Cen.
*/

extern unsigned _stklen=16384; /* Minimum recommend stack size */
#include <stdio.h>
#include <math.h>
#include <dos.h>
#include <mem.h>
#include <alloc.h>
#include <ctype.h>
#include <string.h>
#include <stdlib.h>
#include <plib.h>
#include <plib.glo>


/****************************************************************************/
main()
{
  char
    Buffer[71];

  Calibrate_Delay();            /* Calibrate delay factor */
  Get_Video_Mode("Video.CFG"); /* Get display adapter type */
  Install_Crit_Error();         /* Set up application critical error handler */
  InputAbsolute=AbortPrint=0;  /* Initialize global variables */
```

```
    /* Application code to follow */

    Clr_Scr();
    printf("*****%s*****", Cen("This will be centered between the asters",
         Buffer, 70));

}/*main*/
```

Sample Usage Output

▼

```
*****          This will be centered between the asters           *****
```

Check_Date

Description

▼

Check_Date determines if the date string passed, in the form MM/DD/YY, is a valid calendar date. If the date is valid Check_Date returns true (1); otherwise, it returns false (0).

Routine Declaration

▼

```
char Check_Date(char *Date)
```

Passed Variables

▼

Date String Pointer A pointer to a string of length 8 containing the date to be verified. The date must be in the standard date format MM/DD/YY.

Global Variables

▼

None

Error Codes/ Messages

▼

Check_Date returns true or false. No other errors are created.

Discussion

▼

Check_Date verifies dates entered through library functions such as Input_Date. Check_Date accepts a date in the form MM/DD/YY and pads the month, day, and year with a leading zero if necessary (for example, 1/1/87 is returned as 01/01/87). Verification of the month and day is completed including leap year conditions. Check_Date does not return any error conditions. It only returns true if the date is valid and false if the date is invalid.

Check_Date performs the verification by first separating the month, day, and year from the date passed and converting the string values to numeric values. If the conversion on any of the portions fail, the BadDate is set true to indicate an error in the date. After the values are converted, the month, day, and year are checked for proper ranges. Finally, the numeric dates are returned to string form and concatenated back into a complete calendar date. The value of BadDate is inverted and returned as the function's resulting value.

Limitations and Modifications

▼

The main limitation to Check_Date is that you need to ensure that the date passed is in the proper format. If you pass a date that has had Date_Comp performed on it, Check_Date returns false because Date_Comp alters the date's format to YY/MM/DD. Input_Date allows you to enter dates in either MM/DD/YY, MM-DD-YY, or MMDDYY format and then converts the second and third format to the first format before passing the date to Check_Date.

You may want to modify Check_Date to perform the conversion from the MMDDYY format. This would provide you with the ability to enter either format in any procedure that verifies the date with Check_Date. For an example of how to perform the conversion to the MM/DD/YY format, see Input_Date.

Routine Source Code

▼

```
#include <math.h>
#include <string.h>
#include <stdio.h>
#include <stdlib.h>
#include <ctype.h>
#include <plib.h>

char Check_Date(char *Date)
/*
  This function returns true (1) if the date passed (*Date) is a valid
  date in the form M/D/Y. If it is a valid date it will return it in the
  form MM/DD/YY always. If not, it will return false (0).
*/
{ /* Check_Date */
  char
    Dlmtr,
    BadDate,
    DayStr[6],
    MonthStr[6],
    YearStr[6];

  int
    Md[12] = {31, 28, 31, 30, 31, 30, 31, 31, 30, 31, 30, 31},
    Day,
    Year,
    Month;
```

```
  /* Parse Month, Day, Year */
  BadDate = 0;
  Erase_White(Date);
  if (Pos('-', Date))
    Dlmtr = '-';
  else
    Dlmtr = '/';
  Copy(Date, 1, Pos(Dlmtr, Date) - 1, MonthStr);
  Delete(Date, 1, Pos(Dlmtr, Date));
  Copy(Date, 1, Pos(Dlmtr, Date) - 1, DayStr);
  Delete(Date, 1, Pos(Dlmtr, Date));
  strcpy(YearStr, Date);

  /* Convert & Compare for validity */
  Month = atoi(MonthStr);
  BadDate = (BadDate || !Str_IsInt(MonthStr));
  Day = atoi(DayStr);
  BadDate = (BadDate || !Str_IsInt(DayStr));
  Year = atoi(YearStr);
  BadDate = (BadDate || !Str_IsInt(YearStr));
  if ((Month >= 1) && (Month <= 12) && !BadDate)
    BadDate = !((Day >= 1) && (Day <= (Md[Month - 1] + ((Year % 4) == 0 &&
             Month == 2))) && (Year >= 0) && (Year <= 99));
  else
    BadDate = 1;

  /* Pad Date */
  if (!BadDate)
    sprintf(Date, "%02d/%02d/%02d", Month, Day, Year);
  return(!BadDate);
} /* Check_Date */
```

Sample Usage Source Code

```
/*
  This program will allow the user to input a date and then check
  the validity of the date with the function Check_Date.
*/

extern unsigned _stklen=16384; /* Minimum recommend stack size */
#include <stdio.h>
#include <math.h>
#include <dos.h>
#include <mem.h>
#include <alloc.h>
#include <ctype.h>
#include <string.h>
#include <stdlib.h>
```

```
#include <plib.h>
#include <plib.glo>


/****************************************************************************/
main()
{
  char
    TempDate[9];

  Calibrate_Delay();            /* Calibrate delay factor */
  Get_Video_Mode("Video.CFG"); /* Get display adapter type */
  Install_Crit_Error();         /* Set up application critical error handler */
  InputAbsolute=AbortPrint=0;  /* Initialize global variables */

  /* Application code to follow */

  Clr_Scr();
  TempDate[0] = 0;
  printf("Enter a date, Month/Day/Year(2-digit year): ");
  scanf("%s", TempDate);
  if ( Check_Date(TempDate) )
    printf("%s is a valid date.", TempDate);
  else
    printf("This is not a valid date.");

} /*main*/
```

Sample Usage Output

▼

```
Enter a date, Month/Day/Year(2-digit year): 02/25/88
02/25/88 is a valid date.
```

Clear_Frame

Description

▼

Clear_Frame clears a block of text on the screen to spaces. If used on a color system, it will also set a background color for the specified block and set the global variable Background to that color. The block is defined by its upper left corner and the width and length desired. A call to Get_Video_Mode is required somewhere prior to calling Clear_Frame.

Routine Declaration

▼

```
void Clear_Frame(char WinColor,
                 int  XTL,
```

```
int  YTL,
int  WinWid,
int  WinDep)
```

Passed Variables

▼

WinColor char Specifies the color to be used for the background of the window.

XTL integer Indicates the horizontal (column) position for the upper left corner of the frame to be cleared. Valid values for XTL are 1 through 80.

YTL integer Indicates the vertical (row) position for the upper left corner of the frame to be cleared. Valid values for YTL are 1 through 25.

WinWid integer Indicates the horizontal (column) width, from the XTL position, to be cleared. Valid values for WinWid are 1 through 80.

WinDep integer Indicates the vertical (row) depth, from the Y position, to be cleared. Valid values for WinDep are 1 through 25.

Global Variables

▼

Background char This global variable contains the background color used in the last call to Clear_Frame, Draw_Frame, or Menu.

Error Codes/ Messages

▼

None

Discussion

▼

Clear_Frame is useful in creating windows or pop-up areas on the screen by clearing any text that would be on in the window when the routine is called. Clear_Frame uses a local string of spaces set to the specified window width and a for loop with F_Writes to clear and color the display area. After the display is cleared, the global variable Background is set to the value passed for WinColor.

Limitations and Modifications

▼

No boundary checking is performed by Clear_Frame, so you should use care when specifying the window size parameters. You may want to modify Clear_Frame to check for valid screen positions. If you do additional error checking, evaluate your performance to determine if it will adversely affect your application.

Routine Source Code

▼

```
#include <math.h>
#include <string.h>
```

```
#include <stdio.h>
#include <stdlib.h>
#include <ctype.h>
#include <mem.h>
#include <plib.h>

extern char
  Background;


void Clear_Frame(char WinColor,
                 int XTL,
                 int YTL,
                 int WinWid,
                 int WinDep)
/*
  This procedure will clear the text from a frame with a background of
  WinColor, and will set the global variable Background to WinColor.

  (XTL, YTL) ┌────WinWid───┐
             │             W
             │             i
             │             n
             │             d
             │             e
             │             p
             └─────────────┘
*/
{ /* Clear_Frame */
  char
    ClearString[100];

  int
    C;

  setmem(ClearString, WinWid, 32);
  ClearString[WinWid] = 0;
  YTL--;
  for (C = 1; C <= WinDep; C++)
    F_Write(XTL, YTL + C, WinColor, ClearString);
  Background = WinColor;
} /* Clear_Frame */
```

Sample Usage Source Code

▼

```
/*
  This program will fill the screen with asters, then clear blocks
  in the screen of various sizes.
```

```
*/

extern unsigned _stklen=16384; /* Minimum recommend stack size */
#include <stdio.h>
#include <math.h>
#include <dos.h>
#include <mem.h>
#include <alloc.h>
#include <ctype.h>
#include <string.h>
#include <stdlib.h>
#include <plib.h>
#include <plib.glo>

/*****************************************************************************/
main()
{
  int
    Temp;

  char
    TempString[81]="";

  Calibrate_Delay();            /* Calibrate delay factor */
  Get_Video_Mode("Video.CFG"); /* Get display adapter type */
  Install_Crit_Error();         /* Set up application critical error handler */
  InputAbsolute=AbortPrint=0;  /* Initialize global variables */

  /* Application code to follow */

  Rpt("*", TempString, 80);
  for ( Temp = 1; Temp <= 24 ; Temp++ )
    F_Write(1, Temp, Normal, TempString);

  Clear_Frame(Red, 2, 2, 10, 5);
  Message("Frame X=2, Y=2, Wide=10, Depth=5");
  Delay(2000);

  Clear_Frame(Blue, 40, 6, 25, 8);
  Message("Frame X=40, Y=6, Wide=25, Depth=8");
  Delay(2000);

  Clear_Frame(Green, 5, 12, 14, 7);
  Message("Frame X=5, Y=12, Wide=14, Depth=7");
  Delay(2000);

} /*main*/
```

Sample Usage Output

▼

```
********************************************************************************
*          *********************************************************************
*          *********************************************************************
*          *********************************************************************
*          *********************************************************************
*          ****************************                         ****************
***************************************                         ****************
***************************************                         ****************
***************************************                         ****************
***************************************                         ****************
***************************************                         ****************
****              *********************                         ****************
****              *********************                         ****************
****              **************************************************************
****              **************************************************************
****              **************************************************************
****              **************************************************************
****              **************************************************************
********************************************************************************
********************************************************************************
********************************************************************************
********************************************************************************
********************************************************************************
********************************************************************************
             Frame: X=5, Y=12, Width=14, Depth=7
```

Clr_Scr

Description

▼

Clr_Scr provides an easy method of clearing the entire video display screen to the DOS default color of a black background and positioning the cursor in the upper left corner of the screen.

Routine Declaration

▼

```
void Clr_Scr(void)
```

Passed Variables

▼

None

Global Variables

▼

None

Error Codes/ Messages

▼

None

Discussion

▼

Clr_Scr provides a quick and easy-to-use method of clearing the video display. The routine does not require any parameters and will clear the entire screen and place the cursor in the upper left corner.

Clr_Scr uses two of the library routines to accomplish the clearing. First, Clr_Scr calls Clear_Frame with the attribute set to 0x07, the standard DOS background color, to clear the screen to black. Then Goto_XY is called to position the cursor in the upper left corner of the screen, position 1,1.

Limitations and Modifications

▼

None

Routine Source Code

▼

```
#include <math.h>
#include <string.h>
#include <stdio.h>
#include <stdlib.h>
#include <ctype.h>
#include <mem.h>
#include <plib.h>

void Clr_Scr(void)
/*
  This routine will clear the screen as its Turbo Pascal counterpart
  would. (Clearing the entire screen and positioning the cursor to (1, 1).
*/
{/* Clr_Scr */
  Clear_Frame(0x07, 1, 1, 80, 25);
  Goto_XY(1, 1);
}/* Clr_Scr */
```

Sample Usage Source Code

▼

```
/*
  This program will clear the screen.
*/

extern unsigned _stklen=16384; /* Minimum recommend stack size */
#include <stdio.h>
#include <math.h>
#include <dos.h>
```

```
#include <mem.h>
#include <alloc.h>
#include <ctype.h>
#include <string.h>
#include <stdlib.h>
#include <plib.h>
#include <plib.glo>


/*****************************************************************************/
main()
{
  char
    Check;

  Calibrate_Delay();              /* Calibrate delay factor */
  Get_Video_Mode("Video.CFG"); /* Get display adapter type */
  Install_Crit_Error();           /* Set up application critical error handler */
  InputAbsolute=AbortPrint=0;  /* Initialize global variables */

  /* Application code to follow */

  printf("\nThe screen will be cleared as soon as you press <RETURN>.\n");
  scanf("%c", &Check) ;
  Clr_Scr() ;

} /* main */
```

Sample Usage Output

▼

```
This screen will be cleared as soon as you press <RETURN>.
```

Cnvg_Mess

Description

▼

Cnvg_Mess splits the *Mess into two equal parts and converges the parts from the outside ends of the 25th line until the parts meet in the center. If the string passed is null, the 25th line will be cleared and set to Normal video.

Routine Declaration

▼

```
void Cnvg_Mess(char *Mess)
```

Passed Variables

▼

***Mess String Pointer** A pointer to the string message that is to be converged on the 25th line of the video display. If the string pointed to exceeds 80 characters, it will be truncated to 80 characters.

Global Variables

▼

None

Error Codes/ Messages

▼

None

Discussion

▼

Cnvg_Mess provides an attention-getting way of displaying a message. The message is split into two parts as close to the center of the message as possible. The parts then start from the outer left and right sides of the screen and move toward the center until they meet in the middle of the 25th line.

If the message you pass is Null, Cnvg_Mess clears the 25th line and sets that line's video attributes to Normal.

Limitations and Modifications

▼

Because Cnvg_Mess has to move the strings in from the outer edges of the screen, it is not a fast display routine. For this reason, do not use Cnvg_Mess for messages that are displayed frequently because the user would have to wait for the message to converge.

For additional flexibility, you may add parameters to specify the line number the message is to be displayed on. In addition, you may provide a setting for the width of the convergence window, allowing you to converge messages in any window size you desire.

To further attract the user's attention to the message, you may add a sound function at the beginning or end of the convergence sequence.

Routine Source Code

▼

```
#include <math.h>
#include <string.h>
#include <stdio.h>
#include <stdlib.h>
#include <ctype.h>
#include <plib.h>

extern char
  Normal,
  VidHigh,
  Reverse;

void Cnvg_Mess(char *Mess)
```

```
/*
  This function will converge each half of *Mess from the outside edges of
  the 25th line in Reverse video attribute until they meet centered.
  If *Mess is null then the 25th line is cleared to the Normal
  attribute.
*/
{ /* Cnvg_Mess */
  char
    TStr[100],
    LStr[50],
    RStr[50];

  int
    I;

  if (Mess[0])
  {
    Cen(Mess, TStr, 80);
    for (I = 40; I >= 1; I--)
    {
      F_Write(I + 40, 25, Reverse, Copy(TStr, 41, 41 - I, LStr));
      F_Write(1, 25, Reverse, Copy(TStr, I, 41 - I, RStr));
      Delay(18);
    } /* for I */
  } /* if Mess[0] */
  else
    Message("");
} /* Cnvg_Mess */
```

Sample Usage Source Code

▼

```
/*
  This program will demonstrate Cnvg_Mess.
*/

extern unsigned _stklen=16384; /* Minimum recommend stack size */
#include <stdio.h>
#include <math.h>
#include <dos.h>
#include <mem.h>
#include <alloc.h>
#include <ctype.h>
#include <string.h>
#include <stdlib.h>
#include <plib.h>
#include <plib.glo>


/****************************************************************************/
```

```
main()
{
  Calibrate_Delay();             /* Calibrate delay factor */
  Get_Video_Mode("Video.CFG");  /* Get display adapter type */
  Install_Crit_Error();          /* Set up application critical error handler */
  InputAbsolute=AbortPrint=0;   /* Initialize global variables */

  /* Application code to follow */

  Clr_Scr;
  Cnvg_Mess("This Message will converge on the 25th line.");

} /*main*/
```

Sample Usage Output

```
This message will converge on the 25th line.
```

Common_Chars

Description

Common_Chars treats the two string values as sets of characters. It checks to see if all characters in the first string are contained in the second string. For example, if the first string equals *Madam* and the second string equals *adMm*, the function returns 0 because all the characters in the first string are present in the second. If a character is not present in the second string, the routine returns the offset to the invalid character in the first string.

Routine Declaration

```
int Common_Chars(char *Str1,
                 char *Str2)
```

Passed Variables

***Str1 String Pointer** A pointer to the string group of characters to be located in the string group passed in Str2.

***Str2 String Pointer** A pointer to the string group of characters to be used in verifying the string group passed in Str1.

Global Variables

None

Error Codes/ Messages

▼

None

Discussion

▼

The intended use for Common_Chars is to check the validity of data entered in a field against valid characters for the field. You may find other uses for this routine as you develop your own applications.

Common_Chars uses a nested for loop to increment through the string to be verified and then step through the valid character set contained in Str2. If the null terminator is encountered for the valid set in Str2, the routine assumes that the character being tested is not in the valid character set. The loop terminates and an if condition returns the current position in the string being verified. Otherwise, the routine will continue until a null terminator is encountered for the string being verified. At this point, the if condition will return 0, indicating success. If either string is set to a null prior to calling the routine, a 0 will be returned immediately.

Limitations and Modifications

▼

None

Routine Source Code

▼

```
int Common_Chars(char *Str1,
                 char *Str2)
/*
  This function will make sure that all characters in *Str1 occur in *Str2.
  This is usful for checking things like valid input. If a single
  character in *Str1 does not occur in *Str2, this function will return the
  offset in *Str1 (from 1 not 0) of the character that was not contained in
  *Str2, otherwise it will return 0. If *Str1 or *Str2 has a length of
  zero, this function will also return 0.
*/
{ /* Common_Chars */
  int
    C,
    C1;

  if (Str1[0] && Str2[0])
  {
    for (C = C1 = 0; (Str1[C] && Str2[C1]); C++)
    {
      for (C1 = 0; (Str2[C1] && (Str2[C1] != Str1[C])); C1++);
    } /* for C */
    if (!Str2[C1])
      return(C);
```

```
    else
      return(0);
  } /* if */
  else
    return(0);
} /* Common_Chars */
```

Sample Usage Source Code

▼

```
/*
  This program will allow the user to put in a string that is to be used
  as a set of characters, then input a comparison string and use
  Common_Chars to determine if every character in the second string is
  contained in the first.
*/

extern unsigned _stklen=16384; /* Minimum recommend stack size */
#include <stdio.h>
#include <math.h>
#include <dos.h>
#include <mem.h>
#include <alloc.h>
#include <ctype.h>
#include <string.h>
#include <stdlib.h>
#include <plib.h>
#include <plib.glo>


/****************************************************************************/
main()
{
  char
    StrSet [81] = "" ,
    CompStr [81] = "" ;

  Calibrate_Delay();             /* Calibrate delay factor */
  Get_Video_Mode("Video.CFG"); /* Get display adapter type */
  Install_Crit_Error();          /* Set up application critical error handler */
  InputAbsolute=AbortPrint=0;  /* Initialize global variables */

  /* Application code to follow */

  Clr_Scr() ;
  printf("Enter a character set: ");
  gets(StrSet);
  printf("Enter a comparison string: ");
  gets(CompStr);
```

```
  if (Common_Chars(CompStr, StrSet))
    printf ("\nAll characters are common. \n");
  else
    printf ("\nNot all characters are common. \n");

  } /* main */
```

Sample Usage Output

▼

```
Enter a character set: abc Enter a comparison string: abcd

All characters are common.
```

Copy

Description

▼

Copy produces a substring of a string value. The routine begins at a specified position in the string and retrieves a specified number of characters. A pointer to *DestIn, the new substring, is returned by the routine.

Routine Declaration

▼

```
char *Copy(char *Source,
           int Position,
           int NumChars,
           char *Destin)
```

Passed Variables

▼

***Source String Pointer** A pointer to the original string value to be used in obtaining a substring.

Position integer This field contains the offset to the starting character of the substring. If Position is passed as one, it will start with the first character of the string. If Position is greater than the string length, a null string will be returned.

NumChars integer This field contains the number of characters to be extracted for the substring. If the total of Position and NumChars exceeds the length of the Source string, the substring ends with the last character available in Source.

***Destin String Pointer** A pointer to the buffer space that will contain the substring of Source.

Global Variables

▼

None

Error Codes/ Messages

▼

None

Discussion

▼

Copy relieves some of the tedium and complexity required to obtain substrings in Turbo C. The routine functions identically to the Turbo Pascal copy command, so if you're converting to C from Pascal, you will be familiar with the command.

Copy first checks to insure that the Position specified is within the length of the Source string. If Position exceeds the length, the routine returns a null string. When a valid position is passed, a for loop moves characters from the source string into the Destin string. Upon reaching the NumChars to be moved or the end of the Source text, the loop terminates and the Destin string is null terminated.

Limitations and Modifications

▼

None

Routine Source Code

▼

```
#include <string.h>

char *Copy(char *Source,
           int Position,
           int NumChars,
           char *Destin)
/*
  This function will copy a substring of *Source into *Destin. The
  substring is specified by Position and NumChars. Position can be
  any value from 1 to N, where the substring copied will be from Position
  in *Source and NumChars number of characters. If Position is past the
  end of *Source, Destin will be set null, if Position + NumChars exceeds
  the length of *Source, all characters will be copied that can be.
*/
{ /* Copy */
  int
    C;

  if (Position <= strlen(Source))
  {
    for (C = 0, Position--, NumChars--;
         ((Source[Position]) && (C <= NumChars));
         Position++, C++)
      Destin[C] = Source[Position];
    Destin[C] = 0;
```

```
  } /* if Position */
  else
    Destin[0] = 0;
  return(Destin);
} /* Copy */
```

Sample Usage Source Code

▼

```
/*
  This program will use Copy() to obtain a substring copied from
  another string.
*/

extern unsigned _stklen=16384; /* Minimum recommend stack size */
#include <stdio.h>
#include <math.h>
#include <dos.h>
#include <mem.h>
#include <alloc.h>
#include <ctype.h>
#include <string.h>
#include <stdlib.h>
#include <plib.h>
#include <plib.glo>


/*****************************************************************************/
main()
{
  char
    String [40] = "This is an example of String Copy()." ,
    OpBuff [40] = "" ;

  Calibrate_Delay();             /* Calibrate delay factor */
  Get_Video_Mode("Video.CFG");  /* Get display adapter type */
  Install_Crit_Error();          /* Set up application critical error handler */
  InputAbsolute=AbortPrint=0;    /* Initialize global variables */

  /* Application code to follow */

  Clr_Scr();
  printf("\nThis is the result of Copy (String, 9, 9, OpBuff): \n");
  printf("\n%s\n", String);
  printf("\n%s\n", Copy(String, 9, 9, OpBuff));

} /* main */
```

Sample Usage Output

▼

```
This is the result of Copy (String, 9, 9, OpBuff):

This is an example of String Copy().

an example
```

Copy_File

Description

▼

Copy_File creates a duplicate of the file named in *OFName and names it to *DFName. The filenames may contain the drive and path specifications as well as the file. Upon completion, Copy_File returns true (1) if the copy was successful and false (0) if the copy failed.

Routine Declaration

▼

```
char Copy_File(char *OFName,
               char *DFName)
```

Passed Variables

▼

***OFName String Pointer** A pointer to the string containing the name of the original file to be copied, including any drive and path specifications.

DFName String Pointer A pointer to the string containing the name of the duplicate file to be created by the copy, including any drive and path specifications.

Global Variables

▼

None

Error Codes/ Messages

▼

The true or false value returned by Copy_File indicates an error in the copy process. No other error messages are created.

Discussion

▼

Copy_File is useful for copying files from inside a Turbo C program because Turbo C does not have a command to copy files. The filenames that are passed can contain drive and path specifications. If you don't indicate the drive and path, the current drive and directory will be assumed.

Copy_File starts by opening both the original file and the destination file. The results of the opens are checked to ensure that both files *can* be opened. If either file cannot be opened, the routine returns false (0). Once the files are opened, the data is read from the original and written to the new file. After the transfer is complete, the files are closed and the routine returns true (1).

Limitations and Modifications

There are two main limitations to Copy_File. First, the length of the drive, path, and filenames passed must be less than the DOS limit for path and filename parameters. For more information on the DOS limit to the file environments, consult your DOS manual. The second limitation is that if the destination file exists, it is overwritten, so it is up to you to determine if the file should be overwritten. There are two ways to circumvent this limitation. You can use Created to determine if the file exists prior to calling Copy_File or you can modify Copy_File to prompt the user for a decision on whether or not to overwrite the existing file.

Routine Source Code

```
#include <math.h>
#include <string.h>
#include <stdio.h>
#include <stdlib.h>
#include <ctype.h>
#include <plib.h>

char Copy_File(char *OFName,
               char *DFName)
/*
  This function will make a copy of the file *OFName (Original FileName)
  to *DFName (Duplicate FileName) and return true (1) upon success.
*/
{ /* Copy_File */
  char
    Buffer[2048];

  int
    BytesRead;  /* Temporary variable */

  FILE
    *OFv,                 /* Local file variables */
    *DFv;

  OFv = fopen(OFName, "rb");
  if (OFv != NULL)
  {
    /* If original file exists, copy file */
```

```
    DFv = fopen(DFName, "wb");
    if (DFv != NULL)
    {
      do
      {
        BytesRead = fread(Buffer, 1, 2048, OFv);
        fwrite(Buffer, 1, BytesRead, DFv);
      }while (BytesRead != 0);
      fclose(OFv);
      fclose(DFv);
      return (1);
    } /* if DFv */
    else
      return(0);
  } /* if OFv */
  else
    return(0);
} /* Copy_File */
```

Sample Usage Source Code

```
/*
  This program will allow the user to input a source file and
  destination file then will use the function Copy_file to
  copy the source file to the destination file.
*/

extern unsigned _stklen=16384; /* Minimum recommend stack size */
#include <stdio.h>
#include <math.h>
#include <dos.h>
#include <mem.h>
#include <alloc.h>
#include <ctype.h>
#include <string.h>
#include <stdlib.h>
#include <plib.h>
#include <plib.glo>


/*****************************************************************************/
main()
{
  char
    SourceFile[81]="",
    DestinationFile[81]="";

  Calibrate_Delay();              /* Calibrate delay factor */
```

```
  Get_Video_Mode("Video.CFG"); /* Get display adapter type */
  Install_Crit_Error();        /* Set up application critical error handler */
  InputAbsolute=AbortPrint=0;  /* Initialize global variables */

  /* Application code to follow */

  Clr_Scr();
  printf("Enter the Source filename: ");
  scanf("%s",SourceFile);
  printf("\nEnter the Destination filename: ");
  scanf("%s",DestinationFile);
  if (Copy_File(SourceFile,DestinationFile))
    printf("%s was successfully copied to %s.",SourceFile,DestinationFile);
  else
    printf("%s was not copied to %s.",SourceFile,DestinationFile);

} /*main*/
```

Sample Usage Output ▼

```
Enter the Source filename: scopy.exe

Enter the Destination filename: test.exe
scopy.exe was successfully copied to test.exe.
```

Created

Description ▼

Created determines if a file has been created. The filename may also contain the drive and directory path of the file in question. Created returns true (1) if the file is present and false (0) if the file does not exist.

Routine Declaration ▼

```
char Created(char *FName)
```

Passed Variables ▼

***FName String Pointer** A pointer to the string containing the drive, path, and filename of the file to be checked.

Global Variables ▼

None

Error Codes/ Messages

▼

None

Discussion

▼

Created can be used in conjunction with several of the other file manipulation procedures to determine if the file in question has already been created or needs to be created. Created is a fairly simple routine that uses the Turbo C library routine fopen to attempt to open the file. If the result of the fopen is NULL, Created is set false (0); otherwise, Created is returned as true (1).

Limitations and Modifications

▼

The only limitation to Created is that the length of the drive, directory path, and filename string passed must be less then the maximum DOS length for a file environment. You should consult your DOS manual for the exact length of the filename environment.

Routine Source Code

▼

```
#include <math.h>
#include <string.h>
#include <stdio.h>
#include <stdlib.h>
#include <ctype.h>
#include <plib.h>

char Created(char *FName)
/*
  This function checks to see if the parameter *FName (a path and
  filename) exists, returning true (1) if it exists and false (0)
  if it doesn't exist.
*/
{ /* Created */
  FILE
    *TFin; /* Local file variable */

  TFin = fopen(FName, "rb");
  if (TFin != NULL)
  {
    fclose(TFin);
    return(1);
  } /* if */
  else
    return(0);
} /* Created */
```

Sample Usage Source Code

▼

```
/*
  This program will use the function Created to determine if a file
  the user puts in exists or not.
*/

extern unsigned _stklen=16384; /* Minimum recommend stack size */
#include <stdio.h>
#include <math.h>
#include <dos.h>
#include <mem.h>
#include <alloc.h>
#include <ctype.h>
#include <string.h>
#include <stdlib.h>
#include <plib.h>
#include <plib.glo>


/****************************************************************************/
main()
{
  char
    TempString[81]="";

  Calibrate_Delay();           /* Calibrate delay factor */
  Get_Video_Mode("Video.CFG"); /* Get display adapter type */
  Install_Crit_Error();        /* Set up application critical error handler */
  InputAbsolute=AbortPrint=0;  /* Initialize global variables */

  /* Application code to follow */

  Clr_Scr();
  printf("Enter the filename to check: ");
  scanf("%s", TempString);
  if  (Created(TempString))
    printf("%s is created.", TempString);
  else
    printf("%s is not created.", TempString);

} /*main*/
```

Sample Usage Output

▼

```
Enter the filename to check: test.exe
test.exe does exist.
```

Cursor_Off

Description ▼

Cursor_Off turns off the display of the screen cursor using a call to the ROM BIOS interrupt 10 hex and service 1. The current value of the cursor will be returned so the cursor can be restored later by calling Cursor_On.

Routine Declaration ▼

```
int Cursor_Off()
```

Passed Variables ▼

None

Global Variables ▼

None

Error Codes/ Messages ▼

None

Discussion ▼

Cursor_Off disables the display of the video cursor. This allows you to perform screen displays and printing without having the cursor show on the video display. The cursor is disabled by calling the ROM BIOS interrupt number 10 hex with the AX register set to 0100 hex and the CX register set to 2000 hex.

Interrupt 10 hex handles all the ROM BIOS video and screen control services. These include the video mode, cursor size, scrolling, cursor positioning, character and attribute writing, and many more. Cursor_Off uses service number 1, Set Cursor Size, of interrupt 10 hex to alter the size of the cursor. Two of the system registers must be configured prior to calling this interrupt. The AX register is set with the service number to be executed, service 1 in this case, and the CX register is set to indicate the size and format of the cursor. By setting the high byte of the CX register to 20 hex (32 decimal), the cursor will disappear when service 1 is called. See Cursor_On for setting the visible format of the cursor. For more information on interrupts, consult the reference books listed in the appendix.

Limitations and Modifications ▼

None

Routine Source Code

▼

```
#include <dos.h>
#include <mem.h>

int Cursor_Off()
/*
  This function will turn off the cursor and return the current
  cursor setting.
*/
{ /* Cursor_Off */
  int
    OldCursor;

  union REGS
    Regs;

  setmem(&Regs, sizeof(Regs), 0);
  Regs.h.ah = 0x03; /* read the cursor format */
  int86(0x10, &Regs, &Regs);
  OldCursor = Regs.x.cx;
  setmem(&Regs, sizeof(Regs), 0);
  Regs.h.ah = 0x01; /* Set cursor  */
  Regs.h.ch = 0x20; /* off */
  int86(0x10, &Regs, &Regs);
  return(OldCursor);
} /* Cursor_Off */
```

Sample Usage Source Code

▼

```
/*
  This program will use Cursor_Off and Cursor_On to set and unset
  the cursor.
*/

extern unsigned _stklen=16384; /* Minimum recommend stack size */
#include <stdio.h>
#include <math.h>
#include <dos.h>
#include <mem.h>
#include <alloc.h>
#include <ctype.h>
#include <string.h>
#include <stdlib.h>
#include <plib.h>
#include <plib.glo>


/******************************************************************************/
```

```
main()
{
  char
    Ch;

  int
    Old_Cursor;

  Calibrate_Delay();           /* Calibrate delay factor */
  Get_Video_Mode("Video.CFG"); /* Get display adapter type */
  Install_Crit_Error();        /* Set up application critical error handler */
  InputAbsolute=AbortPrint=0;  /* Initialize global variables */

  /* Application code to follow */

  Clr_Scr();
  printf("The cursor is on here, press < RETURN >:");
  scanf("%c", &Ch);
  Old_Cursor = Cursor_Off();

  printf("The cursor is off here, press < RETURN >:");
  scanf("%c", &Ch);
  Cursor_On(Old_Cursor);

  printf("The cursor is on again, press < RETURN >:");
  scanf("%c", &Ch);

} /*main*/
```

Sample Usage Output

▼

```
The cursor is on here, press < RETURN >:_
The cursor is off here, press < RETURN >:
The cursor is on again, press < RETURN >:_
```

Cursor_On

Description

▼

Cursor_On turns on the display of the screen cursor in the format passed using a call to the ROM BIOS interrupt 10 hex and service 1.

Routine Declaration

▼

```
void Cursor_On(int Cursor)
```

Passed Variables

▼

Cursor integer The value to be used to set the format for the cursor when enabled.

Global Variables

▼

None

Error Codes/ Messages

▼

None

Discussion

▼

Cursor_On enables the display of the video cursor after the cursor has been disabled with Cursor_Off. The cursor is enabled by calling the ROM BIOS interrupt number 10 hex with the appropriate values in the AX and CX register for the type of video display card currently installed.

Interrupt 10 hex handles all the ROM BIOS video and screen control services. These include the video mode, cursor size, scrolling, cursor positioning, character and attribute writing, and many more. Cursor_Off uses service number 1, Set Cursor Size, of interrupt 10 hex to alter the size of the cursor. Two of the system registers are configured prior to calling this interrupt. The AX register is set with the service number to be executed, service 1 in this case, and the CX register is set to the cursor format value passed. For more information on interrupts, consult the Bibliography.

Limitations and Modifications

▼

None

Routine Source Code

▼

```
#include <dos.h>
#include <mem.h>

void Cursor_On(int Cursor)
/*
  This procedure will set the cursor to the value in Cursor.
*/
{ /* Cursor_On */
  union REGS
    Regs;

  setmem(&Regs, sizeof(Regs), 0);
  Regs.h.ah = 0x01; /* set cursor */
  Regs.x.cx = Cursor;
```

```
  int86(0x10, &Regs, &Regs);
} /* Cursor_On */
```

Sample Usage Source Code

▼

See the sample usage for Cursor_Off.

Date_Add

Description

▼

Date_Add adds a specified number of days to the date passed and returns the pointer to *Buffer, which contains the new date in the form MM/DD/YY. For subtraction of date values, see Date_Sub.

Routine Declaration

▼

```
char *Date_Add(char *Date,
               int NumDay,
               char *Buffer)
```

Passed Variables

▼

***Date String Pointer** A pointer to the string date, in the form MM/DD/YY, to which NumDay is to be added.

NumDay integer The number of days to be added to the string date specified in Date.

***Buffer String Pointer** A pointer to the string variable that will contain the final string date.

Global Variables

▼

None

Error Codes/ Messages

▼

None

Discussion

▼

Date_Add and the other date-related routines provide the ability to manipulate and calculate dates. Because many business applications require the ability to determine the time from or to a specific date, date-related routines make the creation of many business-related applications easier.

Date_Add is a simple function. It converts the date passed to a Julian Day

Number and then adds the indicated number of days to the Julian Day Number, converting it back to calendar format. The two function calls used to perform the conversions are Cal_Julian for conversion from calendar to Julian and Julian_Cal for conversion from Julian to calendar.

Limitations and Modifications

▼

Date_Add does not perform any direct error checking on the date passed to the function. However, if a bad date is passed, the function Cal_Julian may result in an error. To compensate, you may make a call to Check_Date to verify the date passed prior to calling the conversion statements. If you are making extensive use of Date_Add, calling Check_Date may cause a degradation in the performance of Date_Add.

Routine Source Code

▼

```
#include <math.h>
#include <string.h>
#include <stdio.h>
#include <stdlib.h>
#include <ctype.h>
#include <plib.h>

char *Date_Add(char *Date,
               int NumDay,
               char *Buffer)
/*
  This function returns a date string in the form MM/DD/YY that is
  *Date plus the number of days NumDay.
*/

{ /* Date_Add */
  Julian_Cal(Cal_Julian(Date) + NumDay, Buffer);
  return(Buffer);
} /* Date_Add */
```

Sample Usage Source Code

▼

```
/*
  This program will allow the user to enter a date and a number of
  days to add to the date, then use Date_Add to calculate and display
  the new date.
*/

extern unsigned _stklen=16384; /* Minimum recommend stack size */
#include <stdio.h>
#include <math.h>
#include <dos.h>
```

```
#include <mem.h>
#include <alloc.h>
#include <ctype.h>
#include <string.h>
#include <stdlib.h>
#include <plib.h>
#include <plib.glo>


/****************************************************************************/
main()
{
  char
    TempDate[9]="" ,
    Buffer[9]="" ;

  int
    NumDays=0;

  Calibrate_Delay();              /* Calibrate delay factor */
  Get_Video_Mode("Video.CFG"); /* Get display adapter type */
  Install_Crit_Error();         /* Set up application critical error handler */
  InputAbsolute=AbortPrint=0;  /* Initialize global variables */

  /* Application code to follow */

  Clr_Scr();
  printf("Enter a date in the form MM/DD/YY: ");
  scanf("%s", TempDate);

  printf("\nEnter the number of days to add to the date: ");
  scanf("%d", &NumDays);
  printf("\n");

  printf ("%s plus %d days = %s. \n", TempDate, NumDays,
        Date_Add (TempDate, NumDays, Buffer) );

} /*main*/
```

Sample Usage Output

▼

```
Enter a date in the form MM/DD/YY: 02/26/88

Enter the number of days to add to date: 300

02/26/88 plus 300 days = 12/22/88.
```

Date_Comp

Description

▼

Date_Comp returns the pointer to *Buffer, a string date in the form YY/MM/DD that has been converted from a specified date in the form MM/DD/YY.

Routine Declaration

▼

```
char *Date_Comp(char *Date,
                char *Buffer)
```

Passed Variables

▼

***Date String Pointer** A pointer to the string date, in the form MM/DD/YY, to be converted to the form YY/MM/DD.

***Buffer String Pointer** A pointer to the string variable that will contain the resulting string date.

Global Variables

▼

None

Error Codes/ Messages

▼

None

Discussion

▼

Date_Comp rearranges the order of the month, day, and year of a string date so the date may be compared against another date. This is of main concern for dates in different years. For example, when a date is in the form MM/DD/YY, the date 12/31/86 is greater than the date 01/01/87. After Date_Comp has been used with these dates, you have 86/12/31 and 87/01/01, which results in the proper comparison.

Date_Comp is also beneficial for indexing data files. We strongly recommend that you always store your date indexes in Date_Comp form. If you don't, you are likely to encounter some peculiar problems as your file grows to include dates that span more than one calendar year.

Limitations and Modifications

▼

Date_Comp does not perform any error checking on the date passed other than to determine if the value passed has any text at all. If the value passed does not have any text, Date_Comp returns a null string.

You may want to modify Date_Comp to ensure that the date string passed is a valid date by using Check_Date, which also ensures that the string date is in the eight-character format. This may affect performance if you are making a significant number of calls to Date_Comp.

Routine Source Code

```
#include <math.h>
#include <string.h>
#include <stdio.h>
#include <stdlib.h>
#include <ctype.h>
#include <plib.h>

char *Date_Comp(char *Date,
                char *Buffer)
/*
  Returns in *Buffer a string date in the form YY/MM/DD from the string
  *Date, where *Date is in the form MM/DD/YY. This is useful for comparing
  differences of dates by simple string-wise comparisons.
*/
{ /* Date_Comp */
  char
    TStr1[6],
    TStr[3];

  /* If the date passed has text, rearrange format */
  if (Is_Text(Date))
    sprintf(Buffer, "%s/%s", Copy(Date, 7, 2, TStr), Copy(Date, 1, 5,
            TStr1));
  else
    Buffer[0] = 0;
  return(Buffer);
} /* Date_Comp */
```

Sample Usage Source Code

```
/*
  This program will demonstrate how to use Date_Comp to compare the
  magnitude of two dates.
*/

extern unsigned _stklen=16384; /* Minimum recommend stack size */
#include <stdio.h>
#include <math.h>
#include <dos.h>
#include <mem.h>
#include <alloc.h>
#include <ctype.h>
#include <string.h>
```

```
#include <stdlib.h>
#include <plib.h>
#include <plib.glo>


/****************************************************************************/
main()
{
  char
    TempDate1[9]="",
    TempDate2[9]="",
    B1[9]="",
    B2[9]="";

  Calibrate_Delay();           /* Calibrate delay factor */
  Get_Video_Mode("Video.CFG"); /* Get display adapter type */
  Install_Crit_Error();        /* Set up application critical error handler */
  InputAbsolute=AbortPrint=0;  /* Initialize global variables */

  /* Application code to follow */

  Clr_Scr();
  printf("Enter the first date in the form MM/DD/YY: ");
  scanf ("%s", TempDate1);
  printf("\nEnter the second date in the form MM/DD/YY: ");
  scanf ("%s", TempDate2);

  if (strcmp(Date_Comp(TempDate1, B1), Date_Comp(TempDate2, B2)) > 0 )
    printf("\n%s is greater than %s.", TempDate1, TempDate2);
  else
    printf("\n%s is less than or equal to %s.\n", TempDate1, TempDate2);

} /*main*/
```

Sample Usage Output

▼

```
Enter the first date in the form MM/DD/YY: 02/25/88

Enter the second date in the form MM/DD/YY: 12/25/88

02/25/88 is less than or equal to 12/25/88.
```

Date_Diff

Description

▼

Date_Diff returns the absolute number of days' difference between the two string dates passed in the form MM/DD/YY. The chronological order of the dates will not affect the result.

Routine Declaration

▼

```
int Date_Diff(char *Date1,
              char *Date2)
```

Passed Variables

▼

***Date1 String Pointer** The first string date, in the form MM/DD/YY, used in finding the absolute number of days' difference from *Date2.

***Date2 String Pointer** The second string date, in the form MM/DD/YY, used in finding the absolute number of days difference from *Date1.

Global Variables

▼

None

Error Codes/ Messages

▼

None

Discussion

▼

Date_Diff is useful in any application in which you need to know how many days are between two particular dates. One example is an invoice-aging report for an accounts receivable system wherein you needed to know how many days had passed since the invoice was issued.

Date_Diff performs the calculation by calling Cal_Julian for each date to obtain the Julian Day Numbers which are then subtracted from each other to obtain the raw number of days. The absolute number of days is then set and the resulting value is returned.

Limitations and Modifications

▼

Date_Diff does not perform any error checking on the dates passed, so if the dates are not in the proper format, errors may result when Cal_Julian is called. To account for this potential error, you may want to check the dates using Check_Date, but this may affect performance if you are calling Date_Diff extensively.

Routine Source Code

▼

```
#include <math.h>
#include <string.h>
#include <stdio.h>
#include <stdlib.h>
#include <ctype.h>
#include <plib.h>
```

```
int Date_Diff(char *Date1,
              char *Date2)
/*
  Returns the number of days' difference between *Date1 and
  *Date2, where *Date1 and *Date2 are in the form MM/DD/YY.
*/
{ /* Date_Diff */
  return(floor(fabs(Cal_Julian(Date1) - Cal_Julian(Date2))));
} /* Date_Diff */
```

Sample Usage Source Code

▼

```
/*
  This program will allow the user to input two dates then use Date_Diff
  to calculate and display the number of days between the two dates.

*/

extern unsigned _stklen=16384; /* Minimum recommend stack size */
#include <stdio.h>
#include <math.h>
#include <dos.h>
#include <mem.h>
#include <alloc.h>
#include <ctype.h>
#include <string.h>
#include <stdlib.h>
#include <plib.h>
#include <plib.glo>

/*****************************************************************************/
main()
{
  char
    TempDate1[9]="",
    TempDate2[9]="";

  Calibrate_Delay();            /* Calibrate delay factor */
  Get_Video_Mode("Video.CFG"); /* Get display adapter type */
  Install_Crit_Error();         /* Set up application critical error handler */
  InputAbsolute=AbortPrint=0;   /* Initialize global variables */

  /* Application code to follow */

  Clr_Scr();
  printf("Enter the first date in the form MM/DD/YY: ");
  scanf ("%s", TempDate1);
  printf("\nEnter the second date in the form MM/DD/YY: ");
```

```
  scanf ("%s", TempDate2);

  printf("\nThe difference between %s and %s is %d days.\n",
       TempDate1, TempDate2, Date_Diff(TempDate1, TempDate2)) ;

} /*main*/
```

Sample Usage Output

▼

```
Enter the first date in the form MM/DD/YY: 08/19/57

Enter the second date in the form MM/DD/YY: 02/26/88

The difference between 08/19/57 and 02/26/88 is 11148 days.
```

Date_Sub

Description

▼

Date_Sub subtracts the specified number of days from the specified string date in the form MM/DD/YY and returns the resulting date in the same format. For addition of date values, see Date_Add.

Routine Declaration

▼

```
char *Date_Sub(char *Date,
               int  NumDay,
               char *Buffer)
```

Passed Variables

▼

***Date String Pointer** A pointer to the string date, in the form MM/DD/YY, from which NumDay is to be subtracted.

NumDay integer The number of days to be subtracted from the string date passed in Date.

***Buffer String Pointer** A pointer to the string variable that will contain the final string date.

Global Variables

▼

None

Error Codes/ Messages

▼

None

Discussion

▼

Date_Sub is a simple function, converting the date passed to a Julian Day Number and then subtracting the number of days from the Julian Day Number and converting the result back to calendar format. The two function calls used to perform the conversions are Cal_Julian for conversion from calendar to Julian and Julian_Cal for conversion from Julian to calendar.

Limitations and Modifications

▼

Date_Sub does not perform any direct error checking on the date passed to the function. However, if a bad date is passed, the function Cal_Julian may result in an error. To account for this, you may want to make a call to Check_Date to verify the date passed prior to calling the conversion statements.

Routine Source Code

▼

```
#include <math.h>
#include <string.h>
#include <stdio.h>
#include <stdlib.h>
#include <ctype.h>
#include <plib.h>

char *Date_Sub(char *Date,
               int NumDay,
               char *Buffer)
/*
  Returns a date string in the form MM/DD/YY that is *Date
  minus the number of days passed in NumDay.
*/

{ /* Date_Sub */
  Julian_Cal(Cal_Julian(Date) - NumDay, Buffer);
} /* Date_Sub */
```

Sample Usage Source Code

▼

```
/*
  This program will allow the user to enter a date and the number
  of days to subtract from the date then use Date_Sub to calculate
  and display the result.
*/

extern unsigned _stklen=16384; /* Minimum recommend stack size */
#include <stdio.h>
#include <math.h>
#include <dos.h>
```

```
#include <mem.h>
#include <alloc.h>
#include <ctype.h>
#include <string.h>
#include <stdlib.h>
#include <plib.h>
#include <plib.glo>


/****************************************************************************/
main()
{
  char
    TempDate[9] = "",
    Buffer[9] = "" ;

  int
    NumDays=0;

  Calibrate_Delay();            /* Calibrate delay factor */
  Get_Video_Mode("Video.CFG"); /* Get display adapter type */
  Install_Crit_Error();         /* Set up application critical error handler */
  InputAbsolute=AbortPrint=0;  /* Initialize global variables */

  /* Application code to follow */


  Clr_Scr();
  printf("Enter a date in the form MM/DD/YY: ");
  scanf ("%s", TempDate);
  printf("\nEnter the number of days to subtract from date: ");
  scanf ("%u", &NumDays);

  printf("\n%s minus %d days = %s.\n", TempDate, NumDays,
        Date_Sub(TempDate, NumDays, Buffer));

} /*main*/
```

Sample Usage Output

▼

```
Enter a date in the form MM/DD/YY: 02/25/88

Enter the number of days to subtract from date: 8888

02/25/88 minus 8888 days = 10/26/63.
```

Day_Of_Week

Description

▼

Day_Of_Week returns the pointer to *Buffer, a string that contains the day of the week corresponding to the string date. The day can be configured in one of the following formats: uppercase abbreviation, upper- and lowercase abbreviation, lowercase abbreviation, uppercase full name, upper- and lowercase full name, or lowercase full name.

Routine Declaration

▼

```
char *Day_Of_Week(char *Date,
                  int  DayCase,
                  char *Buffer)
```

Passed Variables

▼

***Date String Pointer** A pointer to the string date, in the form MM/DD/YY, for which the day of the week is to be determined.

DayCase integer An integer indicating the form in which the day of the week is to be returned. Valid values for DayCase are 1 through 6. Table 2-1 shows sample results from each value for DayCase.

***Buffer String Pointer** A pointer to the string variable that will contain the resulting string.

Global Variables

▼

None

Error Codes/ Messages

▼

None

Discussion

▼

Day_Of_Week calculates and returns the day of the week for any date that Cal_Julian can successfully convert to a Julian Day Number. The date can be

Table 2-1. *DayCase Formats*

DayCase	Result Type	Example of Result
1	Uppercase abbreviation	MON
2	Upper- and lowercase abbreviation	Mon
3	Lowercase abbreviation	mon
4	Uppercase full name	MONDAY
5	Upper- and lowercase full name	Monday
6	Lowercase full name	monday

returned in several formats as shown in table 2-1 and can impart a professional touch to reports and certain types of entry screens in business applications. When you use the day of the week on reports, take into account that the length of the day string returned varies for formats 4 through 6, which return the full name of the day. When using the full Day_Of_Week name on screens and reports, you should ensure that you have sufficient room for the longest day name.

Day_Of_Week returns the textual name of the day by first calculating the number, between 1 and 7, for the day of the week. This number is used to retrieve the textual name from the array DOW. The textual name is then uppercased and truncated as indicated by the DayCase passed.

Limitations and Modifications

▼

As mentioned, some of the routines in the library have parameters that can be used to indicate multiple result formats. This routine and a few others have parameters for determining format styles. Although this may be difficult to read, the additional flexibility justified the potential difficulties in these few cases.

Day_Of_Week has the same limitations with Cal_Julian—you must modify Cal_Julian to properly handle the rollover to the next century.

As with many of the date routines, Day_Of_Week does not perform any error handling on the date. If a bad date is passed, an error may result in the call to Cal_Julian. To correct this, you may want to call Check_Date before calling Cal_Julian, but this may cause a degradation in performance if you make extensive use of Day_Of_Week.

Routine Source Code

▼

```
#include <math.h>
#include <string.h>
#include <stdio.h>
#include <stdlib.h>
#include <ctype.h>
#include <plib.h>

char *Day_Of_Week(char *Date,
                  int DayCase,
                  char *Buffer)
/*
  Returns the day of the week in *Buffer for the calendar date passed
  in *Date in the form MM/DD/YY.
  The following formats are selected by DayCase:
    DayCase = 1  -  MON, TUE, WED, THU...
    DayCase = 2  -  Mon, Tue, Wed, Thu...
    DayCase = 3  -  mon, tue, wed, thu...
    DayCase = 4  -  MONDAY, TUESDAY, WEDNESDAY...
    DayCase = 5  -  Monday, Tuesday, Wednesday...
    DayCase = 6  -  monday, tuesday, wednesday...
```

```
*/
{/* Day_Of_Week */
  char
    DOW[7][10] = {"sunday", "monday", "tuesday", "wednesday",
                  "thursday", "friday", "saturday"};

  strcpy(Buffer, DOW[floor((Cal_Julian(Date) + 2) -
                      (floor((Cal_Julian(Date) + 2) ÷ 7) * 7))]);

  /* If DayCase 1, 2, or 3 copy only first 3 characters of day name */
  if ((DayCase == 1) || (DayCase == 2) || (DayCase == 3))
    Buffer[3] = 0;
  switch (DayCase)
  {
    case 1:
    case 4:
      /* Uppercase full name */
      strupr(Buffer);
    break;

    case 2:
    case 5:
      /* Uppercase first letter only */
      Buffer[0] = Buffer[0] - 32;
    break;
  } /* switch */
  return(Buffer);
} /* Day_Of_Week */
```

Sample Usage Source Code

```
/*
  This program will allow the user to input a date then use the function
  Day_Of_Week to calculate and display the day of the week for the date.
*/

extern unsigned _stklen=16384; /* Minimum recommend stack size */
#include <stdio.h>
#include <math.h>
#include <dos.h>
#include <mem.h>
#include <alloc.h>
#include <ctype.h>
#include <string.h>
#include <stdlib.h>
#include <plib.h>
#include <plib.glo>
```

```
/****************************************************************************/
main()
{
  char
    TempDate[9] = "",
    Buffer[9] = "";

  Calibrate_Delay();            /* Calibrate delay factor */
  Get_Video_Mode("Video.CFG"); /* Get display adapter type */
  Install_Crit_Error();         /* Set up application critical error handler */
  InputAbsolute=AbortPrint=0;  /* Initialize global variables */

  /* Application code to follow */

  Clr_Scr();
  printf("Enter the date in the form MM/DD/YY: ");
  scanf("%s", TempDate);
  printf("\n%s is a %s.\n", TempDate, Day_Of_Week(TempDate, 5, Buffer));

} /*main*/
```

Sample Usage Output

▼

```
Enter the date in the form MM/DD/YY: 02/25/88

02/25/88 is a Thursday.
```

Delay

Description

▼

Delay pauses execution of the program for a specified number of milliseconds. A prior call to Calibrate_Delay is required only once to calibrate the looping constant.

Routine Declaration

▼

```
void Delay(int MilliSecs)
```

Passed Variables

▼

MilliSecs integer This field specifies the number of milliseconds to be consumed by the delay.

Global Variables

▼

None

Error Codes/ Messages

▼

None

Discussion

▼

Delay provides a consistent pause in program execution. Unlike Turbo C version 1.0, Turbo C version 1.5 now provides a routine similar to Delay.

Delay uses a for loop to count through the milliseconds specified and a while loop inside the for loop that acts as a counter calibrated with the global variable CalDelay. CalDelay is set by calling the library routine Cal_Delay.

Limitations and Modifications

▼

None

Routine Source Code

▼

```
extern unsigned int
  CalDelay;

void Delay(int MilliSecs)
/*
  This procedure will wait for MilliSecs # of milliseconds, then continue.
*/
{ /* Delay */
  unsigned int
    C,
    Mil;

  for (C = Mil = 1; C <= MilliSecs; C++, Mil = 1)
  {
    while (Mil <= CalDelay)
      Mil++;
  } /* for */
} /* Delay */
```

Sample Usage Source Code

▼

```
/*
  This program will pause for 3000 milliseconds (3 seconds) to demonstrate
  the Delay routine.
*/

extern unsigned _stklen=16384; /* Minimum recommend stack size */
#include <stdio.h>
```

```
#include <math.h>
#include <dos.h>
#include <mem.h>
#include <alloc.h>
#include <ctype.h>
#include <string.h>
#include <stdlib.h>
#include <plib.h>
#include <plib.glo>

/**************************************************************************/
main()
{
  char
    Check;

  Calibrate_Delay();              /* Calibrate delay factor */
  Get_Video_Mode("Video.CFG");  /* Get display adapter type */
  Install_Crit_Error();         /* Set up application critical error handler */
  InputAbsolute=AbortPrint=0;   /* Initialize global variables */

  /* Application code to follow */

  Clr_Scr();

  printf("\n   Please press < RETURN > to start a 3 second delay. \n");
  scanf("%c", &Check);
  Delay(3000);

  printf("\nTime's up!\n");

} /*  main  */
```

Sample Usage Output

▼

```
Please press < RETURN > to start a 3 second delay.

Time's up!
```

Delete

Description

▼

Delete removes a specified number of characters from a string. The routine requires the starting position of the deletion and the number of characters to be deleted.

Routine Declaration

▼

```
void Delete(char *DlStr,
            int Start,
            int NumChars)
```

Passed Variables

▼

***DlStr String Pointer** A pointer to the string variable that contains the string to be modified.

Global Variables

▼

None

Error Codes/ Messages

▼

None

Discussion

▼

Delete relieves some of the tedium and complexity required to delete portions of a string via Turbo C's string functions. The routine functions identically to the Turbo Pascal delete command, so if you're converting to C from Pascal you may be familiar with the command.

Delete starts by ensuring that the specified start position is within the string. If the start position is after the end of the string, the string is left unchanged. If the start position is a valid location in the specified string, Delete checks to determine if the final location indicated by the start position plus the number of characters to be deleted is within the string. If the ending position falls outside the string, the start position is set to a null terminator. Otherwise, a memory move is done to move the undeleted portion of the string down to the start position.

Limitations and Modifications

▼

None

Routine Source Code

▼

```
#include <string.h>
#include <mem.h>

void Delete(char *DlStr,
            int Start,
            int NumChars)
/*
  This routine will delete NumChars of chars from *DlStr starting at
```

```
  position Start which can be (1..n). If Start is past the actual end of
  the string, nothing is changed. If Start is within the string, but
  NumChars exceeds the length of the string, the string will be terminated
  at Start.
*/
{ /* Delete */
  int
    SLen;

  Start--;
  SLen = strlen(DlStr);

  if (Start <= SLen - 1)
  {
    if (Start + NumChars > SLen - 1)
      DlStr[Start] = 0;
    else
    {
      movmem(DlStr + Start + NumChars, DlStr + Start,
              SLen -  (Start + NumChars) + 1);
    } /* if Start else */
  } /* if Start */
} /* Delete */
```

Sample Usage Source Code

```
/*
  This program will use Delete() to erase a substring from a string.
*/

extern unsigned _stklen=16384; /* Minimum recommend stack size */
#include <stdio.h>
#include <math.h>
#include <dos.h>
#include <mem.h>
#include <alloc.h>
#include <ctype.h>
#include <string.h>
#include <stdlib.h>
#include <plib.h>
#include <plib.glo>


/*****************************************************************************/
main()
{
  char
    String[81] = "";
```

```
  Calibrate_Delay();            /* Calibrate delay factor */
  Get_Video_Mode("Video.CFG"); /* Get display adapter type */
  Install_Crit_Error();         /* Set up application critical error handler */
  InputAbsolute=AbortPrint=0;  /* Initialize global variables */

  /* Application code to follow */

  Clr_Scr();

  printf("\n A substring is deleted from the string in the following.\n");

  strcpy(String, "She says she sells seashells at the seashore.");
  printf("\n    %s\n", String);

  Delete(String, 1, 10) ;
  printf("\nAfter deleting 10 characters starting at position 1:\n%s\n",
      String);

} /*  main  */
```

Sample Usage Output

▼

```
A substring is deleted from the string in the following.

   She says she sells seashells at the seashore.

After deleting 10 characters starting at position 1:
he sells seashells at the seashore.
```

Draw_Frame

Description

▼

Draw_Frame creates a variety of bordered windows with optional titles on the video display. The borders can be composed of single lines, double lines, block characters, and other designs. The title is centered in the top line of the border.

Routine Declaration

▼

```
void Draw_Frame(int TLCX,
                int TLCY,
                int Wide,
                int Len,
                int Lines,
                char *Atr,
                char *Title,
                char WinBack)
```

Passed Variables

▼

TLCX integer The top left corner X (horizontal) position on the screen for the upper left corner of the window. Valid TLCX values are 1 through 79.

TLCY integer The top left corner Y (vertical) position on the screen for the upper left corner of the window. Valid TLCY values are 1 through 24.

Wide integer The horizontal width of the frame to be created. Valid Wide values are 2 through 80.

Len integer The vertical height of the frame to be created. Valid Len values are 2 through 24.

Lines integer The type of border to be drawn around the window. The border types are: 0 for block character border, 1 for single line border, 2 for double line border, 3 for border using +−, 4 for border using +=, and 5 for border using *.

***Atr String Pointer** A pointer to a two-character string that contains the video display attributes for the border and title. There are three video display attributes available with Draw_Frame: N for normal, R for reverse video, and H for high-intensity normal video. The first character of the attribute string controls the border attributes and the second character controls the title attributes. The attributes may be passed in upper- or lowercase letters.

Title String Pointer A pointer to the window title to be centered in the top line of the window. The title has all leading and trailing spaces removed and a single space concatenated onto the beginning and end. If the title is too long for the window, it is truncated to the width of the window.

WinBack char The value to be used for the background color of the window displayed.

Global Variables

▼

None

Error Codes/ Messages

▼

None

Discussion

▼

Draw_Frame is exceptionally useful in creating bordered windows, menus, and entry screens with a consistent look. By setting standards for how you want your screens to look, you can have several different people working on screen designs and be confident they will be compatible in design.

Draw_Frame clears the specified window with the background color indicated, sets the attributes for the text to be displayed, and constructs the frame by creating the top line, bottom line, and side lines. Finally, the title is formatted and displayed.

Limitations and Modifications

▼

As mentioned, some of the routines in the library have parameters that can be used to indicate multiple result formats. This routine and a few others have parameters for determining format styles. In these few cases, the additional flexibility justifies potential reading difficulties.

The main limitations to Draw_Frame are that you can only have six border types and the title has to be centered. You may find that your needs require more flexibility in the way you draw screens. You can compensate for these limitations by either altering Draw_Frame itself to use a different set of borders and different justification on the title or by adding parameters to Draw_Frame for performing optional positioning and styles. The latter method may seem like an excellent solution until you have to remember what all the added parameters are. Long parameter lists are difficult to work with in programs that perform numerous calls to a procedure like Draw_Frame. Because Draw_Frame already requires several parameters, additional parameters can make Draw-_Frame very cumbersome to use.

Routine Source Code

▼

```
#include <math.h>
#include <string.h>
#include <stdio.h>
#include <stdlib.h>
#include <ctype.h>
#include <plib.h>

extern char
  Normal,
  Reverse,
  VidHigh,
  WaitForRetrace;

void Draw_Frame(int TLCX,
                int TLCY,
                int Wide,
                int Len,
                int Lines,
                char *Atr,
                char *Title,
                char WinBack)
/*
  This function will draw a box starting at the Top Left Corner defined
  by TLCX, TLCY that is Wide columns and Len rows large with Lines # of
```

```
  lines (0 - 5, 0 = block, 1 = single, 2 = double, 3 = ±, 4 = +=, 5 = *).
  *Title will appear centered at the top of the box. *Atr is a 2-character
  string, e.g., "NR" where the first character is the Box attribute and the
  second is the *Title attribute. N = Normal, R = Reverse, & H = VidHigh.
  The screen boundary is defined to be from (1, 1) to (80, 25) and the boxes
  definition should not exceed these dimensions. The text inside the box
  will be cleared and the background will be set to WinBack color.
*/
{ /* Draw_Frame */
  char
    BAtr[2],
    Box[6][7] = {"▒▒▒▒▒▒", /* 0 = TL, 1 = BL, 2 = V, 3 = H, 4 = TR, 5 = BR */
                 "┌└│─┐┘",
                 "╔╚║═╗╝",
                 "++|-++",
                 "++|=++",
                 "******"},
    HLine[100],
    TLine[100];


  int
    C,
    RX;

  Wide -= 2;
  Len -= 2;
  if ((Len > 0) && (Wide > 0))
    Clear_Frame(WinBack, TLCX + 1, TLCY + 1, Wide, Len);
  HLine[0] = Box[Lines][0];
  for (C = 1; C <= Wide; HLine[C] = Box[Lines][3], C++);
  HLine[C++] = Box[Lines][4];
  HLine[C] = 0;
  for (C = 0; C <= 1; C++)
  {
    switch (Atr[C])
    {
      case 'N': case 'n': BAtr[C] = Normal;  break;
      case 'R': case 'r': BAtr[C] = Reverse; break;
      case 'H': case 'h': BAtr[C] = VidHigh; break;
    } /* switch */
    if ((WaitForRetrace) && (!C))
      BAtr[C] = (BAtr[C] & 0x0f) | WinBack;
  } /* for C */
  F_Write(TLCX, TLCY, BAtr[0], HLine);
  HLine[0] = Box[Lines][1];
  HLine[Wide + 1] = Box[Lines][5];
  F_Write(TLCX, TLCY + Len + 1, BAtr[0], HLine);
```

```
  Len += TLCY;
  RX = TLCX + Wide + 1;
  HLine[0] = Box[Lines][2];
  HLine[1] = 0;
  for (C = TLCY + 1; C <= Len; C++)
  {
    F_Write(TLCX, C, BAtr[0], HLine);
    F_Write(RX, C, BAtr[0], HLine);
  } /* for C */
  strcpy(TLine, Title);
  Erase_White_End(TLine);
  Erase_White_Begin(TLine);
  if (strlen(TLine) > 0)
  {
    Cen(TLine, HLine, strlen(TLine) + 2);
    RX = (((Wide + 2) - strlen(HLine)) >> 1) + TLCX;
    F_Write(RX, TLCY, BAtr[1], HLine);
  } /* if strlen */
} /* Draw_Frame */
```

Sample Usage Source Code

▼

```
/*
  This program will fill the screen up with asters then use Draw_Frame to
  draw various sizes and styles of boxes in the screen.
*/

extern unsigned _stklen=16384; /* Minimum recommend stack size */
#include <stdio.h>
#include <math.h>
#include <dos.h>
#include <mem.h>
#include <alloc.h>
#include <ctype.h>
#include <string.h>
#include <stdlib.h>
#include <plib.h>
#include <plib.glo>


/******************************************************************************/
main()
{
  int
    Temp=0;

  char
    TempString[81] ="";
```

```
  Calibrate_Delay();           /* Calibrate delay factor */
  Get_Video_Mode("Video.CFG"); /* Get display adapter type */
  Install_Crit_Error();        /* Set up application critical error handler */
  InputAbsolute=AbortPrint=0;  /* Initialize global variables */

  /* Application code to follow */

  Rpt("*", TempString, 80) ;
  for ( Temp = 1; Temp <= 24 ; Temp++ )
    F_Write(1, Temp, Normal, TempString);

  Draw_Frame(2, 2, 15, 5, 1, "NR", "Frame 1", Black) ;
  Message ("Frame X=2, Y=2, Wide=15, Depth=5, Style=1") ;
  Delay (2000);

  Draw_Frame (40, 6, 25, 8, 2, "NR", "Frame 2", Brown) ;
  Message ("Frame X=40, Y=6, Wide=25, Depth=8, Style=2") ;
  Delay (2000);

  Draw_Frame (5, 12, 14, 7, 3, "NR", "Frame 3", Red) ;
  Message ("Frame X=5, Y=12, Wide=14, Depth=7, Style=3") ;
  Delay (2000);

} /*main*/
```

Sample Usage Output

▼

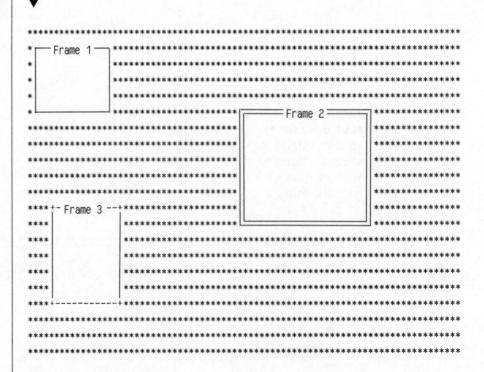

```
********************************************************************************
*┌── Frame 1 ──┐****************************************************************
*│             │****************************************************************
*│             │****************************************************************
*│             │****************************************************************
*└─────────────┘***********************╔════════ Frame 2 ══════╗****************
***************************************║                       ║****************
***************************************║                       ║****************
***************************************║                       ║****************
***************************************║                       ║****************
***************************************║                       ║****************
****+- Frame 3 --+*********************║                       ║****************
****|            |*********************╚═══════════════════════╝****************
****|            |**************************************************************
****|            |**************************************************************
****|            |**************************************************************
****|            |**************************************************************
****+------------+**************************************************************
********************************************************************************
********************************************************************************
********************************************************************************
```

```
********************************************************************************
********************************************************************************
********************************************************************************

           Frame  X=5, Y=12, Width=14, Depth=7, Style=5
```

Ent_Control

Description

▼

Ent_Control manages data entry screens using the library routine Ent_Scr. If multiple pages are being used, Ent_Control controls line incrementation for moving from field to field as well as incrementing or decrementing the page number. Ent_Control returns true (1) if the next line does not exceed the specified LastField value and an Escape has not been pressed. If the LastField has been exceeded or the user presses Escape, Ent_Control returns false (0).

Routine Declaration

▼

```
char Ent_Control(int  LastField,
                 char KeyControl,
                 char PageMode,
                 int  *Page)
```

Passed Variables

▼

LastField integer This field contains the field number of the last field in the entry screen.

KeyControl char If KeyControl is set true (1), any command key (any key that would cause Input_Alpha to exit) causes Ent_Control to return false (0). If KeyControl is set false (0), only an Escape or Enter, on the last field, will cause Ent_Control to return false (0).

PageMode char If PageMode is set true (1), pressing PgUp or PgDn causes the value of *Page to be incremented or decremented and Ent_Control to return false (0). This allows for control of multipage entry screens. If PageMode is false (0), PgUp and PgDn move the pointer to the top option or bottom option on the menu.

***Page integer Pointer** A pointer to the integer that contains the number for the current entry screen page.

Global Variables

▼

FieldLineNum integer Contains the current field number for data entry screens. The value is incremented when Enter or Down is pressed and decremented when Up is pressed.

Error Codes/ Messages

▼

```
Bad key pressed
```

This message appears if a key not specifically trapped is pressed and KeyControl is set false (0).

Discussion

▼

Ent_Control provides a short and easy means within a control structure for creating data entry screens. Using Ent_Control and Ent_Scr, the associated field control routine, you can easily create entry screens that are quick, versatile, and easy to implement. Ent_Control manages multiple pages for an entry screen and a virtually unlimited number of fields per entry screen.

Ent_Control is divided into two main sections. The first manages the field number incrementation if FieldLineNum is currently zero, and adjusts FieldLineNum based on the key pressed and whether or not PageMode has been set true (1). If PageMode is set true (1), the field number is adjusted based on the specific key pressed. If PageMode is false (0), FieldLineNum is set to field 1.

The second section manages the line numbering when FieldLineNum is not zero, and has a separate section for each valid command key that is interpreted. Each key is a case in a switch statement, with a default used to trap any key not specifically interpreted.

Limitations and Modifications

▼

None

Routine Source Code

▼

```
#include <math.h>
#include <string.h>
#include <stdio.h>
#include <stdlib.h>
#include <ctype.h>
#include <plib.h>

extern int
  CurKey,
  FieldLineNum;

char Ent_Control(int LastField,
                 char DataBase,
                 char PageMode,
                 int *Page)
/*
  This routine will handle the control of movement in the entry screens
```

```
  using Ent_Scr. If the user has completed the entry screen, Ent_Control
  will return false (0), if the user is still in the entry screen, it
  will return true (1). If DataBase is true (1), any command key will
  cause Ent_Control to return false (0), otherwise, only a last field
  Enter or an Esc key will cause Ent_Control to return false (0).
  If PageMode is true, PgUp and PgDown will cause *Page to be incremented
  and decremented for using with paged entry screens. Limits must be
  implemented in the actual entry screen itself.
*/
{
  if (!FieldLineNum)
  {
    if (PageMode)
    {
      switch (CurKey)
      {
        case -80: /* Down */
          FieldLineNum = 1;
        break;
        case -72: /* Up */
          FieldLineNum = LastField;
        break;
        default:
          FieldLineNum = 1;
        break;
      } /* switch Curkey */
    } /* if PageMode */
    else
      FieldLineNum = 1;
  } /* if FieldLineNum */
  else
  {
    switch(CurKey)
    {
      case 0:
        FieldLineNum = 1;
      break;
      case -72: /* Up */
        if ((PageMode) && (FieldLineNum <= 1))
        {
          FieldLineNum = LastField + 1;
          (*Page)--;
        } /* if PageMode */
        else
          FieldLineNum -= (FieldLineNum > 1);
      break;
      case -80: /* Down */
        if ((PageMode) && (FieldLineNum >= LastField))
```

```
    {
      FieldLineNum = LastField + 1;
      (*Page)++;
    } /* if PageMode */
    else
      FieldLineNum += (FieldLineNum < LastField);
  break;
  case 13: /* Enter */
    FieldLineNum++;
  break;
  case 27: /* Esc */
    FieldLineNum = LastField + 1;
  break;
  case -73: /* PgUp */
    if (PageMode)
    {
      FieldLineNum = LastField + 1;
      (*Page)--;
    } /* if PageMode */
    else
      FieldLineNum = 1;
  break;
  case -81: /* PgDown */
    if (PageMode)
    {
      FieldLineNum = LastField + 1;
      (*Page)++;
    } /* if PageMode */
    else
      FieldLineNum = LastField;
  break;
  case 9: /* Tab */
  case -15: /* Back Tab */
  default:
    if (DataBase)
      FieldLineNum = LastField + 1;
    else
      Lo_Mess("Bad key pressed");
  break;
 } /* switch CurKey */
} /* if FieldLineNum else */
return(FieldLineNum <= LastField);
} /* Ent_Control */
```

Sample Usage Source Code

▼

See the sample usage in the library routine Ent_Scr for usage of Ent_Control.

Ent_Scr

Description

▼

Ent_Scr manages the entry of a single data field on a data entry screen, and provides entry for any of the data types allowed by Input_Alpha, Input_Num, or Input_Date. The field has an optional prompt and can be placed at any location on the screen by using the positioning parameters. The data entry screen is controlled by a loop using Ent_Control. For additional information, see Ent_Control.

Routine Declaration

▼

```
void Ent_Scr(int  FieldNo,
             int  X,
             int  Y,
             char *Prompt,
             char *RType,
             char *Value)
```

Passed Variables

▼

FieldNo integer This value contains the current field number on the data entry screen. FieldNo is used to control the order in which the fields are manipulated while using the entry screen.

X integer This field contains the horizontal position for the starting position of the field's prompt string (*Prompt). The field (*Value) immediately follows the prompt. Valid values for X are 1 through 80.

Y integer This field contains the vertical position for the starting position of the field's prompt string (*Prompt). Valid values for Y are 1 through 25; however, line 25 should not be used because line 25 is used by the routine Message.

***Prompt String Pointer** A pointer to the string that contains the textual prompt to be displayed in front of the actual data field being manipulated.

***RType String Pointer** A pointer to the string that contains the field type and valid data description used to determine what type of data is to be entered in the field. See Prompt, Input_Alpha, Input_Num, and Input_Date for a complete description of the valid field types.

***Value String Pointer** A pointer to the data string to be modified by the current call to Ent_Scr.

Global Variables

▼

None

Error Codes/ Messages

▼

Any error message generated by Input_Alpha, Input_Date, and Input_Num can occur with calls to Ent_Scr.

Discussion

▼

Ent_Scr creates high-performance data entry screens that are flexible and easy to work with. Ent_Scr allows prompted data entry fields in a variety of formats that can be created in minutes and the ability to perform special processing between fields.

Ent_Scr is divided into two main areas. The first displays the *Prompt and *Value strings when FieldLineNum is set to zero. The second section is divided into smaller sections that handle the specific data types and call the appropriate entry routine (Input_Alpha, Input_Date, or Input_Num).

Limitations and Modifications

▼

None

Routine Source Code

▼

```
#include <math.h>
#include <mem.h>
#include <string.h>
#include <stdio.h>
#include <stdlib.h>
#include <ctype.h>
#include <plib.h>

extern char
  RecChanged,
  Normal,
  Reverse,
  VidHigh;

extern int
  CurKey,
  FieldLineNum;

void Ent_Scr(int FieldNo,
             int X,
             int Y,
             char *Prompt,
             char *RType,
             char *Value)
/*
  This function will, when FieldLineNum = 0, simply write out *Prompt at
```

```
  X, Y in Normal (Blended) with *Value in VidHigh (Blended) following
  it. When FieldLineNum = FieldNo it will allow modification of *Value
  based on *RType (see routine Prompt, "A." not supported). When an Up
  or down key is pressed, it will decrement or increment FieldLineNum
  and exit. If FieldLineNum != FieldNo, then it will simply exit. In
  all cases, the global variable CurKey will contain the last key
  pressed by the user (e.g., a 27 if the user wished to abort and
  pressed <ESC>). *Value may be initialized to a default value.
*/
{ /* Ent_Scr */
  int
    Temp1,
    Temp2,
    Temp3,
    FieldLen;

  float
    Min,
    Max;

  char
    CompStr[85],
    Spec[31],
    ValSet[256],
    TStr1[256];

  if (!FieldLineNum)
  {
    switch (toupper(RType[0]))
    {
      case 'A':
        FieldLen = atoi(Copy(RType, 2, Pos(',', RType) - 2, TStr1));
        F_Write(X, Y, Normal, Prompt);
        F_Write(X + strlen(Prompt), Y, VidHigh, LJ(Value, TStr1, FieldLen));
      break;

      case 'C':
        F_Write(X, Y, Normal, Prompt);
        F_Write(X + strlen(Prompt), Y, VidHigh, LJ(Value, TStr1, 8));
      break;

      case 'Y':
        F_Write(X, Y, Normal, Prompt);
        F_Write(X + strlen(Prompt), Y, VidHigh, LJ(Value, TStr1, 1));
      break;

      case '0': case '1': case '2': case '3': case '4': case '5':
      case '6': case '7': case '8': case '9': case 'I': case 'D':
```

```
        strcpy(Spec, Copy(RType, 1, Pos(',', RType) - 1, TStr1));
        F_WriteXY(X, Y, Normal, Prompt);
        F_Write(X + strlen(Prompt), Y, VidHigh,
                RJ(Value, TStr1, (Pos('-', RType) != 0) +
                   Num_Pattern_Size(Spec, &Temp1, &Temp2, &Temp3)));
      break;
    } /* switch */
  } /* if !FieldLineNum */
  else
  {
    if (FieldLineNum == FieldNo)
    {
      strcpy(CompStr, Value);
      switch (toupper(RType[0]))
      {
        case 'A':
          FieldLen = atoi(Copy(RType, 2, Pos(',', RType) - 2, TStr1));
          if (Pos(',', RType) != strlen(RType))
            strcpy(ValSet, Copy(RType, Pos(',', RType) + 1,
                   strlen(RType) - Pos(',', RType), TStr1));
          else
            ValSet[0] = 0;
          F_WriteXY(X, Y, Normal, Prompt);
          Input_Alpha(FieldLen, ValSet, Value);
          for(Temp1 = strlen(Value); Temp1<FieldLen;
              Value[Temp1] = 32, Temp1++);
          Value[Temp1] = 0;
        break;

        case 'C':
          F_WriteXY(X, Y, Normal, Prompt);
          Input_Date(Value);
        break;

        case 'Y':
          F_WriteXY(X, Y, Normal, Prompt);
          Input_Alpha(1, "YyNn", Value);
          Value[0] = toupper(Value[0]);
        break;

        case '0': case '1': case '2': case '3': case '4': case '5':
        case '6': case '7': case '8': case '9': case 'I': case 'D':
          strcpy(Spec, Copy(RType, 1, Pos(',', RType) - 1, TStr1));
          Min = atof(Copy(RType, Pos(',', RType) + 1,
                     Pos(' ', RType) - (Pos(',', RType) + 1), TStr1));
          Max = atof(Copy(RType, Pos(' ', RType) + 1,
                     strlen(RType) - Pos(' ', RType), TStr1));
          F_WriteXY(X, Y, Normal, Prompt);
```

```
          Erase_White_Begin(Value);
          Input_Num(Value, Spec, Min, Max);
          RJ(Value, TStr1, (Pos('-', RType) != 0) +
             Num_Pattern_Size(Spec, &Temp1, &Temp2, &Temp3));
          strcpy(Value, TStr1);
          if (!Is_Text(Value))
            setmem(Value,(Pos('-', RType) != 0) +
                   Num_Pattern_Size(Spec, &Temp1, &Temp2, &Temp3), 0);
        break;
      } /* end switch */
      if (Is_Text(CompStr) | Is_Text(Value))
        RecChanged = (strcmp(CompStr, Value) != 0) | RecChanged;
    } /* if FieldLineNum */
  } /* if !FieldLineNum else */
} /* Ent_Scr */
```

Sample Usage Source Code

▼

```
/*
  This program will set up a structure to store personal information.
  Then it will allow the user to input the information on a database-style
  data entry screen (made with Ent_Control and Ent_Scr). Finally, it will
  show the information that the user entered into the structure.
*/

extern unsigned _stklen=16384; /* Minimum recommend stack size */
#include <stdio.h>
#include <math.h>
#include <dos.h>
#include <mem.h>
#include <alloc.h>
#include <ctype.h>
#include <string.h>
#include <stdlib.h>
#include <plib.h>
#include <plib.glo>


/*****************************************************************************/
main()
{
  char
    Check,
    Buffer[81];

  int
    Page = 0 ;
```

```
struct PInfo
{
  char
    FName[16],
    LName[16],
    BirthDay[9],
    Weight[4],
    Sex[2];
} P1;


Calibrate_Delay();          /* Calibrate delay factor */
Get_Video_Mode("Video.CFG"); /* Get display adapter type */
Install_Crit_Error();        /* Set up application critical error handler */
InputAbsolute=AbortPrint=0;  /* Initialize global variables */

/* Application code to follow */

Clr_Scr () ;
Draw_Frame(8, 6, 65, 10, 2, "NR", "Enter Personal Information", Blue);
F_Write(1, 20, VidHigh,
      Cen("Use <Up> & <Down> arrows to move, <Esc> when done",
          Buffer, 80));

setmem (&P1, sizeof(P1), 0); /* null out structure */
FieldLineNum = 0;

do
{
  Ent_Scr (1, 10, 8,"Name :   First: ", "A15,", P1.FName);
  Ent_Scr (2, 43, 8,"Last : ", "A15,", P1.LName);
  Ent_Scr (3, 10, 10,"Birthday       : ", "C", P1.BirthDay);
  Ent_Scr (4, 10, 12,"Weight         : ", "3I,0 999", P1.Weight);
  Ent_Scr (5, 10, 14,"Sex (M/F)      : ", "A1,MF", P1.Sex);
}
while (Ent_Control(5, 0, 0, &Page));

Clr_Scr();
printf ("\nYour entry is ( %s, %s, %s, %s, %s ). \n", P1.FName,
      P1.LName, P1.BirthDay, P1.Weight, P1.Sex);

} /* main */
```

Sample Usage Output

▼

```
╔════════════════ Enter Personal Information ══════════════════╗
║                                                              ║
║Name :   First: Joseph          Last : Hope                   ║
```

```
Birthday      : 05/25/62

Weight        : 150

Sex (M/F)     : M
```

```
          Use <Up> & <Down> arrows to move, <Esc> when done


Your entry is ( Joseph, Hope, 05/25/62, 150, M ).
```

Erase_White

Description

▼

Erase_White removes all leading, trailing, and interword white space from the specified string (*St). The characters removed include all ASCII characters with a value less than or equal to 32. When complete, the string pointer is returned.

Routine Declaration

▼

```
char *Erase_White(char *St)
```

Passed Variables

▼

***St String Pointer** A pointer to the string variable that is to have all leading, trailing, and interword white space removed.

Global Variables

▼

None

Error Codes/ Messages

▼

None

Discussion

▼

Erase_White removes white space by moving only valid nonwhite space characters to the left side of the string while searching to the right for the next nonwhite space character. Because Erase_White alters and searches the same string, it significantly improves the performance of this routine over the method of creating a second copy of the original string and then moving characters from one to the other.

Erase_White removes all spaces from the passed string by using a for loop to step through the original string. Each character is checked to see if it is a white space character. If it is not a white space character, it is moved to the next available position on the left side of the string. The next available position is maintained in the variable C1, which is incremented each time a valid character is moved to the left. Finally, Erase_White returns the pointer to the string.

Limitations and Modifications

▼

The main limitation to Erase_White is that it is destructive to the original string. You may want to create another routine that is nondestructive.

Routine Source Code

▼

```
char *Erase_White(char *St)
/*
  This function will remove all blank space (Tabs, spaces,
  anything <= ascii 32) from *St and will return the pointer to *St.
*/
{ /* Erase_White */
  int
    C,
    C1;

  for (C = C1 = 0; St[C]; C++)
  {
    if ((unsigned)St[C] > 32)
    {
      St[C1] = St[C];
      C1++;
    } /* if */
  } /* for */
  St[C1] = 0;
  return(St);
} /* Erase_White */
```

Sample Usage Source Code

▼

```
/*
  This program will use Erase_White to remove all spaces from a string.
*/

extern unsigned _stklen=16384; /* Minimum recommend stack size */
#include <stdio.h>
#include <math.h>
```

```
#include <dos.h>
#include <mem.h>
#include <alloc.h>
#include <ctype.h>
#include <string.h>
#include <stdlib.h>
#include <plib.h>
#include <plib.glo>


/*****************************************************************************/
main()
{
  char
    TempString[81] = "";

  Calibrate_Delay();              /* Calibrate delay factor */
  Get_Video_Mode("Video.CFG");  /* Get display adapter type */
  Install_Crit_Error();          /* Set up application critical error handler */
  InputAbsolute=AbortPrint=0;    /* Initialize global variables */

  /* Application code to follow */

  Clr_Scr();
  strcpy(TempString, "  ** This is the original String **  ");
  printf("Original --%s--\n", TempString);
  Erase_White(TempString);
  printf("\nErased --%s--\n", TempString);

} /*main*/
```

Sample Usage Output

▼

```
Original --  ** This is the original String **  --

Erased --**ThisistheoriginalString**--
```

Erase_White_Begin

Description

▼

Erase_White_Begin removes all leading white space from the passed string. The characters removed include all ASCII characters with a value less than or equal to 32. Erase_White_Begin returns a pointer to the string when complete.

Routine Declaration

▼

```
char *Erase_White_Begin(char *St)
```

Passed Variables

▼

***St String Pointer** A pointer to the string variable that is to have all leading white space removed.

Global Variables

▼

None

Error Codes/ Messages

▼

None

Discussion

▼

Erase_White_Begin removes all leading white space from the string by using a while to examine each character from an incrementing counter offset. After the first nonwhite space is found, a while loop moves the remaining characters beyound the counter offset to the left. Finally, the string pointer is returned.

Limitations and Modifications

▼

To correct the limitation of altering the original string, you may develop a new routine that creates a new string. There may be a slight, but acceptable, performance disadvantage in this method.

Routine Source Code

▼

```
char *Erase_White_Begin(char *St)
/*
  This function will remove all blank space (Tabs, spaces,
  anything <= ascii 32) from the beginning of *St and will
  return the pointer to *St.
*/
{ /* Erase_White_Begin */
  int
    C,
    C1;

  C1 = 0;
  for (C = 0; (((unsigned)St[C] <= 32) && (St[C])); C++);
  if (St[C])
  {
    while (St[C])
```

```
    {
      St[C1] = St[C];
      C1++;
      C++;
    } /* while */
  } /* if */
  St[C1] = 0;
  return(St);
} /* Erase_White_Begin */
```

Sample Usage Source Code

▼

```
/*
  This program will use Erase_White_Begin to remove all the spaces
  from the beginning of a string.
*/

extern unsigned _stklen=16384; /* Minimum recommend stack size */
#include <stdio.h>
#include <math.h>
#include <dos.h>
#include <mem.h>
#include <alloc.h>
#include <ctype.h>
#include <string.h>
#include <stdlib.h>
#include <plib.h>
#include <plib.glo>


/****************************************************************************/
main()
{
  char
    TempString[81] = "";

  Calibrate_Delay();            /* Calibrate delay factor */
  Get_Video_Mode("Video.CFG"); /* Get display adapter type */
  Install_Crit_Error();         /* Set up application critical error handler */
  InputAbsolute=AbortPrint=0;  /* Initialize global variables */

  /* Application code to follow */

  Clr_Scr();
  strcpy(TempString, "   ** This is the original String **   ");
  printf("Original --%s--\n", TempString) ;
  Erase_White_Begin(TempString);
  printf("\nBegin Erased --%s--\n", TempString) ;
```

```
} /*main*/
```

Sample Usage Output

▼

```
Original --  ** This is the original String **  --

Begin Erased --** This is the original String **  --
```

Erase_White_End

Description

▼

Erase_White_End removes all trailing white space from the passed string. The characters removed include all ASCII characters with a value less than or equal to 32. Erase_White_End returns the string pointer when complete.

Routine Declaration

▼

```
char *Erase_White_End(char *St)
```

Passed Variables

▼

***St String Pointer** A pointer to the string variable that is to have all trailing white spaces removed.

Global Variables

▼

None

Error Codes/ Messages

▼

None

Discussion

▼

Erase_White_End removes all trailing white space from the string passed by using a for loop to determine where the last nonwhite space is located and decrementing a counter offset. A null terminator is placed after the last nonwhite space character, and Erase_White_End returns the string pointer.

Limitations and Modifications

▼

To correct the limitation of altering the original string, you may develop a new routine that creates a new string. There may be a slight, but acceptable, performance disadvantage in this method.

Routine Source Code

```
char *Erase_White_End(char *St)
/*
  This function will remove all blank space (Tabs, spaces,
  anything  <= ascii 32) from the end of *St and will return
  the pointer to *St.
*/
{ /* Erase_White_End */
  int
    C;

  if (St[0])
  {
    for (C = 0; St[0]; C++); /* Get length of *St */
    for (C--; ((C > 0) && ((unsigned)St[C] <= 32)); C--);
    if ((unsigned)St[C] > 32)
      St[C + 1] = 0;
    else
      St[C] = 0;
  } /* if */
  return(St);
} /* Erase_White_End */
```

Sample Usage Source Code

```
/*
  This program will use Erase_White_End to remove all the spaces
  at the end of a string.
*/

extern unsigned _stklen=16384; /* Minimum recommend stack size */
#include <stdio.h>
#include <math.h>
#include <dos.h>
#include <mem.h>
#include <alloc.h>
#include <ctype.h>
#include <string.h>
#include <stdlib.h>
#include <plib.h>
#include <plib.glo>


/****************************************************************************/
main()
{
  char
```

```
    TempString[81] = "";

  Calibrate_Delay();          /* Calibrate delay factor */
  Get_Video_Mode("Video.CFG"); /* Get display adapter type */
  Install_Crit_Error();        /* Set up application critical error handler */
  InputAbsolute=AbortPrint=0;  /* Initialize global variables */

  /* Application code to follow */

  Clr_Scr();
  strcpy(TempString, "  ** This is the original String **  ");
  printf ("Original --%s--\n", TempString);

  Erase_White_End (TempString);
  printf ("\nEnd Erased --%s--\n", TempString);

} /*main*/
```

Sample Usage Output

▼

```
Original --  ** This is the original String **  --

End Erased --  ** This is the original String **--
```

F_Write

Description

▼

F_Write is an assembly language routine designed to write text directly to video memory with a specified display attribute. A call to Get_Video_Mode must be made at some time prior to any calls to F_Write. If you do not call Get-_Video_Mode prior to using F_Write, your system may lock up and force you to reboot.

Routine Declaration

▼

```
void F_Write(unsigned int Col,
             unsigned int Row,
             char Attribute,
             char *St)
```

Passed Variables

▼

Col unsigned int The horizontal position on the screen for the first character of the string to be displayed. Valid values for Col are 1 through 80.

Row unsigned int The vertical position on the screen for the first character of the string to be displayed. Valid values for Row are 1 through 25.

Attribute char The video attribute to be used in displaying the string.

***St String Pointer** A pointer to the character string to be displayed. The string should typically not exceed a length of 80 characters.

Global Variables

▼

BaseOfScreen Designates the base memory address of the video display memory for the current type of video display. See Get_Video_Mode for the exact calculation and setup for BaseOfScreen. F_Write does not alter the value of BaseOfScreen.

WaitForRetrace Flags F_Write's looping structure synchronizing the display of characters with the video retracing done on color systems. If this synchronization is not accomplished, you may see video flickering during screen updates.

Error Codes/ Messages

▼

None

Discussion

▼

F_Write was created because of the slow performance of Turbo C's display routine (i.e., printf). With F_Write and a for loop displaying a predefined string 80 characters long, you may rewrite the entire screen on a monochrome AT system (8mHz) 500 times in approximately eight seconds. The same process performed by routines provided with Turbo C would take almost seven minutes. Another difference between the F_Write and Turbo C display routines is that a call to F_write does not affect the current cursor position. If you do need to move the cursor to the end of the displayed string, you can use the related library routine F_WriteXY. Because F_WriteXY causes a performance loss that may be important in large screen updates, you may want to experiment with the two routines to determine which is best for your main display calls.

The actual mechanics of F_Write are fairly simple. The routine loads the video attribute value passed into the high-order byte of the AX register (AH). Next, a character is moved from the string to the low-order byte of the AX register (AL), and F_Write moves the entire register to the video display memory. The location in memory is based on the value in BaseOfScreen and the offset calculated from the column and row values passed for the string to be displayed. The process of loading and displaying characters is repeated until the entire string is displayed. The actual move can be performed by two different portions of the assembly language code, determined by the global variable WaitForRetrace. If WaitForRetrace is false (monochrome systems), the data is moved immediately. If WaitForRetrace is true (color systems), the routine waits for the vertical and horizontal control address of the video display adapter to be set. Because of this delay, displaying text on color systems is slower, but without the retrace checking on a color system, flicker would occur whenever you update the screen.

F_Write is written in assembly language and requires a Microsoft Assembler or comparable assembler to generate the object file that can be linked into the Turbo C library.

Limitations and Modifications

▼

There are two main limitations to F_Write. First, F_Write does not perform any boundary checking on the column and row positions passed. If you add boundary checking to the routine, performance is diminished while doing large numbers of small string displays. Performance isn't affected so much if you are displaying large strings, because the boundaries are only checked prior to the display and not during.

The second limitation is directly linked to the first. Because there is no boundary checking, if you display a string that exceeds the boundaries of video memory, you may overwrite other memory used by the system. Because memory problems are difficult to debug, avoid using line 25 other than through the Message routine.

Routine Source Code

▼

```
#pragma inline
#include <stddef.h>

extern int
  BaseOfScreen;

extern char
  WaitForRetrace;

void F_Write(unsigned int X,
             unsigned int Y,
             char Attribute,
             char *St)
/*
  This routine will write *St in Attribute quickly directly to video
  memory based on the global variables BaseOfScreen (B000 for mono and
  B800 for color) and WaitForRetrace (1 if color, 0 if mono). These variables
  must be set first by calling Get_Video_Mode or hard coding the values.
*/

{ /* F_Write */
#ifdef __LARGE__
  asm push  ds
#endif
  asm mov   al, 00h
#ifdef __SMALL__
```

```
  asm push  ds
  asm pop   es
  asm mov   di, St
#endif
#ifdef __LARGE__
  asm les   di, St
#endif
  asm mov   bx, di      /* Get length of string */
  asm mov   cx, 0ffffh
  asm cld
  asm repne scasb
  asm sub   di, bx
  asm mov   bx, di
  asm dec   bx
#ifdef __SMALL__
  asm mov   si, St
#endif
#ifdef __LARGE__
  asm push  ds
  asm lds   si, St
#endif
  asm mov   ax, Y        /* Calculate BaseOfScreen offset for X and Y */
  asm dec   ax
  asm mov   cx, 0004h
  asm shl   ax, cl
  asm mov   cx, bx
  asm mov   bx, ax
  asm shl   ax, 1h
  asm shl   ax, 1h
  asm add   ax, bx
  asm mov   bx, X
  asm dec   bx
  asm add   ax, bx
  asm shl   ax, 1h
  asm mov   di, ax
#ifdef __LARGE__
  asm pop   ds
#endif
  asm mov   dx, BaseOfScreen     /* Load screen values and determine which */
  asm mov   es, dx               /* output routine to use */
  asm mov   al, WaitForRetrace
#ifdef __SMALL__
  asm mov   si, St
#endif
#ifdef __LARGE__
  asm lds   si, St
#endif
  asm jcxz  Exit
```

```
  asm mov   ah, Attribute
  asm cld
  asm rcr   al, 1h
  asm jnc   Mono
  asm mov   dx, 03DAh
  GetNext:                /* Output to color card */
  asm lodsb
  asm mov   bx, ax
  asm mov   ah, 09h
  asm cli
  WaitH:
  asm in    al, dx
  asm rcr   al, 1h
  asm jc    WaitH
  WaitV:
  asm in    al, dx
  asm and   al, ah
  asm jz    WaitV
  asm mov   ax, bx
  asm stosw
  asm sti
  asm loop  GetNext
  asm jmp   Exit
  Mono:                   /* Output to a mono card */
  asm lodsb
  asm stosw
  asm loop  Mono
  Exit:
#ifdef __LARGE__
  asm pop   ds
#endif
} /* F_Write */
```

Sample Usage Source Code

▼

```
/*
  This program will use F_Write to quickly display asters on the screen first
  in the Reverse attribute, then Normal attribute 20 times.
*/

extern unsigned _stklen=16384; /* Minimum recommend stack size */
#include <stdio.h>
#include <math.h>
#include <dos.h>
#include <mem.h>
#include <alloc.h>
#include <ctype.h>
#include <string.h>
```

```
#include <stdlib.h>
#include <plib.h>
#include <plib.glo>


/****************************************************************************/
main()
{
  char
    TempString[81] = "";

  int
    Temp1,
    Temp2,
    ScreenColor;

  Calibrate_Delay();             /* Calibrate delay factor */
  Get_Video_Mode("Video.CFG");  /* Get display adapter type */
  Install_Crit_Error();          /* Set up application critical error handler */
  InputAbsolute=AbortPrint=0;   /* Initialize global variables */

  /* Application code to follow */

  Rpt("*", TempString, 80) ;
  for(Temp1 = 1; Temp1 <= 20; Temp1++)
  {
    if (ScreenColor = Normal)
      ScreenColor = Reverse;
    else
      ScreenColor = Normal;
    for(Temp2 = 1; Temp2 <= 24; Temp2++)
      F_Write(1, Temp2, ScreenColor, TempString);

    Delay(100) ;
  }

} /*main*/
```

Sample Usage Output

▼

```
********************************************************************************
********************************************************************************
********************************************************************************
********************************************************************************
********************************************************************************
********************************************************************************
********************************************************************************
********************************************************************************
```

```
******************************************************************************************
******************************************************************************************
******************************************************************************************
******************************************************************************************
******************************************************************************************
******************************************************************************************
******************************************************************************************
******************************************************************************************
******************************************************************************************
******************************************************************************************
******************************************************************************************
******************************************************************************************
******************************************************************************************
******************************************************************************************
******************************************************************************************
******************************************************************************************
```

F_WriteXY

Description

▼

F_WriteXY displays a string of text to the video display with a specified attribute and places the cursor at the end of the displayed string. This routine calls F_Write, which requires a call to Get_Video_Mode at some point prior to the use of this routine. For more information on the restrictions of using this routine, see F_Write.

Routine Declaration

▼

```
void F_WriteXY(int X,
               int Y,
               char Atr,
               char *St)
```

Passed Variables

▼

Col integer   The horizontal position on the screen for the first character of the string to be displayed. Valid values for Col are 1 through 80.

Row integer   The vertical position on the screen for the first character of the string to be displayed. Valid values for Row are 1 through 25.

Atr char   The video attribute to be used to display the string.

***St String Pointer**   A pointer to the character string to be displayed. The string should typically not exceed a length of 80 characters.

Global Variables

None

Error Codes/Messages

None

Discussion

F_WriteXY allows a single operation that quickly writes to the video display and leaves the cursor at the end of the displayed string. The operation of the routine is simple. It first calls F_Write to display the string and then uses the library routine Goto_XY to move the cursor. The cursor placement causes this routine to be slower than a direct call to F_Write. Use F_WriteXY only when you need to place the cursor after the write.

Limitations and Modifications

Because F_WriteXY calls F_Write, it has the same boundary checking limitations as F_Write. (See F_Write for a complete discussion of these limitations.) You may want to modify this routine to perform boundary checking for those occasions in which you need to write near the end of your video page. As mentioned in F_Write, checking the boundaries will reduce performance. Weigh the benefits against the performance loss for your particular application.

Routine Source Code

```
#include <math.h>
#include <string.h>
#include <stdio.h>
#include <stdlib.h>
#include <ctype.h>
#include <plib.h>

void F_WriteXY(int X,
               int Y,
               char Atr,
               char *St)
/*
  Writes *St as an F_Write but places cursor at the end of the Line.
*/
{ /* F_WriteXY */
  F_Write(X, Y, Atr, St);
  X += strlen(St);
  if (X > 80)
  {
    Y++;
```

```
    X -= 80;
  }
  Goto_XY(X, Y);
} /* F_WriteXY */
```

Sample Usage Source Code

▼

```
/*
  This program will use F_WriteXY to display ten asters and position the
  cursor appropriately. Then use printf to output text immediately following
  each set of asters (7 sets).
*/

extern unsigned _stklen=16384; /* Minimum recommend stack size */
#include <stdio.h>
#include <math.h>
#include <dos.h>
#include <mem.h>
#include <alloc.h>
#include <ctype.h>
#include <string.h>
#include <stdlib.h>
#include <plib.h>
#include <plib.glo>

/*****************************************************************************/
main()
{
  char
    TempString[81] = "";

  int
    Temp;

  Calibrate_Delay();            /* Calibrate delay factor */
  Get_Video_Mode("Video.CFG"); /* Get display adapter type */
  Install_Crit_Error();         /* Set up application critical error handler */
  InputAbsolute=AbortPrint=0;  /* Initialize global variables */

  /* Application code to follow */

  Clr_Scr();
  Rpt("*", TempString, 10) ;
  for(Temp = 1; Temp < 8; Temp++)
  {
    F_WriteXY((Temp-1) * 10, Temp, Normal, TempString);
    printf ("At the end of the F_WriteXY");
```

```
  }

} /*main*/
```

Sample Usage Output

▼

```
f_wrtxy.txt
*********At the end of the F_WriteXY
         **********At the end of the F_WriteXY
                   **********At the end of the F_WriteXY
                             **********At the end of the F_WriteXY
                                       **********At the end of the F_WriteXY
                                                 **********At the end of the F_W
riteXY                                                     **********At the end
of the F_WriteXY
```

Flush_KB_Buffer

Description

▼

Flush_KB_Buffer removes all characters currently in the keyboard buffer. The characters removed from the buffer are not stored or returned.

Routine Declaration

▼

```
void Flush_KB_Buffer()
```

Passed Variables

▼

None

Global Variables

▼

None

Error Codes/ Messages

▼

None

Discussion

▼

Flush_KB_Buffer removes all characters, including control and function keystrokes, from the keyboard buffer used by DOS. Use Flush_KB_Buffer to eliminate any leftover keystrokes at the end of routines, useful when your program is waiting for the user to press a key in response to a prompt. If you don't flush the buffer at key points, improper actions could result from previous keystrokes.

Use extreme caution in placing calls to Flush_KB_Buffer, because frequent calls can reduce the efficiency of your user's input.

Flush_KB_Buffer uses two library routines, Look_One_Char and Get_One_Char, to remove the characters from the buffer. The routine executes a while statement that continues as long as Look_One_Char returns a key value. In the while statement is a Get_One_Char that extracts a character from the keyboard buffer. When Look_One_Char returns false (0), the while statement stops execution and the routine ends.

Limitations and Modifications

▼

Flush_KB_Buffer's main limitation is the loss of performance when used with input routines. Scrutinize carefully where you place calls to Flush_KB_Buffer in your applications.

Consider creating a related function that returns the characters extracted from the buffer, and review Get_One_Char, used for character retrieval, and Look_One_Char, used to examine the next character in the buffer.

Routine Source Code

▼

```
#include <math.h>
#include <string.h>
#include <stdio.h>
#include <stdlib.h>
#include <ctype.h>
#include <plib.h>

extern int
  CurKey;

void Flush_KB_Buffer()
/*
  Removes all characters waiting in keyboard buffer.
*/
{/* Flush_KB_Buffer */
  while (Look_One_Char() != 0)
    Get_One_Char();
}/* Flush_KB_Buffer */
```

Sample Usage Source Code

▼

```
/*
  This program will demonstrate the effects of Flush_KB_Buffer.
*/

extern unsigned _stklen=16384; /* Minimum recommend stack size */
#include <stdio.h>
#include <math.h>
```

```
#include <dos.h>
#include <mem.h>
#include <alloc.h>
#include <ctype.h>
#include <string.h>
#include <stdlib.h>
#include <plib.h>
#include <plib.glo>


/******************************************************************************/
main()
{
  char
    KeyBuff [255] = "" ;

  Calibrate_Delay();            /* Calibrate delay factor */
  Get_Video_Mode("Video.CFG"); /* Get display adapter type */
  Install_Crit_Error();         /* Set up application critical error handler */
  InputAbsolute=AbortPrint=0;  /* Initialize global variables */

  /* Application code to follow */

  Clr_Scr();
  printf("Type in anything now until you hear beeps, then stop and wait.\n");
  Delay(10000) ;
  printf("Below is what you typed as echoed by gets(). Now press enter.\n");
  gets(KeyBuff);

  printf ("Now type in anything again, same as before.\n");
  Delay (10000);
  Flush_KB_Buffer();

  printf ("The buffer was flushed before gets() could use it. As\n") ;
  printf ("you can see, nothing was echoed below. Now press enter.\n") ;
  gets(KeyBuff) ;

} /*main*/
```

Sample Usage Output

▼

```
Type in anything now until you hear beeps, then stop and wait.
Below is what you typed as echoed by gets(). Now press enter.
hhhhhhhhhhhhhhh
Now type in anything again, same as before.
The buffer was flushed before gets() could use it. As
you can see, nothing was echoed below. Now press enter.
```

Get_One_Char

Description

Get_One_Char reads a keystroke from the keyboard buffer and sets the global variable CurKey to the value of that keystroke. Any keys that are function keys, cursor keys, or alternate keys have a negative value equal to the magnitude of the second scan code. Get_One_Char sets Curkey equal to this value and returns the value. If a key has not been pressed, Get_One_Char waits until a character is pressed.

Routine Declaration

```
int Get_One_Char(void)
```

Passed Variables

None

Global Variables

CurKey Contains the value of the keyboard keystroke retrieved by Get-_One_Char or Look_One_Char. If the keystroke is a prefixed keystroke (a two-byte scan code), CurKey contains a negative value equal to the significant byte of the scan codes. For example, pressing A returns a 65 in CurKey and pressing F1 returns −59.

Error Codes/ Messages

None

Discussion

Get_One_Char provides a standardized method for acquiring keyboard input. In addition to returning a key value, it sets the global variable CurKey, used in several other routines in the library. Working with CurKey, instead of creating new variables for each data input, provides you with consistency in your programming methods involving data entry. If you use the other data entry routines in the library, you normally won't need to use Get_One_Char. However, you may want to use the value returned in CurKey to determine how the user exited a data entry routine.

Get_One_Char uses ROM BIOS interrupt 16 hex service 0, Read Next Keyboard Character, to retrieve the scan code for the character currently waiting. Once the scan code is retrieved, the AL register is checked to determine if it contains a nonzero value. If it does, AL contains the character's scan code. If AL is zero, the key was a function or command key and the scan code is contained in AH, which is made negative for use in the system. Curkey is set to the proper value and the value is returned.

Limitations and Modifications

None

Routine Source Code

```
#include <dos.h>
#include <mem.h>

extern int
  CurKey;

int Get_One_Char(void)
/*
  This function removes a character from the keyboard buffer and
  returns its ascii value. If the key is a prefixed key (function key)
  then the ascii value returned is negative. Additionally, the
  global variable CurKey is set to the value returned. Note: This function
  will wait for a key if one has not been pressed yet.
*/
{ /* Get_One_Char */
  union REGS
    Regs;

  setmem(&Regs, sizeof(Regs), 0);
  int86(0x16, &Regs, &Regs);
  if (Regs.h.al)
  {
    CurKey = (int)Regs.h.al;
    return((int)Regs.h.al);
  } /* if */
  else
  {
    CurKey = -(int)Regs.h.ah;
    return(-(int)Regs.h.ah);
  } /* if else */
} /* Get_One_Char */
```

Sample Usage Source Code

```
/*
  This program will demonstrate the usage of Get_One_Char.
*/

extern unsigned _stklen=16384; /* Minimum recommend stack size */
#include <stdio.h>
#include <math.h>
#include <dos.h>
```

```
#include <mem.h>
#include <alloc.h>
#include <ctype.h>
#include <string.h>
#include <stdlib.h>
#include <plib.h>
#include <plib.glo>


/****************************************************************************/
main()
{
  Calibrate_Delay();           /* Calibrate delay factor */
  Get_Video_Mode("Video.CFG"); /* Get display adapter type */
  Install_Crit_Error();        /* Set up application critical error handler */
  InputAbsolute=AbortPrint=0;  /* Initialize global variables */

  /* Application code to follow */

  Clr_Scr();
  printf("Press any key.\n");
  Get_One_Char();
  printf("Curkey value for the key you just pressed is %d\n",CurKey);

} /*main*/
```

Sample Usage Output

▼

```
Press any key.
Curkey value for the key you just pressed is 104
```

Get_Time

Description

▼

Get_Time returns a string pointer (*Buffer) containing the current system time. The returned time can be in several formats. The formats are: 1 for HHMMSSFF, 2 for HH:MM:SS:FF, 3 for HHMMa, and 4 for hH:MM am/pm.

Routine Declaration

▼

```
char *Get_Time(int  TimeFormat,              char *Buffer)
```

Passed Variables

▼

TimeFormat integer The format for the returned time string. Valid values for

TimeFormat are 1 through 4. Table 2-2 lists the abbreviations used in the format descriptions, and table 2-3 lists the formats for each value of TimeFormat. Time formats 1 and 2 are in 24-hour or military format. Time formats 3 and 4 are in 12-hour am/pm format.

Global Variables

▼

None

Error Codes/ Messages

▼

None

Discussion

▼

Get_Time retrieves the current system time in several formats (see table 2-3), which provide an excellent range of styles for the returned string. Because you will probably discover other formats that meet the needs of particular applications, we put the actual formats into a switch statement.

The Get_Time routine is divided into two steps: get the time using Turbo C's gettime, then format the time string indicated by the format number selected.

Limitations and Modifications

▼

The only limitation to Get_Time are the formats for the returned time. Correct this limitation by adding any formats you need.

Table 2-2. ***Time Format Abbreviations***

Abbreviation	Meaning
HH	Two digits for the hours
hH	One or two digits for the hours
MM	Two digits for the minutes
SS	Two digits for the seconds
FF	Two digits for the hundredths of a second
a	One character for a.m. or p.m.

Table 2-3. ***TimeFormat Formats***

Format No.	General Format	Example
1	HHMMSSFF	09301550
2	HH:MM:SS:FF	09:30:15:50
3	HHMMa	0930a
4	hH:MM am/pm	9:30 am

Routine Source Code

```
#include <math.h>
#include <dos.h>
#include <string.h>
#include <stdio.h>
#include <stdlib.h>
#include <ctype.h>
#include <plib.h>

char *Get_Time(int TimeFormat,
               char *Buffer)
/*
  This function gets the system time and returns it in the format
  specified by TimeFormat:
    if TimeFormat =
      1:
        HHMMSSFF - where HH is 24 hr 00 to 23, MM is minutes 00 to 59,
                   SS is seconds 00 to 59 and FF is hundredths of seconds
                   00 to 99.
      2:
        HH:MM:SS:FF - same as 1 with colons.
      3:
        HHMMa - where HH is the 12 hr 1 to 12 and MM is minutes 00 59
                and a is am or pm indicator (a/p), e.g., 13:30 would
                be '0130p'.
      4:
        hH:MM am/pm - where H is the 12 hr 1 to 12, MM is minutes
                      00 to 59 and am/pm is the am or pm indicator,
                      e.g., 13:30 would be '1:30 pm' - 11:45 would
                      be '11:45 am'.
*/
{ /* Get_Time */
  char
    TStr[16],
    TStr1[16];

  struct time
    TimeBlk;

  /* Retrieve system time */
  gettime(&TimeBlk);
  /* Set up initial time string of HHMMSSFF */
  sprintf(Buffer, "%02d%02d%02d%02d", TimeBlk.ti_hour, TimeBlk.ti_min,
          TimeBlk.ti_sec, TimeBlk.ti_hund);
  switch (TimeFormat)
  {
    case 1: /* HHMMSSFF */
```

```
      break;

      case 3: /* HHMMa/p */
        /* If time is in PM */
        if (strcmp(Copy(Buffer, 1, 2, TStr), "12") > 0)
          sprintf(Buffer, "%02d%sp", atoi(Copy(Buffer, 1, 2, TStr)) - 12,
                  Copy(Buffer, 3, 2, TStr1));
        else /* if time is in AM */
        {
          if (strcmp(Copy(Buffer, 1, 2, TStr), "01") < 0)
            sprintf(Buffer, "12%sa", Copy(Buffer, 3, 2, TStr));
          else
            sprintf(Buffer, "%sa", Copy(Buffer, 1, 4, TStr));
        } /* if strcomp else */
      break;

      case 2:/* HH:MM:SS:FF or hH:MM: am/pm */
      case 4:
        Insert(":", Buffer, 3);
        Insert(":", Buffer, 6);
        Insert(":", Buffer, 9);
        if (TimeFormat == 4)
        {
          if (strcmp(Copy(Buffer, 1, 2, TStr), "12") > 0)
            sprintf(Buffer, "%d%s pm", atoi(Copy(Buffer, 1, 2, TStr)) - 12,
                    Copy(Buffer, 3, 3, TStr1));
          else
          {
            if (strcmp(Copy(Buffer, 1, 2, TStr), "01") < 0)
              sprintf(Buffer, "12%s am", Copy(Buffer, 3, 3, TStr));
            else
            {
              if (strcmp(Copy(Buffer, 1, 2, TStr), "10") < 0)
                sprintf(Buffer, "%s am", Copy(Buffer, 2, 4, TStr));
              else
                sprintf(Buffer, "%s am", Copy(Buffer, 1, 5, TStr));
            } /* if strcomp else */
          } /* if strcomp else */
        } /* if TimeFormat */
      break; /* case 2, 4 */
  } /* switch TimeFormat */
  return(Buffer);
} /* Get_Time */
```

Sample Usage Source Code

▼

```
/*
  This program will demonstrate the use of Get_Time and the results of
```

```
  its various formats.
*/

extern unsigned _stklen=16384; /* Minimum recommend stack size */
#include <stdio.h>
#include <math.h>
#include <dos.h>
#include <mem.h>
#include <alloc.h>
#include <ctype.h>
#include <string.h>
#include <stdlib.h>
#include <plib.h>
#include <plib.glo>


/***************************************************************************/
main()
{
  int
    Formatloop = 0;

  char
    TimeBuffer[12] = "";

  Calibrate_Delay();              /* Calibrate delay factor */
  Get_Video_Mode("Video.CFG");    /* Get display adapter type */
  Install_Crit_Error();           /* Set up application critical error handler */
  InputAbsolute=AbortPrint=0;     /* Initialize global variables */

  /* Application code to follow */
  Clr_Scr();
  for (Formatloop = 1; Formatloop <= 4; Formatloop++)
    printf("%s\n", Get_Time(Formatloop, TimeBuffer));
} /*main*/
```

Sample Usage Output

▼

```
14302299
14:30:22:99
0230p
2:30 pm
```

Get_Video_Mode

Description

▼

Get_Video_Mode determines the type of video display currently installed and sets the associated global variables used by the video display routines. Note:

You must call this routine at some point in your application prior to calling the video display routines or your system may lock up and require a reboot.

Routine Declaration

▼

```
void Get_Video_Mode(char *FName)
```

Passed Variables

▼

***FName String Pointer** A pointer to the string containing the name of the file with the video configuration information.

Global Variables

▼

BaseOfScreen Designates the base memory address of the video display memory for the current type of video display. BaseOfScreen is set to B000 hex for monochrome systems and B800 hex for color systems.

WaitForRetrace Tells the video display routine's looping structure that it has to synchronize the display of characters with the video retracing done on color systems. If this synchronization is not accomplished, you are likely to see video flickering during screen updates.

Error Codes/ Messages

▼

When Get_Video_Mode determines that a color system is installed, it attempts to read the file *FName. This file contains the values for normal, high-intensity, reverse video attributes, and background colors. If Get_Video_Mode does not find the file, a message is displayed saying that the default values are being set. You can create or change the values in your configuration file with the sample utility program VIDEOCFG included in Chapter 5.

Discussion

▼

Get_Video_Mode uses ROM BIOS interrupt 10 hex, service 0F hex, to determine what type of video display is installed on the system. If 7 is returned in the AL register, the system has a monochrome card installed. All other values indicate a color card is present. There are three global attributes used for writing out screen text: Normal, VidHigh, and Reverse. The remaining global attribute variables are background colors.

The program flow used in Get_Video_Mode follows these steps: acquire the type of video card installed, set the variable BaseOfScreen, set the variable WaitForRetrace, and set the color or monochrome attributes from the file or to hard-set values.

Limitations and Modifications

▼

Because this library does not deal with graphics, Get_Video_Mode determines if the system contains a monochrome card or a color card. This routine only checks for a 7 in the AL register after the interrupt call. If you need to determine if other types of displays are present, refer to the table in *The Peter Norton Programmer's Guide to the IBM PC* (Norton 1985).

Routine Source Code

▼

```
#include <dos.h>
#include <mem.h>
#include <math.h>
#include <string.h>
#include <stdio.h>
#include <stdlib.h>
#include <ctype.h>
#include <plib.h>

extern int
  BaseOfScreen;

extern char
  WaitForRetrace,
  Normal,
  VidHigh,
  Reverse,
  Black,
  Blue,
  Green,
  Cyan,
  Red,
  Magenta,
  Brown,
  White,
  BWhite,
  Background;

void Get_Video_Mode(char *FName)
/*
  This procedure will set all the video values. If *FName is available,
  it will be read and the values from it will be placed in the video
  variables. If it is not present, it will display a message on the 25th
  line stating such and check which kind of card is installed to set
  defaults to.
*/

{ /* Get_Video_Mode */
  struct VidCfgType
  {
    char
      Normal,
```

```
    VidHigh,
    Reverse,
    Black,
    Blue,
    Green,
    Cyan,
    Red,
    Magenta,
    Brown,
    White,
    BWhite,
    Background;
}; /* struct */

struct VidCfgType
  CfgVid;

union REGS
  ProcReg;

FILE
  *Cfg;

memset(&ProcReg, 0x00, sizeof(ProcReg));
ProcReg.h.ah = 0x0f;
int86(0x10, &ProcReg, &ProcReg);
switch (ProcReg.h.al)
{
  case 0x07: /* Mono */
    BaseOfScreen = 0xb000; /* Mono */
    WaitForRetrace = 0x00;
    Normal = 0x07;
    VidHigh = 0x0f;
    Reverse = 0x70;
    Black = Blue = Green = Cyan = Red =
    Magenta = Brown = White = BWhite = 0x07;
    Background = Black;
  break;
  case 0x00: /* CGA */
  case 0x01:
  case 0x02:
  case 0x03:
  case 0x04:
  case 0x05:
  case 0x06:
    BaseOfScreen = 0xb800;
    WaitForRetrace = 0x01;
    Normal = 0x17;
```

```
    VidHigh = 0x3f;
    Reverse = 0x57;
    Black = 0x00;
    Blue = 0x10;
    Green = 0x20;
    Cyan = 0x30;
    Red = 0x40;
    Magenta = 0x50;
    Brown = 0x60;
    White = 0x70;
    BWhite = 0xf0;
    Background = Blue;
  break;

  case 0x08: /* EGA */
  case 0x09:
  case 0x0a:
  case 0x0d:
  case 0x0e:
  case 0x0f:
    BaseOfScreen = 0xb800;
    WaitForRetrace = 0x01;
    Normal = 0x17;
    VidHigh = 0x3f;
    Reverse = 0x41;
    Black = 0x00;
    Blue = 0x10;
    Green = 0x20;
    Cyan = 0x30;
    Red = 0x40;
    Magenta = 0x50;
    Brown = 0x60;
    White = 0x70;
    BWhite = 0xf0;
    Background = Blue;
  break;
} /* switch */
if (WaitForRetrace)
{
  Cfg = fopen(FName, "rb");
  if (Cfg != NULL)
  {
    fread(&CfgVid, 1, sizeof(CfgVid), Cfg);
    Background = CfgVid.Background;
    Normal = CfgVid.Normal;
    VidHigh = CfgVid.VidHigh;
    Reverse = CfgVid.Reverse;
    Black = CfgVid.Black;
```

```
      Blue = CfgVid.Blue;
      Green = CfgVid.Green;
      Cyan = CfgVid.Cyan;
      Red = CfgVid.Red;
      Magenta = CfgVid.Magenta;
      Brown = CfgVid.Brown;
      White = CfgVid.White;
      BWhite = CfgVid.BWhite;
      Background = CfgVid.Background;
      fclose(Cfg);
    } /* if Cfg */
    else
    {
      if (WaitForRetrace == 0x01)
      {
        F_Write(1, 25, VidHigh, "Could not find ");
        F_Write(16, 25, VidHigh, FName);
        Delay(1000);
      } /* if WaitForRetrace */
    } /* if Cfg else */
  } /* if WaitForRetrace */
} /* Get_Video_Mode */
```

Sample Usage Source Code

▼

```
/*
  This program will check what kind of card (color or mono) is installed
  and set the global variables BaseOfScreen and WaitForRetrace. If the system
  is color, Get_Video_Mode will attempt to open the file Video.Cfg and use
  its contents to set the globals Normal, Reverse, and VidHigh. If the file
  cannot be found then defaults will be used for setting Normal, Reverse, and
  VidHigh and a message explaining so will be displayed.
*/

extern unsigned _stklen=16384; /* Minimum recommend stack size */
#include <stdio.h>
#include <math.h>
#include <dos.h>
#include <mem.h>
#include <alloc.h>
#include <ctype.h>
#include <string.h>
#include <stdlib.h>
#include <plib.h>
#include <plib.glo>


/*****************************************************************************/
```

```
main()
{
  Calibrate_Delay();           /* Calibrate delay factor */
  Get_Video_Mode("Video.CFG"); /* Get display adapter type */
  Install_Crit_Error();        /* Set up application critical error handler */
  InputAbsolute=AbortPrint=0;  /* Initialize global variables */

  /* Application code to follow */

  Clr_Scr() ;
  Get_Video_Mode ("Video.CFG") ;
  if ( WaitForRetrace )
    printf ("Color system, screen base set to: %u\n",BaseOfScreen) ;
  else
    printf ("Mono system, screen base set to: %u\n", BaseOfScreen) ;

} /*main*/
```

Sample Usage Output

▼

```
Color system, screen base set to: 47104
```

Goto_XY

Description

▼

Goto_XY moves the cursor position to a specified column and row coordinate on the video display. No error checking is performed on out-of-range screen positioning.

Routine Declaration

▼

```
void Goto_XY(int X,
             int Y)
```

Passed Variables

▼

X integer The horizontal position to be used to place the cursor. Valid values for X are 1 through 80.

Y integer The vertical position to be used to place the cursor. Valid values for Y are 1 through 25.

Global Variables

▼

None

Error Codes/ Messages

None

Discussion

Goto_XY positions the cursor by calling ROM BIOS interrupt 10 hex, Video Services, service 2 hex, Set Cursor Position, the DH register with the desired Y position, and the DL register with the desired X register. Once the registers are loaded, the interrupt routine is called. Turbo C version 1.5 contains a similar library routine that you may want to use.

Limitations and Modifications

Because Goto_XY does not perform any error checking, it is possible to pass screen positions not on the physical screen. This causes unpredictable results, so you may want to add range checking to your application. If you do, determine how the additional code will affect performance in your application.

Routine Source Code

```
#include <dos.h>
#include <mem.h>

void Goto_XY(int X,
             int Y)
/*
  This procedure will set the cursor to the location (X, Y) where
  X (1..80) and Y (1..25).
*/
{ /* Goto_XY */
  union REGS
    Regs;

  X--;
  Y--;
  setmem(&Regs, sizeof(Regs), 0);
  Regs.h.ah = 0x02; /* set cursor position */
  Regs.h.dh = (char)Y;
  Regs.h.dl = (char)X;
  int86(0x10, &Regs, &Regs);
} /* Goto_XY */
```

Sample Usage Source Code

```
/*
  This program will use the routine Goto_XY to bounce the cursor around the
  screen until a key is pressed.
```

```
*/

extern unsigned _stklen=16384; /* Minimum recommend stack size */
#include <stdio.h>
#include <math.h>
#include <dos.h>
#include <mem.h>
#include <alloc.h>
#include <ctype.h>
#include <string.h>
#include <stdlib.h>
#include <plib.h>
#include <plib.glo>


/****************************************************************************/
main()
{
  int
    X,
    Y,
    XDir,
    YDir;

  Calibrate_Delay();            /* Calibrate delay factor */
  Get_Video_Mode("Video.CFG"); /* Get display adapter type */
  Install_Crit_Error();         /* Set up application critical error handler */
  InputAbsolute=AbortPrint=0;  /* Initialize global variables */

  /* Application code to follow */

  Clr_Scr() ;
  Message("Cursor will bounce until a key is pressed to stop");

  X = 10;
  Y = 13;
  XDir = YDir = 1;
  while (!Look_One_Char())
  {
    Goto_XY(X, Y);
    X += XDir;
    Y += YDir;
    if ((X > 79) || (X < 2))
      XDir = -XDir;
    if ((Y > 24) || (Y < 2))
      YDir = -YDir;

    Delay(30);
```

```
  }
  Get_One_Char(); /* Remove key from buffer */
} /*  main  */
```

Sample Usage Output

▼

```
Cursor will bounce until a key is pressed to stop
```

Help_File

Description

▼

Help_File provides an on-screen help system for any application. The information displayed in the help window is taken from a text file specified in the calling parameter (*HFName). The help window consumes the entire screen and provides a 20-line by 78-character display window for the text. The text on the display prior to calling Help_File is saved and restored internally by Help_File.

Routine Declaration

▼

```
void Help_File(char *HFName,
               char *HTitle)
```

Passed Variables

▼

***HFName String Pointer** A pointer to the string containing the drive, directory path, and filename of the text file displayed in the help window.

***HTitle String Pointer** A pointer to the title string to be displayed on the top of the screen during the viewing of the help text.

Global Variables

▼

None

Error Codes/ Messages

▼

```
First Page
```

This message appears on line 25 when the user attempts to PageUp past the first page of the text file.

```
Last Page
```

This message appears on line 25 when the user attempts to PageDown past the last page of the text file.

```
Not enough memory to load file.
```

This message appears on line 25 when the routine attempts to load a text file that will not fit into the available memory.

```
Error - (Help_File) could not find file XXXXXXXXXX
```

This message will appear on line 25 when the routine cannot open the specified file XXXXXXXXXX. If the drive and directory path are specified with the filename, verify that the text file is on the specified drive.

Discussion

▼

Creating meaningful help systems for custom applications is not always an easy task. Help_File uses modifiable text files, allowing the user to change the help text to meet specific needs after the application has been installed. Help_File can also be used to view other types of text files in any application. Having the text on disk rather than residing in memory frees up more space for temporary processing variables and program modules.

Help_File begins by saving the current display with a call to Save_Screen. Then an attempt is made to open the specified text file. If the open is successful, the file is loaded into memory as a linked list of lines. If the load is successful, the first page of text is displayed for the user and the routine waits for the user's next command. Valid commands are PageUp, PageDown, and Escape to exit. Any other key is shown as a Bad Key Pressed. Once the user exits the view process, the screen is restored and the routine exits. If either the open or the load is unsuccessful, a message is issued to the user and the routine exits.

Limitations and Modifications

▼

You may find other uses for the quick load and display capabilities of Help_file, some of which require that smaller portions of the screen be consumed. Consider altering Help_File to have run-time definable window size and window placement. This would provide a flexible and dynamic text viewing routine.

Routine Source Code

▼

```
#include <stdio.h>
#include <mem.h>
#include <dos.h>
#include <alloc.h>
#include <ctype.h>
#include <string.h>
#include <plib.h>
```

```
extern char
  Blue,
  Normal,
  Reverse,
  VidHigh;

extern int
  CurKey;

typedef struct LPT
{
  struct LPT
    far *FL,
    far *BL;
  char
    Txt[81];
} LinePtrType;

void Help_File(char *HFName,
               char *HTitle)
/*
  This routine will save the screen, load the file *HFName (if present)
  and allow the user to peruse through it with the PgUp and PgDown keys;
  pressing Esc will restore the screen and terminate the routine.
*/
{ /* Help_File */

  char
    NotDone,
    OutMem;

  int
    WindowDepth,
    OldCursor,
    C;

  char
    TStr[81],
    LineStr[81],
    OldScreen[4000];

  LinePtrType
    *CLine, /* Current Line */
    *NLine, /* New Line */
    *FLine, /* First Line */
    *TScr;  /* Top of Screen */

  FILE
```

```
    *TxtF;

  WindowDepth = 20;
  OldCursor = Cursor_Off();
  Save_Screen(OldScreen);
  Clear_Frame(Blue, 1, 1, 80, 25);
  CLine = NLine = FLine = TScr = NULL;
  TxtF = fopen(HFName, "rb");
  if (TxtF != NULL)
  {
    Message("Loading help file - Please wait...");
    OutMem = 0;
    NotDone = 1;
    while ((NotDone) && (!(OutMem)))
    {
      NotDone = Read_Line(TxtF, LineStr, 80);
      if (NotDone)
      {
        NLine = (LinePtrType *)farmalloc(sizeof(LinePtrType));
        OutMem = (NLine == NULL);
        if (!OutMem)
        {
          if (FLine == NULL)
            FLine = NLine;
          NLine -> BL = CLine;
          if (CLine != NULL)
            CLine -> FL = NLine;
          CLine = NLine;
          strcpy(CLine -> Txt, LineStr);
        } /* if !OutMem */
      } /* if NotDone */
    } /* while NotDone */
    CLine -> FL = NULL;
    TScr = FLine;
    CLine = TScr;
    fclose(TxtF);
    Message("");
    if (!OutMem)
    {
      Draw_Frame(1, 1, 80, WindowDepth + 2, 1, "NR", HTitle, Blue);
      F_Write(1, 23, VidHigh, Cen("<PageUp> & <PageDown>, <Esc> to exit",
              TStr, 80));
      do
      {
        Clear_Frame(Blue, 2, 2, 78, WindowDepth);
        CLine = TScr;
        for (C = 1; C <= WindowDepth; C++)
        {
```

```
        if (CLine != NULL)
        {
          F_Write(2, C + 1, Blend(VidHigh), CLine -> Txt);
          CLine = CLine -> FL;
        } /* if CLine */
      } /* for C */
      Get_One_Char();
      Message("");
      switch(CurKey)
      {
        case -73: /* PageUp */
          if (TScr == FLine)
            Lo_Mess("First Page");
          for (C = 1; C <= WindowDepth; C++)
          {
            if (TScr != FLine)
              TScr = TScr -> BL;
          } /* for C */
        break;

        case -81: /* PageDown */
          CLine = TScr;
          for (C = 1; C <= WindowDepth; C++)
          {
            if (TScr != NULL)
              TScr = TScr -> FL;
          } /* if TScr */
          if (TScr == NULL)
          {
            TScr = CLine;
            Lo_Mess("Last Page");
          } /* if TScr */
        break;

      }/* switch */
    }while (CurKey != 27); /* do */
  } /* if !OutMem */
  else
    Lo_Mess("Not enough memory to load file.");
  while (FLine != NULL)
  {
    CLine = FLine -> FL;
    farfree(FLine);
    FLine = CLine;
  } /* while FLine */
} /* if TxtF */
else
{
```

```
    sprintf(TStr, "Error - (Help_File) could not find file %s.", HFName);
    Cnvg_Mess(TStr);
    for (C = 1; C<=100; C++)
    {
      Beep_Lo();
      Beep_Hi();
    }
  } /* if TxtF else */
  Restore_Screen(OldScreen);
  Cursor_On(OldCursor);
}/* Help_File */
```

Sample Usage Source Code

▼

```
/*
  This program will use Help_File to display any text file.
*/

extern unsigned _stklen=16384; /* Minimum recommend stack size */
#include <stdio.h>
#include <math.h>
#include <dos.h>
#include <mem.h>
#include <alloc.h>
#include <ctype.h>
#include <string.h>
#include <stdlib.h>
#include <plib.h>
#include <plib.glo>

/****************************************************************************/
main()
{
  char
    Title[81] = "",
    FName[81] = "";

  Calibrate_Delay();           /* Calibrate delay factor */
  Get_Video_Mode("Video.CFG"); /* Get display adapter type */
  Install_Crit_Error();        /* Set up application critical error handler */
  InputAbsolute=AbortPrint=0;  /* Initialize global variables */

  /* Application code to follow */
  Goto_XY(1, 25);
  printf("Enter the name of the file you wish to view:");
  scanf("%s", FName);
  Help_File(FName, Title);
```

```
} /*main*/
```

Sample Usage Output

▼

```
        Enter the name of the file you wish to view: Hlpfile.exc

─────────────── Showing I:\c\cbook\hlpfile.exc as follows: ───────────────
/*
  This program will use Help_File to display any text file.
*/

extern unsigned _stklen=16384; /* Minimum recommend stack size */
#include <stdio.h>
#include <math.h>
#include <dos.h>
#include <mem.h>
#include <alloc.h>
#include <ctype.h>
#include <string.h>
#include <stdlib.h>
#include <plib.h>
#include <plib.glo>


/**************************************************************************/
main()
{

                    <PageUp> & <PageDown>, <Esc> to exit
```

Hi_Mess

Description

▼

Hi_Mess calls Beep_Hi to produce a high-pitch tone and calls Message to display the specified message on the 25th line of the video display. Beep_Hi is typically used for reporting nonfatal operational errors. For example, if a data record is missing during a file update, call Hi_Mess to display the error.

Routine Declaration

▼

```
void Hi_Mess(char *Mess)
```

Passed Variables

▼

***Mess String Pointer** A pointer to the string to be displayed by Message. The string can be a maximum of 80 characters long.

Global Variables

None

Error Codes/ Messages

None

Discussion

Hi_Mess provides a consistent method of informing the end user of nonfatal operational errors, including missing data records, missing files for copies or erasures, general informational errors, etc. Message displays the string passed on the message line (line 25). Any message on line 25 will be cleared by the display of the new message.

Hi_Mess calls Message to display the string prior to calling Beep_Hi, ensuring that the message will be on the screen for at least the length of the Beep_Hi. Your program needs to account for any additional time for the message and for clearing the message at some point after the completion of Hi_Mess.

Limitations and Modifications

Hi_Mess doesn't have any specific limitations, but there are several ways you may want to modify the routine, adding a delay time to the parameter list to ensure a constant time for the display of the message, for instance. However, this may impede the performance of data entry under some applications. Clearing the message line after the Beep_Hi is also possible, but be careful to allow sufficient time for the user to read the message. (You can appreciate this concern if you have ever used a program that doesn't allow you to read the error message before it is cleared!)

Routine Source Code

```
#include <math.h>
#include <string.h>
#include <stdio.h>
#include <stdlib.h>
#include <ctype.h>
#include <plib.h>

void Hi_Mess(char *Mess)
/*
  Same as Lo_Mess but with Beep_Hi.
*/
{ /* Hi_Mess */
  Message(Mess);
  Beep_Hi();
} /* Hi_Mess */
```

Sample Usage Source Code

▼

```
/*
  This program will use Hi_Mess to beep and display a message in
  reverse video on the 25th line, then wait 3 seconds before exiting.
*/

extern unsigned _stklen=16384; /* Minimum recommend stack size */
#include <stdio.h>
#include <math.h>
#include <dos.h>
#include <mem.h>
#include <alloc.h>
#include <ctype.h>
#include <string.h>
#include <stdlib.h>
#include <plib.h>
#include <plib.glo>

/****************************************************************************/
main()
{
  Calibrate_Delay();           /* Calibrate delay factor */
  Get_Video_Mode("Video.CFG"); /* Get display adapter type */
  Install_Crit_Error();        /* Set up application critical error handler */
  InputAbsolute=AbortPrint=0;  /* Initialize global variables */

  /* Application code to follow */

  Hi_Mess("They shoot horses, don't they!");
  Delay(3000);

} /*main*/
```

Sample Usage Output

▼

```
They shoot horses, don't they!
```

Input_Alpha

Description

▼

Input_Alpha allows entry and updating of any alphanumeric data field (string variable). The routine has complete field editing and manipulation capabilities, and any prompts must be displayed and the cursor positioned prior to calling Input_Alpha. Input_Alpha assumes that the current cursor position is the location for the entry of the field. Fields can be initialized to a value prior to calling Input_Alpha. The value in the specified field is displayed prior to accepting modification commands.

Routine Declaration

▼

```
void Input_Alpha(int Size,
                 char *ValSet,
                 char *St)
```

Passed Variables

▼

Size integer The width of the screen field for displaying and updating the value specified in *St. Valid values for Size are 1 through 80.

***ValSet String Pointer** A pointer to the set of characters considered valid keystrokes for entering data into the field. If ValSet is passed as a null string, the set defined in the local constant DefValSet is used as the valid character set.

***St String Pointer** A pointer to the string value to be displayed and modified.

Global Variables

▼

CurKey The value of the last keyboard keystroke retrieved by Get_One_Char that caused Input_Alpha to exit. If the keystroke is a prefixed keystroke (a two-byte scan code), CurKey contains a negative value equal to the significant byte of the scan codes. For example, pressing A returns a 65 in CurKey and pressing F1 returns −59.

Error Codes/ Messages

▼

```
End of field
```

This message is displayed on the 25th line when the Right Arrow cursor key is pressed and the cursor is at the right end of the field.

```
Beginning of field
```

This message is displayed on the 25th line when the Left Arrow cursor key or Backspace key is pressed and the cursor is at the left end of the field.

```
Nothing to delete
```

This message will be displayed on the 25th line if the Delete key is pressed when the cursor is located to the right of the last character in the field.

```
No room in field left to insert
```

This message will be displayed on the 25th line if the Insert key is pressed and the field is already filled to the maximum size.

```
Invalid input X only VVVVV allowed
```

This message will be displayed on the 25th line when the user presses a standard character key not in the valid set of characters defined in ValSet. X indicates the character pressed and VVVVV shows the valid set of characters.

Discussion

▼

Input_Alpha accommodates data entry for a variety of field types. The other data entry routines, Input_Date, Input_Num, and Prompt all use Input_Alpha for the actual entry of the data. Other entry routines primarily handle the setup before entry by Input_Alpha and verification of the data returned. The ValSet passed to Input_Alpha by the other routines limits the type of characters entered to meet the needs of the type of field being requested. For example, Input_Date only allows 0123456789/- for valid characters, while Input_Num allows 0123456789-.

Input_Alpha starts by initializing the cursor position variables and displaying the starting value of the field to be updated. Next, Input_Alpha starts a while loop, conditioned on the variable Done, used to continue keyboard processing until an exit condition is triggered by function and control keys not specifically trapped. The while loop manages the editing operations based on the specific key value pressed by the operator. When the operator triggers an exit condition, the updated field is displayed in VidHigh and the routine exits.

The following command keys are used in Input_Alpha:

Ins Inserts a space at the current cursor position in the field.

Del Deletes the character the cursor is on.

→ Moves the cursor one character to the right in the field without disturbing the field's contents.

← Moves the cursor one character to the left in the field without disturbing the field's contents.

BackSpace Deletes the character to the immediate left of the cursor.

Home Moves the cursor to the first character of the field.

End Moves the cursor to the next open space past the very last character in the field. If the field is full, the cursor is positioned at the last character of the field.

Ctrl BackSpace Deletes the contents of the entire field.

All other keys not in the printable set cause the procedure to exit, leaving the parameter StIn in its latest form. The key causing the exit remains in the global value CurKey.

Limitations and Modifications

▼

You may want to implement your own desires for entry methods and modify Input_Alpha's command keys or display characteristics to meet the needs of your application.

Routine Source Code

▼

```
#include <mem.h>
#include <math.h>
#include <string.h>
#include <stdio.h>
#include <stdlib.h>
#include <ctype.h>
#include <plib.h>

extern int
  CurKey;

extern char
  InputAbsolute,
  Normal,
  Reverse,
  VidHigh;

void Input_Alpha(int Size,
                 char *ValSet,
                 char *St)
/*
  This sets a block in Reverse attribute that is Size long from the
  current cursor position with *St in it (if *St isn't null). Then it
  accepts modification to *St from the user with all the following
  editing abilities:
    Ins         - Pressing this key will insert a space from where the
                  cursor is.
    Del         - Pressing this key will remove the character the cursor
                  is on.
    →           - Pressing the right arrow will move the cursor one
                  character to the right of its current position.
    ←           - Pressing the left arrow key will move the cursor one
                  character to the left of its current position.
    Home        - Pressing the Home key will position the cursor at the
                  beginning of the field.
    End         - Pressing the End key will place the cursor at the end of
                  the textual content of the field.
    BackSpace   - Pressing the backspace key will delete the character to
                  the left of the cursor unless the cursor is at the end of
                  the field or the field is only 1 wide, then the character
```

```
                above the cursor is deleted.
    ^BackSpace - Pressing a control backspace will clear the field and
                place cursor at the beginning of the field.

  All other keys that are control keys (function keys, return, esc, etc.)
  will terminate this routine with *St in its most recent state and the
  control key pressed will be left in the global variable CurKey. Any data
  keys (printable) will be placed in the field directly above the cursor
  and the cursor will be advanced one unless it is against the end of the
  field. If the key is not in *Valset then the key will not be accepted, and
  an error message will be displayed. If *Valset is null, then all
  characters from 32 to 127 will be accepted. If the global variable
  InputAbsolute is true (1) then *St will be returned exactly as it was
  input by the user, without erase-whiting any part. *St will always be
  returned with nulls (0s) after the initial null for the remaining
  size of the string; this allows for reliable results when working
  with file management utilities such as BTrieve.
*/
{ /* Input_Alpha */
  int
    C,
    CurX,
    CurY,
    CurPos,
    LastPos;

  char
    Done,
    TStr1[256],
    TStr2[256];

  CurX = WhereX();
  CurY = WhereY();
  LastPos = CurX + Size - 1;
  CurPos = CurX;
  F_Write(CurX, CurY, Reverse, LJ(St, TStr1, Size));
  Done = 0;
  while (!Done)
  {
    if (!InputAbsolute)
      Erase_White_End(St);
    Get_One_Char();
    Message("");
    switch(CurKey)
    {
      case -75: /* Left */
        CurPos -= (CurPos > CurX);
      break;
```

```
case -77: /* Right */
  CurPos += (CurPos < LastPos);
break;

case 127: /* CtrlBkSpace */
  St[0] = 0;
  CurPos = CurX;
break;

case -82: /* Ins */
  if (strlen(St) < Size)
  {
    C = strlen(St) - (CurPos - CurX) + 1;
    movmem(St + (CurPos - CurX), St + (CurPos -
           CurX + 1), C > 0 ? C : 0);
    St[CurPos - CurX] = ' ';
  } /* if strlen(St) */
break;

case -83: /* Del */
  if (strlen(St) > CurPos - CurX)
  {
    C = strlen(St) - (CurPos - CurX);
    movmem(St + (CurPos - CurX + 1), St + (CurPos - CurX),
           C > 0 ? C : 0);
  } /* if strlen(St) */
break;

case -71: /* Home */
  CurPos = CurX;
break;

case -79: /* End */
  Erase_White_End(St);
  CurPos = CurX + strlen(St) - (strlen(St) == Size);
break;

case 8: /* BackSpace */
  if ((Size == 1) || (strlen(St) == Size))
  {
    St[CurPos - CurX] = 0;
  } /* if Size */
  else
  {
    if (CurPos != CurX)
    {
      C = strlen(St) - (CurPos - CurX) + 1;
      movmem(St + (CurPos - CurX), St + (CurPos - CurX - 1),
```

```
              C > 0 ? C : 0);
          CurPos-- ;
        } /* if CurPos! */
      } /* if Size else */
    break;

    default:
      if (CurKey > 0 && CurKey != 13 && CurKey != 27 && CurKey != 9)
      {
        for (C = 0; (ValSet[C] != (char)CurKey && ValSet[C]); C++ );
        if (ValSet[C] || !ValSet[0])
        {
          TStr1[0] = (char)CurKey;
          TStr1[1] = 0;
          Replace(TStr1, St, CurPos - CurX + 1);
          CurPos += (CurPos - CurX + 1 < Size);
        } /* if ValSet[C] */
        else
        {
          LJ(ValSet, TStr1, 50);
          if (TStr1[49] != ' ')
            for (C = 47; C <= 49; TStr1[C] = '.', C++ );
          else
            Erase_White_End(TStr1);
          sprintf(TStr2, "Bad entry '%c', only '%s' allowed.",
                  (char)CurKey, TStr1);
          Lo_Mess(TStr2);
        } /* if ValSet[C] else */
      } /* if CurKey */
      else
        Done = 1;
    break;
  } /* switch CurKey */
  if (!Done)
  {
    if (!InputAbsolute)
      Erase_White_End(St);
    F_Write(CurX, CurY, Reverse, LJ(St, TStr1, Size));
    Goto_XY(CurPos, CurY);
  } /* if !Done */
} /* while !Done */
C = strlen(St);
if (C <= Size)
  setmem(St + C + 1, Size - C, 0);
F_Write(CurX, CurY, VidHigh, LJ(St, TStr1, Size));
} /* Input_Alpha */
```

Sample Usage Source Code

▼

```
/*
  This program will use Input_Alpha to demonstrate Input_Alpha's Input,
  Error trapping and editing facilities. When a key allowing the user
  to exit is used, the key pressed will be shown at the bottom.
*/

extern unsigned _stklen=16384; /* Minimum recommend stack size */
#include <stdio.h>
#include <math.h>
#include <dos.h>
#include <mem.h>
#include <alloc.h>
#include <ctype.h>
#include <string.h>
#include <stdlib.h>
#include <plib.h>
#include <plib.glo>


/****************************************************************************/
main()
{
  char
    TempVar[41] = "";

  Calibrate_Delay();            /* Calibrate delay factor */
  Get_Video_Mode("Video.CFG"); /* Get display adapter type */
  Install_Crit_Error();         /* Set up application critical error handler */
  InputAbsolute=AbortPrint=0;  /* Initialize global variables */

  /* Application code to follow */

  Clr_Scr();
  strcpy(TempVar, "This is the Default Setting");
  F_WriteXY(1, 5, Normal, "Enter Something: ");
  Input_Alpha(40, "", TempVar);
  printf("\nThe Key you used to exit - CurKey= %d.", CurKey);

} /*main*/
```

Sample Usage Output

▼

```
Enter Something: This is the Default Setting
The Key you used to exit - CurKey= 13.
```

Input_Date

Description

▼

Input_Date enters or modifies fields that are considered calendar dates. The date is checked for validity based on valid days available in the year indicated by the year value entered. The actual entry is accomplished by a call to Input_Alpha. For more information on the workings of the entry function, see Input_Alpha.

Routine Declaration

▼

```
void Input_Date(char *Date)
```

Passed Variables

▼

***Date String Pointer** A pointer to the string date variable to be entered or modified by the call to Input_Date. If a value is preset before calling Input_Date, it must be in the format MM/DD/YY.

Global Variables

▼

CurKey Contains the value of the last keyboard keystroke retrieved by Get_One_Char that caused Input_Alpha to exit. If the keystroke is prefixed (a two-byte scan code), CurKey contains a negative value equal to the significant byte of the scan codes. For example, pressing A returns a 65 in CurKey and pressing F1 returns −59.

Error Codes/ Messages

▼

```
Bad Date, re-enter or erase (MM/DD/YY or MMDDYY)
```

This message is displayed on the 25th line of the screen if the date entered is not a valid calendar date. For example, the date 13/01/87 triggers the error message because there is no thirteenth month.

Discussion

▼

Input_Date enters and changes valid calendar dates. This routine verifies that the month and day entered are valid for the year entered, including checks for leap years. The actual entry of the field is accomplished by a call to Input_Alpha with the valid character set passed as 1234567890/-. The date entered can be in two different forms. The first uses slashes or dashes to separate the month, day, and year, with one or two digits entered for each portion of the date. The second option allows the user to enter all six digits—two month, two day, and two year—without slashes or dashes. Input_Date will insert the slashes at the appropriate positions.

Input_Date starts by storing the current cursor position, used if repetitive calls to Input_Alpha are required. Next, Input_Date calls Input_Alpha with length and valid set configured for date values. Upon returning a value from Input_Alpha, Input_Date formats the value to a standard pattern that the routine Check_Date can accept and evaluate for a valid date. If the date is validated by Check_Date, the value is output in VidHigh and the routine exits. Otherwise, the looping structure of Input_Date is used to start the cycle over for entry of another date. Input_Date also allows for blank data fields.

Limitations and Modifications

▼

None

Routine Source Code

▼

```
#include <math.h>
#include <string.h>
#include <stdio.h>
#include <stdlib.h>
#include <ctype.h>
#include <plib.h>

extern char
  Reverse,
  Normal,
  VidHigh;

void Input_Date(char *Date)
/*
  This procedure will display *Date as it is passed in at the current
  x, y cursor locations and accept changes to Date, then check for
  validity of *Date and exit or continue prompting if *Date is bad.
  *Date will always be returned as a valid 8-character date in the
  form MM/DD/YY or as nothing.
*/
{ /* Input_Date */
  char
    GoodDate,
    OldDate[9],
    TStr1[10],
    TStr2[10],
    TStr3[10];

  int
    IX,
    IY;

  /* Initialize */
```

```
  IX = WhereX();
  IY = WhereY();
  strcpy(OldDate, Date);

  /* Display and get changes to Date */
  GoodDate = 0;
  while (!GoodDate)
  {
    Goto_XY(IX, IY);
    strcpy(Date, OldDate);
    Input_Alpha(8, "1234567890/-", Date);
    strcpy(OldDate, Date);
    Erase_White(Date);
    if ((strlen(Date) == 6) && (Str_IsInt(Date)))
      sprintf(Date, "%Fs/%Fs/%Fs", Copy(Date, 1, 2, TStr1),
              Copy(Date, 3, 2, TStr2), Copy(Date, 5, 2, TStr3));
    if (!Date[0])
      GoodDate = 1;
    else
      GoodDate = Check_Date(Date);
    if (!GoodDate)
      Lo_Mess("Bad Date, re-enter or erase (MM/DD/YY or MMDDYY)");
  } /* while !GoodDate */

  /* Display Full Date if any */
  F_Write(IX, IY, VidHigh, Date);
} /* Input_Date */
```

Sample Usage Source Code

▼

```
/*
  This program will use Input_Date to demonstrate Input_Date's Input,
  Error trapping and editing facilities. When a key allowing the user
  to exit is used, the key pressed will be shown at the bottom.
*/

extern unsigned _stklen=16384; /* Minimum recommend stack size */
#include <stdio.h>
#include <math.h>
#include <dos.h>
#include <mem.h>
#include <alloc.h>
#include <ctype.h>
#include <string.h>
#include <stdlib.h>
#include <plib.h>
#include <plib.glo>
```

```
/****************************************************************************/
main()
{
  char
    TempVar[9] = "" ;

  Calibrate_Delay();            /* Calibrate delay factor */
  Get_Video_Mode("Video.CFG"); /* Get display adapter type */
  Install_Crit_Error();         /* Set up application critical error handler */
  InputAbsolute=AbortPrint=0;  /* Initialize global variables */

  /* Application code to follow */

  Clr_Scr();
  strcpy(TempVar, "01/01/88"); /* Default date (could be null also) */
  F_WriteXY(1, 5, Normal, "Enter any date: ");
  Input_Date(TempVar);
  printf("\nThe key you used to exit (CurKey) was = %d", CurKey);

} /*main*/
```

Sample Usage Output

▼

```
Enter any date: 02/26/88
The key you used to exit - CurKey= 13
```

Input_Num

Description

▼

Input_Num enters numeric values with a specified pattern and range for the number. The number entered can also have a minimum and maximum range value specified. The actual entry of the field is accomplished by a call to the routine Input_Alpha. For more information on the function of the entry procedure, see Input_Alpha.

Routine Declaration

▼

```
void Input_Num(char *Num,
               char *Pattern,
               float Min,
               float Max)
```

Passed Variables

▼

***Num String Pointer** A pointer to the string variable that contains the number displayed and modified.

***Pattern String Pointer** A pointer to the pattern to be used to display the entered number. The pattern definition consists of a combination of I, D, ., and a number for integer digits. The I is used to indicate the integer or whole number portion of the value to be entered. You can specify the maximum number of integer digits by preceding the I with a number between 1 and 9. If you don't prefix the I with a number, 10 integer digits will be assumed. If you want a decimal portion to the number, insert the decimal point after the integer definition and the required number of Ds for each decimal position. When the user enters the number, any unfilled decimal positions are padded with zeros. For example, for the pattern I.DD, if 8 is entered, 8.00 would be displayed when the user presses Return. If you enter Ds instead of an integer definition, the exact number of digits specified must be entered by the user to match the pattern and obtain a correct entry.

The following examples show some sample patterns:

I.DD Allows up to 10 integer positions and two decimal positions. If the decimals are not entered, Input_Num inserts zeros for the empty positions.

DDDD Requires that all four digits be entered. This type of format works very well for fields like the time of day where you need the hours and minutes in an exact format (e.g., 436 would be invalid, but 0436 would be valid).

DD.DD Requires two leading integer digits and an optional decimal amount. If the two leading integer digits are not filled, a bad number indication results.

6I.DDDD Allows up to six integer digits and up to four decimal digits. Both the integers and decimals can be variable in the length entered.

8I Allows the entry of eight integer digits with no decimal places.

Min float Contains the minimum value that can be entered in the associated field. If the value the user entered is less than Min, an error notifies the user of the range.

Max float Contains the maximum value that can be entered in the associated field. If the value the user enters is greater than Max, an error notifies the user of the range.

Global Variables

▼

CurKey Contains the value of the last keystroke retrieved by Get_One_Char that caused Input_Alpha to exit. If the keystroke is prefixed (a two-byte scan code), CurKey contains a negative value equal to the significant byte of the scan codes. For example, pressing A returns a 65 in CurKey and pressing F1 returns −59.

Error Codes/ Messages

▼

```
Error, entry must fit pattern XXXXX, please re-enter
```

This message is displayed on the 25th line of the display if the value entered by the user does not fit the pattern specified in Pattern.

```
Bad number, re-enter
```

This message is displayed on the 25th line of the display if the text entered by the user cannot be converted to a numeric variable.

```
Error, entry must be between XXXXX and YYYYY, please re-enter
```

This message is displayed on the 25th line of the display if the value entered by the user is not within the minimum and maximum range specified in the call to Input_Num.

Discussion

▼

Input_Num enters and verifies numeric information. The flexibility provided by the pattern and range checking capabilities designed into Input_Num allow you to create very finite entry fields that can range from integers with up to 10 digits to very small decimal values. See the description of the parameter Pattern in the section on passed variables for an in-depth description of the types of patterns available.

Input_Num starts by determining the size of the field to be modified. Next, the pattern is analyzed for potential negative numbers, the valid character set is established for the proper value range, and Input_Alpha is called. When the value is returned from Input_Alpha, the string is converted to a numeric value and validated against the specified minimum and maximum values. If the number is invalid, the process of entry is repeated. Otherwise, the numeric value is patterned, converted back to a string representation, and the routine exits.

Limitations and Modifications

▼

None

Routine Source Code

▼

```
#include <stdio.h>
#include <string.h>
#include <stdlib.h>
#include <plib.h>

extern char
  VidHigh;
```

```
extern int
  CurKey;

void Input_Num(char *Num,
               char *Pattern,
               float Min,
               float Max)
/*
  This procedure accepts a number in the range of Min and Max obeying
  the format of *Pattern where if *Pattern = (examples of typical
  patterns :
  1: 'I.DD'     up to 10 integers may be entered with up to 2 decimals.
  2: 'DDDD'     4 digits must be entered.
  3: 'DD.DD'    2 integers must be entered and up to 2 decimals may be
                specified.
  4: '6I.DDDD' up to 6 integers may be entered and up to 4 decimals may
                be specified.
  5: '8I'       up to 8 integers may be entered.)

  The 'D' before a decimal point (if any) means that exact pattern must
  be entered as in examples 2 & 3. A single 'I' with no number in front
  will default to '10I' as in example 1. A valid negative sign is
  indicated in the Min and Max range settings (if Min is negative, a
  negative sign may be entered).
*/
{ /* Input_Num */

  char
    Redo,
    TStr[50],
    TStr1[50],
    TStr2[50],
    EMess[100];

  int
    OrX,
    OrY,
    Decs,
    Digs,
    Ints,
    FSize,
    C;

  float
    NumF;

  OrX = WhereX();
  OrY = WhereY();
```

```
/* Get size of field for Input_Alpha */
FSize = Num_Pattern_Size(Pattern, &Ints, &Digs, &Decs) + (Min < 0);
Redo = 1;
while (Redo)
{
  Goto_XY(OrX, OrY);
  /* Decide if In_Alpha gets invalid set */
  if (Min < 0.0)
  {
    /* Decide if In_Alpha gets a decimal point in the valid set */
    if (Decs > 0.0)
      Input_Alpha(FSize, "-0123456789.", Num);
    else
      Input_Alpha(FSize, "-0123456789", Num);
  } /* if Min */
  else
  {
    if (Decs > 0.0)
      Input_Alpha(FSize, "0123456789.", Num);
    else
      Input_Alpha(FSize, "0123456789", Num);
  } /* if Min else */
  Message("");
  /* If there is a number to process */
  if (Is_Text(Num))
  {
    /* Convert to number */
    NumF = atof(Num);
    /* See if entry is within valid range */
    if ((NumF < Min) || (NumF > Max))
    {
      sprintf(TStr1, "%1.6f", Min);
      sprintf(TStr2, "%1.6f", Max);
      /*Strip trailing 0's from ranges*/
      C = strlen(TStr1) - 1;
      for (; (TStr1[C] == '0'); TStr1[C] = 0, C--);
      if (TStr1[C] == '.')
        TStr1[C] = 0;
      C = strlen(TStr2) - 1;
      for (; (TStr2[C] == '0'); TStr2[C] = 0, C--);
      if (TStr2[C] == '.')
        TStr2[C] = 0;
      sprintf(EMess, "Error, number must be between %s and %s.", TStr1,
              TStr2);
      Lo_Mess(EMess);
    } /* if NumF */
    else
    {
```

```
      /* See if the number is a valid number */
      if ((Num_Chars('.', Num) > 1) ||
          (Num_Chars('-', Num) > 1) ||
          (Pos('-', Num) > 1))
        Hi_Mess("Bad number, please re-enter.");
      else
      {
        if (Decs)
        {
          /*Strip leading 0's*/
          C = 0;
          while ((Num[C] == '0') || (Num[C] == '-'))
            Delete(Num, C+1, 1);
        }
        /*Prevent lockup condition*/
        if ((!Decs) && (Pos('.', Num) != 0))
          Delete(Num, Pos('.', Num), 25);
        /* See if done */
        if ((Digs != 0) || (Decs != 0))
        {
          /* See if the number fits the pattern */
          if (((Digs) && (Num_Ints(Num) != Digs)) ||
              ((Decs) && (Num_Decs(Num) > Decs)))
          {
            sprintf(EMess, "Error, entry must fit the pattern '%s'.",
                    Pattern);
            Lo_Mess(EMess);
          } /* if Digs */
          else
            Redo = 0;
        } /* if Digs! */
        else
          Redo = 0;
      } /* if Num_Chars else */
    } /* if NumF else */
  } /* if Is_Text(Num) */
  else
    Redo = 0;
} /* while Redo */
/* Format and pad the number */
if (Is_Text(Num))
{
  if ((Num_Decs(Num) == 0) && (Decs) && (Num[strlen(Num) - 1] != '.'))
  {
    C = strlen(Num);
    Num[C] = '.';
    Num[C + 1] = 0;
  } /* if Num_Decs */
```

```
    while (Num_Decs(Num) != Decs)
    {
      C = strlen(Num);
      Num[C] = '0';
      Num[C + 1] = 0;
    } /* while Num_Decs */
  } /* if Is_Text */
  F_Write(OrX, OrY, VidHigh, RJ(Num, TStr, FSize));
} /* Input_Num */
```

Sample Usage Source Code

▼

```
/*
  This program will use Input_Num to demonstrate Input_Num's Input,
  Error trapping and editing facilities. When a key allowing the user
  to exit is used, the key pressed will be shown at the bottom.
*/

extern unsigned _stklen=16384; /* Minimum recommend stack size */
#include <stdio.h>
#include <math.h>
#include <dos.h>
#include <mem.h>
#include <alloc.h>
#include <ctype.h>
#include <string.h>
#include <stdlib.h>
#include <plib.h>
#include <plib.glo>


/****************************************************************************/
main()
{
  char
    TempVar[11] = "";

  Calibrate_Delay();            /* Calibrate delay factor */
  Get_Video_Mode("Video.CFG"); /* Get display adapter type */
  Install_Crit_Error();         /* Set up application critical error handler */
  InputAbsolute=AbortPrint=0;   /* Initialize global variables */

  /* Application code to follow */

  Clr_Scr();
  strcpy(TempVar, "500");
  F_WriteXY(1, 5, Normal, "Enter a Number: ");
  Input_Num(TempVar, "6I.DDD", 0., 999999.999);
```

```
} /*main*/
```

Sample Usage Output

▼

```
Enter a Number: 500.000
```

Insert

Description

▼

Insert inserts the string *OBStr into another string (*TrgStr) at a specific location. If the position is beyond the end of the specified string, the string value being inserted is appended to the very end of the *TrgStr string.

Routine Declaration

▼

```
void Insert(char *ObStr,
            char *TrgStr,
            int  Position)
```

Passed Variables

▼

***ObStr String Pointer** A pointer to the string that is to be inserted into *TrgStr.

***TrgStr String Pointer** A pointer to the string that is to have *ObStr inserted into it.

Position integer The position within *TrgStr at which *ObStr is to be inserted. If Position is greater than the length of *TrgStr, *ObStr is inserted between the end of *TrgStr and the null terminator. Position is referenced from 1 to the length of *TrgStr, instead of from 0 to the length of *TrgStr minus 1.

Global Variables

▼

None

Error Codes/ Messages

▼

None

Discussion

▼

Insert provides an easy method of placing a substring within a specified string at a desired location. The routine provides very little error checking other than to ensure that if the specified position is beyond the end of the target string, the substring is merely appended to the target string rather than being inserted.

Insert starts by decrementing the Position to put it in the 0 to n range rather than the 1 to n + 1 range passed. Then an if condition is used to determine if the Position specified is beyond the length of the target string. If Position is out of range, Turbo C's routine strcat concatenates the substring onto the end of the target string. If Position is within the target string, Turbo C's routine movmem adjusts the target string and places the substring within the target string.

Limitations and Modifications

▼

None

Routine Source Code

▼

```
#include <string.h>
#include <mem.h>

void Insert(char *ObStr,
            char *TrgStr,
            int Position)
/*
  This routine will insert *ObStr in *TrgStr at Position. If the length
  of *TrgStr is less than Position, *ObStr will be concatenated onto the
  Position which starts at 1.
*/
{ /* Insert */
  int
    ObLen,
    TrgLen;

  Position--;
  TrgLen = strlen(TrgStr);
  if (Position <= TrgLen)
  {
    ObLen = strlen(ObStr);
    movmem(TrgStr + Position, TrgStr + ObLen + Position,
           TrgLen - Position + 1);
    movmem(ObStr, TrgStr + Position, ObLen);
  } /* if Position */
  else
    strcat(TrgStr, ObStr);
} /* Insert */
```

Sample Usage Source Code

▼

```
/*
  This program will insert string A into string B by using Insert().
*/
```

```
extern unsigned _stklen=16384; /* Minimum recommend stack size */
#include <stdio.h>
#include <math.h>
#include <dos.h>
#include <mem.h>
#include <alloc.h>
#include <ctype.h>
#include <string.h>
#include <stdlib.h>
#include <plib.h>
#include <plib.glo>


/******************************************************************************/
main()
{
  char
    StrA[81] = "",
    StrB[81] = "";

  Calibrate_Delay();             /* Calibrate delay factor */
  Get_Video_Mode("Video.CFG"); /* Get display adapter type */
  Install_Crit_Error();          /* Set up application critical error handler */
  InputAbsolute=AbortPrint=0;   /* Initialize global variables */

  /* Application code to follow */

  Clr_Scr();
  printf("\n See, the following string is inserted with something .\n");
  strcpy(StrB, "She sells seashells at the seashore.");
  strcpy(StrA, " says he");
  printf("\nThis is String B ---%s---\n", StrB);

  Insert(StrA, StrB, 4);
  printf("\nThis is String A ---%s---\n", StrA) ;
  printf("\nThis is the result of String A inserted into B at position 4\n%s\n",
         StrB);

} /*  main  */
```

Sample Usage Output

▼

```
See, the following string is inserted with something.

This is String B ---She sells seashells at the seashore.---

This is String A --- says he---
```

```
This is the result of String A inserted into B at position 4
She says he sells seashells at the seashore.
```

Install_Crit_Error

Description

▼

Install_Crit_Error resets the DOS error vector to the routine Critical-_Error_Handler. Critical_Error_Handler is included in this section because it should never be called directly by an application. The call to Install_Crit_Error should be made once and only once during an application. A subsequent call to Install_Crit_Error can cause problems in the error handling routine. When your application is ended, the DOS error vector is reset to the normal error handler incorporated in DOS.

Routine Declaration

▼

```
void Install_Crit_Error(void)
```

Passed Variables

▼

None

Global Variables

▼

AbortPrint Disables printing when the printer is no longer available or the user has selected to halt printing. The Critical_Error_Handler sets this variable true (1) if the user selects to Stop Print.

CritOperation Returns the number of the operation selected by the user. The operations are: 1 for Stop Print or Try again, 2 for Exit to DOS, or 3 for Ignore error. CritOperation 2 never actually returns equal to 2 because, when this option is selected by the user, the program is terminated and the user returned to DOS. Note: your application should initialize CritOperation to 0 and reset it to 0 after any critical errors are returned, in order to properly detect additional errors.

Error Codes/ Messages

▼

```
Diskette is write-protected:Unknown unit:
Drive not ready:
Data Error (CRC):
Bad request structure length:
Seek error:
Unknown media type:
```

```
Sector not found:
Printer off-line:
Write fault:
Read fault:
General failure:
```

These errors are displayed on the 25th line of the screen with either of two options after the message:

```
Try Again  Exit to DOS  Ignore error
Try Again  Stop Print  Ignore error
```

Users select the operation they want and the error is handled appropriately. To select an error handler option, users must press the left or right arrow or the first letter of the option to highlight and a carriage return to select the option. For further information on these messages, consult the DOS Technical Reference Manual.

Discussion

▼

Install_Crit_Error uses the Turbo C routine harderr to redirect critical errors trapped by DOS to the associated library routine Critical_Error_Handler. Critical_Error_Handler manages the message display and user interface for any of the potential critical errors. For a complete description of the errors and their causes, consult the DOS Technical Reference Manual.

Critical_Error_Handler starts by saving the current video screen, CurKey, and the cursor format for restoration when the routine is completed. Then, on the 25th line, the DOS error message referenced in the ErrMess array is displayed left justified and the user options are displayed to the right of the ErrMess in a horizontal menu format. User responses are interpreted until the user presses <ENTER>, at which time Critical_Error_Handler attempts to perform the option selected by the user. If the option is option 1 or 3, the global variable CritOperation is set to the selected option. If the error was caused by a printer off-line condition, the global variable AbortPrint is set appropriately. Finally, Critical_Error_Handler restores the screen, CurKey, and the cursor's format and exits the routine.

Limitations and Modifications

▼

None

Routine Source Code

▼

```
#include <math.h>
#include <string.h>
```

```
#include <stdio.h>
#include <stdlib.h>
#include <ctype.h>
#include <dos.h>
#include <plib.h>

extern char
  AbortPrint;

extern char
  Normal,
  Reverse,
  VidHigh;

extern int
  CritOperation,
  CurKey;

/*
  This is the routine that actually handles the critical error and interacts
  with the user. The routine that installs this routine follows it.
*/
int Critical_Error_Handler(int ErrVal,
                           int AX,
                           int BP,
                           int SI)
/*
  This routine will function as a library compatible critical error
  handler with all messages and selections taking place on the 25th line.
*/
{ /* Critical_Error_Handler */
  char
    ITag[3][16] = {"Try again", "Exit to DOS", "Ignore error"},
    OldScreen[4001],
    ErrMess[13][40] = {"Diskette is write-protected:",
                       "Unknown unit:",
                       "Drive not ready:",
                       "Unknown command:",
                       "Data Error (CRC):",
                       "Bad request structure length:",
                       "Seek error:",
                       "Unknown media type:",
                       "Sector not found:",
                       "Printer off-line:",
                       "Write fault:",
                       "Read fault:",
                       "General failure:"};
```

```
int
  OldCur,
  OldCurKey,
  IPtr;

Save_Screen(OldScreen);
OldCur = Cursor_Off();
OldCurKey = CurKey;
if (ErrVal == 9)
  strcpy(ITag[1], "Stop Print");
Message("");
F_Write(1, 25, VidHigh, ErrMess[ErrVal]);
F_Write(39, 25, VidHigh, ITag[0]);
F_Write(54, 25, VidHigh, ITag[1]);
F_Write(69, 25, VidHigh, ITag[2]);
for (IPtr = 1; IPtr<=6; IPtr++)
{
  Beep_Lo();
  Beep_Hi();
}
IPtr = 0;
do
{
  F_Write(IPtr * 15 + 39, 25, Reverse, ITag[IPtr]);
  Get_One_Char();
  F_Write(IPtr * 15 + 39, 25, VidHigh, ITag[IPtr]);
  switch(CurKey)
  {
    case -75: /*left*/
    IPtr -= (IPtr>0);
    break;
    case -77: /*right*/
    IPtr += (IPtr<2);
    break;
    case 'S':
    case 's':
    if (ErrVal == 9)
      IPtr = 0;
    break;
    case 'T':
    case 't':
    if (ErrVal != 9)
      IPtr = 0;
    break;
    case 'Q':
    case 'q':
    IPtr = 1;
    break;
```

```
      case 'C':
      case 'c':
      IPtr = 2;
      break;
    } /* switch CurKey */
  } while (CurKey != 13);
  Cursor_On(OldCur);
  IPtr++;
  CurKey = OldCurKey;
  Restore_Screen(OldScreen);
  if (ErrVal == 9)
  {
    switch(IPtr)
    {
      case 1:
        CritOperation = 1;
        return(1);
      break;

      case 2:
        AbortPrint = 1;
        CritOperation = 2;
        hardretn(ErrVal);
      break;

      case 3:
        CritOperation = 3;
        hardretn(ErrVal);
      break;
    } /* switch IPtr */
  } /* if ErrVal */
  else
  {
    switch(IPtr)
    {
      case 1:
        CritOperation = 1;
        return(1);
      break;

      case 2:
        CritOperation = 2;
        return(2);
      break;

      case 3:
        CritOperation = 3;
        return(0);
```

```
      break;
    } /* switch IPtr */
  }  /* if ErrVal else */
} /* Critical_Error_Handler */

void Install_Crit_Error(void)
/*
  This routine will install the critical error handler.
*/
{ /* Install_Crit_Error */
  harderr(Critical_Error_Handler);
} /* Install_Crit_Error */
```

Sample Usage Source Code

▼

```
/*
  This program will use Install_Crit_Error to load in Critical_Error_Handler,
  and try to copy a file into empty Drive A; then we can see that the DOS
  error's handling control has been taken over.
*/

extern unsigned _stklen=16384; /* Minimum recommend stack size */
#include <stdio.h>
#include <math.h>
#include <dos.h>
#include <mem.h>
#include <alloc.h>
#include <ctype.h>
#include <string.h>
#include <stdlib.h>
#include <plib.h>
#include <plib.glo>


/******************************************************************************/
main()
{
  char
    Check ;

  Calibrate_Delay();            /* Calibrate delay factor */
  Get_Video_Mode("Video.CFG"); /* Get display adapter type */
  Install_Crit_Error();         /* Set up application critical error handler */
  InputAbsolute=AbortPrint=0;   /* Initialize global variables */

  /* Application code to follow */

  Clr_Scr ();
```

```
    printf("\nTo show how Critical_Error_Handler works,");
    printf("please remove any diskette that \n may be in drive A:");
    printf("\n\n          When you are ready, please press <RETURN>. \n");
    scanf("%c", &Check);

    printf("\n\n  Now we try to copy A:TTTTT.TTT to A:CCCCC.CCC, ");
    printf("and watch how the DOS error comes out.");
    Delay (2000);
    Copy_File ("A:TTTTT.TTT", "A:CCCCC.CCC");

} /*  main  */
```

Sample Usage Output

```
   To show how Critical_Error_Handler works, please remove any diskette that
may be in drive A:

          When you are ready, please press <RETURN>.




  Now we try to copy A:TTTTT.TTT to A:CCCCC.CCC, and watch how the DOS error comes
out.






  Drive not ready:            Try again       Exit to DOS       Ignore error
```

Is_Text

Description

Is_Text determines if the specified string contains any characters that are not a space (ASCII 32 decimal). If any characters are found, the routine returns true (1); otherwise, it returns false (0).

Routine Declaration

```
char Is_Text(char *Txt)
```

Passed Variables

***Txt String Pointer** A pointer to the string to be checked for nonspace characters.

Global Variables

▼

None

Error Codes/ Messages

▼

None

Discussion

▼

Is_Text provides an easy method of determining if a string contains textual data and conditioning routine calls that must have information in parameters before processing. For example, you shouldn't use Date_Diff to calculate the difference between two dates if either is blank or only contains spaces.

Is_Text steps forward through the specified string with a for loop that continues until it reaches the end of the string or a nonspace character. If the for loop is able to step through the entire string, the routine returns false (0); otherwise, the routine returns true (1).

Limitations and Modifications

▼

Is_Text's main limitation is that the routine does not distinguish between text characters, graphics characters, and control codes. In most cases, this limitation does not present a problem, since most data is entered through a controlling routine like Input_Alpha. However, you may want to create a different function for checking entire strings for the type of characters the string contains.

Routine Source Code

▼

```
char Is_Text(char *Txt)
/*
  This function will return true (1) if any character in the string
  *Txt is anything > ascii 32; if not, it will return false (0).
*/
{ /* Is_Text */
  int T;

  for (T = 0; (Txt[T] && ((unsigned)Txt[T]) <= 32); T++);
  return(Txt[T] != 0);
} /* Is_Text */
```

Sample Usage Source Code

▼

```
/*
  It is sometimes necessary to consider a string of spaces the same as
  a null string. This program will allow the user to enter a string
  from the keyboard and to display with Is_Text whether or not the entry
  was considered text.
```

```
*/

extern unsigned _stklen=16384; /* Minimum recommend stack size */
#include <stdio.h>
#include <math.h>
#include <dos.h>
#include <mem.h>
#include <alloc.h>
#include <ctype.h>
#include <string.h>
#include <stdlib.h>
#include <plib.h>
#include <plib.glo>

/*****************************************************************************/
main()
{
  char
    TempStr[256] = "";

  Calibrate_Delay();           /* Calibrate delay factor */
  Get_Video_Mode("Video.CFG"); /* Get display adapter type */
  Install_Crit_Error();        /* Set up application critical error handler */
  InputAbsolute=AbortPrint=0;  /* Initialize global variables */

  /* Application code to follow */

  Clr_Scr();
  printf("Enter something, spaces or nothing on the line below.\n");
  gets(TempStr);
  if (Is_Text(TempStr))
    printf("Worthwhile text was entered.");
  else
    printf("Meaningless text or nothing was entered.");

} /* main */
```

Sample Usage Output

▼

```
Enter something, spaces or nothing on the line below.
  ±*/ @$%# ^&!¦ (<>) {:;,.} ? [] abcd ABCD  O.K.!
Worthwhile text was entered.
```

Julian_Cal

Description

▼

Julian_Cal converts the passed Julian Day Number to the standard calendar format MM/DD/YY, then returns the pointer to *Buffer, which contains the conversion result. This routine is the inverse of the process taken in Cal_Julian, which converts a calendar date to a Julian Day Number.

Routine Declaration

▼

```
char *Julian_Cal(float JDN,
                 char  *Buffer)
```

Passed Variables

▼

JDN float The float number that contains the Julian Day Number.

***Buffer String Pointer** A pointer to the string variable that will contain the resulting string.

Global Variables

▼

None

Error Codes/ Messages

▼

None

Discussion

▼

Julian_Cal provides an easy method of reversing the process taken in Cal_Julian. Cal_Julian converts a standard date in the form MM/DD/YY into its Julian Day Number representation, i.e., the number of days since January 1, 4713 B.C. (Julian Calendar). The Julian Day Number allows easy calculation of the other dates by adding or subtracting the number of days and then converting the Julian Day Number back to calendar format.

The conversion routine separates the process into three main steps. The first step calculates the numeric values for the day, month, and year from the Julian Day Number. The second portion converts the numeric day, month, and year to strings to be concatenated into the standard format MM/DD/YY. The final step ensures that the string day, month, and year are two digits in length and concatenates them into the final format, which is placed in the buffer before the pointer is returned.

Limitations and Modifications

▼

Julian_Cal's only limitation is that it is limited to the current century by the line itoa(Y - 1900, YS, 10). This statement subtracts the value 1900 from the year value calculated from the Julian Day Number. This only creates a problem when we reach the next century. However, if you want to add a correction for this problem now, there are several alternatives. First, you could retrieve the system date at the beginning of the application and derive the century. A problem with this method is that if the user does not set the system date it will show the ROM date retrieved at startup. Another alternative is to change the routine to interpret any date over 50 as being in the 1900s and any date under 50 as being in the 2000s. This again has an imposed limitation, but if you expect your users to update their software in the next 10 or 12 years, you can change the offset then.

Routine Source Code

▼

```
#include <math.h>
#include <string.h>
#include <stdio.h>
#include <stdlib.h>
#include <ctype.h>
#include <plib.h>

char *Julian_Cal(float JDN,
                 char *Buffer)
/*
  Returns a calendar date string in the standard form MM/DD/YY from the
  Julian real parameter JDN.
*/
{ /* Julian_Cal */
  int
    D,                /* Temporary variables */
    Y,
    M;

  float
    N1,
    N2,
    Y1,
    M1;

  N1 = (JDN - 1721119.0) + 2.0;
  Y1 = floor((N1 - 0.2) ÷ 365.25);
  N2 = N1 - floor(365.25 * Y1);
  M1 = floor((N2 - 0.5) ÷ 30.6);
  D  = (N2 - 30.6 * M1 + 0.5);
  Y  = (Y1 + (M1 > 9));
  M  = (M1 + 3 - ((M1 > 9) * 12));
  /* Offset for the 20th century */
  Y -= 1900;
  sprintf(Buffer, "%02d/%02d/%02d", M, D, Y);
```

```
  return(Buffer);
} /* Julian_Cal */
```

Sample Usage Source Code

▼

```
/*
  This program will use Input_Num to allow the user to input a number of
  days since year 4713 B.C., Jan. 1, noon, then use Julian_Cal to determine
  what the date is for that number of days.
*/

extern unsigned _stklen=16384; /* Minimum recommend stack size */
#include <stdio.h>
#include <math.h>
#include <dos.h>
#include <mem.h>
#include <alloc.h>
#include <ctype.h>
#include <string.h>
#include <stdlib.h>
#include <plib.h>
#include <plib.glo>


/*****************************************************************************/
main()
{
  float
    Days = 0.0;

  char
    DateBuffer[20] = "";

  Calibrate_Delay();            /* Calibrate delay factor */
  Get_Video_Mode("Video.CFG"); /* Get display adapter type */
  Install_Crit_Error();         /* Set up application critical error handler */
  InputAbsolute=AbortPrint=0;   /* Initialize global variables */

  /* Application code to follow */

  do
  {
    Clr_Scr();
    printf("Enter a number of days from 4713 B.C. (2415033 - 2451550): ");
    scanf("%f", &Days);
  }
  while((Days < 2.415033e+6) || (Days > 2.4651550e+6));
```

```
  printf("\nThat date is: %s \n", Julian_Cal(Days, DateBuffer));

} /*main*/
```

Sample Usage Output

▼

```
Enter a number of days from 4713 B.C. (2415033 - 2451550): 2450000

That date is: 09/26/95
```

LJ

Description

▼

LJ left justifies the string *LStr in the string buffer for the field of spaces FWdth wide. If the string exceeds the specified length, it is truncated to the field width. Leading spaces on the passed string are not removed. The pointer to the buffer returns upon completion.

Routine Declaration

▼

```
char *LJ(char *LStr,
         char *Buffer,
         int FWdth)
```

Passed Variables

▼

***LStr String Pointer** A pointer to the string to be left justified in a field of spaces FWdth characters wide.

***Buffer String Pointer** A pointer to the string variable that will contain the resulting string.

FWdth integer The integer value that specifies the width of the returned string value.

Global Variables

▼

None

Error Codes/ Messages

▼

None

Discussion

▼

LJ provides an easy, consistent method for left justifying strings in specified fields of spaces, which is extremely useful in creating fixed-length concatenations of fields for output in printed or disk forms. In using the library, you will particularly need to use LJ for any fields in data files that are used as key indexes. This ensures that comparisons or substring extractions of indexes will have a full field of characters to manipulate.

LJ uses an if to determine if the specified string is longer than the allowed field. If the string is too long, it is truncated with a copy command executed within a for loop. If the string is within the boundaries of the field length, the string is copied into the Buffer by a for loop and a second for loop adds the appropriate number of spaces onto the end of the original string. The number of spaces used is the difference between the string length and the specified width.

Limitations and Modifications

▼

The only real limitation to LJ is that it does not strip any leading spaces from the passed string. If you find your application requires the leading spaces to be stripped, use a call to the procedure Erase_White_Begin. Evaluate the performance differences this may cause to ensure that it won't dramatically impede your application's performance.

Routine Source Code

▼

```
char *LJ(char *LStr,
         char *Buffer,
         int FWdth)
/*
  This function will set *LStr in *Buffer left justified in a field
  FWdth wide with space character fills. If FWdth is smaller than the
  length of *LStr, *Buffer will contain the truncated version of
  *LStr(from 0 to FWdth - 1).
  It will return the pointer to *Buffer.
*/
{ /* LJ */
  int
    T,
    LS;

  for (LS = 0; LStr[LS]; LS++);
  if (LS <= FWdth)
  {
    FWdth--;
    for (T = 0; LStr[T]; T++)
      Buffer[T] = LStr[T];
    for (; T <= FWdth; T++)
      Buffer[T] = ' ';
    Buffer[T] = 0;
  } /* if LS */
  else
  {
```

```
    FWdth--;
    for (T = 0; T <= FWdth; T++)
      Buffer[T] = LStr[T];
    Buffer[T] = 0;
  } /* if LS else */
  return(Buffer);
} /* LJ */
```

Sample Usage Source Code

▼

```
/*
  This program will allow the user to input a string into
  TempStr and a number into FWidth. It will then use LJ to
  left justify TempStr into a field of spaces that is FWidth
  long.
*/

extern unsigned _stklen=16384; /* Minimum recommend stack size */
#include <stdio.h>
#include <math.h>
#include <dos.h>
#include <mem.h>
#include <alloc.h>
#include <ctype.h>
#include <string.h>
#include <stdlib.h>
#include <plib.h>
#include <plib.glo>


/****************************************************************************/
main()
{
  int
    FWidth = 0;

  char
    LeftStr[81] = "",
    TempStr[81] = "";

  Calibrate_Delay();            /* Calibrate delay factor */
  Get_Video_Mode("Video.CFG");  /* Get display adapter type */
  Install_Crit_Error();         /* Set up application critical error handler */
  InputAbsolute=AbortPrint=0;   /* Initialize global variables */

  /* Application code to follow */

  Clr_Scr();
```

```
printf("Enter something: ");
gets(TempStr);
printf("\n\nEnter field width: ");
scanf("%u", &FWidth);

printf("\n*******%s*******\n", LJ(TempStr, LeftStr, FWidth));

} /*  main  */
```

Sample Usage Output

▼

```
Enter something: This is an LJ test.


Enter field width: 25

*******This is an LJ test.      *******
```

Lo_Mess

Description

▼

Lo_Mess provides a consistent method of reporting data entry errors to the user. Such errors include bad keystrokes and bad data entered for fields that require specific types of data, such as dates and word contents. The routine sounds a low-pitch tone and displays a specified string on the 25th line using the routine Message.

Routine Declaration

▼

```
void Lo_Mess(char *Mess)
```

Passed Variables

▼

***Mess String Pointer** A pointer to the message line to be displayed on the 25th line of the screen.

Global Variables

▼

None

Error Codes/ Messages

▼

None

Discussion

Lo_Mess provides a consistent means of informing the user of errors made when entering data. Lo_Mess is primarily used with the input routines (Input_Alpha, Prompt, Input_Num, and Input_Date). The types of errors that trigger a call to Lo_Mess include: pressing a key not in the field's valid set of characters, entering a bad date, or entering a number that is out of range.

Limitations and Modifications

Lo_Mess doesn't really have any specific limitations, but there are several ways to modify the routine, adding a delay time to the parameter list to ensure a constant time for the display of the message, for instance. However, this may impede the performance of data entry under some applications. Clearing the message line after the Beep_Lo is also possible, but be careful to allow sufficient time for the user to read the message. (You can appreciate this concern if you have ever used a program that doesn't allow you to read the error message before it is cleared!)

Routine Source Code

```
#include <math.h>
#include <string.h>
#include <stdio.h>
#include <stdlib.h>
#include <ctype.h>
#include <plib.h>

void Lo_Mess(char *Mess)
/*
  This function will write *Mess as a message preceded by a Beep_Lo.
*/
{ /* Lo_Mess */
  Message(Mess);
  Beep_Lo();
} /* Lo_Mess */
```

Sample Usage Source Code

```
/*
  This program will use Lo_Mess to beep and display a message in
  reverse video on the 25th line.
*/

extern unsigned _stklen=16384; /* Minimum recommend stack size */
#include <stdio.h>
#include <math.h>
#include <dos.h>
```

```
#include <mem.h>
#include <alloc.h>
#include <ctype.h>
#include <string.h>
#include <stdlib.h>
#include <plib.h>
#include <plib.glo>


/*****************************************************************************/
main()
{
  Calibrate_Delay();             /* Calibrate delay factor */
  Get_Video_Mode("Video.CFG"); /* Get display adapter type */
  Install_Crit_Error();         /* Set up application critical error handler */
  InputAbsolute=AbortPrint=0;  /* Initialize global variables */

  /* Application code to follow */
  Clr_Scr();
  Lo_Mess("They shoot horses, don't they!");
  Delay (3000) ;

} /* main */
```

Sample Usage Output

▼

```
They shoot horses, don't they!
```

Look_One_Char

Description

▼

Look_One_Char reads the value of the next keystroke in the keyboard buffer and returns the appropriate value for the waiting keystroke. Any keys that use a two-byte scan code returns a negative value equal to the significant scan value. Unlike Get_One_Char, Look_One_Char only determines the value of the keystroke. It does not remove the character from the buffer. If a key has not been pressed, Look_One_Char returns zero.

Routine Declaration

▼

```
int Look_One_Char(void)
```

Passed Variables

▼

None

Global Variables

▼

None

Error Codes/ Messages

▼

None

Discussion

▼

Look_One_Char provides the means to look ahead into the keyboard buffer without actually disturbing the characters stored there. But unlike Get-_One_Char, Look_One_Char does not wait for a key to be pressed. If a key is not pressed, the routine returns zero. The value returned is either the ASCII value of a character or the negative value of the significant scan code if a two-byte scan code is used for the keystroke.

Look_One_Char uses service 1 (Report if a character is ready) of ROM BIOS interrupt 16 hex (Keyboard Services). This interrupt call sets the Zero Flag (bit 2) to 0 if a character is present and 1 if there is not a character in the keyboard buffer. If a character is present, it is checked for being a prefixed key. A positive value is returned if it is not a prefixed key and a negative value if it is. Prefixed keys return a 0 in the AL register and the key's scan code in the AH register. Nonprefixed keys return the scan code in the AL register.

Limitations and Modifications

▼

None

Routine Source Code

▼

```
#include <dos.h>
#include <mem.h>

int Look_One_Char(void)
/*
  This function returns the ascii value of characters waiting in the keyboard
  buffer. If the key is a prefixed key (function key), then the ascii value
  returned is negative. If a character is not present, then 0 is returned.
  Note that this function does not remove the character from the keyboard
  buffer as Get_One_Char does.

*/
{ /* Look_One_Char */
  union REGS
    Regs;

  setmem( &Regs, sizeof(Regs), 0);
  Regs.h.ah = 0x01;
```

```
  int86(0x16, &Regs, &Regs);
  if (!(Regs.x.flags & 0x0040))
  {
    if (Regs.h.al)
    {
      return((int)Regs.h.al);
    } /* if Regs */
    else
      return(-(int)Regs.h.ah);
  } /* if ! */
  else
    return(0);
} /* Look_One_Char */
```

Sample Usage Source Code

▼

```
/*
  This program will use Look_One_Char() to show what the first character
  in the keyboard buffer is without removing it from the buffer.
*/

extern unsigned _stklen=16384; /* Minimum recommend stack size */
#include <stdio.h>
#include <math.h>
#include <dos.h>
#include <mem.h>
#include <alloc.h>
#include <ctype.h>
#include <string.h>
#include <stdlib.h>
#include <plib.h>
#include <plib.glo>


/*****************************************************************************/
main()
{
  char
    S[11] = "";

  Calibrate_Delay();            /* Calibrate delay factor */
  Get_Video_Mode("Video.CFG"); /* Get display adapter type */
  Install_Crit_Error();         /* Set up application critical error handler */
  InputAbsolute=AbortPrint=0;   /* Initialize global variables */

  /* Application code to follow */

  Clr_Scr();
```

```
  printf("Press 3 character keys followed by <Enter> and wait.\n");
  Delay(10000);
  printf("\n\nAscii of the first character you typed is: %d.\n",
        Look_One_Char());
  gets(S);
  printf("All of what you typed is: '%s'.\n", S);

} /* main */
```

Sample Usage Output

▼

```
Press 3 character keys followed by <Enter> and wait.


Ascii of the first character you typed is: 79.
Oka
All of what you typed is: 'Oka'.
```

M_D_Y

Description

▼

M_D_Y provides six different formats for returning the textual representation of a specified date in the form MM/DD/YY. The formats available in M_D_Y are shown in table 2-4.

Routine Declaration

▼

```
char *M_D_Y(char *Date,
            int  MDYCase,
            Char *Buffer)
```

Passed Variables

▼

***Date String Pointer** A pointer to the string date, in the form MM/DD/YY, for conversion to textual format.

Table 2-4. *MDYCase Formats*

MDYCase	Result
1	October 18, 1987
2	Sunday, October 18, 1987
3	Sun, October 18, 1987
4	Oct 18, 1987
5	Sun, Oct 18, 1987
6	18th day of October 1987

MDYCase integer The integer number that specifies the type of format to be used in the conversion. For the sample date 10/18/87, M_D_Y provides the formats listed in table 2-4.

***Buffer String Pointer** A pointer to the string variable that will contain the resulting string.

Global Variables

▼

None

Error Codes/ Messages

▼

None

Discussion

▼

The need for a routine that could provide several reporting formats of dates led to the development of M_D_Y. The formats can be used for report titling, screen display, or legal documents that require the display of the month and day from a date.

The routine is primarily comprised of a switch statement that is sectioned by MDYCase. Each section of the switch creates the results for a particular format. The cases make calls to other date routines to retrieve the month and day formats required. For more information on acquiring month and date formats, see the routines Month_Of_Year and Day_Of_Week.

Limitations and Modifications

▼

As mentioned, some routines in the library have parameters that can be used to indicate multiple result formats. This routine and a few others have parameters for determining format styles. Although this can be difficult to read, the additional flexibility justifies the potential difficulties in these few cases.

M_D_Y is one of the few routines in the library that require you to pass a variable for the style of results desired. In routines like M_D_Y, it is more space efficient to lump the formats together rather than provide six separate routines. If you prefer separate routines, break the cases out into different modules.

With the six formats available, most reporting needs have been addressed. However, you may find other formats that your applications require. Adding new cases to the switch statement can be accomplished easily. Other date routines in the library also make the assembly of new formats easy.

Routine Source Code

▼

```
#include <math.h>
#include <string.h>
#include <stdio.h>
```

```
#include <stdlib.h>
#include <ctype.h>
#include <plib.h>


char *M_D_Y(char *Date,
            int MDYCase,
            char *Buffer)
/*
  Returns the English spelling of the parameter *Date (MM/DD/YY) in the
  format selected by MDYCase:
    MDYCase = 1  -  January 18, 1987
    MDYCase = 2  -  Wednesday, September 18, 1987
    MDYCase = 3  -  Wed, September 18, 1987
    MDYCase = 4  -  Jan 18, 1987
    MDYCase = 5  -  Wed, Jan 18, 1987
    MDYCase = 6  -  18th day of January, 1987
*/
{ /* M_D_Y */
  char
    TStr1[30],
    TStr2[30],
    TStr3[30],
    Sufx[3],
    Day[3],
    DCh;

  Copy(Date, 4 + (Date[3] == '0'), 2 - (Date[3] == '0'), Day);
  switch (MDYCase)
  {
    case 1:
      sprintf(Buffer, "%s %s, 19%s", Month_Of_Year(Date, 5, TStr1), Day,
              Copy(Date, 7, 2, TStr2));
    break;
    case 2:
      sprintf(Buffer, "%s, %s %s, 19%s", Day_Of_Week(Date, 5, TStr1),
              Month_Of_Year(Date, 5, TStr2), Day, Copy(Date, 7, 2, TStr3));
    break;
    case 3:
      sprintf(Buffer, "%s, %s %s, 19%s", Day_Of_Week(Date, 2, TStr1),
              Month_Of_Year(Date, 5, TStr2),
              Day, Copy(Date, 7, 2, TStr3));
    break;
    case 4:
      sprintf(Buffer, "%s %s, 19%s", Month_Of_Year(Date, 2, TStr1), Day,
              Copy(Date, 7, 2, TStr2));
    break;
    case 5:
```

```
      sprintf(Buffer, "%s, %s %s, 19%s", Day_Of_Week(Date, 2, TStr1),
              Month_Of_Year(Date, 2, TStr2), Day,
              Copy(Date, 7, 2, TStr3));
    break;
    case 6:
      if (strlen(Day) == 1)
        DCh = Day[0];
      else
        DCh = Day[1];
      if ((Day[0] != '1') || (strlen(Day) == 1))
      {
        switch (DCh)
        {
          case '1':
            strcpy(Sufx, "st");
          break;
          case '2':
            strcpy(Sufx, "nd");
          break;
          case '3':
            strcpy(Sufx, "rd");
          break;
          default :
            strcpy(Sufx, "th");
          break;
        } /* switch DCh */
      } /* if Day[0] */
      else
        strcpy(Sufx, "th");
      sprintf(Buffer, "%s%s day of %s, 19%s", Day, Sufx,
              Month_Of_Year(Date, 5, TStr1),
              Copy(Date, 7, 2, TStr2));
    break;
  } /* switch MDYCase */
  return(Buffer);
} /*M_D_Y*/
```

Sample Usage Source Code

▼

```
/*
  This program will use M_D_Y to print today's date in all the available
  formats M_D_Y has.
*/

extern unsigned _stklen=16384; /* Minimum recommend stack size */
#include <stdio.h>
#include <math.h>
#include <dos.h>
```

```
#include <mem.h>
#include <alloc.h>
#include <ctype.h>
#include <string.h>
#include <stdlib.h>
#include <plib.h>
#include <plib.glo>

/***************************************************************************/
main()
{
  int
    Format = 0;
  char
    TBuffer[9] = "",
    Buffer[40] = "";

  Calibrate_Delay();            /* Calibrate delay factor */
  Get_Video_Mode("Video.CFG"); /* Get display adapter type */
  Install_Crit_Error();         /* Set up application critical error handler */
  InputAbsolute=AbortPrint=0;   /* Initialize global variables */

  /* Application code to follow */

  Clr_Scr();
  for (Format = 1; Format <= 6; Format++)
    printf("Today in format # %u is %s.\n", Format,
           M_D_Y(Today(TBuffer), Format, Buffer));

} /*  main  */
```

Sample Usage Output

▼

```
Today in format # 1 is February 26, 1988.
Today in format # 2 is Friday, February 26, 1988.
Today in format # 3 is Fri, February 26, 1988.
Today in format # 4 is Feb 26, 1988.
Today in format # 5 is Fri, Feb 26, 1988.
Today in format # 6 is 26th day of February, 1988.
```

Menu

Description

▼

Menu creates menus from either a data file or from a string of commands passed. The menu can have items on a horizontal and/or vertical layout and options are selected by cursoring to the option or by typing the starting portion of the option tag. When a text string is passed, the string must contain the following format: /Xposition/Yposition/Itemtag/. . . . When a data filename is used, the file contains a series of data records in the form of a char that contains the X position, an integer that contains the Y position, and a text string up to 80 characters in length. The records are separated into two sections, delimited by a tag record with a null tag. The first section of records contains the actual selectable tags and related positions. The second section contains nonselectable, display-only tags and their associated positions. Data files can be created using the program Make Menu (see Chapter 5).

Routine Declaration

▼

```
void Menu(char *Command,
          int  *IPtr,
          char *STag,
          char CaseSense,
          int  WinX,
          int  WinY,
          int  WinWid,
          int  WinDep,
          char BkGrnd)
```

Passed Variables

▼

***Command String Pointer** A pointer to the menu command string or filename to be used in displaying the menu.

***IPtr integer Pointer** A pointer to the number of the menu option selected by the user. If the value passed in IPtr is a negative value, all function or control keys pressed, other than option selection keys, exit the menu and their value is returned in CurKey. Also, IPtr is converted to a positive integer and used as the initial option. If the value passed is positive, the number is used for the initial option and all function or control keys pressed, other than option selection keys, display a Bad key pressed message.

***STag String Pointer** A pointer to the literal text value of the option selected is returned in this variable.

CaseSense char Determines if the characters entered by the user are to be case-sensitive when being compared to the item tag strings. If CaseSense is zero, the case does not matter in the search for a matching tag. If CaseSense is one, the case of the user's selection must match the desired item tag string.

WinX integer The starting horizontal position of the window defined to contain the menu. Valid values for WinX are 1 through 79.

WinY integer The starting vertical position for the window defined to contain the menu. Valid values for WinY are 1 through 25. Line 25 should not be used in your menu because it is also used by Menu for displaying error messages.

WinWid integer The horizontal width of the window defined for the menu. Valid values for WinWid are 1 through 80.

WinDep integer The vertical height of the window defined for the menu. Valid values for WinDep are 1 through 25, but line 25 should not be used because it is used to display error messages.

BkGrnd char Specifies the background color to be used for the window that contains the menu.

Global Variables

▼

CurKey Contains the value of the last keyboard keystroke retrieved by Get_One_Char that caused Input_Alpha to exit. If the keystroke is prefixed (a two-byte scan code), CurKey contains a negative value equal to the significant byte of the scan codes. For example, pressing A returns a 65 in CurKey and pressing F1 returns −59.

Error Codes/ Messages

▼

```
F.N.F. :Menu - File XXXXX not found.
```

This error is displayed on the 25th line of the display if the specified menu text file cannot be found, causing the application to terminate after the message has completed.

```
Bad Key Pressed
```

This message is displayed on the 25th line if an invalid key is pressed by the user.

```
Not enough memory to load Menu
```

This message occurs if there is not enough free memory to load all the menu tags. The application terminates after the message is displayed.

Discussion

▼

Creating easy-to-use and easy-to-program menus has always been a hassle for application developers. Menu provides a means to overcome that frustration. The routine can accommodate menus that require vertical and horizontal directions and multiple window menus. You can define a menu that requires several full window displays and Menu will handle the pagination when the user moves from one window to the next. When selecting options, the user can use the Up, Down, Left, and Right cursor keys to move to the option desired, or start entering letters or numbers of the option desired and Menu will locate the first match to the characters entered.

Menu begins by determining if a string command parameter or a filename for a data file was passed. If a string command was passed, Menu parses out the tag position parameters and the tags and places them into a linked list of TagRecType structures.

If a data file was specified, Menu reads the records in the form of TagDef, and places the data into a linked list of TagRecType structures. When a blank tag is encountered in the data file, all subsequent records read are placed into a separate linked list of TagRecType used for display-only tags.

Once Menu's local variables are initialized, the routine Paint_Menu displays the current set of tags within the defined window. Once the menu is displayed, the current tag is rewritten to the menu using the Reverse attribute. Menu then waits for the user to enter a keystroke, rewrites the tag in the Normal attribute Blended with BackGround, and begins interpretation of the keystroke. If the keystroke is a cursor movement (Up, Down, Left, Right, PgDn, or PgUp), each cursor direction searches for the closest tag in the coordinate list. If the closest tag is on another menu page or a PgDn/PgUp is pressed, Paint_Menu is called to display the new menu page. This loop continues until the user either selects a tag with a Return or exits the menu with an escape or command key. After the selection, the linked lists are dissolved and Menu returns the appropriate selected values.

Limitations and Modifications

▼

Even though Menu has numerous features and capabilities, it lacks error detection, so it is up to the programmer to ensure that the menu text is correct. You may want to improve on the error trapping in Menu, but be careful of adversely affecting the performance.

Routine Source Code

▼

```
#include <stddef.h>
#include <stdlib.h>
#include <stdio.h>
#include <mem.h>
#include <dos.h>
#include <alloc.h>
#include <ctype.h>
#include <string.h>
#include <plib.h>

extern char
  Reverse,
  VidHigh,
  Normal;

extern int
  CurKey;

typedef struct
{
```

```
  char
    X1;
  int
    Y1;
  char
    Str[81];
} TagDef;

typedef struct TRT
{
  struct TRT
    far *FLink,
    far *BLink;
  char
    X,
    Y,
    StrTxt[81];
} TagRecType;

/*
  This routine is used by the routine Menu.
*/
void Paint_Menu(TagRecType far *FTag,
                TagRecType far *FTTag,
                int WindowY,
                int WinX,
                int WinY,
                int WinDep)
/*
  This function will clear the defined window and show the menu items
  contained in it.
*/
{ /* Paint_Menu */
  char
    First;

  TagRecType
    far *ITag;

  TagRecType
    WorkBuff;

  int
    WinBot;

  WinBot = WindowY + WinDep - 1;
  for(First = 0; First < 2; First++)
  {
```

```
    if (First)
      ITag = FTTag;
    else
      ITag = FTag;

    while ((ITag != NULL) && (ITag -> Y <= WinBot))
    {
      if (ITag -> Y >= WindowY && ITag -> Y <= WinBot)
      {
#ifdef __SMALL__
        movedata(FP_SEG(ITag), FP_OFF(ITag), (int)_DS, (int) & WorkBuff,
                 sizeof(WorkBuff));
        F_Write(ITag -> X + WinX - 1, ITag -> Y - WindowY + WinY,
                Blend(Normal), WorkBuff.StrTxt);
#endif
#ifdef __LARGE__
        F_Write(ITag -> X + WinX - 1, ITag -> Y - WindowY + WinY,
                Blend(Normal), ITag -> StrTxt);
#endif
      } /* if ITag */
      ITag = ITag -> FLink;
    } /* while ITag */
  } /* for First */
} /* Paint_Menu */

void Menu(char *Command,
          int *IPtr,
          char *STag,
          char CaseSense,
          int WinX,
          int WinY,
          int WinWid,
          int WinDep,
          char BkGrnd)
/*
  If Command does not start with a '/' then it is assumed that Command
  contains the name of a menu description file, in which case the menu
  description file is read and executed.  The menu description file is
  a file of records of type TagDef. The first set of tags in the
  description file are the actual tags. Then there is a tag with a
  null string as a delimiter to the next set of tags which are merely
  text tags (they cannot be selected, only displayed). And, finally,
  there is another tag with a null string to indicate the end. This file can
  be created using the utility 'makmenu'. If the menu description
  file is not available, an error will be displayed to the user, STag
  will be set null, IPtr will be set to 0 and this routine will exit.

  If Command starts with a '/' then it is assumed that Command contains
```

the actual Tags and is interpreted like this: "/X1/Y1/Tag1/X2/Y2/Tag2/..." where the Xs & Ys are the coordinates for the Tags - note that the sequence must end with a '/'. By the way, no display-only tags can be entered in this method. Only the menu description files can have display-only tags.

IPtr is the Tag (sometimes called Item) pointer. It will place the Tag selector initially on the value it contains. This value can be from 1 to N (number of Tags) or -1 to -N, but it must always be initialized to something valid. Tags are referenced in the order a page of text would be read, from left to right and down. For instance, the command "/1/1/Set up/10/1/Initialize/1/5/Enter Data/10/5/Print Report/50/10/Exit/" tags numbering would be as follows:

Tag	Tag number
Set up	1
Initialize	2
Enter Data	3
Print Report	4
Exit	5

In this case it is only a coincidence that the numbering follows in the order the commands are presented. The number follows the way the tags coordinates would place them on a page and consequently be read. If IPtr happened to be set to 3 when the menu was entered, it would come up initially with the selector on the tag "Enter Data". If the user selected "Print Report" it would be returned set to 4.

STag merely returns the Tag that was selected, so in the last example, STag would be set to "Print Report".

This routine will exit when the user presses any nonprintable key other than the Backspace, Up, Down, Right, Left, Page up, and Page down. These keys would be, for example, Enter, Esc, F1 - F10 (nonshifted, shifted, or alternate) and control codes. However, if IPtr is initialized to the negative value of its intended value, only the Enter and Esc keys may be used to exit this routine, all other keys will invoke an error prompt; IPtr will still be returned as a positive number. In either case, the key used to exit the routine will be stored in the global variable CurKey.

All selectable and display-only tags will be displayed where they fall relative to the window defined by WinX, WinY, Wdth and Lnth. Pagination within the window will be handled automatically. The Page up or Page down keys may be used if more than one window is available or when a window boundary is reached via the Up or Down keys.

```
  Pagination will also occur for the appropriate direction. The user
  may select tags with the cursor keys, or may type the actual name of
  the tag. As each character is typed, the chain of selectable tags
  will be scanned for the first match to what has currently been entered
  by the user, which will be displayed on the 25th line in the Reverse
  attribute. If CaseSense is 1 then Tags and entries are case
  sensitive; if CaseSense is 0 then all is case insensitive. However
  STag will still return the literal tag in its exact case. The
  backspace key will remove the last character typed in the string
  accumulation.
*/
{ /* Menu */
  char
    Ch,
    NotFound,
    NotDone,
    *CmdPtr,
    *SStr,
    TagStr[256],
    TStr[256],
    ErrMess;

  int
    TTagCount,
    Ind,
    WindowY,
    TY,
    OldCur;

  TagRecType
    far *TTag,
    far *FTag,
    far *FTTag,
    far *ITag,
    far *CTag;

  TagRecType
    WorkBuff;

  TagDef
    FileTag;

  FILE
    *MnFl;

  TTagCount = 0;
  /* Determine if Menu description or Menu description file. */
  if (Command[0] == '/') /* Menu Description */
```

```
  {
    /* Read in the string definition */
    CmdPtr = Command;
    CmdPtr++;
    ITag = FTTag = NULL;
    do
    {
      TTag = (TagRecType far *)farmalloc((unsigned long)sizeof(TagRecType));
      if (TTag != NULL)
      {
        if (ITag != NULL)
          ITag -> FLink = TTag;
        else
          FTag = TTag;
        TTag -> BLink = ITag;
        ITag = TTag;
        for (SStr = TStr; (*CmdPtr != '/' && *CmdPtr); /* Parse X */
             *SStr = *CmdPtr, SStr++, CmdPtr++);
        CmdPtr++;
        *SStr = 0;
        ITag -> X = atoi(TStr);
        for (SStr = TStr; (*CmdPtr != '/' && *CmdPtr);  /* Parse Y */
            *SStr = *CmdPtr, SStr++, CmdPtr++);
        CmdPtr++;
        *SStr = 0;
        ITag -> Y = atoi(TStr);
        for (SStr = TStr; (*CmdPtr != '/' && *CmdPtr);  /* Parse Tag */
            *SStr = *CmdPtr, SStr++, CmdPtr++);
        CmdPtr++;
        *SStr = 0;
#ifdef __SMALL__
        movedata(_DS, (int)TStr, FP_SEG(ITag -> StrTxt), FP_OFF(ITag -
> StrTxt),
                 (int)(SStr - TStr) + 1);
#endif
#ifdef __LARGE__
        strcpy(ITag -> StrTxt, TStr);
#endif
        ITag -> FLink = NULL;
      }/*end if*/
      else
        Bomb_Mess("Not enough memory to load Menu");
    } while (*CmdPtr);
  } /* if Command[0] */
  else
  {
    /* Read the file definition */
    ITag = NULL;
```

```
    MnFl = fopen(Command, "rb");
    if (MnFl != NULL)
    {
      do
      {
        TTag = (TagRecType far *)
                farmalloc((unsigned long)sizeof(TagRecType));
        if (TTag != NULL)
        {
          if (ITag != NULL)
            ITag -> FLink = TTag;
          else
            FTag = TTag;
          TTag -> BLink = ITag;
          ITag = TTag;
          fread( & FileTag, sizeof(TagDef), 1, MnFl);
          ITag -> X = FileTag.X1;
          ITag -> Y = FileTag.Y1;
#ifdef __SMALL__
          movedata(_DS, (int)FileTag.Str, FP_SEG(ITag -> StrTxt),
                  FP_OFF(ITag -> StrTxt), strlen(FileTag.Str) + 1);
#endif
#ifdef __LARGE__
          strcpy(ITag -> StrTxt, FileTag.Str);
#endif
        }
        else
        {
          fclose(MnFl);
          Bomb_Mess("Not enough memory to load Menu");
        }
      } while(ITag -> StrTxt[0] != 0);
      ITag -> BLink -> FLink = NULL;
      ITag = NULL;
      do
      {
        TTag = (TagRecType far *)farmalloc((unsigned long)sizeof(TagRecType));
        if (TTag != NULL)
        {
          if (ITag != NULL)
            ITag -> FLink = TTag;
          else
            FTTag = TTag;
          TTag -> BLink = ITag;
          ITag = TTag;
          fread(&FileTag, sizeof(TagDef), 1, MnFl);
          ITag -> X = FileTag.X1;
          ITag -> Y = FileTag.Y1;
```

```
#ifdef __SMALL__
          movedata(_DS, (int)FileTag.Str, FP_SEG(ITag -> StrTxt),
                   FP_OFF(ITag -> StrTxt), strlen(FileTag.Str) + 1);
#endif
#ifdef __LARGE__
          strcpy(ITag -> StrTxt, FileTag.Str);
#endif
        }
        else
        {
          fclose(MnFl);
          Bomb_Mess("Not enough memory to load Menu");
        }
        TTagCount++;
      } while(ITag -> StrTxt[0] != 0);
      if (TTagCount == 1)
      {
        farfree(FTTag);
        FTTag = NULL;
      }
      ITag -> BLink -> FLink = NULL;
      fclose(MnFl);
    } /* if MnFl */
    else
    {
      sprintf(TStr, "F.N.F. :Menu - File %s not found", Command);
      Bomb_Mess(TStr);
    } /* if MnFl else */
  } /* if Command[0] else */
  /* loaded successfully */
  Clear_Frame(BkGrnd, WinX, WinY, WinWid, WinDep);
  WindowY = 1;
  if (*IPtr < 0)
  {
    ErrMess = 0;
    *IPtr *= -1;
  } /* if *IPtr */
  else
  {
    ErrMess = 1;
  } /* if IPtr else */
  CTag = FTag;
  for (Ind = 1; (CTag != NULL) && (Ind < *IPtr); Ind++)
  {
    if (CTag -> Y > WindowY + WinDep - 1)
      WindowY += WinDep;
    CTag = CTag -> FLink;
  } /* for Ind */
```

```
  Paint_Menu(FTag, FTTag, WindowY, WinX, WinY, WinDep);
  NotDone = 1;
  TagStr[0] = 0;
  OldCur = Cursor_Off();
  do
  {
#ifdef __SMALL__
    movedata(FP_SEG(CTag), FP_OFF(CTag), _DS, (int) & WorkBuff,
               sizeof(WorkBuff));
    F_Write(CTag -> X + WinX - 1, CTag -> Y - WindowY + WinY, Reverse,
               WorkBuff.StrTxt);
#endif
#ifdef __LARGE__
    F_Write(CTag -> X + WinX - 1, CTag -> Y - WindowY + WinY, Reverse,
               CTag -> StrTxt);
#endif
    Get_One_Char();
    if (CurKey > 31 && CurKey < 128)
    {
      Ch = CurKey;
      CurKey =  -255;
    } /* if CurKey */
    else
    {
      if (CurKey != 8)
        TagStr[0] = 0;
    } /* if CurKey else */
    Message("");
#ifdef __SMALL__
    F_Write(CTag -> X + WinX - 1, CTag -> Y - WindowY + WinY,
              Blend(Normal),  WorkBuff.StrTxt);
#endif
#ifdef __LARGE__
    F_Write(CTag -> X + WinX - 1, CTag -> Y - WindowY + WinY,
              Blend(Normal), CTag -> StrTxt);
#endif
    switch (CurKey)
    {
      case 8: /*Backspace*/
        TagStr[strlen(TagStr) > 0 ? strlen(TagStr) - 1 : 0] = 0;
        Message(TagStr);
      break;
      case  -75: /* Left Arrow */
        ITag = CTag -> BLink;
        if ((ITag -> Y == CTag -> Y) && (ITag != NULL))
          CTag = ITag;
      break;
      case  -77: /* Right Arrow */
```

```
    ITag = CTag -> FLink;
    if ((ITag -> Y == CTag -> Y) && (ITag != NULL))
      CTag = ITag;
  break;
  case  -72: /* Up Arrow */
    ITag = CTag -> BLink;
    while ((ITag != NULL) && (ITag -> Y == CTag -> Y))
      ITag = ITag -> BLink;
    if (ITag != NULL)
    {
      if (ITag -> Y >= WindowY) /* Find Closest */
      {
        TY = ITag -> Y;
        while ((ITag != NULL) && (ITag -> Y == TY) &&
                  (ITag -> X > CTag -> X))
          ITag = ITag -> BLink;
        if ((ITag != NULL) && (ITag -> Y == TY))
        {
          if ((CTag -> X - ITag -> X > ITag -> FLink -> X -
                 CTag -> X) && (ITag -> FLink -> Y  ==  TY))
            CTag = ITag -> FLink;
          else
            CTag = ITag;
        } /* if ITag */
        else
        {
          if (ITag != NULL)
            CTag = ITag -> FLink;
        } /* if ITag else */
      } /* if ITag */
      else
      { /* New Window */
        WindowY -= WinDep;
        Clear_Frame(BkGrnd, WinX, WinY, WinWid, WinDep);
        Paint_Menu(FTag, FTTag, WindowY, WinX, WinY, WinDep);
        CTag = ITag;
      } /* if ITag else */
    } /* if ITag */
  break;
  case  -73: /* Page Up */
    ITag = CTag;
    while ((ITag -> BLink != NULL) && (ITag -> Y >= WindowY))
      ITag = ITag -> BLink;
    if (ITag != NULL)
    {
      WindowY -= (WindowY > 1) ? WinDep : 0;
      CTag = ITag;
      Clear_Frame(BkGrnd, WinX, WinY, WinWid, WinDep);
```

```
      Paint_Menu(FTag, FTTag, WindowY, WinX, WinY, WinDep);
    } /* if ITag */
  break;
  case  -81: /* Page Down */
    ITag = CTag;
    while ((ITag != NULL) && (ITag -> Y <= WindowY + WinDep - 1))
      ITag = ITag -> FLink;
    if (ITag != NULL)
    {
      WindowY += WinDep;
      CTag = ITag;
      Clear_Frame(BkGrnd, WinX, WinY, WinWid, WinDep);
      Paint_Menu(FTag, FTTag, WindowY, WinX, WinY, WinDep);
    } /* if ITag */
  break;
  case  -80: /* Down Arrow */
    ITag = CTag -> FLink;
    while ((ITag != NULL) && (ITag -> Y == CTag -> Y))
      ITag = ITag -> FLink;
    if (ITag != NULL)
    {
      if (ITag -> Y <= WindowY + WinDep - 1) /* Find Closest */
      {
        TY = ITag -> Y;
        while ((ITag != NULL) && (ITag -> Y == TY) && (ITag -> X <
                CTag -> X))
          ITag = ITag -> FLink;
        if ((ITag != NULL) && (ITag -> Y == TY))
        {
          if ((ITag -> X - CTag -> X > CTag -> X - ITag ->
                BLink -> X) && (ITag -> BLink -> Y  ==  TY))
            CTag = ITag -> BLink;
          else
            CTag = ITag;
        } /* if ITag */
        else
        {
          if (ITag != NULL)
            CTag = ITag -> BLink;
        } /* if ITag else */
      } /* if ITag */
      else
      { /* New Window */
        WindowY += WinDep;
        Clear_Frame(BkGrnd, WinX, WinY, WinWid, WinDep);
        Paint_Menu(FTag, FTTag, WindowY, WinX, WinY, WinDep);
        CTag = ITag;
      } /* if ITag else */
```

```
    } /* if ITag */
  break;
  case 13: /* Return/Enter */
  case 27: /* Escape */
    NotDone = 0;
  break;

  case -255: /* Any Alpha */
    TagStr[strlen(TagStr) + 1] = 0;
    TagStr[strlen(TagStr)] = Ch;
    ITag = FTag;
    Ind = 0;
    Message(TagStr);
    NotFound = 1;
    while((ITag != NULL) && (NotFound))
    {
      if (CaseSense)
      {
        while ((ITag -> StrTxt[Ind] == TagStr[Ind]) && (TagStr[Ind]))
          Ind++;
      } /* if CaseSense */
      else
      {
        while ((toupper(ITag -> StrTxt[Ind]) == toupper(TagStr[Ind]))
              && (TagStr[Ind]))
          Ind++;
      } /* if CaseSense else */
      if (TagStr[Ind])
      {
        Ind = 0;
        ITag = ITag -> FLink;
      } /* if TagStr[Ind] */
      else
        NotFound = 0;
    } /* while ITag */
    if (NotFound == 0)
    {
      if (ITag -> Y > WinDep)
        WindowY = ITag -> Y/WinDep;
      Clear_Frame(BkGrnd, WinX, WinY, WinWid, WinDep);
      Paint_Menu(FTag, FTTag, WindowY, WinX, WinY, WinDep);
      CTag = ITag;
    } /* if NotFound */
  break;

  default:
    if (ErrMess)
    {
```

```
          Lo_Mess("Bad key pressed.");
        } /* if ErrMess */
        else
          NotDone = 0;
      break;
    } /* switch CurKey */
  } while (NotDone);
  Cursor_On(OldCur);
#ifdef __SMALL__
  for (Ind = 0; (CTag -> StrTxt[Ind]) && (Ind < 80); Ind++);
  movedata(FP_SEG(CTag -> StrTxt), FP_OFF(CTag -> StrTxt), _DS,
           (int)STag, Ind + 1);
#endif
#ifdef __LARGE__
  strcpy(STag, CTag -> StrTxt);
#endif
  for(*IPtr = 0; CTag != NULL; CTag = CTag -> BLink, *IPtr = *IPtr + 1);
  while (FTag != NULL)
  {
    ITag = FTag -> FLink;
    farfree(FTag);
    FTag = ITag;
  } /* while FTag */
  while (FTTag != NULL)
  {
    ITag = FTTag -> FLink;
    farfree(FTTag);
    FTTag = ITag;
  } /* while FTag */
} /* end Menu */
```

Sample Usage Source Code

▼

```
/*
  This program will use Menu in its literal mode to handle a simple
  menu, then it will use Menu in its file mode to handle a menu and
  text from the file EXAMPLE.MNU.
*/

extern unsigned _stklen=16384; /* Minimum recommend stack size */
#include <stdio.h>
#include <math.h>
#include <dos.h>
#include <mem.h>
#include <alloc.h>
#include <ctype.h>
#include <string.h>
#include <stdlib.h>
```

```
#include <plib.h>
#include <plib.glo>


/****************************************************************************/
main()
{
  char
    SelTag1[81] = "",
    SelTag2[81] = "";

  int
    Sel1 = 0,
    Sel2 = 0,
    ExitKey1 = 0,
    ExitKey2 = 0;

  Calibrate_Delay();            /* Calibrate delay factor */
  Get_Video_Mode("Video.CFG"); /* Get display adapter type */
  Install_Crit_Error();         /* Set up application critical error handler */
  InputAbsolute=AbortPrint=0;  /* Initialize global variables */

  /* Application code to follow */
  Clr_Scr();
  Sel1 = 1;
  Menu("/1/1/A - First/1/2/B - Second/1/3/C - Third/", &Sel1, SelTag1,
      0, 5, 5, 30, 3, Red);
  ExitKey1 = CurKey;

  Sel2 = 1;
  Menu ("Example.Mnu", &Sel2, SelTag2, 1, 5, 10, 70, 5, Green);
  ExitKey2 = CurKey;

  Goto_XY(1, 15);
  printf("Menu 1 Selected # %d option %s and exited with %d .\n",
        Sel1, SelTag1, ExitKey1);
  printf("Menu 2 Selected # %d option %s and exited with %d .\n",
        Sel2, SelTag2, ExitKey2);

} /*  main  */
```

Use the sample utility Make Menu to enter these tag definitions for file example.mnu:

```
Selectable Tags:
  #  Coords     Tag
   1 (1,2) -    1 ---->
   2 (35,2) -   9 ---->
```

```
 3 (1,3) -   2 ---->
 4 (35,3) -  10---->
 5 (1,4) -   3 ---->
 6 (35,4) -  11---->
 7 (1,5) -   4 ---->
 8 (35,5) -  12---->
 9 (1,6) -   5 ---->
10 (35,6) -  13---->
11 (1,7) -   6 ---->
12 (1,8) -   7 ---->
13 (1,9) -   8 ---->

Display only Tags:
Coords        Tag
(5,1) -       Diagnostics
(39,1) -      Burn In Test
(10,2) -      System Checkout
(44,2) -      Memory Burn In
(10,3) -      Memory Test
(44,3) -      Damage Duress
(10,4) -      Failure Analysis
(44,4) -      Fault Knockout
(10,5) -      Gallop Pattern
(44,5) -      Bad Tracking
(10,6) -      Range Extreme test
(44,6) -      EMI
(10,7) -      Vibration Curve
(10,8) -      Self Diagnosis
(10,9) -      Exit
```

Sample Usage Output

▼

```
    A - First
    B - Second
    C - Third


        Diagnostics                      Burn In Test
    1 ----> System Checkout          9 ----> Memory Burn In
    2 ----> Memory Test              10----> Damage Duress
    3 ----> Failure Analysis         11----> Fault Knockout
    4 ----> Gallop Pattern           12----> Bad Tracking
Menu 1 Selected # 1 option A - First and exited with 13.
Menu 2 Selected # 1 option 1 ----> and exited with 13.
```

Message

Description

▼

Message displays the string *Mess on the 25th line of the video display in reverse video. If the passed string is null (""), the 25th line is cleared to Normal video.

Routine Declaration

▼

```
void Message(char *Mess)
```

Passed Variables

▼

***Mess String Pointer** A pointer to the string to be displayed on the 25th line of the video display. If the string exceeds 80 characters, it is truncated to 80 characters before being displayed.

Global Variables

▼

None

Error Codes/ Messages

▼

None

Discussion

▼

Message informs the user of errors and notable information. The routine uses the 25th line of the video display to output messages. Therefore, we recommend that you avoid using line 25.

Message uses an if-else statement to conditionalize the message output for valid messages and null messages. F_Write outputs all text from Message.

Limitations and Modifications

▼

None

Routine Source Code

▼

```
#include <math.h>
#include <string.h>
#include <stdio.h>
#include <stdlib.h>
#include <ctype.h>
#include <plib.h>

extern char
```

```
  Normal,
  VidHigh,
  Reverse;

void Message(char *Mess)
/*
  This function will write *Mess on the 25th line of the screen centered
  in the reverse attribute.
*/
{ /* Message */
  char TStr[85];

  if (Mess[0])
    F_Write(1, 25, Reverse, Cen(Mess, TStr, 80));
  else
    F_Write(1, 25, Normal, Rpt(" ", TStr, 80));
} /* Message */
```

Sample Usage Source Code

▼

```
/*
  This program will use Message to display a message in
  reverse video on the 25th line.
*/

extern unsigned _stklen=16384; /* Minimum recommend stack size */
#include <stdio.h>
#include <math.h>
#include <dos.h>
#include <mem.h>
#include <alloc.h>
#include <ctype.h>
#include <string.h>
#include <stdlib.h>
#include <plib.h>
#include <plib.glo>

/*****************************************************************************/
main()
{
  Calibrate_Delay();              /* Calibrate delay factor */
  Get_Video_Mode("Video.CFG");  /* Get display adapter type */
  Install_Crit_Error();           /* Set up application critical error handler */
  InputAbsolute=AbortPrint=0;     /* Initialize global variables */

  /* Application code to follow */

  Clr_Scr();
```

```
  Message("They shoot horses, don't they!");
  Delay (3000);

} /* main */
```

Sample Usage Output

▼

```
They shoot horses, don't they!
```

Month_Of_Year

Description

▼

Month_Of_Year returns the textual name of the month in *Buffer for the date passed in *Date. The date passed must be in the form MM/DD/YY. Month_Of_Year provides six different formats for the text returned. The formats range from all uppercase full names to all lowercase abbreviations. For a complete list of the format options, see table 2-5.

Routine Declaration

▼

```
char *Month_Of_Year(char *Date,
                    int  MonthCase,
                    char *Buffer)
```

Passed Variables

▼

***Date String Pointer** A pointer to the string date, in the form MM/DD/YY, that provides the month number for conversion.

MonthCase integer The integer value that indicates the format for the returned month name. The formats available and their corresponding format numbers are shown in table 2-5.

***Buffer String Pointer** A pointer to the string variable that contains the resulting string.

Table 2-5. *MonthCase Formats*

MonthCase	Result
1	JAN, FEB, MAR, APR . . .
2	Jan, Feb, Mar, Apr . . .
3	jan, feb, mar, apr . . .
4	JANUARY, FEBRUARY, MARCH, APRIL . . .
5	January, February, March, April . . .
6	january, february, march, april . . .

Global Variables

None

Error Codes/Messages

None

Discussion

Month_Of_Year is primarily used by other date-related routines to format dates. You may find other uses in specific applications for direct calls to Month-_Of_Year. The actual mechanics of Month_Of_Year are performed by retrieving the month text from a constant string array, based on the month number passed in the string date variable *Date. Once the date has been parsed out of the date variable, the month text is truncated if MonthCase is 1, 2, or 3. Finally, the case of the text is set based on MonthCase.

Limitations and Modifications

As mentioned, some of the routines in the library have parameters that can be used to select multiple result formats. This routine and a few others have parameters for determining format styles. Although this can be difficult to read, the additional flexibility justified the potential difficulties in these few cases.

The only limitations to Month_Of_Year are the formats available for the textual names. These can easily be eliminated by adding new formats to the routine to meet your application's needs.

Routine Source Code

```
#include <math.h>
#include <string.h>
#include <stdio.h>
#include <stdlib.h>
#include <ctype.h>
#include <plib.h>

char *Month_Of_Year(char *Date,
                    int MonthCase,
                    char *Buffer)
/*
  Returns the month of year for the parameter Date (MM/DD/YY)
  in the format specified by the MonthCase:
    MonthCase = 1  -  JAN, FEB, MAR, APR...
    MonthCase = 2  -  Jan, Feb, Mar, Apr...
    MonthCase = 3  -  jan, feb, mar, apr...
    MonthCase = 4  -  JANUARY, FEBRUARY, MARCH, APRIL...
    MonthCase = 5  -  January, February, March, April...
```

```
   MonthCase = 6  -  january, february, march, april...
*/
{ /* Month_Of_Year */
  /* Month names constant */
  char
    MOY[12][10]  =  {"january", "february", "march", "april",
                     "may", "june", "july", "august",
                     "september", "october", "november", "december"},
    TmpMonth[3];

  int
    MonthNo;

  MonthNo = atoi(Copy(Date, 1, 2, TmpMonth));
  strcpy(Buffer, MOY[MonthNo - 1]);
  if (MonthCase < 4)
    Buffer[3] = 0;
  switch (MonthCase)
  {
    case 1:
    case 4:
      strupr(Buffer);
    break;
    case 2:
    case 5:
      Buffer[0] = Buffer[0] - 32;
    break;
  } /* switch MonthCase */
  return(Buffer);
} /* Month_Of_Year */
```

Sample Usage Source Code

▼

```
/*
  This program will use Month_Of_Year to print today's month in all the
  available formats Month_Of_Year has.
*/

extern unsigned _stklen=16384; /* Minimum recommend stack size */
#include <stdio.h>
#include <math.h>
#include <dos.h>
#include <mem.h>
#include <alloc.h>
#include <ctype.h>
#include <string.h>
#include <stdlib.h>
#include <plib.h>
```

```
#include <plib.glo>

/****************************************************************************/
main()
{
  int
    Format =0;

  char
    TBuffer[9] = "",
    Buffer[40] = "";

  Calibrate_Delay();            /* Calibrate delay factor */
  Get_Video_Mode("Video.CFG"); /* Get display adapter type */
  Install_Crit_Error();         /* Set up application critical error handler */
  InputAbsolute=AbortPrint=0;  /* Initialize global variables */

  /* Application code to follow */

  Clr_Scr();
  for(Format = 1; Format <= 6; Format++)
    printf ("The month in format # %d is %s .\n", Format,
          Month_Of_Year(Today(TBuffer), Format, Buffer));

} /*  main  */
```

Sample Usage Output

▼

```
The month in format # 1 is FEB.
The month in format # 2 is Feb.
The month in format # 3 is feb.
The month in format # 4 is FEBRUARY.
The month in format # 5 is February.
The month in format # 6 is february.
```

Move_Scrn_Mem

Description

▼

Move_Scrn_Mem transfers a contiguous portion of memory to another location in memory. The memory areas can be any location, but the routine is designed to accommodate transfers to and from video memory. If the global variable WaitForRetrace is true, the routine accounts for possible screen flicker by synchronizing with the horizontal and vertical retrace signals from the video adapter. A call to Get_Video_Mode must be made somewhere in your application prior to calling Move_Scrn_Mem. Get_Video_Mode sets the correct value for

WaitForRetrace based on the type of video display adapter installed in the system.

Routine Declaration

```
void Move_Scrn_Mem(char far *Source,
                   char far *Dest,
                   unsigned Len)
```

Passed Variables

***Source Far Character Pointer** A pointer to the beginning of the memory block to be moved to the memory block pointed to by *Dest.

***Dest Far Character Pointer** The pointer for the beginning of the memory block that is to receive the memory area pointed to by *Source.

Len unsigned integer The number of bytes of memory to be moved from *Source to *Dest.

Global Variables

WaitForRetrace Tells the video display routines that they must synchronize the manipulation of video characters with the video retracing done on color systems. If this synchronization is not accomplished, you are likely to see video flickering during screen manipulations.

Error Codes/ Messages

None

Discussion

Move_Scrn_Mem provides the capability to copy portions of the memory to or from video memory and working memory. This is useful in creating copies or restoring copies of the video display prior to or after overlaying windows or other information.

Move_Scrn_Mem is written in assembly language and requires a Microsoft Assembler or comparable assembler to generate the object file that can be linked into the Turbo C library.

Limitations and Modifications

One excellent use for Move_Scrn_Mem is to save screen windows. Since video memory is contiguous, you need to move each line of video memory from the text window separately. Note: video memory contains two bytes for each character displayed. The first contains the display attributes for the character byte that follows.

Routine Source Code

```
#pragma inline

extern char
  WaitForRetrace;


void Move_Scrn_Mem(char far *Source,
                   char far *Dest,
                   unsigned Len)
/*
   Moves data to and from screen memory, doing snow control if necessary.
*/
{ /* Move_Scrn_Mem */

  unsigned char Right;

  Right = ((unsigned long)Source < (unsigned long)Dest);
  asm push ds
  asm push es
  asm mov al, WaitForRetrace
  asm lds si, Source
  asm les di, Dest
  asm cmp al, 1
  asm mov cx, Len
  asm jcxz Exit
  asm mov al, Right
  asm je Color

  Mono:
  asm cmp al, 1
  asm je MRightToLeft
  asm cld
  asm jmp short MMoveByte

  MRightToLeft:
  asm std
  asm dec cx
  asm add si, cx
  asm add di, cx
  asm inc cx

  MMoveByte:
  asm movsb
  asm loop MMoveByte
  asm jmp short Exit
```

```
  Color:
  asm mov dx, 3dah
  asm cmp al, 1
  asm sti
  asm je CRightToLeft
  asm cld
  asm jmp short CMoveByte

  CRightToLeft:
  asm std
  asm dec cx
  asm add si, cx
  asm add di, cx
  asm inc cx

  CMoveByte:
  asm in al, dx
  asm rcr al, 1
  asm jb CMoveByte
  asm cli
  j1:
  asm in al, dx
  asm rcr al, 1
  asm jnb j1
  asm movsb
  asm sti
  asm loop CMoveByte

  Exit:
  asm pop es
  asm pop ds

} /* Move_Scrn_Mem */
```

Sample Usage Source Code

▼

```
/*
  This program will clear the screen, write something on the top line,
  capture what was written on the top line with Move_From_Screen and
  write the captured version out. Next it will fill the array TempLine
  with attributes and characters, then write TempLine to the screen with
  Move_Scrn_Mem.
*/

extern unsigned _stklen=16384; /* Minimum recommend stack size */
#include <stdio.h>
#include <math.h>
#include <dos.h>
```

```
#include <mem.h>
#include <alloc.h>
#include <ctype.h>
#include <string.h>
#include <stdlib.h>
#include <plib.h>
#include <plib.glo>


/****************************************************************************/
main()
{
  int
    C = 0;

  char
    *P,
    TempStr[81] = "",
    TempLine[160] = "";

  Calibrate_Delay();            /* Calibrate delay factor */
  Get_Video_Mode("Video.CFG"); /* Get display adapter type */
  Install_Crit_Error();         /* Set up application critical error handler */
  InputAbsolute=AbortPrint=0;  /* Initialize global variables */

  /* Application code to follow */
  Clr_Scr();
  Goto_XY(1, 1);
  printf("This text is only here on the screen: ");
  P = MK_FP(BaseOfScreen, 0); /*Make a pointer to screen memory*/

  Move_Scrn_Mem(P, TempLine, 160);
  Goto_XY(1, 10);
  for (C = 0; C <= 39; C++) /* Print out every other byte */
    printf("%c", TempLine [C*2]);
  printf ("\n Press <RETURN> to continue \n");

  scanf ("%c",&P);   /* just wait */
  Clr_Scr();
  Goto_XY(1, 1);
  strcpy(TempStr, "This is a test, Dumb de de de Dumb");
  P = MK_FP (BaseOfScreen, 0) ;
  for(C = 0; C < strlen(TempStr) * 2; C++) /* set up atr/char string */
  {
    if (!(C & 0x0001))
      TempLine[C] = TempStr[C/2];
    else
      TempLine[C] = Normal;
```

```
  }
  Move_Scrn_Mem(TempLine, P, strlen(TempStr) * 2);

} /* main */
```

Sample Usage Output

```
This text is only here on the screen:




This text is only here on the screen:
 Press <RETURN> to continue




This is a test, Dumb de de de Dumb
```

No_Sound

Description

No_Sound disables a tone initiated by the Sound() routine in the library. No_Sound does not require any parameters when called and can be called at any time.

Routine Declaration

```
void No_Sound(void)
```

Passed Variables

None

Global Variables

None

Error Codes/ Messages

None

Discussion

No_Sound uses the Turbo C routine outportb to change bits 0 and 1 of port 97 hex 61 to zeros for disabling the sound. Bit 0 controls the timer signal to the speaker and bit 1 controls the pulsing of the speaker. Both bits must be disabled to turn off the speaker enabled by a call to Sound. Both No_Sound and Sound are available with the Turbo C version 1.5 library. If you are using Turbo C version 1.0, you can achieve identical results with these library routines.

Limitations and Modifications

▼

None

Routine Source Code

▼

```
#include <dos.h>

void No_Sound(void)
/*
  This procedure will disable the Sound(Freq) procedure so that no more
  tone is produced.
*/
{ /* No_Sound */
  outportb(0x61, (inportb(0x61) & 0xfc));
} /* No_Sound */
```

Sample Usage Source Code

▼

See the sample usage for the library routine Sound() for an example of using No_Sound.

Num_Chars

Description

▼

Num_Chars determines the number of occurrences of a particular character in a string. The routine only searches for single characters, not whole strings.

Routine Declaration

▼

```
int Num_Chars(char Ch,
              char *St)
```

Passed Variables

▼

Ch char The character used to search the string pointed to by *St.

***St String Pointer** A pointer to the string to be searched by the Num_Chars.

Global Variables

None

Error Codes/ Messages

None

Discussion

Num_Chars was primarily implemented to aid the library routines that need to determine the number of occurrences of a character in a string. For example, Num_Chars counts the number of Ds in a numeric pattern to determine the number of decimals or absolute digits required.

Num_Chars uses a for loop to step the specified string and increments the counter NumChs for each found occurrence of the search character.

Limitations and Modifications

The only limitation to Num_Chars is that it will only count single character occurrences. If you want to count the occurrences of multiple character strings, you could create a routine using Str_Pos, which finds a string within another string.

Routine Source Code

```
int Num_Chars(char Ch,
              char *St)
/*
  This function will return the number of occurrences of Ch in *St.
*/
{ /* Num_Chars */
  int
    C,
    NumChs;

  for (C = NumChs = 0; St[C]; C++)
  {
    NumChs += (St[C] == Ch);
  } /* for C */
  return(NumChs);
} /* Num_Chars */
```

Sample Usage Source Code

```
/*
  This program will use Num_chars() to count out how many times that
  a certain character appears in a certain string.
```

```
*/

extern unsigned _stklen=16384; /* Minimum recommend stack size */
#include <stdio.h>
#include <math.h>
#include <dos.h>
#include <mem.h>
#include <alloc.h>
#include <ctype.h>
#include <string.h>
#include <stdlib.h>
#include <plib.h>
#include <plib.glo>

/****************************************************************************/
main()
{
  char
    String[81] = "",
    Check;

  Calibrate_Delay();            /* Calibrate delay factor */
  Get_Video_Mode("Video.CFG"); /* Get display adapter type */
  Install_Crit_Error();         /* Set up application critical error handler */
  InputAbsolute=AbortPrint=0;  /* Initialize global variables */

  /* Application code to follow */

  Clr_Scr();
  printf("\n\nHere is sentence, please input a character to check how");
  printf("\noften it appears in the sentence.");
  strcpy (String, "She sells seashells at the seashore.");
  printf ("\n\n\n        The sentence is     %s \n", String);
  printf ("\n\n\n        What is the scan character? ");
  scanf ("%c", &Check);

  printf ("\n\n\n\nThe number of times it appears is %d.\n",
        Num_Chars (Check, String));

} /*  main  */
```

Sample Usage Output

▼

```
Here is sentence, please input a character to check how
often it appears in the sentence.



         The sentence is     She sells seashells at the seashore.
```

```
What is the scan character? l
```

```
The number of times it appears is 4.
```

Num_Decs

Description

Num_Decs returns the number of decimal places in the string representation of a numeric value. If no decimals are present, the routine returns zero.

Routine Declaration

```
int Num_Decs(char *Num)
```

Passed Variables

***Num String Pointer** A pointer to the number represented in string form to be used in determining the number of decimal places.

Global Variables

None

Error Codes/ Messages

None

Discussion

Num_Decs aids the data entry routines in verifying that the values entered meet the specified pattern. Num_Decs uses a for loop to step through the specified string and searches for the first occurrence of a decimal point. Once the decimal point is found, the digits beyond that point are accumulated. The accumulation line is also conditioned by the flag set when the decimal point is found.

Limitations and Modifications

None

Routine Source Code

```
int Num_Decs(char *Num)
/*
```

```
  This function will return the number of digits to the right of the
  decimal point in the string *Num; if none exist, it returns 0.
*/
{ /* Num_Decs */
  char
    DecFlag;

  int
    C,
    Decs;

  for (C = Decs = DecFlag = 0; Num[C]; C++)
  {
    DecFlag = (DecFlag || (Num[C] == '.'));
    Decs += (DecFlag && (Num[C] > 47 && Num[C] < 58));
  } /* for */
  return(Decs);
} /* Num_Decs */
```

Sample Usage Source Code

▼

For a sample usage of this routine, see the sample usage for the library routine Num_Ints.

Num_Ints

Description

▼

Num_Ints returns the number of integer digits in a string representation of a numeric value. If no integer values are present, the routine returns zero.

Routine Declaration

▼

```
int Num_Ints(char *Num)
```

Passed Variables

▼

***Num String Pointer** A pointer to the numeric string representation to be used in determining the number of integer decimal places.

Global Variables

▼

None

Error Codes/ Messages

▼

None

Discussion

▼

Num_Ints aids the data entry routines in verifying that the values entered meet the specified pattern. Num_Ints uses a for loop to step through the specified string and searches for the first occurrence of a decimal point. Any numeric digits up to the decimal point are counted and the total number of digits is returned by the routine.

Limitations and Modifications

▼

None

Routine Source Code

▼

```
int Num_Ints(char *Num)
/*
  This function will return the number of integers in the string *Num
  (representing a number). If no integers are present, 0 will return.
*/
{ /* Num_Ints */
  int
    Ints,
    C;

  for (C = Ints = 0; ((Num[C]) && (Num[C] != '.')); C++)
  {
    Ints += (Num[C] > 47 && Num[C] < 58);
  } /* for C */
  return(Ints);
} /* Num_Ints */
```

Sample Usage Source Code

▼

```
/*
  This program will figure out the integer part's length of a number
  in string form.
*/

extern unsigned _stklen=16384; /* Minimum recommend stack size */
#include <stdio.h>
#include <math.h>
#include <dos.h>
#include <mem.h>
#include <alloc.h>
#include <ctype.h>
#include <string.h>
#include <stdlib.h>
#include <plib.h>
```

```
#include <plib.glo>


/****************************************************************************/
main()
{
  char
    NumStr[21] = "";

  Calibrate_Delay();            /* Calibrate delay factor */
  Get_Video_Mode("Video.CFG"); /* Get display adapter type */
  Install_Crit_Error();         /* Set up application critical error handler */
  InputAbsolute=AbortPrint=0;  /* Initialize global variables */

  /* Application code to follow */

  Clr_Scr();
  strcpy(NumStr, "123456.7890");

  printf ("\n\nThe number is  %s ", NumStr );
  printf ("\n\nIts integer part's length is %d ", Num_Ints(NumStr));
  printf ("\n\nIts decimal part's length is %d\n", Num_Decs(NumStr));

} /*  main  */
```

Sample Usage Output

▼

```
The number is 123456.7890

Its integer part's length is 6

Its decimal part's length is 4
```

Num_Pattern_Size

Description

▼

Num_Pattern_Size returns the maximum field length required to enter a number with the pattern specified. Num_Pattern_Size also returns the maximum number of optional integer digits, absolute required integer digits, and decimal places specified in the pattern. The pattern specifications available are described in the routines Input_Num and Prompt.

Routine Declaration

▼

```
int Num_Pattern_Size(char *Pattern,
                     int  *Ints,
```

```
int *Digs,
int *Decs)
```

Passed Variables

▼

***Pattern String Pointer** A pointer to the string value containing the pattern for the numeric field. For a complete description of the patterns available, see Input_Num.

***Ints integer Pointer** A pointer to the integer value that will contain the maximum number of integer digits allowed by the pattern.

***Digs integer Pointer** A pointer to the integer value that will contain the absolutely required number of integer digits specified by the pattern.

***Decs integer Pointer** A pointer to the integer value that will contain the maximum number of decimal places allowed by the pattern.

Global Variables

▼

None

Error Codes/ Messages

▼

None

Discussion

▼

Num_Pattern_Size provides a consistent means of evaluating the patterns passed to Input_Num for numeric fields. The values returned from Num_Pattern_Size are used to specify the length of the field used for entering numbers.

Num_Pattern_Size determines if the pattern contains Ds (absolute digits). If any exist, the routine counts them, designated by a D or d, to the left of the decimal point. If the pattern doesn't contain Ds to specify the integer portion of the pattern, the routine checks for the integer specifier, which can have two forms. The first is the single letter I or i, which defaults the integer length to 10 digits. The second case is the letter I preceded by a number between one and nine that specifies the number of integer places. If a decimal point is encountered, the routine counts the number of decimal digits, designated by D or d, to the right of the decimal point. The number of integer digits is added to the number of decimal places, plus space for a decimal point and minus sign, if needed to return the total field width.

Limitations and Modifications

▼

Num_Pattern_Size has two primary limitations. First, the routine only calculates patterns that contain up to 10 integer digits: 9,999,999,999. This should be adequate for most applications, but if you need larger numbers you need to modify the routine's calculations.

The second limitation occurs in the routine's error trapping capabilities. To increase the performance of the routine, it was designed to perform only minimal error trapping. Thus, it is possible to pass patterns to Num_Pattern_Size that could result in erroneous lengths. The programmer must ensure that the patterns used are within the appropriate ranges.

Routine Source Code

▼

```
int Num_Pattern_Size(char *Pattern,
                     int *Ints,
                     int *Digs,
                     int *Decs)
/*
  This function will return the field size of a numeric pattern (as
  described in the function Input_Num) and its components where *Ints is
  the number of Integers, *Digs is the number of absolute integers, and
  *Decs is the number of decimal places.
*/
{ /* Num_Pattern_Size */
  int
    C;


  /* interpret pattern */
    /* count Digits */
  C = *Digs = *Ints = *Decs = 0;
  for (; (Pattern[C] == 'D' || Pattern[C] == 'd'); C++);
  *Digs = C;
    /* count I's */

  if ((Pattern[C] > 47) && (Pattern[C] < 58))
  {
    *Ints = Pattern[C] - 48;
    C++;
    C++;
  } /* if Pattern */
  else
  {
    if (Pattern[C] == 'I' || Pattern[C] == 'i')
    {
      C++;
      *Ints = 10;
    } /* if Pattern */
  } /* if Pattern else */
    /* count Decs */
  if (Pattern[C] == '.')
  {
    C++;
```

```
    *Decs = C;
    for (; (Pattern[C] == 'D' || Pattern[C] == 'd'); C++);
    *Decs = C - (*Decs);
  } /* if Pattern */

  C = (*Digs) + (*Ints);
  C += (*Decs != 0) + (*Decs);
  return(C);
} /* Num_Pattern_Size */
```

Sample Usage Source Code

▼

```
/*
  This program will allow you to enter a pattern which would be passed
  to Input_Num & Prompt for numeric fields, and then print out the size
  and specifications about the pattern you have just entered.
*/

extern unsigned _stklen=16384; /* Minimum recommend stack size */
#include <stdio.h>
#include <math.h>
#include <dos.h>
#include <mem.h>
#include <alloc.h>
#include <ctype.h>
#include <string.h>
#include <stdlib.h>
#include <plib.h>
#include <plib.glo>


/*****************************************************************************/
main()
{
  char
    Pattern[10] = "",
    Check;

  int
    FWidth,
    Ints,
    Digs,
    Decs;

  Calibrate_Delay();             /* Calibrate delay factor */
  Get_Video_Mode("Video.CFG");   /* Get display adapter type */
  Install_Crit_Error();          /* Set up application critical error handler */
  InputAbsolute=AbortPrint=0;    /* Initialize global variables */
```

```
  /* Application code to follow */

  Clr_Scr();
  printf("\n   Please enter a numeric field pattern here: ");
  scanf("%s", Pattern);
  FWidth = Num_Pattern_Size (Pattern, &Ints, &Digs, &Decs);
  printf("\n\nThis is the information derived from the pattern:\n");
  printf("\nThe width of the pattern is %d \n", FWidth);
  printf("\nThe number of optional integer digits is %d \n", Ints);
  printf("\nThe number of absolute integer digits is %d \n", Digs);
  printf("\nThe number of decimal digits is %d .\n", Decs);

} /*  main  */
```

Sample Usage Output

▼

```
Please enter a numeric field pattern here: 8I.DDDD

This is the information derived from the pattern:

The width of the pattern is 13

The number of optional integer digits is 8

The number of absolute integer digits is 0

The number of decimal digits is 4.
```

Num_To_Word

Description

▼

Num_To_Word converts a numeric value into its English bank note representation. For example, 100.95 would be converted to: One hundred dollars and 95 cents. Valid values for the numeric data passed are −999,999,999.99 to +999,999,999.99. Any values passed that are out of range return ***Overflow***.

Routine Declaration

▼

```
char *Num_To_Word(float Num,
                  char  *Buffer)
```

Passed Variables

▼

Num float The real number to be converted to English bank note format.

***Buffer String Pointer** A pointer to the string variable that will contain the resulting string.

Global Variables

▼

None

Error Codes/ Messages

▼

Numeric value overflow, positive or negative, is the only error trapped by Num_To_Word. If an overflow occurs, Num_To_Word returns the string ***Overflow***.

Discussion

▼

In business applications, such as payroll and accounts payable, it is often necessary to write checks. Num_To_Word provides the ability to output the values in English for inclusion on checks or other monetary reports. The routine accommodates positive and negative values up to 999,999,999.99. This limit should not impose a restriction on most applications.

Num_To_Word first converts the float number passed to a string number with two decimal places. This string is then stripped of all leading spaces and the location of the decimal place is assigned to the variable Dot. Num_To_Word uses three constant string arrays to build the textual value returned. The appropriate constant is concatenated to the string Engl based on evaluating the position in reference to the decimal point's location in the string. After the decimal position is established, Num_To_Word uses a while loop and a switch statement to walk character by character through the number string and parse out the proper constant to concatenate to NumStr. The cents are inserted as a numeric value rather than as English text; this conforms to common practice.

Limitations and Modifications

▼

Num_to_Word has one limitation in that the number cannot exceed 999,999,999.99. To most applications, this is not a major concern. However, this limitation can be corrected by adding additional cases to the routine to accommodate the larger value sets.

Routine Source Code

▼

```
#include <math.h>
#include <string.h>
#include <stdio.h>
#include <stdlib.h>
#include <ctype.h>
#include <plib.h>

char *Num_To_Word(float Num,
```

```
                char *Buffer)

/*
  This function accepts a float (Num) and returns a pointer to *Buffer,
  which is set to the amount of Num in English bank note form. Valid
  ranges of Num are -999,999,999.99 to +999,999,999.99. Numbers outside of
  this range will produce (return) the overflow message "***OVERFLOW***".
*/
{ /* Num_To_Word */
  char
    Ones[10][7] = {{""}, {"One "}, {"Two "}, {"Three "},
                   {"Four "}, {"Five "}, {"Six "},
                   {"Seven "}, {"Eight "}, {"Nine "}},
    Teens[10][10] = {{"Ten "}, {"Eleven "}, {"Twelve "},
                     {"Thirteen "}, {"Fourteen "}, {"Fifteen "},
                     {"Sixteen "}, {"Seventeen "}, {"Eighteen "},
                     {"Nineteen "}},
    Tens[10][9] = {{""}, {""}, {"Twenty "}, {"Thirty "}, {"Forty "},
                   {"Fifty "}, {"Sixty "}, {"Seventy "}, {"Eighty "},
                   {"Ninety "}},
    NStr[256], /* String convert num to string form with two
                    decimal places */
    TStr1[256],
    TStr2[256];

  int
    Dot,    /* Position of Decimal */
    Ind;    /* Index of String converted */


  sprintf(NStr, "%22.2f", Num);  /*Convert number to string*/
  Buffer[0] = 0;                 /*Null Buffer*/

  Erase_White_Begin(NStr);
  if (NStr[0] == '-')
  {
    strcpy(Buffer, "Negative ");
    Delete(NStr, 1, 1);
  } /* if NStr[0] */

  Dot = Pos('.', NStr);
  Dot--;

  if ((Dot == 1) && (NStr[0] == '0')) /* 0.00 */
    strcat(Buffer, "Zero ");

  if (Dot <= 9)
  {
```

```
    Ind = 1;
    while (Ind <= Dot)
    {
      switch ((Dot - Ind + 1) % 3)
      {
        case 0:
          if (NStr[Ind - 1] != '0')
          {
            strcat(Buffer, Ones[NStr[Ind - 1] - 48]);
            strcat(Buffer, "Hundred ");
          } /* if NStr */
        break;

        case 1:
          strcat(Buffer, Ones[NStr[Ind - 1] - 48]);
        break;

        case 2:
          if (NStr[Ind - 1] == '1')
          {
            Ind++;
            strcat(Buffer, Teens[NStr[Ind - 1] - 48]);
          } /* if NStr */
          else
            strcat(Buffer, Tens[NStr[Ind - 1] - 48]);
        break;
      } /* switch */
      Ind++;
      if ((Dot - Ind) == 5)
        strcat(Buffer, "Million ");
      if (((Dot - Ind) == 2) && (Pos('M', Buffer) + 7 != strlen(Buffer)))
        strcat(Buffer, "Thousand ");
    } /* while Ind */

    if ((strcmp(Buffer, "Negative One ") != 0)  &&
       (strcmp(Buffer, "One ") != 0))
    {
      sprintf(TStr2, "Dollars and %s Cents",
              Copy(NStr, Dot + 2, 2, TStr1));
      strcat(Buffer, TStr2);
    } /* if strcmp */
    else
    {
      sprintf(TStr2, "Dollar and %s Cents", Copy(NStr, Dot + 2, 2, TStr1));
      strcat(Buffer, TStr2);
    } /* if strcmp else */
  } /* if Dot */
  else
```

```
  {
    strcpy(Buffer, "***OVERFLOW***");
  } /* if Dot else */
  return(Buffer);
} /* Num_to_word */
```

Sample Usage Source Code

▼

```
/*
  This program will take a number from the user and write it out
  in English bank note form using Num_To_Word.
*/

extern unsigned _stklen=16384; /* Minimum recommend stack size */
#include <stdio.h>
#include <math.h>
#include <dos.h>
#include <mem.h>
#include <alloc.h>
#include <ctype.h>
#include <string.h>
#include <stdlib.h>
#include <plib.h>
#include <plib.glo>


/****************************************************************************/
main()
{
  float
    NumIn = 0.0 ;
  char
    Buffer [81] = "" ;

  Calibrate_Delay();            /* Calibrate delay factor */
  Get_Video_Mode("Video.CFG"); /* Get display adapter type */
  Install_Crit_Error();         /* Set up application critical error handler */
  InputAbsolute=AbortPrint=0;  /* Initialize global variables */

  /* Application code to follow */

  Clr_Scr();
  printf("Enter a dollar amount: ");
  scanf("%f", &NumIn);
  printf("\nIn English, that's:\n\n  %s.\n", Num_To_Word(NumIn, Buffer));

} /*  main  */
```

Sample Usage Output

▼

```
Enter a dollar amount: 5500

In English, that's:

  Five Thousand Five Hundred Dollars and 00 Cents.
```

Pattern

Description

▼

Pattern provides the ability to format string represented numbers. Pattern converts the string number *RlStr to the specified number of digits and decimal places and returns the patterned string number. The number will be right justified in the string returned (*Buffer).

Routine Declaration

▼

```
char *Pattern(char *RlStr,
              int  FldWdth,
              int  NumDecs,
              char *Buffer)
```

Passed Variables

▼

***RlStr String Pointer** A pointer to the string number to be patterned to the width and number of decimal places specified.

FldWdth integer The width of the field in which the number is to be right justified.

NumDecs integer The number of decimals the formatted number is to contain.

***Buffer String Pointer** A pointer to the string variable that will contain the resulting string.

Global Variables

▼

None

Error Codes/ Messages

▼

None

Discussion

▼

Pattern allows the formatting of numeric output inside calls to output routines. Pattern requires that a string number be passed instead of a true numeric value.

This was instituted because the library primarily deals with string representations of numbers.

The actual functioning of Pattern is simple. Pattern uses the Turbo C routine sprintf to convert the number to a formatted output. However, since sprintf cannot use parameters in its format sequence, Pattern first assembles the complete format string which can be passed into sprintf.

Limitations and Modifications

▼

Pattern is only limited by Turbo C's limit on the length of float and double float variables.

Routine Source Code

▼

```
#include <math.h>
#include <dos.h>
#include <string.h>
#include <stdio.h>
#include <stdlib.h>
#include <ctype.h>
#include <plib.h>

char *Pattern(char *RlStr,
              int FldWdth,
              int NumDecs,
              char *Buffer)
/*
  Returns a reformatted string of the parameter *RlStr that is in a field
  FldWdth wide and has NumDecs number of decimals showing (or precision).
  Error conditions encountered in the function Str_Real are possible.
*/
{ /* Pattern */
  double
    TF;
  char
    TStr0[10],
    TStr1[10];

  TF = atof(RlStr);
  strcpy(TStr0, "%");
  itoa(FldWdth, TStr1, 10);
  strcat(TStr0, TStr1);
  strcat(TStr0, ".");
  itoa(NumDecs, TStr1, 10);
  strcat(TStr0, TStr1);
  strcat(TStr0, "f");
  sprintf(Buffer, TStr0, TF);
  return(Buffer);
```

```
} /* Pattern */
```

Sample Usage Source Code

```
/*
  This program will take a string number from the user, a field width,
  and number of decimal places, then use Pattern to adjust the field width
  and decimal places of the string and display it.
*/

extern unsigned _stklen=16384; /* Minimum recommend stack size */
#include <stdio.h>
#include <math.h>
#include <dos.h>
#include <mem.h>
#include <alloc.h>
#include <ctype.h>
#include <string.h>
#include <stdlib.h>
#include <plib.h>
#include <plib.glo>

/****************************************************************************/
main()
{
  int
    Width = 0,
    Decimals = 0;

  char
    Buffer[81] = "",
    NumIn[81] = "";

  Calibrate_Delay();           /* Calibrate delay factor */
  Get_Video_Mode("Video.CFG"); /* Get display adapter type */
  Install_Crit_Error();        /* Set up application critical error handler */
  InputAbsolute=AbortPrint=0;  /* Initialize global variables */

  /* Application code to follow */

  Clr_Scr();

  printf("Enter a number: ");
  scanf("%s", NumIn);
  printf("\nEnter a field width: ");
  scanf("%u", &Width);
  printf("\nEnter the number of decimal places: ");
  scanf("%u", &Decimals);
```

```
  printf("\nThe number you entered: %s Patterned is: %s .\n", NumIn,
       Pattern(NumIn, Width, Decimals, Buffer));

} /* main */
```

Sample Usage Output

▼

```
Enter a number: 4567.890

Enter a field width: 10

Enter the number of decimal places: 2

The number you entered: 4567.890 Patterned is: 4567.89.
```

Pos

Description

▼

Pos finds the first occurrence of a character in a specified string value. When the character is found, Pos returns the position in the string, with the first character represented as position 1. If the character is not found, Pos returns zero.

Routine Declaration

▼

```
int Pos(char Ch,
        char *St)
```

Passed Variables

▼

Ch char The character to be located in the string value pointed to by *St.

***St String Pointer** A pointer to the string to be scanned for an occurrence of Ch.

Global Variables

▼

None

Error Codes/ Messages

▼

None

Discussion

▼

Pos provides an easier method of finding the position of a character within a string than those provided with Turbo C. The routine is used extensively throughout the library. Pos considers the offset 0 to be position 1 in the string being scanned, and starts by determining if the first character of the string is the character being searched for or the end of the string (a null). If the first character is the search character, Pos returns 1 and if the first character is a null, Pos returns 0. If the first character is not the search character, a for loop is used to step through the string until the character is found or the end of the string is reached. If the character is found, the character's position is incremented by one and returned. Otherwise, zero is returned indicating the character was not found.

Limitations and Modifications

▼

Pos has two limitations. First, it only finds the first occurrence of the character, so you may want to create a new routine that uses Pos and a temporary copy of the string that can be deleted to find the next occurrence.

The second limitation is that Pos only finds a single character, not a string value. If you need to locate strings within strings, you should use the library routine Str_Pos.

Routine Source Code

▼

```
int Pos(char Ch,
        char *St)
/*
  This function will return the position of Ch in *St, starting from
  position 1. If Ch is not in *St or *St is null, Pos will return 0.
*/
{ /* Pos */
  int
    C;

  if ((St[0] != Ch) && (St[0]))
  {
    for (C = 0; (St[C] && St[C] != Ch); C++);
    if (St[C])
    {
      C++;
      return(C);
    } /* if St[C] */
    else
      return(0);
  } /* if St[0] */
  else
  {
```

```
    if (St[0])
      return(1);
    else
      return(0);
  } /* if St[0] else */
} /* Pos */
```

Sample Usage Source Code

▼

```
/*
  This program will use Pos() to get the first position of a character
  in a string.
*/

extern unsigned _stklen=16384; /* Minimum recommend stack size */
#include <stdio.h>
#include <math.h>
#include <dos.h>
#include <mem.h>
#include <alloc.h>
#include <ctype.h>
#include <string.h>
#include <stdlib.h>
#include <plib.h>
#include <plib.glo>

/****************************************************************************/
main()
{
  char
    String[81] = "",
    Check;

  Calibrate_Delay();            /* Calibrate delay factor */
  Get_Video_Mode("Video.CFG"); /* Get display adapter type */
  Install_Crit_Error();         /* Set up application critical error handler */
  InputAbsolute=AbortPrint=0;   /* Initialize global variables */

  /* Application code to follow */

  Clr_Scr();
  Check = 'a';
  strcpy(String, "She sells seashells at the seashore. ");

  printf("\n\n\n\n") ;
  printf("The specified string is: %s \n\n", String);
  printf("The character is: %c \n\n", Check);
  printf("The 1st %c's position is: %d.\n\n", Check, Pos(Check, String));
```

```
} /* main */
```

Sample Usage Output

▼

```
The specified string is: She sells seashells at the seashore.

The character is: a

The 1st a's position is: 13.
```

Print

Description

▼

Print outputs a line of text to the printer followed by a specified number of linefeeds, and discards all output if the global variable AbortPrint is true (1). Therefore, AbortPrint must be set false (0) initially. If the printer goes off-line for any reason and Critical_Error_Handler has been installed, AbortPrint may be set true (1) at the user's discretion.

Routine Declaration

▼

```
void Print(char *Str,
           int LineFeeds)
```

Passed Variables

▼

***Str String Pointer** A pointer to the text string to be output to the printer.

LineFeeds integer The number of line feeds following text output. A zero leaves the printer on the same print line and at the last horizontal position printed.

Global Variables

▼

AbortPrint Used by printer output routines to indicate the current print condition. If AbortPrint is true (1), all subsequent output will be discarded until AbortPrint is set false (0).

Error Codes/ Messages

▼

All possible errors generated by Print are handled through Install_Crit_Error. See that library routine for a description of the possible errors.

Discussion

▼

Print provides the capability of outputting preformatted lines of text to the LST device (printer), but does not perform any formatting of the actual string. When a printer error occurs, the library routine Critical_Error_Handler intervenes to manage the error and user response. For more information on the error handling, see Install_Crit_Error.

Print starts by checking to determine if AbortPrint is set false (0). If so, a for loop is used to output the string character by character through the library routine Print_Char. Once the string has been sent, a second for loop is used to output the specified number of line feed/carriage return combinations.

Limitations and Modifications

▼

Care should be taken when using Print with the related routine Print_At, which maintains the printer's carriage location for referencing the next output. If you call Print in the middle of a series of Print_At calls, you may cause erratic location positioning in subsequent calls to Print_At.

Routine Source Code

▼

```
#include <math.h>
#include <string.h>
#include <stdio.h>
#include <stdlib.h>
#include <ctype.h>
#include <plib.h>

extern char
  AbortPrint;

void Print(char *Str,
           int LineFeeds)
/*
  This routine will Print *Str through Print_Char followed by LineFeeds
  number of return line feeds.
*/
{ /* Print */
  int
    StrLen,
    C;

  if (AbortPrint == 0)
  {
    StrLen = strlen(Str);
    for (C = 0; C < StrLen; C++)
      Print_Char(Str[C]);
    for (C = 1; C <= LineFeeds; C++)
    {
      Print_Char(13);
      Print_Char(10);
    } /* for C */
```

```
  } /* if AbortPrint */
} /* Print */
```

Sample Usage Source Code

▼

```
/*
  This program will use Print to output text to a Lpt1.
  Note: If the Printer should go off-line during print, no
        rude DOS error will corrupt the program's workings.
*/

extern unsigned _stklen=16384; /* Minimum recommend stack size */
#include <stdio.h>
#include <math.h>
#include <dos.h>
#include <mem.h>
#include <alloc.h>
#include <ctype.h>
#include <string.h>
#include <stdlib.h>
#include <plib.h>
#include <plib.glo>

/*****************************************************************************/
main()
{
  int
    C=0;
  char
    Check = ' ';

  Calibrate_Delay();            /* Calibrate delay factor */
  Get_Video_Mode("Video.CFG"); /* Get display adapter type */
  Install_Crit_Error();         /* Set up application critical error handler */
  InputAbsolute=AbortPrint=0;  /* Initialize global variables */

  /* Application code to follow */

  Clr_Scr();
  printf("\n\n\nWhen Printer is ready, please press <Enter>.\n");
  scanf("%c", Check);
  printf("\n");

  Print("The next Print will be On the same line. ", 0);
  Print("Because of 0 line feeds. ", 1);
  for (C = 1; C <= 5; C++)
    Print ("This is a test that should come out Lpt1 ", 1);
```

```
} /* main */
```

Sample Usage Output

▼

```
When Printer is ready, please press <Enter>.
```

Print_At

Description

▼

Print_At provides the ability to output strings on a single print line at exact locations without having to perform intricate concatenations. Print_At prints a text string at a specified horizontal position on the print line and advances the paper a specified number of vertical print lines after the output.

Routine Declaration

▼

```
void Print_At(int X,
              int LineFeeds,
              char *Strng)
```

Passed Variables

▼

X integer The horizontal location on the current print line. If this location is less than the current value of PrintAtX, a carriage return, without a line feed, is performed to reset the printer to the left edge of the print line, followed by X number of spaces.

LineFeeds integer The number of line feeds performed after the text is printed. If you want to continue printing on the same print line, LineFeeds should be set to zero.

***Strng String Pointer** A pointer to the text string to be printed at the X value indicated.

Global Variables

▼

PrintAtX Contains the current column position of the printer's printhead in relation to the left side of the page. If other print routines are used between calls to Print_At, this value should be adjusted accordingly or it may reflect an incorrect position.

Error Codes/ Messages

▼

All possible errors generated by Print_At are handled through Install_Crit_Error. See that library routine for a description of the possible errors.

Discussion

Print_At is useful in producing columnized reports and documents, because it allows you to specify the exact column for the location of the output. A call to Print_At(0,0,'') should be executed prior to the first output of actual data to initialize the printer and the global variable PrintAtX, which contains the current column position on the printed page. Using Print_At instead of other output routines makes your source code a little longer, but the time saved for any modifications is worth it.

The code for Print_At is very short since the actual output is performed with calls to Print. The routine verifies that the X position is positive and performs a carriage return without a line feed if the X position is to the left of PrintAtX. Then, print is called with a string padded with the appropriate number of spaces. This is followed by a call to Print with the number of line feeds desired.

Limitations and Modifications

Print_At was designed to primarily print information after the current printhead position. If your output is sent to a position to the left of the current printhead position, Print_At seeks the printhead to the left margin and moves out to the required print position. If your report does this consistently, the print speed slows considerably.

Routine Source Code

```
#include <string.h>
#include <plib.h>

extern int
  PrintAtX;

void Print_At(int X,
              int LineFeeds,
              char *Strng)
/*
  This procedure uses the global variable PrintAtX to store the current
  position of the printhead. The parameter X is the position at which
  to start printing parameter *Strng. LineFeeds may only be 0 or
  positive since most printers cannot reverse line feed anyway.
  Caution should be used in printing at positions that are less than
  the value of PrintAtX on the same line as this method is inefficient
  in printing. If LineFeeds is given a value other than 0, it will
  cause LineFeeds # of return line feeds and reset PrintAtX to one. If
  this procedure is used with another printing procedure, misalignment
  may occur if PrintAtX is not cared for.

  IMPORTANT: A  Print_At(0, 0, "");
```

```
  should always be done in the beginning to reset the carriage of the
  printer and initialize PrintAtX. Note: This routine uses the
  procedure Print.
*/
{ /* Print_At */
  char
    ReturnStr[2] = {13, 0},
    TStr0[256];

  if (X > 0)
  { /* Print as usual */
    if (X < PrintAtX)
    {
      Print(ReturnStr, 0);
      PrintAtX = 1;
    } /* if X */
    Print(Rpt(" ", TStr0, X - PrintAtX), 0);
    PrintAtX = X + strlen(Strng);
    if (LineFeeds > 0)
      PrintAtX = 1;
    Print(Strng, LineFeeds);
  } /* if X */
  else          /* Recalibrate printer and reset PrintAtX */
  {
    Print(ReturnStr, 0);
    PrintAtX = 1;
    Print("", LineFeeds);
  } /* if X else */
} /* Print_At */
```

Sample Usage Source Code

▼

```
/*
  This program will use Print_At to output text to a Lpt1.
  Note: If the printer should go off-line during print, no
       rude DOS error will corrupt the program's workings.
*/

extern unsigned _stklen=16384; /* Minimum recommend stack size */
#include <stdio.h>
#include <math.h>
#include <dos.h>
#include <mem.h>
#include <alloc.h>
#include <ctype.h>
#include <string.h>
#include <stdlib.h>
#include <plib.h>
```

```
#include <plib.glo>

/****************************************************************************/
main()
{
  int
    I = 0,
    J = 0;

  char
    Check = '';

  Calibrate_Delay();              /* Calibrate delay factor */
  Get_Video_Mode("Video.CFG");   /* Get display adapter type */
  Install_Crit_Error();           /* Set up application critical error handler */
  InputAbsolute=AbortPrint=0;     /* Initialize global variables */

  /* Application code to follow */

  Clr_Scr();
  printf("\n\n\nWhen Printer is ready, please press <Enter>.\n");
  scanf("%c", &Check);
  printf("\n");

  Print_At (0, 0, "");  /*Initialize printer and PrintAtX*/
  for (I = 1; I <= 5; I++)
  {
    for (J = 1; J <= 5; J++)
      Print_At(J * 5, 0, "XXX");
    Print_At(1, 1, "");
  }

}  /*  main  */
```

Sample Usage Output

▼

```
When Printer is ready, please press <Enter>.
```

Note: The following output will appear five times, consecutively, on the printer.
XXX   XXX   XXX   XXX   XXX

Print_Char

Description

▼

Print_Char sends a character to the current DOS printer, allowing the user to use DOS to set the output destination to any device that can be routed through DOS operations.

Routine Declaration

▼

```
void Print_Char(char PrntCh)
```

Passed Variables

▼

Ch char The character to be output to a DOS printer.

Global Variables

▼

None

Error Codes/ Messages

▼

All possible errors generated by Print_Char are handled through Install-_Crit_Error. See that library routine for a description of the possible errors.

Discussion

▼

Print_Char sends a single character to the current DOS printer. For printing complete strings, use Print or Print_At.

Print_Char uses an if condition based on AbortPrint to determine if the passed character should be output to the printer. If the printer is not ready, Install_Crit_Error prompts the user for the desired operation. Otherwise, Print_Char uses the DOS interrupt 21 hex, Function Call Interrupt, service 05 hex, Print Character, to output the character.

Limitations and Modifications

▼

None

Routine Source Code

▼

```
#include <dos.h>
#include <math.h>
#include <string.h>
#include <stdio.h>
#include <stdlib.h>
#include <ctype.h>
#include <plib.h>

extern char
  AbortPrint;

void Print_Char(char PrntCh)
/*
  This routine uses the dos call 0x21 to output PrntCh.
*/
```

```
{ /* Print_Char */
  union REGS
    Regs;

  if (AbortPrint == 0)
  {
    Regs.h.ah = 0x05; /* Print char */
    Regs.h.dl = PrntCh;
    int86(0x21, &Regs, &Regs);
  } /* if AbortPrint */
} /* Print_Char */
```

Sample Usage Source Code

▼

See the source code in Print for an example usage for this routine.

Print_Codes

Description

▼

Print_Codes sends the ASCII characters equal to the string representation of numeric values contained in the specified string. For example, if the string contains 65 66 67, Print_Codes outputs ABC.

Routine Declaration

▼

```
void Print_Codes(char *Sequence)
```

Passed Variables

▼

***Sequence String Pointer** A pointer to the string that contains the numeric representation to be output to the current DOS printer. The values must be separated by a space or they will not be properly interpreted.

Global Variables

▼

None

Error Codes/ Messages

▼

```
Print_Codes: Bad Number, Ignoring XX
```

This message is generated if the parameters passed contain any characters that cannot be converted to numeric values in a character range. This is not a fatal error, but uses the Beep_Bomb() sound.

All other possible errors generated by Print_Codes are handled through Install_Crit_Error. See that library routine for a description of the possible errors.

Discussion

▼

Print_Codes provides an easy means of outputting stored printer configurations without having to convert from ASCII characters to string for user entry.

Print_Codes begins by ensuring that the last character in the string is a space, providing consistent parsing of the character code representations. Next, a while loop is used to repeat the parsing and conversion process until all the parameters have been printed. Inside the while loop, Print_Codes finds the first space in the parameter string and copies the numeric representation to a temporary variable that is stripped of spaces. The temporary code is then converted to a numeric value and any errors in the conversion process trigger an error message. If the conversion is successful, the code is written to the printer using Print_Char and the parameter is removed from the parameter string by a call to Delete.

Limitations and Modifications

▼

Because most of the library routines use Beep_Bomb() as an indication of fatal errors, you may want to derive another very distinctive error routine instead of using Beep_Bomb() in this routine.

Routine Source Code

▼

```
#include <stdio.h>
#include <stdlib.h>
#include <mem.h>
#include <dos.h>
#include <alloc.h>
#include <ctype.h>
#include <string.h>
#include <plib.h>

void Print_Codes(char *Sequence)
/*
  This procedure will print out the ascii sequence in the string
  *Sequence. i.e., if Sequence = "84 73 110", Print_Codes will print
  "TIn".
*/
{ /* Print_Codes */
  char
    Temp[81],
    Temp1[81],
    TSeq[1000];
```

```
  int
    ErCode,
    AscCode;


  strcpy(TSeq, Sequence);
  if (TSeq[0])
  {
    if (TSeq[strlen(TSeq)-1] != ' ')
      strcat(TSeq, " ");
    while ((strlen(TSeq) > 0) && (Pos(' ', TSeq) != 0))
    {
      Copy(TSeq, 1, Pos(' ', TSeq) - 1, Temp);
      Erase_White(Temp);
      if (Temp[0])
      {
        if (!Common_Chars(Temp, "0123456789"))
        {
          ErCode = 0;
          AscCode = atoi(Temp);
        } /* if !Common_Chars */
        else
          ErCode = 1;
        if ((!ErCode) && (AscCode >= 0) && (AscCode <= 255))
        {
          Print_Char(AscCode);
        } /* if !ErCode */
        else
        {
          sprintf(Temp1, "Print_Codes: Bad number, Ignoring %s", Temp);
          Message(Temp1);
          Beep_Bomb();
        } /* if !ErCode else */
      } /* if Temp[0] */
      Delete(TSeq, 1, Pos(' ', TSeq));
    } /* while strlen */
  } /* if TSeq */
} /* Print_Codes */
```

Sample Usage Source Code

```
/*
  This program will use Print_Code to print a string
  containing ascii numbers onto the printer in character form.
  This routine is extremely useful for setting up configurable
  printer command applications.
*/
```

```
extern unsigned _stklen=16384; /* Minimum recommend stack size */
#include <stdio.h>
#include <math.h>
#include <dos.h>
#include <mem.h>
#include <alloc.h>
#include <ctype.h>
#include <string.h>
#include <stdlib.h>
#include <plib.h>
#include <plib.glo>


/****************************************************************************/
main()
{
  char
    TempString[81]="";

  Calibrate_Delay();           /* Calibrate delay factor */
  Get_Video_Mode("Video.CFG"); /* Get display adapter type */
  Install_Crit_Error();        /* Set up application critical error handler */
  InputAbsolute=AbortPrint=0;  /* Initialize global variables */

  /* Application code to follow */

  Clr_Scr();
  strcpy(TempString,"65 66 67 68 69 70");
  Print("The original String = ",0);
  Print(TempString,1);
  Print("The equivalent ASCII characters = ",0);
  Print_Codes(TempString);
  Print("",1);

} /*main*/
```

Sample Usage Output

▼

Note: All output will appear on the printer.

```
The original string = 65 66 67 68 69 70
The equivalent ASCII characters = ABCDEF
```

Prompt

Description

▼

Prompt acquires string data in the form of alphanumeric, date, and numeric. Unlike the Ent_Scr routine, Prompt does not require any additional control structure to function. Prompt acquires data as a stand-alone routine call or can be used for elementary entry screens.

Routine Declaration

▼

```
void Prompt(int  X,
         int  Y,
         char Attr,
         char *Prompt,
         char *RType,
         char *Value)
```

Passed Variables

▼

X integer The horizontal position for the start of the prompt and field display. Valid values for X are 1 through 79.

Y integer The vertical position for the start of the prompt and field display. Valid values for Y are 1 through 25. However, line 25 should be avoided because Prompt also uses this line to display its error messages.

Attr char The video display attributes to be used in displaying the prompt associated with the field to be entered (Normal, Reverse, and VidHigh).

***Prompt String Pointer** A string pointer to the text string to be displayed to the left of the area used to enter the field. The length of the field and prompt added to the X position should not exceed 80. If it does, the line will wrap around to the next screen line and may cause entry problems.

***RType String Pointer** A string pointer that identifies the type and limits of the data field being entered. (For additional information on patterns, see Input_Alpha, Input_Num, and Input_Date.) Some valid pattern examples are:

> **A30,** for Alpha numeric field 30 long and any ASCII character from 32 to 127.
>
> **A11,EFGefg** for Alpha numeric field 11 long and ASCII characters EFGefg. Any length is allowed up to 80.
>
> **A.,** same as A1, except the first key pressed is taken as the entry unless it is not in the valid set of characters specified. No need for user to press Return. If Escape is pressed, CurKey contains an Escape. If not, CurKey is set to an Enter. Value is always returned in uppercase.
>
> C for a date in the form MM/DD/YY.
>
> **6I.DD,0 55545.50** for a number with six integer places, two decimal places and a valid range from 0 to 55545.50. All standard numeric specifiers are allowed.
>
> **YN** for a Y/N (Yes/No) response. Lowercase entries are valid but will be converted to uppercase for Value.

P for PROMPT to be displayed. Any key may be pressed by the user to continue. Value will always return null (length of 0).

***Value String Pointer** A pointer to the actual variable to be displayed and modified. If this parameter has a value upon calling Prompt, the value is displayed prior to allowing modification.

Global Variables

CurKey Contains the value of the last keyboard keystroke retrieved by Get_One_Char that caused Input_Alpha to exit. If the keystroke is prefixed (a two-byte scan code), CurKey contains a negative value equal to the significant byte of the scan codes. For example, pressing A returns a 65 in CurKey and pressing F1 returns −59.

Error Codes/ Messages

All messages from Input_Alpha, Input_Num, and Input_Date can also appear.

Discussion

Prompt provides a flexible method of acquiring information in an application from the user. Prompt can enter alphanumeric data with the same patterning styles used in Input_Alpha, Input_Num, and Input_Date. The main difference is that you must specify the screen location and the prompt to be displayed with the field to be entered. Prompt is primarily intended for acquiring single fields of information prior to performing special processing. You can use it to create small special entry screens, but we don't recommend it for large entry screens because you would need to create all the control structure for performing sophisticated entry screens. (See Ent_Scr for a discussion of large entry screens.)

Prompt basically consists of a large case statement that is based on the type of field to be entered as specified in the parameter *RType. The first character of *RType identifies whether the field will be alphanumeric, numeric, date, prompt only, or Yes/No only. Each of these conditions has a separate section that sets up the parameters to be passed to one of the input routines (Input_Alpha, Input_Num, or Input_Date.)

Limitations and Modifications

Prompt provides very little error trapping for the patterns passed in *RType. You may want to add additional format checking to Prompt to aid in eliminating program errors. This may have an adverse affect on the performance of your routines, so evaluate any differences that may be caused in your application.

Routine Source Code

```
#include <math.h>
#include <stdlib.h>
```

```
#include <string.h>
#include <stdio.h>
#include <ctype.h>
#include <plib.h>
extern char
  Normal,
  Reverse,
  VidHigh;
extern int
  CurKey;

void Prompt(int X,
            int Y,
            char Attr,
            char *Prompt,
            char *RType,
            char *Value)
/*
  This function will write *Prompt at X, Y in Attr attribute and accept
  a value as specified by *RType via Input_Alpha to *Value. *Value will
  default to whatever *Value is set to before calling this function.
  Set *RType to:
    'A30,'                  For alphanumeric field 30 long and any ascii
                            character from 32 to 127.

    'A11,EFGefg'            For alphanumeric field 11 long and ascii
                            characters EFGefg are valid.  Any length is
                            allowed up to 80.

    'A.,'                   Same as A1 except that the first key pressed is
                            taken as the entry unless it is not in the
                            valid set of characters specified. No need for
                            user to press return. If Esc is pressed, CurKey
                            will contain an Esc.  If not, CurKey will be
                            set to an Enter.  Value will be returned in
                            uppercase always.

    'C'                     For a date in the form MM/DD/YY.

    '6I.DD,0 55545.50'      For a number with six integer places, two
                            decimal places and a valid range from 0 to
                            55545.50. All standard numeric specifiers are
                            allowed.

    'YN'                    For a Y/N (Yes/No) response. Lowercase entries
                            are valid but will be converted to uppercase for
                            Value.

    'P'                     For *Prompt to be displayed and any key may be
```

```
                    pressed by the user to continue. Value will
                    always return null (length of 0).

  In all cases, the global variable CurKey will contain the last key
  pressed by the user, i.e., an <ESC> if the user wished to abort.
  *Value may be initialized to a default value.

  Note: Caution should be used when placing a prompt on the 25th line
  because this may conflict with error messages displayed by Input_Alpha,
  Input_Date, etc. The 'P' *RType should be the only *RType used on
  the 25th line.
*/
{ /* Prompt */
  char
    Ch,
    Spec[31],
    ValSet[256],
    TStr1[256];

  int
    FieldLen;

  float
    Min,
    Max;

  switch (toupper(RType[0]))
  {
    case 'A':
      if (RType[1] != '.')
      {
        FieldLen = atoi(Copy(RType, 2, Pos(',', RType) - 2, TStr1));
        if (Pos(',', RType) != strlen(RType))
          strcpy(ValSet, Copy(RType, Pos(',', RType) + 1,
                 strlen(RType) - Pos(',', RType), TStr1));
        else
          ValSet[0] = 0;
        do
        {
          F_WriteXY(X, Y, Attr, Prompt);
          Input_Alpha(FieldLen, ValSet, Value);
          if (CurKey != 13 && CurKey != 27)
            Lo_Mess("Bad key pressed");
        } while (CurKey != 13 && CurKey != 27);
      } /* if *RType */
      else
      {
        ValSet[0] = 0;
```

```
      if (Pos(',', RType) != strlen(RType))
      {
        strcpy(ValSet, Copy(RType, Pos(',', RType) + 1,
               strlen(RType) - Pos(',', RType), TStr1));
      } /* if Pos */
      else
      {
        for (FieldLen = 32; FieldLen <= 90; ValSet[FieldLen - 32] = FieldLen,
           FieldLen++);
        ValSet[FieldLen - 32] = 0;
        F_WriteXY(X, Y, Attr, Prompt);
        F_Write(WhereX(), WhereY(), Reverse, LJ(Value, TStr1, 1));
        do
        {
          Get_One_Char();
          Ch = toupper(CurKey>0?CurKey:0);
          if ((Pos(Ch, ValSet) == 0)&&(CurKey != 27)&&(CurKey != 13))
          {
            sprintf(TStr1, "Invalid input '%c' only '%s' allowed",
                    Ch, ValSet);
            Lo_Mess(TStr1);
          } /* if Pos */
        } while (Pos(Ch, ValSet) != 0 && CurKey != 27 && CurKey != 13);
        if (CurKey != 27)
          CurKey = 13;
        Value[0] = Ch;
        Value[1] = 0;
        F_Write(WhereX(), WhereY(), VidHigh, Value);
        Delay(500);
      } /* if Pos else */
    } /* if *RType else*/
  break;

  case 'C':
    do
    {
      F_WriteXY(X, Y, Attr, Prompt);
      Input_Date(Value);
      if (CurKey != 13 && CurKey != 27)
        Lo_Mess("Bad key pressed");
    } while (CurKey != 13 && CurKey != 27);
  break;

  case 'Y':
    do
    {
      F_WriteXY(X, Y, Attr, Prompt);
      Input_Alpha(1, "YyNn", Value);
```

```
      if (CurKey != 13 && CurKey != 27)
        Lo_Mess("Bad key pressed");
    } while (CurKey != 13 && CurKey != 27);
    Value[0] = toupper(Value[0]);
  break;

  case 'P':
    F_WriteXY(X, Y, Attr, Prompt);
    Get_One_Char();
  break;

  case '0': case '1': case '2': case '3': case '4': case '5':
  case '6': case '7': case '8': case '9': case 'I': case 'D':
    strcpy(Spec, Copy(RType, 1, Pos(',', RType) - 1, TStr1));
    Min = atof(Copy(RType, Pos(',', RType) + 1, Pos(' ', RType) -
                (Pos(',', RType) + 1), TStr1));
    Max = atof(Copy(RType, Pos(' ', RType) + 1, strlen(RType) -
                Pos(' ', RType), TStr1));
    do
    {
      F_WriteXY(X, Y, Attr, Prompt);
      Input_Num(Value, Spec, Min, Max);
      if (CurKey != 13 && CurKey != 27)
        Lo_Mess("Bad key pressed");
    } while (CurKey != 13 && CurKey != 27);
  break;
 } /* switch */
} /* Prompt */
```

Sample Usage Source Code

▼

```
/*
  This program will use Prompt to get a general alpha input, a number,
  then a date with the default for the date set to the current date
  using Today.
*/

extern unsigned _stklen=16384; /* Minimum recommend stack size */
#include <stdio.h>
#include <math.h>
#include <dos.h>
#include <mem.h>
#include <alloc.h>
#include <ctype.h>
#include <string.h>
#include <stdlib.h>
#include <plib.h>
#include <plib.glo>
```

```
/******************************************************************************/
main()
{
  char
    TempStr [81] = "" ;

  Calibrate_Delay();              /* Calibrate delay factor */
  Get_Video_Mode("Video.CFG"); /* Get display adapter type */
  Install_Crit_Error();           /* Set up application critical error handler */
  InputAbsolute=AbortPrint=0;  /* Initialize global variables */

  /* Application code to follow */

  Clr_Scr();
  Prompt(1, 1, Normal,"Enter a something: ","A50,", TempStr);
  TempStr[0] = '';
  Prompt(1, 3, Normal, "Now enter a number: ",
       "9I.DD,-125 9999999999.99", TempStr);
  Today(TempStr);
  Prompt(1, 5, Normal, "Now enter a date or press return: ",
       "C,", TempStr );

} /*  main  */
```

Sample Usage Output

▼

```
Enter a something: This is a prompt() test.

Now enter a number: 10.00

Now enter a date or press return: 02/26/88
```

RJ

Description

▼

RJ returns a pointer to a copy of the specified string that has been right justified in a field of spaces of a specified length. If the string is longer than the specified field width, RJ truncates the right portion of the string to fit within the field size.

Routine Declaration

▼

```
char *RJ(char *RStr,
         char *Buffer,
         int  FieldWdth)
```

Passed Variables

▼

***RStr String Pointer** A pointer to the string value to be right justified in a field of spaces.

***Buffer String Pointer** A pointer to the string variable that will contain the resulting string.

FieldWdth integer The width of the field in which *RStr is to be right justified.

Global Variables

▼

None

Error Codes/ Messages

▼

None

Discussion

▼

RJ provides an easy consistent method for right justifying strings in specified fields of spaces. The ability to right justify text is useful in creating fixed-length concatenations of fields for output in printed or disk forms. In using the library, you will particularly need to use RJ for any fields in data files used as numeric key indexes. This ensures that numeric values will be compared as numeric representations and not their actual textual representations. RJ also simplifies the printing of long concatenations of several strings by allowing you to right justify the strings in the concatenation.

RJ uses an if to determine if the string passed is longer than the allowed field. If the string is too long, the left portion is copied into *Buffer using a for loop that moves characters from the end of *RStr into *Buffer. If the string is within the boundaries of the field length, the appropriate number of spaces is inserted into the new string and the original string is moved in after the spaces. The number of spaces used is the difference between the string length and the specified width.

Limitations and Modifications

▼

The only real limitation to RJ is that it does not strip any trailing spaces from the passed string. If you find that your application requires this, use a call to the procedure Erase_White_End to remove the trailing spaces. You should evaluate the performance differences this may cause to ensure that it won't dramatically impede your application's performance.

Routine Source Code

▼

```
char *RJ(char *RStr,
         char *Buffer,
         int FieldWidth)
```

```
/*
  This function will set LStr in *Buffer right justified in a field
  FieldWidth wide with space character fills. If FieldWidth is smaller
  than the length of LStr, *Buffer will contain the truncated version of
  *RStr(from lenstr(*RStr) downto lenstr(*RStr) - FieldWidth).
  It will return the pointer to *Buffer.
*/
{ /* RJ */
  int
    T,
    T1,
    LR;

  for (LR = 0; RStr[LR]; LR++);
  if (LR <= FieldWidth)
  {
    T1 = FieldWidth-LR-1;
    for (T = 0; T <= T1; T++)
      Buffer[T] = ' ';
    for (T1 = 0, FieldWidth--; T <= FieldWidth; T++, T1++)
      Buffer[T] = RStr[T1];
    Buffer[T] = 0;
  } /* if LR */
  else
  {
    Buffer[FieldWidth] = 0;
    for (FieldWidth--, LR--; FieldWidth >= 0; FieldWidth--, LR--)
      Buffer[FieldWidth] = RStr[LR];
  } /* if LR else */
  return(Buffer);
} /* RJ */
```

Sample Usage Source Code

▼

```
/*
  This program will allow the user to input a string into
  TempStr and a number into FWidth. It will then use RJ to
  right justify TempStr in a field of FWidth.
*/

extern unsigned _stklen=16384; /* Minimum recommend stack size */
#include <stdio.h>
#include <math.h>
#include <dos.h>
#include <mem.h>
#include <alloc.h>
```

```
#include <ctype.h>
#include <string.h>
#include <stdlib.h>
#include <plib.h>
#include <plib.glo>


/****************************************************************************/
main()
{
  int
    FWidth = 0;

  char
    RightStr[81] = "",
    TempStr[81] = "";

  Calibrate_Delay();              /* Calibrate delay factor */
  Get_Video_Mode("Video.CFG"); /* Get display adapter type */
  Install_Crit_Error();           /* Set up application critical error handler */
  InputAbsolute=AbortPrint=0;  /* Initialize global variables */

  /* Application code to follow */

  Clr_Scr();

  printf("Enter something: ");
  gets(TempStr);
  printf("\nEnter field width: ");
  scanf("%u", &FWidth);

  printf ("\n*******%s*******\n", RJ(TempStr, RightStr, FWidth));

} /*  main  */
```

Sample Usage Output

▼

```
Enter something: This is an RJ test.

Enter field width: 30

*******           This is an RJ test.*******
```

Range_Max

Description

▼

Range_Max returns the maximum end of a numeric range passed in a string form of minimum maximum, e.g., 1.25 5.55.

Routine Declaration

▼

```
float Range_Max(char *Rng)
```

Passed Variables

▼

***Rng String Pointer** A pointer to the string containing the minimum and maximum range values in the format min max.

Global Variables

▼

None

Error Codes/ Messages

▼

None

Discussion

▼

Range_Max can be used to retrieve the maximum range value for a string range definition (e.g., −10.5 10.5). This range style is used when specifying numeric ranges for Prompt or Ent_Scr.

Range_Max uses the library routine Copy to pull out the maximum portion of the range string. The positions required to execute the command are calculated inside the call to Copy by the library routine Pos and a numeric calculation of the string length. Once the value has been parsed, it is converted to a real value by atof.

Limitations and Modifications

▼

None

Routine Source Code

▼

```
#include <math.h>
#include <dos.h>
#include <string.h>
#include <stdio.h>
#include <stdlib.h>
#include <ctype.h>
```

```
#include <plib.h>

float Range_Max(char *Rng)
/*
  This function will return the maximum side of a string range, e.g., if
  *Rng = '1.25 550.5' then Range_Max will return the real 550.5.
*/

{ /* Range_Max */
  char
    TStr[20];

  return(atof(Copy(Rng, Pos(' ', Rng) + 1,
              strlen(Rng) - Pos(' ', Rng), TStr)));
} /*Range_Max*/
```

Sample Usage Source Code

```
/*
  This program will allow the user to input a string that has
  a low number separated by a space, then a high number, together
  representing a numerical range. Then it will use Range_Max to
  parse and display the maximum number in the range.

*/

extern unsigned _stklen=16384; /* Minimum recommend stack size */
#include <stdio.h>
#include <math.h>
#include <dos.h>
#include <mem.h>
#include <alloc.h>
#include <ctype.h>
#include <string.h>
#include <stdlib.h>
#include <plib.h>
#include <plib.glo>


/*****************************************************************************/
main()
{
  char
    StrRange[81] = "";

  Calibrate_Delay();            /* Calibrate delay factor */
  Get_Video_Mode("Video.CFG"); /* Get display adapter type */
  Install_Crit_Error();         /* Set up application critical error handler */
```

```
  InputAbsolute=AbortPrint=0;  /* Initialize global variables */

  /* Application code to follow */

  Clr_Scr();

  printf("\nEnter a range (Min Max): ");
  gets(StrRange);
  printf("The maximum of this range is %f ", Range_Max(StrRange));

} /*  main  */
```

Sample Usage Output

▼

```
Enter a range (Min Max): 0 6000
The maximum of this range is 6000.000000
```

Range_Min

Description

▼

Range_Min returns the minimum portion of a numeric range passed in a string form of minimum maximum, e.g., 1.25 5.55.

Routine Declaration

▼

```
float Range_Min(char *Rng)
```

Passed Variables

▼

***Rng String Pointer** A pointer to the string containing the minimum and maximum range values in the format min max.

Global Variables

▼

None

Error Codes/ Messages

▼

None

Discussion

▼

Range_Min can be used to retrieve the minimum range value for a string range definition (e.g., 0 100). This range style is used when specifying numeric range values for Prompt or Ent_Scr.

Range_Min uses the library routine Copy to pull out the minimum portion of the range string. The positions required to execute the command are calculated inside the call to Copy by the library routine Pos and a numeric calculation of the string length. Once the value has been parsed, it is converted to a real value by atof.

Limitations and Modifications

None

Routine Source Code

```
#include <math.h>
#include <dos.h>
#include <string.h>
#include <stdio.h>
#include <stdlib.h>
#include <ctype.h>
#include <plib.h>

float Range_Min(char *Rng)
/*
  This function will return the minimum side of a string range, e.g., if
  Rng = "1.25 550.5" then Range_Min will return the float 1.25.
*/

{ /* Range_Min */
  char
    TStr[20];

  return(atof(Copy(Rng, 1, Pos(' ', Rng) - 1, TStr)));
} /* Range_Min */
```

Sample Usage Source Code

```
/*
  This program will allow the user to input a string that has
  a low number separated by a space, then a high number, together
  representing a numerical range. Then it will use Range_Min to
  parse and display the minimum number in the range.

*/

extern unsigned _stklen=16384; /* Minimum recommend stack size */
#include <stdio.h>
#include <math.h>
#include <dos.h>
#include <mem.h>
```

```
#include <alloc.h>
#include <ctype.h>
#include <string.h>
#include <stdlib.h>
#include <plib.h>
#include <plib.glo>


/*****************************************************************************/
main()
{
  char
    StrRange [81] = "";

  Calibrate_Delay();          /* Calibrate delay factor */
  Get_Video_Mode("Video.CFG"); /* Get display adapter type */
  Install_Crit_Error();       /* Set up application critical error handler */
  InputAbsolute=AbortPrint=0; /* Initialize global variables */

  /* Application code to follow */

  Clr_Scr();
  printf("\nEnter a range (Min Max): ");
  gets(StrRange);
  printf("The minimum of this range is %f ", Range_Min(StrRange));

} /*  main  */
```

Sample Usage Output

▼

```
Enter a range (Min Max): -234  500
The minimum of this range is -234.000000
```

Read_Line

Description

▼

Read_Line provides a consistent means of reading a line from a text file into a specified variable buffer. Read_Line will return a true (1) if the end of the file is not reached and a false (0) if the end of the file is reached.

Routine Declaration

▼

```
void Read_Line(FILE *RFile,
               char *Line,
               int  MaxLineSize)
```

Passed Variables

▼

***RFile Stream Buffer Pointer** A pointer to the structure defining the current file read.

***Line String Pointer** A pointer to the string variable that is to receive the string read from *RFile.

MaxLineSize integer The maximum length of data read before the read is terminated.

Global Variables

▼

None

Error Codes/ Messages

▼

None

Discussion

▼

Read_Line provides a reliable and consistent means of reading lines out of text streams from disk. For example, both fscanf and fgets leave unwanted characters in the string and occasionally read beyond the end of the file. Read_Line solves both of these problems and is easier to work with.

Read_Line uses a do-while loop to read a character at a time from the specified file. The loop terminates when it encounters a ^Z (ASCII 26), a carriage return/line feed (ASCII 13 10), the end of the file, or the MaxLineSize limit. Once one of the conditions halts the loop, the halting if condition is returned.

Limitations and Modifications

▼

Read_Line is intended for reading standard text files only. Attempting to use Read_Line for anything other than standard ASCII file may result in unpredictable line parsing.

Routine Source Code

▼

```
#include <stdio.h>

char Read_Line(FILE *RFile,
               char *Line,
               int MaxLineSize)
/*
  This routine will read a line from *RFile into Line as delimited
  by a 13 10. The 13 and 10 will not be placed in *Line. If the length
  of *Line reaches MaxLineSize, *Line will be terminated at that point
  and in either case Read_Line will return true (1). If, while reading,
  the end of file is detected, Read_Line will terminate *Line and
```

```
  return false (0).
*/
{/* Read_Line */
  int
    Ch,
    C;

  C = 0;
  do
  {
    while ((Ch = getc(RFile)) == 10); /*Discard LF's*/
    if ((Ch != 26) && (Ch != 13) && (Ch != -1))
    {
      Line[C] = Ch;
      C++;
    } /* if Ch */
  } while ((Ch != 26) && (Ch != 13) && (C < MaxLineSize) && (Ch != -1));
  Line[C] = 0;
  return ( ((Ch != 26) && (Ch != -1)) );
} /* Read_Line */
```

Sample Usage Source Code

```
/*
  This program will create a text file, then print it out, by using
  Read_Line(), Write_String(), and Write_Line().
*/

extern unsigned _stklen=16384; /* Minimum recommend stack size */
#include <stdio.h>
#include <math.h>
#include <dos.h>
#include <mem.h>
#include <alloc.h>
#include <ctype.h>
#include <string.h>
#include <stdlib.h>
#include <plib.h>
#include <plib.glo>


/****************************************************************************/
main()
{
  FILE
    *RFile;

  char
```

```
  Line[129] = "";

 Calibrate_Delay();             /* Calibrate delay factor */
 Get_Video_Mode("Video.CFG"); /* Get display adapter type */
 Install_Crit_Error();          /* Set up application critical error handler */
 InputAbsolute=AbortPrint=0;  /* Initialize global variables */

 /* Application code to follow */

 Clr_Scr();

 RFile = fopen("Test.txt", "wb");
 Write_Line(RFile, "Hi there this is line 1.");
 Write_String(RFile, "And this is");
 Write_String(RFile, " line ");
 Write_Line(RFile, "number 2.");
 Write_Line(RFile, "This is line 3.");
 fputc(26, RFile);     /*  terminate the ascii file   */
 fclose(RFile);

 RFile = fopen("Test.txt", "rb");
 printf("\n\n\n\n") ;
 while(Read_Line(RFile, Line, 128))
   printf("%s\n", Line);
 printf("%s\n", Line);
 fclose(RFile);

} /*  main  */
```

Sample Usage Output

▼

```
Hi there this is line 1.
And this is line number 2.
This is line 3.
```

Replace

Description

▼

Replace overwrites a portion of an existing string with the text from a specified string. The overwrite can occur anywhere within the existing string or past the end of the existing string. If the overwrite goes beyond the end of the existing string, the existing string is lengthened to accommodate the new size. If the overwrite begins after the end of the existing string, spaces are placed between the previous end of the string and the starting position of the overwrite.

Routine Declaration

```
char *Replace(char *Src,
              char *Target,
              int Position)
```

Passed Variables

***Src String Pointer** A pointer to the string value that is to overwrite a portion of the string Target.

***Target String Pointer** A pointer to the existing string to be partially overwritten with the string value in Source (*Src).

Position integer The starting position in Target for the overwrite using Source (*Src).

Global Variables

None

Error Codes/ Messages

None

Discussion

Replace was developed out of a need in several library routines for a routine that could overwrite text within strings. Replace does not insert any text between existing characters, but rather overwrites the values in the existing string or lengthens the string to accommodate new text that exceeds the current length of the string.

Replace first determines if the starting position for the overwrite is past the end of the target string. If it is, spaces are added between the difference and then the replace string, with a null at the end, is attached to the end of the original. If the position is within the original length, the replace string is simply written over the original characters and the string is returned.

Limitations and Modifications

None

Routine Source Code

```
char *Replace(char *Src,
              char *Target,
              int Position)
/*
  This function will place *Src into *Target at Position in *Target (in an
```

```
  overwrite fashion). If Position exceeds the length of *Target, spaces
  will be appended to *Target to fill the difference. The pointer to *Target
  will be returned.
*/
{ /* Replace */
  int
    T,
    LT;

  for (LT = 0; Target[LT]; LT++);
  if (Position <= LT)
  {
    Position--;
    for (T = 0; Src[T]; T++, Position++)
    {
      Target[Position] = Src[T];
    } /* for T */
    LT--;
    if (Position > LT)
      Target[Position] = 0;
  } /* if Position */
  else
  {
    Position--;
    for (; LT < Position; LT++)
      Target[LT] = ' ';
    for (T = 0; Src[T]; Position++, T++)
      Target[Position] = Src[T];
    Target[Position] = 0;
  } /* if Position else */
  return(Target);
} /* Replace */
```

Sample Usage Source Code

▼

```
/*
  This program will take string A and place string B in it at the
  beginning, middle, and beyond the end of string A by using Replace().
*/

extern unsigned _stklen=16384; /* Minimum recommend stack size */
#include <stdio.h>
#include <math.h>
#include <dos.h>
#include <mem.h>
#include <alloc.h>
#include <ctype.h>
#include <string.h>
```

```
#include <stdlib.h>
#include <plib.h>
#include <plib.glo>


/*****************************************************************************/
main()
{
  char
    A[81] = "",
    B[81] = "";

  Calibrate_Delay();           /* Calibrate delay factor */
  Get_Video_Mode("Video.CFG"); /* Get display adapter type */
  Install_Crit_Error();        /* Set up application critical error handler */
  InputAbsolute=AbortPrint=0;  /* Initialize global variables */

  /* Application code to follow */

  Clr_Scr();
  strcpy(A, "This is an example of Replace ");
  strcpy(B, "Wow");
  printf("%s\n", A);
  Replace(B, A, 1);
  printf("%s\n", A);
  Replace(B, A, 20);
  printf("%s\n", A);
  Replace(B, A, 40);
  printf("%s\n", A);

} /*  main  */
```

Sample Usage Output

▼

```
This is an example of Replace
Wows is an example of Replace
Wows is an example WowReplace
Wows is an example WowReplace          Wow
```

Restore_Screen

Description

▼

Restore_Screen copies the information contained in the specified buffer area of 4000 characters back into video memory. The global variable WaitForRetrace is used to determine if the routine should adjust for possible screen flicker with color systems. A call to Get_Video_Mode must be made prior to calling Restore_Screen. This will initialize the global variables WaitForRetrace and BaseOfScreen.

Routine Declaration

```
void Restore_Screen(char *WinBuff)
```

Passed Variables

***WinBuff String Pointer** A pointer to the char buffer used to contain the stored copy of video memory.

Global Variables

BaseOfScreen Designates the base memory address of the video display memory for the current type of video display. See Get_Video_Mode for the exact calculation and setup for BaseOfScreen.

WaitForRetrace Flags the video display routines to synchronize the display of characters with the video retracing done on color systems. If this synchronization is not done, video flickering may occur during screen updates.

Error Codes/ Messages

None

Discussion

Restore_Screen is primarily used by library routines like Help_File and Calculator that require temporary control of the video screen and must restore the screen to its original condition upon exit. Save_Screen saves both the text and the video attributes attached to each character on the screen. Restore_Screen restores the text in the same manner, so if you assemble data into a buffer area on your own you need to use both video bytes.

Restore_Screen uses the library routine Move_Scrn_Mem to perform the actual restoration. The source is the string pointed to by WinBuff and the destination is the base of video memory, established in the global variable BaseOfScreen. The length of the move is 4000 bytes, the sum of 2000 text bytes and 2000 attribute bytes. Because of the near and far pointer system implemented in Turbo C, the routine has two sections, one for small code model programs and one for large code model programs.

Limitations and Modifications

None

Routine Source Code

```
#include <stddef.h>
#include <dos.h>
```

```
#include <math.h>
#include <string.h>
#include <stdio.h>
#include <stdlib.h>
#include <ctype.h>
#include <plib.h>

extern int
  BaseOfScreen;

void Restore_Screen(char *WinBuff)
/*
  This function will restore the screen saved in the array pointed to
  by *WinBuff.
*/
{ /* Restore_Screen */
#ifdef __SMALL__
  Move_Scrn_Mem(MK_FP((unsigned int)_DS, (unsigned int)WinBuff),
                MK_FP((unsigned int)BaseOfScreen, 0x0000), 4000);
#endif
#ifdef __LARGE__
  Move_Scrn_Mem(WinBuff, MK_FP((unsigned int)BaseOfScreen, 0x0000), 4000);
#endif
} /* Restore_Screen */
```

Sample Usage Source Code

▼

See the sample program for Save_Screen for an example usage of this routine.

Rpt

Description

▼

Rpt creates a string that is composed of a certain number of repetitions of the specified string or character and returns a pointer to the created string.

Routine Declaration

▼

```
char *Rpt(char *RStr,
          char *Buffer,
          int Repts)
```

Passed Variables

▼

***RStr String Pointer** A pointer to the textual value to repeat a specified number of times.

***Buffer String Pointer** A pointer to the string variable that will contain the resulting string.

Repts integer The number of repetitions of the value in Strng to be concatenated together and returned from the function.

Global Variables

▼

None

Error Codes/ Messages

▼

None

Discussion

▼

Rpt is one of the most widely used routines in the library because of its ability to fill in areas of fields and variables. Because Rpt is used so often, the name is short and sweet, saving considerable typing during the creation of applications. Rpt creates repeating strings of a single character or string values. Rpt's most common use is to create a string of spaces to pad variables to a specified length. This can be done in concatenations or in output routines such as Print.

Rpt uses a for loop to repeat the required number of repetitions based on the value passed. The actual insertion is performed in a while loop that is repeated for each occurrence of the for loop. Once the for loop has completed, a null is appended to the end of the new string to terminate the string.

Limitations and Modifications

▼

None

Routine Source Code

▼

```
char *Rpt(char *RStr,
          char *Buffer,
          int Repts)
/*
  This procedure will fill *Buffer with Repts number of *RStr.
  and return the (far) pointer to Buffer.
*/
{ /* Rpt */
  int
    C,
    C1,
    C2;

  for (C = C1 = C2 = 0; C < Repts; C++, C1 = 0)
  {
```

```
    while (RStr[C1])
      {
        Buffer[C2] = RStr[C1];
        C1++;
        C2++;
      } /* while RStr[C1] */
    } /* for C */
  Buffer[C2] = 0;
  return(Buffer);
} /* Rpt */
```

Sample Usage Source Code

▼

```
/*
  This program will use Rpt to print out 60 asters and 20 'DOCs.
*/

extern unsigned _stklen=16384; /* Minimum recommend stack size */
#include <stdio.h>
#include <math.h>
#include <dos.h>
#include <mem.h>
#include <alloc.h>
#include <ctype.h>
#include <string.h>
#include <stdlib.h>
#include <plib.h>
#include <plib.glo>


/****************************************************************************/
main()
{
  char
    RStr [81] = "" ;

  Calibrate_Delay();            /* Calibrate delay factor */
  Get_Video_Mode("Video.CFG"); /* Get display adapter type */
  Install_Crit_Error();         /* Set up application critical error handler */
  InputAbsolute=AbortPrint=0;  /* Initialize global variables */

  /* Application code to follow */

  Clr_Scr();
  printf("%s\n", Rpt ("*", RStr, 60) );
  printf("%s\n", Rpt ("DOC", RStr, 20) );

}  /*  main  */
```

Sample Usage Output

▼

```
************************************************************
DOCDOCDOCDOCDOCDOCDOCDOCDOCDOCDOCDOCDOCDOCDOCDOCDOCDOCDOCDOC
```

Save_Screen

Description

▼

Save_Screen moves the information contained in video memory to a specified memory buffer. The global variable WaitForRetrace determines if the routine should adjust for possible screen flicker with color systems. A call to Get-_Video_Mode must be made at some point prior to calling Restore_Screen. This initializes the global variables WaitForRetrace and BaseOfScreen.

Routine Declaration

▼

```
void Save_Screen(char *WinBuff)
```

Passed Variables

▼

***WinBuff String Pointer** A pointer to the memory area that is to contain a copy of the screen memory. The memory buffer must be large enough to accommodate 4000 characters of data.

Global Variables

▼

BaseOfScreen Designates the base memory address of the video display memory for the current type of video display. See Get_Video_Mode for the exact calculation and setup for BaseOfScreen.

WaitForRetrace Flags the video display routines to synchronize the display of characters with the video retracing done on color systems. If this synchronization is not accomplished, video flickering may occur during screen updates.

Error Codes/ Messages

▼

None

Discussion

▼

Save_Screen is primarily used by library routines such as Help_File and Calculator that require temporary control of the video screen and must restore the screen to its original condition upon exit. Save_Screen saves both the text and the video attributes attached to each character on the screen. Restore_Screen restores the text in the same manner, so if you assemble data into memory buffers on your own you need to use both video bytes.

Save_Screen uses the library routine Move_Scrn_Mem to perform the actual movement to the storage buffer. The source is the video memory and the destination is the memory area pointed to by WinBuff. The length of the move is 4000 bytes, the sum of 2000 text bytes and 2000 attribute bytes. Because of the near and far pointer system implemented in Turbo C, the routine has two sections of the move, one for small code model programs and one for large code model programs.

Limitations and Modifications

▼

None

Routine Source Code

▼

```
#include <stddef.h>
#include <dos.h>
#include <math.h>
#include <string.h>
#include <stdio.h>
#include <stdlib.h>
#include <ctype.h>
#include <plib.h>

extern int
  BaseOfScreen;

void Save_Screen(char *WinBuff)
/*
  This function will save the entire text screen into the array pointed to
  by *WinBuff.
*/
{ /* Save_Screen */
#ifdef __SMALL__
  Move_Scrn_Mem(MK_FP((unsigned int)BaseOfScreen, 0x0000),
                MK_FP((unsigned int)_DS, (unsigned int)WinBuff), 4000);
#endif
#ifdef __LARGE__
  Move_Scrn_Mem(MK_FP((unsigned int)BaseOfScreen, 0x0000), WinBuff, 4000);
#endif
} /* Save_Screen */
```

Sample Usage Source Code

▼

```
/*
  This program will write text to the screen, use Save_Screen to save the
  screen, clear the screen, then use Restore_Screen to bring back the original.
*/
```

```
extern unsigned _stklen=16384; /* Minimum recommend stack size */
#include <stdio.h>
#include <math.h>
#include <dos.h>
#include <mem.h>
#include <alloc.h>
#include <ctype.h>
#include <string.h>
#include <stdlib.h>
#include <plib.h>
#include <plib.glo>


/*****************************************************************************/
main()
{
  char
    Check = ' ',
    WinBuff[4000] = "";
  int
    Cn = 0;

  Calibrate_Delay();            /* Calibrate delay factor */
  Get_Video_Mode("Video.CFG"); /* Get display adapter type */
  Install_Crit_Error();         /* Set up application critical error handler */
  InputAbsolute=AbortPrint=0;  /* Initialize global variables */

  /* Application code to follow */

  Clr_Scr();
  for(Cn = 1; Cn <= 20; Cn++)
    printf("This is to fill up the screen for 20 lines. \n");
  printf("This is the original screen. Press <RETURN> to save it.\n");
  scanf("%c", &Check);

  Save_Screen(WinBuff);
  Clr_Scr();
  printf("The screen has been cleared!!!!!!!!! \n\n\n");
  printf("Press <RETURN> to restore the original screen. \n");
  scanf("%c", &Check);
  Restore_Screen(WinBuff);

  Goto_XY(1, 24);

} /*  main  */
```

Sample Usage Output

▼

```
This is to fill up the screen for 20 lines.
This is to fill up the screen for 20 lines.
```

```
This is to fill up the screen for 20 lines.
This is to fill up the screen for 20 lines.
This is to fill up the screen for 20 lines.
This is to fill up the screen for 20 lines.
This is to fill up the screen for 20 lines.
This is to fill up the screen for 20 lines.
This is to fill up the screen for 20 lines.
This is to fill up the screen for 20 lines.
This is to fill up the screen for 20 lines.
This is to fill up the screen for 20 lines.
This is to fill up the screen for 20 lines.
This is to fill up the screen for 20 lines.
This is to fill up the screen for 20 lines.
This is to fill up the screen for 20 lines.
This is to fill up the screen for 20 lines.
This is to fill up the screen for 20 lines.
This is to fill up the screen for 20 lines.
This is to fill up the screen for 20 lines.
This is the original screen. Press <RETURN> to save it.


The screen has been cleared!!!!!!!!!


Press <RETURN> to restore the original screen.
```

Scroll_Mess

Description ▼

Scroll_Mess horizontally scrolls a line of text from right to left inside of a defined single line window. You can define the attributes for the text and designate whether the text should stop in the window or scroll out the left side of the window.

Routine Declaration ▼

```
void Scroll_Mess(int XL,
                 int XR,
                 int Y,
                 char Atr,
                 char StopEOL,
                 char *Mess)
```

Passed Variables ▼

XL integer The left horizontal column number for the scroll window. The value for XL must be at least one less than the value for XR. Valid values are 1 through 79.

XR integer The right horizontal column number for the scroll window. The value for XR must be at least one greater than XL. Valid values for XR are 2 through 80.

Y integer The vertical position on the screen for the one-line window used to display the message. Valid values for Y are 1 through 25.

Atr char The video attribute to be used for the displayed text.

StopEOL integer If this value is true (1), the text stops when it reaches the left side of the window. Any other value for StopIt causes the text to continue to scroll off the left side of the window.

***Mess String Pointer** A pointer to the textual message scrolled through the defined window.

Global Variables

▼

None

Error Codes/ Messages

▼

None

Discussion

▼

Scroll_Mess displays attention-getting messages on the screen. The text scrolls from right to left in marquee style. Scroll_Mess is particularly useful in title pages and demonstrations where you need to get the user's attention.

Scroll_Mess first calculates a delay factor proportional to the size of the line window used. This allows the user more time to read text in a small line window. After the delay is set, *Mess is checked to ensure that a real message was passed. Then a for loop and F_Write are used to display the actual message using the calculated delay between writes. Like Cnvg_Mess, this routine was primarily designed to provide special effects.

Limitations and Modifications

▼

One primary limitation of Scroll_Mess is the line window size passed by the call. If you specify a window too small, the message wil be difficult to read.

You may want to modify the routine to have a passed value for the delay instead of the calculated value. This provides additional control but requires more thought in each call to the routine.

Routine Source Code

▼

```
#include <math.h>
#include <string.h>
```

```
#include <stdio.h>
#include <stdlib.h>
#include <ctype.h>
#include <plib.h>

extern char
  Normal,
  Reverse,
  VidHigh;

void Scroll_Mess(int XL,
                 int XR,
                 int Y,
                 char Atr,
                 char StopEOL,
                 char *Mess)
/*
  This routine will display Mess in a marquee style (scrolling from
  right to left) in line Y between XL and XR (XL must always be at least
  1 less than XR) in Atr attribute. If StopEOL is true (1), the last
  displayable portion of *Mess will remain on the screen, any other value
  for StopEOL and the entire *Mess will be scrolled through until it is all
  gone. If *Mess is longer than what will fit in the space defined by
  XL & XR then it will be scrolled all the way through as it would if
  StopEOL was set to something other than 1.
*/
{ /* Scroll_Mess */
  char
    TStr1[85],
    TStr2[85],
    TStr3[85];

  int
    Lim,
    I,
    Len,
    Bot,
    Dly;


  Len = XR - XL;
  Dly = 20 + (int)( ((float)(300 / Len)) * (float)3);
  if (StopEOL != 1)
    StopEOL = 2;
  if (Mess[0])
  {
    Bot = 1;
    Lim = StopEOL * strlen(Mess) + ((strlen(Mess) < Len) *
```

```
          (Len - strlen(Mess)));
    for (I = 1; I <= Lim; I++)
    {
      if (I > Len)
        Bot++;
      F_Write(XL, Y, Atr, RJ(LJ(Copy(Mess, Bot, I, TStr1), TStr2, I),
              TStr3, Len));
      Delay(Dly);
    } /* for I */
  } /* if Scroll_Mess */
  else
    F_Write(XL, Y, Normal, Rpt(" ", TStr1, Len));
} /* Scroll_Mess */
```

Sample Usage Source Code

```
/*
  This program will scroll text through three different line sizes.
  The first time it will scroll text entirely through the line,
  the second time it will leave the line shown. This is primarily a
  special effects routine.
*/

extern unsigned _stklen=16384; /* Minimum recommend stack size */
#include <stdio.h>
#include <math.h>
#include <dos.h>
#include <mem.h>
#include <alloc.h>
#include <ctype.h>
#include <string.h>
#include <stdlib.h>
#include <plib.h>
#include <plib.glo>


/*****************************************************************************/
main()
{
  int
    C = 0;

  Calibrate_Delay();           /* Calibrate delay factor */
  Get_Video_Mode("Video.CFG"); /* Get display adapter type */
  Install_Crit_Error();        /* Set up application critical error handler */
  InputAbsolute=AbortPrint=0;  /* Initialize global variables */

  /* Application code to follow */
```

```
  Clr_Scr();

  for (; C <= 1; C++)
  {
    Scroll_Mess(1, 70, 3, Normal, C, "This is a test of Scroll_Mess.");
    Scroll_Mess(1, 35, 5, Reverse, C, "This is a test of Scroll_Mess.");
    Scroll_Mess(1, 10, 7, VidHigh, C, "This is a test of Scroll_Mess.");
  }
  Goto_XY (1, 24); /*Don't let DOS trample screen when done */

} /*  main  */
```

Sample Usage Output

▼

```
This is a test of Scroll_Mess.

This is a test of Scroll_Mess.
```

Set_Window_Attr

Description

▼

Set_Window_Attr changes the video attributes for a block of text on the screen defined by the passed window limits—its starting horizontal and vertical positions and its width and length.

Routine Declaration

▼

```
void Set_Window_Attr(char Atr,
                     int  X,
                     int  Y,
                     int  Wid,
                     int  Len)
```

Passed Variables

▼

Atr char The video attribute to be used to change the defined screen window.

X integer The horizontal position of the upper left corner of the window. Valid values for X are 1 through 80.

Y integer The vertical position for the upper left corner of the window. Valid values for Y are 1 through 25.

Wid integer The horizontal width of the window. Valid values for Wid are 1 through 80.

Len integer The vertical length of the window. Valid values for Len are 1 through 25.

Global Variables

▼

None

Error Codes/ Messages

▼

None

Discussion

▼

Set_Window_Attr provides a high-performance method of changing the video attributes for portions of video memory. This can be used to intensify or subdue the current working area of an entry form. With some thought, numerous uses can be derived for Set_Window_Attr in your applications.

Set_Window_Attr starts by decrementing the window width and length so the offsets start at zero instead of one. Next a for loop is used to step through the proper number of lines required for the specified window length and a Move_Scrn_Mem call is used to move the specified attribute to screen memory. Because the pointers are different for the memory models, the Move_Scrn_Mem call is conditioned for a small and large code model.

Limitations and Modifications

▼

Set_Window_Attr does not provide any limit checking on the window dimensions passed. Without the error checking, there is a possibility of writing to memory outside of the video memory area. This can cause problems and you should weigh the value of error checking against increased performance in your application.

Routine Source Code

▼

```
#include <Dos.H>
#include <math.h>
#include <string.h>
#include <stdio.h>
#include <stdlib.h>
#include <ctype.h>
#include <plib.h>

extern int
  BaseOfScreen;

void Set_Window_Attr(char Atr,
                     int  X,
                     int  Y,
```

```
                    int Wid,
                    int  Len)
/*
  This function will change the attributes in screen memory of the
  window defined by the parameters X, Y, Wid, Len.
*/
{ /* Set_Window_Attr */
  union HiLoPtr
  {
    char far *FPtr;
    unsigned int Words[2];
  }; /* union */

  char
    far *LL;
  union HiLoPtr
    ScOfs;
  unsigned int
    TmpOfs,
    CX,
    CY;


  ScOfs.Words[1] = BaseOfScreen;
  Wid--;
  Len--;
  for (CY = Y; CY <= Y + Len; CY++)
  {
    TmpOfs = ((CY - 1) * 160) + ((X - 1) * 2) + 1;
    for (CX = 0; CX <= Wid; CX++)
    {
      ScOfs.Words[0] = TmpOfs + (CX << 1);
#ifdef __SMALL__
      LL = MK_FP(_DS, (unsigned int) & Atr);
      Move_Scrn_Mem(LL, ScOfs.FPtr, 1);
#endif
#ifdef __LARGE__
      Move_Scrn_Mem(&Atr, ScOfs.FPtr, 1);
#endif
    } /* for CX */
  } /* for CY */
} /* Set_Window_Attr */
```

Sample Usage Source Code

▼

```
/*
  This program will write text onto the screen, then it will use the
```

```
  procedure Set_Window_Attr to change the background of the text in a
  window starting at 1,1 that is 60 wide and 10 deep from Normal to reverse
  and back again until the user presses a key.
*/

extern unsigned _stklen=16384; /* Minimum recommend stack size */
#include <stdio.h>
#include <math.h>
#include <dos.h>
#include <mem.h>
#include <alloc.h>
#include <ctype.h>
#include <string.h>
#include <stdlib.h>
#include <plib.h>
#include <plib.glo>


/****************************************************************************/
main()
{
  int
    C = 0;

  Calibrate_Delay();            /* Calibrate delay factor */
  Get_Video_Mode("Video.CFG"); /* Get display adapter type */
  Install_Crit_Error();         /* Set up application critical error handler */
  InputAbsolute=AbortPrint=0;  /* Initialize global variables */

  /* Application code to follow */

  Clr_Scr();
  for (C = 1; C <= 10; C++)
    printf("This text will appear and change from reverse to Normal.\n");
  do
  {
    Set_Window_Attr(Reverse, 1, 1, 60, 10);
    Delay(500);
    Set_Window_Attr(Normal, 1, 1, 60, 10);
    Delay(500);
  }
  while (!Look_One_Char());

  Goto_XY(1, 24); /*Don't let DOS trample screen */
  Get_One_Char(); /*Remove char waiting in keyboard buffer*/

} /*  main  */
```

Sample Usage Output

▼

```
This text will appear and change from reverse to Normal.
This text will appear and change from reverse to Normal.
This text will appear and change from reverse to Normal.
This text will appear and change from reverse to Normal.
This text will appear and change from reverse to Normal.
This text will appear and change from reverse to Normal.
This text will appear and change from reverse to Normal.
This text will appear and change from reverse to Normal.
This text will appear and change from reverse to Normal.
This text will appear and change from reverse to Normal.
```

Show_Dir

Description

▼

Show_Dir provides an easy method for displaying directories and allowing a user to pick files from the list if necessary.

Routine Declaration

▼

```
char Show_Dir(char *FName)
```

Passed Variables

▼

***FName String Pointer** A pointer to the string that contains the desired path and filename, including wildcards, for the directory to be displayed.

Global Variables

▼

CurKey Contains either a 13 decimal (Enter key) if a carriage return is pressed, or a 27 decimal (Escape key) if the escape is pressed.

Error Codes/ Messages

▼

```
Searching and sorting directory information, please wait...
```

This message is displayed while the directory listing is being assembled.

```
Bad key pressed
```

This error message is displayed when an invalid key is pressed by the user.

```
Not enough memory to show directory
```

This error message appears when there is not enough far heap memory available to load the directory listing.

```
No file(s) or path not found - press any key
```

This error message appears when the specified file or path, in FName, has no matching files or does not exist.

Discussion

▼

Show_Dir provides an easy transparent method for scanning and selecting filenames from file directories. The routine accepts a filename or wildcard set and path name for the desired group of filenames. All subdirectories in the listing are shown with an asterisk (*) in front of the subdirectory name. The filename being pointed to is shown in reverse video, and when a return or escape is pressed, the filename currently highlighted is returned with the full path and CurKey set to the keystroke. CurKey can then be checked to determine if the filename is used or discarded. If a subdirectory is selected, the subdirectory name is appended to the path passed in FName and the string *.* is appended after the subdirectory name.

Show_Dir begins by saving the current screen and the current cursor setting and turning off the cursor. Then, the path is extracted from FName and the first directory entry is located using Turbo C's routine findfirst. If findfirst is unsuccessful, a message informs the user and the routine exits, returning false (0).

If findfirst is successful, the directory entries fitting the specification are counted using the Turbo C routine findnext. This number allocates the required memory for the listing. If the allocation is unsuccessful, the user is informed of the problem and the routine exits, returning false (0).

After the allocation, the list of files is loaded and sorted. The list is then displayed and the user begins selection of a desired filename. When the user presses escape or enter, the current highlighted filename is appended to the path and FName is set to the assembled string. The original screen and cursor are restored and the routine returns true (1).

Limitations and Modifications

▼

A suggested modification for Show_Dir is implementation of a more efficient sorting method for the list. Currently, Show_Dir uses a simple bubble sort for this operation. One option would be to sort a list of pointers rather than the text list.

Routine Source Code

▼

```
#include <math.h>
#include <mem.h>
#include <alloc.h>
#include <dos.h>
```

```
#include <dir.h>
#include <string.h>
#include <stdio.h>
#include <stdlib.h>
#include <ctype.h>
#include <plib.h>

extern char
  Green,
  Blue,
  Reverse,
  VidHigh,
  Normal;

extern int
  CurKey;

char Show_Dir(char *FName)
/*
  This routine will save the current screen and cursor, then draw a
  window in which files can be viewed and selected.  When Return or Esc
  is entered, the file currently selected will be concatenated onto the
  Path and returned.  If the directory procedure was successful, it
  will return a 1, if it wasn't, e.g., there was not enough memory to
  show the directory, it will return a 0.
*/
{ /* Show_Dir */
  char
    Done,
    Stat,
    *FN,
    *Blk,
    *SFN,
    *CFN,
    *TFN,
    TStr[81],
    OldScreen[4000],
    PathStr[60];

  int
    C,
    X,
    Y,
    FNum,
    OldCursor;

  struct
  {
```

```
  char
    Unused1[21],
    Attr,
    Unused2[8],
    Name[13];
} FInfo;

Save_Screen(OldScreen);
OldCursor = Cursor_Off();

if ((Pos('\\', FName)) || (Pos(':', FName)))
{
  if (Pos('\\', FName))
  {
    for (C = strlen(FName) - 1; (FName[C] != '\\'); C--);
    Copy(FName, 1, C+1, PathStr);
  }
  else
    Copy(FName, 1, 2, PathStr);
}
else
  PathStr[0] = 0;

if (!findfirst(FName, &FInfo, FA_DIREC))
{
  Message("Searching and Sorting Directory Information, Please wait...");
  FNum = 1;
  while (!findnext(&FInfo))
    FNum++;

  Blk = FN = farmalloc(13 * FNum);
  if (FN != NULL)
  {
    /*Load all the files*/
    CFN = FN;
    if (!findfirst(FName, &FInfo, 0))
    {
      do
      {
        strcpy(CFN, FInfo.Name);
        CFN += 13;
      }while (!findnext(&FInfo));
    }
    if (!findfirst(FName, &FInfo, FA_DIREC))
    {
      do
      {
        if (FInfo.Attr == FA_DIREC)
```

```
        {
          strcpy(CFN, "*");
          strcat(CFN, FInfo.Name);
          CFN += 13;
        }
      }while (!findnext(&FInfo));
    }
    /* Sort names (Bubble sort)*/
    CFN = FN;
    FNum--;
    while (((CFN - FN) / 13) < FNum)
    {
      if (strcmp(CFN, CFN+13) > 0)
      {
        strcpy(TStr, CFN);
        strcpy(CFN, CFN+13);
        strcpy(CFN + 13, TStr);
        CFN -= 13 * (CFN != FN);
      }
      else
        CFN += 13;
    }/*while ((CFN - FN / 13) <= FNum)*/
    FNum++;
    Message("");
    if (!strcmp(FN, "*."))
    {
      FN += 13;
      FNum--;
      if (!strcmp(FN, "*..."))
      {
        FN += 13;
        FNum--;
      }
    }
    TFN = SFN = CFN = FN;
    /*Display all files and allow selection*/
    Draw_Frame(2, 8, 78, 16, 2, "RN", "", Blue);
    sprintf(TStr, "Directory of %s    %d files", FName, FNum);
    Draw_Frame(10, 10, 60, 9, 1, "NR", TStr, Blue);
    Draw_Frame(3, 20, 76, 3, 2, "HN", "", Blue);
    F_Write(6, 21, Normal,
    "<Up>, <Down>, <Right>, <Left> - movements / <Enter>, <Esc> - return");
    Clear_Frame(Green, 12, 12, 56, 5);
    TFN = CFN;
    for (Y = 12; ((TFN - FN) / 13 != FNum) && (Y <= 16); Y++)
    {
      for (X = 12; ((TFN - FN) / 13 != FNum) && (X <= 54); X += 14)
      {
```

```
      F_Write(X, Y, Blend(Normal), TFN);
      TFN += 13;
    }
  }
  Done = 0;
  while (!Done)
  {
    /* Allow selection */
    F_Write( ((((SFN - CFN) / 13) % 4) * 14) + 12,
         (((SFN - CFN) / 13) / 4) + 12,
         Reverse, SFN);
    Get_One_Char();
    Message("");
    F_Write( ((((SFN - CFN) / 13) % 4) * 14) + 12,
         (((SFN - CFN) / 13) / 4) + 12,
         Blend(Normal), SFN);
    switch (CurKey)
    {
      case -75: /*Left*/
        if ((((SFN - CFN) / 13) % 4) != 0)
          SFN -= 13;
      break;
      case -77: /*Right*/
        if (((((SFN - CFN) / 13) % 4) != 3) &&
          (((SFN - FN) + 13) / 13 < FNum))
          SFN += 13;
      break;
      case -72: /*Up*/
        if (((SFN - CFN) / 13 <= 3) && (CFN != FN))
        {
          CFN -= 52;
            Clear_Frame(Green, 12, 12, 56, 5);
            TFN = CFN;
            for (Y = 12; ((TFN - FN) / 13 != FNum) && (Y <= 16); Y++)
            {
              for (X = 12; ((TFN - FN) / 13 != FNum) && (X <= 54); X += 14)
              {
                F_Write(X, Y, Blend(Normal), TFN);
                TFN += 13;
              }
            }
        }
        if ((SFN - FN) / 13 > 3)
          SFN -= 52;
      break;
      case -80: /*Down*/
        if (((SFN - CFN) / 13 >= 16) && (((CFN - FN)+ 260) / 13 <= FNum))
        {
```

```
          CFN += 52;
            Clear_Frame(Green, 12, 12, 56, 5);
            TFN = CFN;
            for (Y = 12; ((TFN - FN) / 13 != FNum) && (Y <= 16); Y++)
            {
              for (X = 12; ((TFN - FN) / 13 != FNum) && (X <= 54); X += 14)
              {
                F_Write(X, Y, Blend(Normal), TFN);
                TFN += 13;
              }
            }
        }
        if (((SFN - FN) + 52) / 13 < FNum)
          SFN += 52;
        else
            SFN = FN + (13 * (FNum - 1));
      break;
      case 13: /*Enter*/
      case 27: /*Esc*/
        Done = 1;
        if (SFN[0] != '*')
            strcat(PathStr, SFN);
        else
        {
          strcat(PathStr, SFN+1);
          strcat(PathStr, "\\*.*");
        }
          strcpy(FName, PathStr);
        Stat = 1;
      break;
      default:
        Lo_Mess("Bad Key Pressed");
    }/* switch(CurKey) */
  }/* while !Done*/
  farfree(Blk);
 }
 else
 {
   Hi_Mess("Not enough memory to show directory");
   Delay(2000);
   Stat = 0;
 }
}/* if findfirst */
else
{
  Lo_Mess("No file(s) or path not found - press any key.");
  Get_One_Char();
  Stat = 0;
```

```
  }
  Restore_Screen(OldScreen);
  Cursor_On(OldCursor);
  return(Stat);
} /* Show_Dir */
```

Sample Usage Source Code

▼

```
extern unsigned _stklen=16384; /* Minimum recommend stack size,
                                  32768 minimum recommended for
                                  use with Btrieve */
#include <stdio.h>
#include <math.h>
#include <dos.h>
#include <mem.h>
#include <alloc.h>
#include <ctype.h>
#include <string.h>
#include <stdlib.h>
#include <plib.h>
#include <plib.glo>
/* #include <plib.btv> */ /* - remove comment for Btrieve usage*/

/****************************************************************************/
main()
{
  /* Application variables declarations */
  char
    TStr[81];

  /* Initialize library values */
  Calibrate_Delay();           /* Calibrate delay factor */
  Get_Video_Mode("Video.CFG"); /* Get display adapter type */
  Install_Crit_Error();        /* Set up application critical error handler */
  InputAbsolute=AbortPrint=0;  /* Initialize global variables */
  Clr_Scr();
  /* Application code to follow */
  CurKey = 0;
  TStr[0] = 0;
  while (CurKey != 27)
  {
    Prompt(1, 1, Normal, "Enter Path: ", "A65,", TStr);
    if (CurKey != 27)
      Show_Dir(TStr);
  }
  /* End of application code */
  Clr_Scr();
} /*main*/
```

Sample Usage Output

```
Enter Path: c:\*.*
```

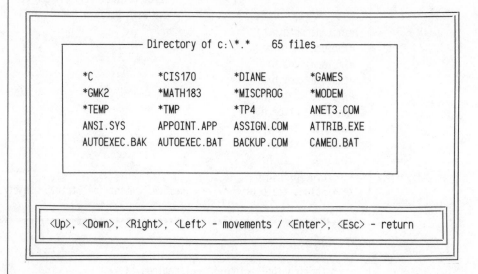

```
             Directory of c:\*.*     65 files

  *C            *CIS170       *DIANE        *GAMES
  *GMK2         *MATH183      *MISCPROG     *MODEM
  *TEMP         *TMP          *TP4          ANET3.COM
  ANSI.SYS      APPOINT.APP   ASSIGN.COM    ATTRIB.EXE
  AUTOEXEC.BAK  AUTOEXEC.BAT  BACKUP.COM    CAMEO.BAT

<Up>, <Down>, <Right>, <Left> - movements / <Enter>, <Esc> - return
```

Sound

Description

Sound provides the computer speaker with a specific tone frequency. The tone continues until the library routine No_Sound is called to disable the speaker.

Routine Declaration

```
void Sound(int Freq)
```

Passed Variables

Freq integer The frequency of the tone to be enabled on the speaker.

Global Variables

None

Error Codes/ Messages

▼

None

Discussion

▼

Sound provides an audible tone generation from within Turbo C. If you have Turbo C version 1.5 or later, the library included with version 1.5 has other versions of Sound and No_Sound which function identically to the routines in this library. If you don't have version 1.5, you can use these routines and the calls will be compatible when you upgrade to the newer version of Turbo C.

Sound starts by calculating the timer frequency, then uses the Turbo C routine outportb to set up the 8253 Timer Chip for programming. The 8253 Timer Chip is programmed through the port addresses 43 hex and 42 hex. These addresses are then used to send the low- and high-order bytes of the calculated frequency to the 8253. After the 8253 is loaded, the speaker is turned on with the last outportb call.

Limitations and Modifications

▼

None

Routine Source Code

▼

```
#include <dos.h>

void Sound(int Freq)
/*
  This procedure will make the speaker produce a Freq frequency tone
  until the procedure No_Sound() is called.
*/
{ /* Sound */
  int
    Count;

  Count = 1193280 / Freq;
  /* get timer ready to program */
  outportb(0x43, 0x0306);
  /* output lower order of count */
  outportb(0x42, Count&0x00ff);
  /* high order */
  outportb(0x42, Count >> 8);
  /* turn speaker on */
  outportb(0x61, (inportb(0x61) | 0x03));
} /* Sound */
```

Sample Usage Source Code

▼

For a sample use of this routine, see the library routine Beep_Bomb.

Str_IsInt

Description

▼

Str_IsInt is used to determine if the specified string is a proper representation of an integer value. The routine will return true (1) if the string is a valid representation and false (0) if it is invalid.

Routine Declaration

▼

```
char Str_IsInt(char *PNum)
```

Passed Variables

▼

***PNum String Pointer** A pointer to the string variable that contains the string to be validated.

Global Variables

▼

None

Error Codes/ Messages

▼

None

Discussion

▼

Str_IsInt provides a means of ensuring that the string representation of an integer does not contain any invalid characters for an integer conversion.

Str_IsInt uses a for loop to step through the specified string searching for characters that are in the range of ASCII 48 to ASCII 57. If the character is not within the range, the for loop terminates, and the counter C is checked to see if it is zero. If it is not zero, the entire string has failed the range test and Str_IsInt returns false (0); otherwise, true (1) is returned.

Limitations and Modifications

▼

Str_IsInt does not determine if the string contains an integer that is too large to be interpreted by Turbo C. You may want to add more checking to the routine for out-of-range integer values.

Routine Source Code

▼

```
char Str_IsInt(char *PNum)
/*
  This function will return true (1) if the string *PNum contains only an
  integer. It will return false (0) if *PNum is null.
```

```
*/
{ /* Str_IsInt */
  char
    BInt;

  int
    C;

  BInt = 1;
  for (C = 0; PNum[C]; C++)
  {
    BInt = (BInt && (PNum[C] > 47 && PNum[C] < 58));
  } /* for C */
  if (C != 0)
    return(BInt);
  else
    return(0);
} /* Str_IsInt */
```

Sample Usage Source Code

▼

```
/*
  This program will check whether or not a string the user inputs
  is an integer.
*/

extern unsigned _stklen=16384; /* Minimum recommend stack size */
#include <stdio.h>
#include <math.h>
#include <dos.h>
#include <mem.h>
#include <alloc.h>
#include <ctype.h>
#include <string.h>
#include <stdlib.h>
#include <plib.h>
#include <plib.glo>

/*****************************************************************************/
main()
{
  char
    Check[81] = "";

  Calibrate_Delay();            /* Calibrate delay factor */
  Get_Video_Mode("Video.CFG"); /* Get display adapter type */
  Install_Crit_Error();         /* Set up application critical error handler */
  InputAbsolute=AbortPrint=0;   /* Initialize global variables */
```

```
/* Application code to follow */

Clr_Scr();
printf("\n\n\n  The following will check if the string you enter is an\n");
printf("  integer or not.\n");
printf("\n\n\n          Enter a string: ");
scanf("%s", Check);
if (Str_IsInt(Check))
  printf("\n\n\n          This is an integer.\n");
else
  printf("\n\n\n          This is not an integer.\n");

} /*  main  */
```

Sample Usage Output

▼

```
The following will check if the string you enter is an
integer or not.



       Enter a string: 123409.3



       This is not an integer.
```

Str_Pos

Description

▼

Str_Pos finds the first occurrence of a string in another specified string value. When the string is found, Str_Pos returns the position in the string, with the first character represented as position 1. If the string is not found, Str_Pos returns zero.

Routine Declaration

▼

```
int Str_Pos(char *SearchStr,
            char *TargStr,
            char CaseFlag)
```

Passed Variables

▼

***SearchStr String Pointer** A pointer to the string to be located in the string value pointed to by *TargStr.

***TargStr String Pointer** A pointer to the string to be scanned for an occurrence of *SearchStr.

CaseFlag integer This integer determines if the search is case-sensitive. If CaseFlag is 1, the case of the letters will not matter in the search.

Global Variables

▼

None

Error Codes/ Messages

▼

None

Discussion

▼

Str_Pos provides an easier method of finding the position of a character within a string than those provided with Turbo C. Like Pos, the routine is simple to use. Str_Pos returns the character's position based on 1 as the first available position.

Str_Pos starts by determining if the first character of the string is the end of the string (a null). If so, Str_Pos returns 0. Otherwise, Str_Pos begins the search for the specified substring. The search is performed through a while loop that ends when either string's null terminator is reached. If the target string's null is reached, the substring is found and Str_Pos returns the starting position of the substring. If the string being searched ends first, the substring was not found and Str_Pos returns 0.

Limitations and Modifications

▼

Str_Pos has one primary limitation—it only finds the first occurrence of the substring. If you want to find all occurrences, you may want to create a new routine that uses Str_Pos and a temporary copy of the string that can be deleted to find the next occurrence.

Routine Source Code

▼

```
#include <ctype.h>

int Str_Pos(char *SearchStr,
            char *TargStr,
            char CaseFlag)
/*
  This function is similar to Pos except that this function will search for
  one string in another and, if CaseFlag is 1, case will not matter.
*/
{ /* Str_Pos */
  int
```

```
    C,
    C1;

  C = C1 = 0;
  if (SearchStr[0] == 0 || TargStr[0] == 0)
  {
    return(0);
  } /* if SearchStr[0] */
  else
  {
    while (TargStr[C] && SearchStr[C1])
    {
      if (CaseFlag)
      {
        if (toupper(TargStr[C]) == toupper(SearchStr[C1]))
          C1++;
        else
          C1 = 0;
        C++;
      } /* if CaseFlag */
      else
      {
        if (TargStr[C] == SearchStr[C1])
          C1++;
        else
          C1 = 0;
        C++;
      } /* if CaseFlag else */
    } /* while TargStr[0] */
    if (SearchStr[C1] == 0)
      return(C - C1 + 1);
    else
      return(0);
  } /* if SearchStr[0] else */
} /* Str_Pos */
```

Sample Usage Source Code

```
/*
  This program will use Str_Pos() to find out the position at which
  the first string is contained inside the second string.
*/

extern unsigned _stklen=16384; /* Minimum recommend stack size */
#include <stdio.h>
#include <math.h>
#include <dos.h>
#include <mem.h>
```

```
#include <alloc.h>
#include <ctype.h>
#include <string.h>
#include <stdlib.h>
#include <plib.h>
#include <plib.glo>


/*****************************************************************************/
main()
{
  char
    Str1[81] = "",
    Str2[81] = "";

  Calibrate_Delay();            /* Calibrate delay factor */
  Get_Video_Mode("Video.CFG"); /* Get display adapter type */
  Install_Crit_Error();         /* Set up application critical error handler */
  InputAbsolute=AbortPrint=0;  /* Initialize global variables */

  /* Application code to follow */

  Clr_Scr();
  printf("\n\nNow please enter two strings. \n\n\n");
  printf("\n\nThe first string:  ");
  gets(Str1);
  printf("\n\nThe second string:  ");
  gets(Str2);

  if (Str_Pos(Str1, Str2, 0))
  {
    printf("\n\n\n\nThe second string contains the first from the\n");
    printf("character #%d.\n", Str_Pos(Str1,Str2,0));
  }
  else
    printf ("\n\n\n\nThe second string does not contain the first one.\n");

} /*  main  */
```

Sample Usage Output

▼

```
Now please enter two strings.




The first string:  test
```

```
The second string:  This is a test of Str_Pos
```

```
The second string contains the first from the
character #11.
```

Time_Add

Description

▼

Time_Add adds a specified number of hours to a time passed in a 24-hour format HHMM. (HH contains the hour and MM contains the minutes.) The number of hours to be added are in decimal format. For example, to add 1 hour and 30 minutes, pass 1.5.

Routine Declaration

▼

```
char *Time_Add(char  *Time,
               float Hrs,
               char  *Buffer)
```

Passed Variables

▼

***Time String Pointer** A pointer to the time of day to be added to the associated number of hours. The format for the hours is HHMM, where HH is the hour of the day in the range of 0 through 24 and MM is the minutes of the hour in the range of 0 through 59.

Hrs float The number of hours to be added to the time passed in Time.

***Buffer String Pointer** A pointer to the string variable that will contain the resulting string.

Global Variables

▼

None

Error Codes/ Messages

▼

None

Discussion

▼

Time_Add provides an easy means of determining the ending time of an event when the start time and duration are known. This is useful in applications that have to provide appointment or event scheduling.

Time_Add converts the time passed to a float number with the integer portion containing the hours and the fractional portion containing the hundredths of an hour, based on the minutes. The number of hours passed are then added to the converted time and the new time is checked to see if it wraps past midnight (24.00). If so, the time is adjusted for the new day. The float number representation is then translated back to the four-position string format and returned.

Limitations and Modifications

▼

If you pass a time greater than 2400, Time_Add will only compensate for the value after the addition of the hours passed. The resulting time may not be correct. You can compensate for this by adding additional error checking into Time_Add or in your application prior to calling Time_Add.

Routine Source Code

▼

```
#include <math.h>
#include <dos.h>
#include <string.h>
#include <stdio.h>
#include <stdlib.h>
#include <ctype.h>
#include <plib.h>

char *Time_Add(char *Time,
               float Hrs,
               char *Buffer)
/*
  This routine will accept a Time in the 24-hour format of HHMM and Hrs
  in terms of hours, e.g., 1.25 hours, and add the hours to the time,
  returning a pointer to *Buffer with the resulting time (e.g., "1330"
  Time_Add("1300", 0.5);).
*/
{ /* Time_Add */
  float
    TimeHours;

  char
    TStr1[15],
    TStr2[15];

  TimeHours = atof(Copy(Time, 1, 2, TStr1)) +
              (atof(Copy(Time, 3, 2, TStr2)) / 60);
  TimeHours += Hrs;
  if (TimeHours >= 24.0)
    TimeHours -= 24.0;
  sprintf(Buffer, "%02g%02g", floor(TimeHours),
```

```
        floor((TimeHours - floor(TimeHours)) * 60 + 0.5));
  return(Buffer);
} /* Time_Add */
```

Sample Usage Source Code

```
/*
  This program will allow the user to enter a time, then allow the
  user to enter the number of hours to be added to the time,
  and then use Time_Add to calculate and display the results.

*/

extern unsigned _stklen=16384; /* Minimum recommend stack size */
#include <stdio.h>
#include <math.h>
#include <dos.h>
#include <mem.h>
#include <alloc.h>
#include <ctype.h>
#include <string.h>
#include <stdlib.h>
#include <plib.h>
#include <plib.glo>


/****************************************************************************/
main()
{
  char
    TBuff[5] = "",
    Time[5] = "";

  float
    Hours = 0.0;

  Calibrate_Delay();            /* Calibrate delay factor */
  Get_Video_Mode("Video.CFG"); /* Get display adapter type */
  Install_Crit_Error();         /* Set up application critical error handler */
  InputAbsolute=AbortPrint=0;   /* Initialize global variables */

  /* Application code to follow */

  Clr_Scr();
  printf("Enter a time in the form HHMM: ");
  scanf("%s", Time);
  printf("\nEnter the number of hours to be added to the time: ");
  scanf("%f", &Hours);
```

```
    printf("\n%s plus %f hours = %s.\n", Time, Hours,
           Time_Add(Time, Hours, TBuff));

} /* main */
```

Sample Usage Output

▼

```
Enter a time in the form HHMM: 1345

Enter the number of hours to be added to time: 1.5

1345 plus 1.500000 hours = 1515.
```

Time_Diff

Description

▼

Time_Diff determines the number of hours and hundredths of hours of absolute difference between two specified times. The order in which the times are passed does not matter because the smaller is always taken as the start time and the larger is taken as the end time. The times must be in the standard military (24-hour) time format HHMM, where HH is the hour and MM is the minutes.

Routine Declaration

▼

```
float Time_Diff(char *Tim1,
                char *Tim2)
```

Passed Variables

▼

***Tim1 String Pointer** A pointer to the time of day string to be used in determining the number of hours difference with *Tim2.

***Tim2 String Pointer** A pointer to the time of day string to be used in determining the number of hours difference with *Tim1.

Global Variables

▼

None

Error Codes/ Messages

▼

None

Discussion

▼

Time_Diff was developed to provide an easy means of determining the duration of an event when the start and end times of the event are known. This can be useful in applications such as time billing or time scheduling.

Time_Diff is simple to operate, using Turbo C's atof routine to convert the hours to a floating point value and the minutes divided by 60 to a floating point value for both times. These values are then subtracted and their absolute value is returned.

Limitations and Modifications

▼

The main limitation to Time_Diff shows up when you want to subtract a start time from an end time that is after midnight. For example, if you want the difference between 2330 and 0100 with 2330 as the start time and 0100 as the end time, you need to add 2400 to 0100. Otherwise, the result returns as the difference between 0100 and 2330. By adding the 2400 to the ending time, you can properly sequence the desired begin and end times.

Routine Source Code

▼

```
#include <math.h>
#include <dos.h>
#include <string.h>
#include <stdio.h>
#include <stdlib.h>
#include <ctype.h>
#include <plib.h>

float Time_Diff(char *Tim1,
                char *Tim2)
/*
  This function will return the difference of the two times in the 24-hour
  form HHMM in terms of hours.
*/
{ /* Time_Diff */
  char
    TStr1[15],
    TStr2[15];

  float
    T1,
    T2;

  T1 = atof(Copy(Tim1, 1, 2, TStr1)) +
       (atof(Copy(Tim1, 3, 2, TStr2)) / 60);
  T2 = atof(Copy(Tim2, 1, 2, TStr1)) +
       (atof(Copy(Tim2, 3, 2, TStr2)) / 60);
  return(fabs(T1 - T2));
} /* Time_Diff */
```

Sample Usage Source Code

▼

```
/*
  This program will allow the user to enter two times in the form
```

```
  HHMM, then use Time_Diff() to calculate the number of hours
  difference, and then display the results.
*/

extern unsigned _stklen=16384; /* Minimum recommend stack size */
#include <stdio.h>
#include <math.h>
#include <dos.h>
#include <mem.h>
#include <alloc.h>
#include <ctype.h>
#include <string.h>
#include <stdlib.h>
#include <plib.h>
#include <plib.glo>

/**************************************************************************/
main()
{
  char
    Time1[5] = "",
    Time2[5] = "";

  Calibrate_Delay();            /* Calibrate delay factor */
  Get_Video_Mode("Video.CFG"); /* Get display adapter type */
  Install_Crit_Error();         /* Set up application critical error handler */
  InputAbsolute=AbortPrint=0;  /* Initialize global variables */

  /* Application code to follow */

  Clr_Scr();
  printf("Enter the first time in the form HHMM: ");
  scanf("%s", Time1);
  printf("Enter the second time in the form HHMM: ");
  scanf("%s", Time2);
  printf("\nThe number of hours difference is %10.3f\n",
       Time_Diff(Time1, Time2));

  } /*  main  */
```

Sample Usage Output

▼

```
Enter the first time in the form HHMM: 0930
Enter the second time in the form HHMM: 2218

The number of hours difference is 12.800
```

Time_Sub

Description

▼

Time_Sub subtracts a specified number of hours from a time passed in a 24-hour format HHMM. (HH contains the hour and MM contains the minutes.) The number of hours to be subtracted are in decimal format. For example, to subtract 1 hour and 30 minutes, pass 1.5.

Routine Declaration

▼

```
char *Time_Sub(char  *Time,
               float Hrs,
               char  *Buffer)
```

Passed Variables

▼

***Time String Pointer** A pointer to the time of day that is to have the associated number of hours subtracted from it. The format for the hours is HHMM, where HH is the hour of the day in the range of 0 through 24 and MM is the minutes of the hour in the range of 0 through 59.

Hrs float The number of hours to be subtracted from the time passed in Time.

***Buffer String Pointer** A pointer to the string variable that will contain the resulting string.

Global Variables

▼

None

Error Codes/ Messages

▼

None

Discussion

▼

Time_Sub provides an easy means of determining the beginning time of an event when the end time and duration are known. This is useful in applications that have to provide appointment or event scheduling.

Time_Sub converts the time passed to a real number with the integer portion containing the hours and the fractional portion containing the hundredths of an hour, based on the minutes. The number of hours passed are then subtracted from the converted time and the new time is checked to see if it starts before midnight (24.00). If so, the time is adjusted for the previous day. The real number representation is then translated back to the four-position string format and returned.

Limitations and Modifications

▼

If you pass a time greater than 2400, Time_Sub compensates only for the value after the subtraction of the hours passed. The resulting time may not be correct. You can modify this by adding additional error checking into Time_Sub or in your application prior to calling Time_Sub.

Routine Source Code

▼

```
#include <math.h>
#include <dos.h>
#include <string.h>
#include <stdio.h>
#include <stdlib.h>
#include <ctype.h>
#include <plib.h>

char *Time_Sub(char *Time,
               float Hrs,
               char *Buffer)
/*
  This routine will accept a *Time in the 24-hour format of HHMM and
  Hrs in terms of hours, e.g., 1.25 hours, subtract the hours from the
  time, and return the resulting time in *Buffer (returning the pointer
  to *Buffer), e.g., "1230" = Time_Sub("1300",0.5);
*/
{ /* Time_Sub */
  float
    TimeHours;

  char
    TStr1[15],
    TStr2[15];

  TimeHours = atof(Copy(Time, 1, 2, TStr1)) +
              (atof(Copy(Time, 3, 2, TStr2)) / 60);
  TimeHours -= Hrs;
  if (TimeHours < 0.0)
    TimeHours += 24.0;
  sprintf(Buffer, "%2g%2g", floor(TimeHours),
                floor((TimeHours - floor(TimeHours)) * 60 + 0.5));
  return(Buffer);
} /* Time_Sub */
```

Sample Usage Source Code

▼

```
/*
  This program will allow the user to enter a time, then allow the
```

```
  user to enter the number of hours to be subtracted from the time,
  and then use Time_Sub to calculate and display the results.
*/

extern unsigned _stklen=16384; /* Minimum recommend stack size */
#include <stdio.h>
#include <math.h>
#include <dos.h>
#include <mem.h>
#include <alloc.h>
#include <ctype.h>
#include <string.h>
#include <stdlib.h>
#include <plib.h>
#include <plib.glo>


/***************************************************************************/
main()
{
  char
    TBuff[5] = "",
    Time[5] = "";

  float
    Hours = 0.0;

  Calibrate_Delay();            /* Calibrate delay factor */
  Get_Video_Mode("Video.CFG"); /* Get display adapter type */
  Install_Crit_Error();         /* Set up application critical error handler */
  InputAbsolute=AbortPrint=0;  /* Initialize global variables */

  /* Application code to follow */

  Clr_Scr();
  printf("Enter a time in the form HHMM: ");
  scanf("%s", Time);
  printf("\nEnter the number of hours to subtract from the time: ");
  scanf("%f", &Hours);

  printf("\n%s minus %f hours = %s.\n", Time, Hours,
        Time_Sub(Time, Hours, TBuff));

} /*  main  */
```

Sample Usage Output

▼

```
Enter a time in the form HHMM: 2215

Enter the number of hours to subtract from the time: 15
```

```
2215 minus 15.000000 hours =  715.
```

Today

Description

▼

Today returns the current date maintained by DOS. The date returned is in the string form MM/DD/YY. If the date is not set at startup, the date reflects the default date from the ROM BIOS.

Routine Declaration

▼

```
char *Today(char *Buffer)
```

Passed Variables

▼

***Buffer String Pointer** A pointer to the string variable that will contain the resulting string.

Global Variables

▼

None

Error Codes/ Messages

▼

None

Discussion

▼

Today provides an easy method of obtaining the current system date in the format used by related library routines. The date returned is an eight-character string in the form MM/DD/YY containing the month, day, and last two digits of the year.

Today uses the Turbo C routine getdate to retrieve the current date from the system. The date is then formatted to the standard library format MM/DD/YY and returned from the routine.

Limitations and Modifications

▼

None

Routine Source Code

▼

```
#include <math.h>
#include <dos.h>
#include <string.h>
```

```
#include <stdio.h>
#include <stdlib.h>
#include <ctype.h>
#include <plib.h>

char *Today(char *Buffer)
/*
  Returns the system date in the form MM/DD/YY.
*/
{/* Today */
  struct date
    DateBlock;

  getdate(&DateBlock);
  sprintf(Buffer, "%02d/%02d/%02d", DateBlock.da_mon, DateBlock.da_day,
                                    DateBlock.da_year - 1900);
  return(Buffer);
}/* Today */
```

Sample Usage Source Code

▼

```
/*
  This program will use Today to retrieve the system's date in the form
  MM/DD/YY and display it.
*/

extern unsigned _stklen=16384; /* Minimum recommend stack size */
#include <stdio.h>
#include <math.h>
#include <dos.h>
#include <mem.h>
#include <alloc.h>
#include <ctype.h>
#include <string.h>
#include <stdlib.h>
#include <plib.h>
#include <plib.glo>

/****************************************************************************/
main()
{
  char
    DBuff [9] = "";

  Calibrate_Delay();            /* Calibrate delay factor */
  Get_Video_Mode("Video.CFG"); /* Get display adapter type */
  Install_Crit_Error();         /* Set up application critical error handler */
  InputAbsolute=AbortPrint=0;   /* Initialize global variables */
```

```
  /* Application code to follow */

  Clr_Scr () ;
  printf ("Today is %s \n", Today(DBuff) );

} /*  main  */
```

Sample Usage Output

▼

```
Today is 12/27/88
```

Undate_Comp

Description

▼

Undate_Comp returns a string in the form MM/DD/YY that has been converted from the string date passed in the form YY/MM/DD. This routine is used to reverse the process performed by the library routine Date_Comp.

Routine Declaration

▼

```
char *Undate_Comp(char *CDate,
                  char *Buffer)
```

Passed Variables

▼

***CDate String Pointer** The string date in the form YY/MM/DD to be converted to the form MM/DD/YY.

***Buffer String Pointer** A pointer to the string variable that will contain the resulting string.

Global Variables

▼

None

Error Codes/ Messages

▼

None

Discussion

▼

Undate_Comp is primarily used to reverse the date manipulation performed by the routine Date_Comp. Date_Comp takes a date in the form MM/DD/YY and returns a date in the form YY/MM/DD. On the other hand, Undate_Comp takes a date in the form YY/MM/DD and returns a date in the form MM/DD/YY.

Undate_Comp first checks to ensure that the string passed contains text by using a call to Is_Text. If a text value is present, it is assumed to be in the YY/MM/DD format, and is rearranged, and the pointer *Buffer is returned. If the date passed was blank, a blank string is returned.

Limitations and Modifications

▼

Since Undate_Comp does not check the string value passed for any validity other than its existence, you may want to add format error checking to the routine. You should also take care in passing Undate_Comp values that have not been Date_Comp'd. This results in a string in the form DD/YY/MM, because Undate_Comp considers the first two characters as the year value.

Routine Source Code

▼

```
#include <math.h>
#include <string.h>
#include <stdio.h>
#include <stdlib.h>
#include <ctype.h>
#include <plib.h>

char *Undate_Comp(char *CDate,
                  char *Buffer)
/*
  Returns a string date in the form MM/DD/YY from *CDate where
  *CDate is in the form YY/MM/DD. This is useful for displaying a date
  in date standard format that had been 'Date_Comp'd.
*/
{/* Undate_Comp */
  char
    TStr1[6],
    TStr2[3];

  if (Is_Text(CDate))
    sprintf(Buffer, "%s/%s", Copy(CDate, 4, 5, TStr1),
            Copy(CDate, 1, 2, TStr2));
  else
    Buffer[0] = 0;
  return(Buffer);
}/* Undate_Comp */
```

Sample Usage Source Code

▼

```
/*
  This program will use Undate_Comp to put a date in the form of
  YY/MM/DD into the familiar form MM/DD/YY.
*/
```

```
extern unsigned _stklen=16384; /* Minimum recommend stack size */
#include <stdio.h>
#include <math.h>
#include <dos.h>
#include <mem.h>
#include <alloc.h>
#include <ctype.h>
#include <string.h>
#include <stdlib.h>
#include <plib.h>
#include <plib.glo>

/**************************************************************************/
main()
{
  char
    DBuff[9] = "",
    DCDate[9] = "";

  Calibrate_Delay();             /* Calibrate delay factor */
  Get_Video_Mode("Video.CFG");  /* Get display adapter type */
  Install_Crit_Error();          /* Set up application critical error handler */
  InputAbsolute=AbortPrint=0;    /* Initialize global variables */

  /* Application code to follow */

  Clr_Scr();
  strcpy(DCDate, "88/12/31");
  printf ("The familiar form of %s is %s.\n", DCDate,
        Undate_Comp(DCDate, DBuff));

} /*  main  */
```

Sample Usage Output

▼

```
The familiar form of 88/12/31 is 12/31/88.
```

WhereX

Description

▼

WhereX obtains the current horizontal position of the screen cursor. The horizontal position value is returned in the range of 1 to 80.

Routine Declaration

▼

```
int WhereX(void)
```

Passed Variables

▼

None

Global Variables

▼

None

Error Codes/ Messages

▼

None

Discussion

▼

WhereX was written for Turbo C version 1.0, which does not contain a similar routine. Turbo C version 1.5 and later do contain similar routines, with almost the same name.

WhereX uses service 3 hex, Read Cursor Position, of ROM BIOS interrupt 10 hex, Video Services, to obtain the cursor position. The routine starts by loading the service number into the AH register and calls the Turbo C routine int86 to execute the interrupt. Upon return from the interrupt, the DL register contains the X position value in the range 0 to 79. The DL is incremented by 1 to put the position in the range of 1 to 80 and then returned.

Limitations and Modifications

▼

None

Routine Source Code

▼

```
#include <dos.h>
#include <mem.h>

int WhereX(void)
/*
  This procedure will return the Y position of the cursor (1..25).
*/
{ /* WhereX */
  union REGS
    Regs;

  setmem(&Regs, sizeof(Regs), 0);
  Regs.h.ah = 0x03; /* Read cursor position */
  int86(0x10, &Regs, &Regs);
  Regs.h.dl++;
  return((int)Regs.h.dl);
} /* WhereX */
```

Sample Usage Source Code

```
/*
  This program will use WhereX() to get the horizontal position of the cursor.
*/

extern unsigned _stklen=16384; /* Minimum recommend stack size */
#include <stdio.h>
#include <math.h>
#include <dos.h>
#include <mem.h>
#include <alloc.h>
#include <ctype.h>
#include <string.h>
#include <stdlib.h>
#include <plib.h>
#include <plib.glo>


/******************************************************************************/
main()
{
  char
    Buff [3] = "" ,
    Check ;

  Calibrate_Delay();            /* Calibrate delay factor */
  Get_Video_Mode("Video.CFG"); /* Get display adapter type */
  Install_Crit_Error();         /* Set up application critical error handler */
  InputAbsolute=AbortPrint=0;  /* Initialize global variables */

  /* Application code to follow */
  Clr_Scr();
  F_Write(1, 1, Normal, "Just press <RETURN> to find out the");
  F_Write(1, 2, Normal, "cursor's vertical position.");
  scanf("%c", &Check);

  Goto_XY(55, 10);
  F_Write(52, 12, Normal, "(  ,--)");
  F_Write(56, 12, VidHigh, itoa(WhereX(), Buff, 10));
  F_Write(1, 20, Normal, "Press <RETURN> to exit.");
  scanf("%c", &Check);

} /* main */
```

Sample Usage Output

```
Just press <RETURN> to find out the
cursor's vertical position.
```

(,55)

```
Press <RETURN> to exit.
```

WhereY

Description ▼

WhereY obtains the current vertical position of the screen cursor. The vertical position value is returned in the range of 1 to 25.

Routine Declaration ▼

```
int WhereY(void)
```

Passed Variables ▼

None

Global Variables ▼

None

Error Codes/ Messages ▼

None

Discussion ▼

WhereY was written for Turbo C version 1.0, which does not contain a similar routine. Turbo C version 1.5 and later do contain similar routines, with almost the same name.

WhereY uses service 3 hex, Read Cursor Position, of ROM BIOS interrupt 10 hex, Video Services, to obtain the cursor position. The routine starts by loading the service number into the AH register and calls the Turbo C routine int86 to execute the interrupt. Upon return from the interrupt, the DH register contains the Y position value in the range 0 to 24. The DH is incremented by 1 to put the position in the range of 1 to 25 and then returned.

Limitations and Modifications ▼

None

Routine Source Code

```
#include <dos.h>
#include <mem.h>

int WhereY(void)
/*
  This procedure will return the Y position of the cursor (1..25).
*/
{ /* WhereY */
  union REGS
    Regs;

  setmem(&Regs, sizeof(Regs), 0);
  Regs.h.ah = 0x03; /*Read cursor position*/
  int86(0x10, &Regs, &Regs);
  Regs.h.dh++;
  return((int)Regs.h.dh);
} /* WhereY */
```

Sample Usage Source Code

```
/*
  This program will use WhereY() to get the vertical position of the cursor.
*/

extern unsigned _stklen=16384; /* Minimum recommend stack size */
#include <stdio.h>
#include <math.h>
#include <dos.h>
#include <mem.h>
#include <alloc.h>
#include <ctype.h>
#include <string.h>
#include <stdlib.h>
#include <plib.h>
#include <plib.glo>

/*****************************************************************************/
main()
{
  char
    Buff[3] = "",
    Check;

  Calibrate_Delay();            /* Calibrate delay factor */
  Get_Video_Mode("Video.CFG"); /* Get display adapter type */
  Install_Crit_Error();         /* Set up application critical error handler */
```

```
  InputAbsolute=AbortPrint=0;  /* Initialize global variables */

  /* Application code to follow */

  Clr_Scr();
  F_Write(1, 1, Normal,"Just press <RETURN> to find out the");
  F_Write(1, 2, Normal, "cursor's vertical position.");
  scanf("%c", &Check);

  Goto_XY(55, 12);
  F_Write(52, 14, Normal, "(--,  )");
  F_Write(56, 14, VidHigh, itoa(WhereY(), Buff, 10));
  F_Write(1, 20, Normal, "Press <RETURN> to exit.");

  scanf ("%c", &Check);

} /* main */
```

Sample Usage Output

▼

```
Just press <RETURN> to find out the
cursor's vertical position.









                                                    (--,12)





Press <RETURN> to exit.
```

Write_Line

Description

▼

Write_Line provides a consistent means of writing a line of text to a text file from a specified string. After the line is written, it is terminated by writing an ASCII 13 (CR) and ASCII 10 (LF).

Routine Declaration

▼

```
void Write_Line(FILE *RFile,
                char *Line)
```

Passed Variables

▼

***RFile Stream Buffer Pointer** A pointer to the structure defining the current file to be written to by Write_Line.

***Line String Pointer** A pointer to the string variable that contains the string to be written to *RFile.

Global Variables

▼

None

Error Codes/ Messages

▼

None

Discussion

▼

Write_String provides a reliable means of writing lines of text to files, because the routines provided in the Turbo C library are unclear as to how to consistently write and read text lines.

Write_Line uses a for loop to output the string with the Turbo C routine putc that continues until the end of the string is encountered. Once the string has been output, an ASCII 13 and ASCII 10 are written to the file to terminate the string. Write_Line does not return any indicators for completion, because errors are trapped by the critical error handler installed with Install_Crit_Error.

Limitations and Modifications

▼

None

Routine Source Code

▼

```
#include <stdio.h>
void Write_Line(FILE *RFile,
                char *Line)
/*
  This function will write Line out to RFile padding with 13 & 10s on the
  end.
*/
{/* Write_Line */
  int
    C;

  for (C = 0; (Line[C]) ; putc(Line[C], RFile), C++);
  putc(13, RFile);
  putc(10, RFile);
```

```
}/* Write_Line */
```

Sample Usage Source Code

▼

For sample usage of this routine, see the sample usage for the library routine Read_Line.

Write_String

Description

▼

Write_String provides a consistent means of writing a string of text to a text file from a specified string. The line written is not terminated in any way and there is no line terminator (CR LF) or file terminator (Ctrl Z) attached after the string. See the library routine Write_Line for line termination.

Routine Declaration

▼

```
void Write_String(FILE *RFile,
                  char *Line)
```

Passed Variables

▼

***RFile Stream Buffer Pointer** A pointer to the structure defining the current file to be written to by Write_String.

***Line String Pointer** A pointer to the string variable that contains the string to be written to *RFile.

Global Variables

▼

None

Error Codes/ Messages

▼

None

Discussion

▼

Write_String provides a reliable means of writing strings to files, because the routines provided in the Turbo C library are unclear as to how to consistently write and read text.

Write_String uses a for loop to output the string with the Turbo C routine putc that continues until the end of the string is encountered. Write_String does not return any indicators for completion, because errors are trapped by the critical error handler installed with Install_Crit_Error.

Limitations and Modifications

None

Routine Source Code

```
#include <stdio.h>
void Write_String(FILE *RFile,
                  char *Line)
/*
  This function will write *Line out to *RFile without padding with
  13 & 10s on the end.
*/
{/* Write_String */
  int
    C;

  for (C = 0; (Line[C]) ; putc(Line[C], RFile), C++);
}/* Write_String */
```

Sample Usage Source Code

For sample usage of this routine, see the sample usage for the library routine Read_Line.

3 Btrieve File System Routines

Add_Record Adds a new record to a Btrieve data file.

Change_Record Updates a data record in a Btrieve data file.

Close_File Closes a Btrieve data file.

Delete_Record Deletes a data record from a Btrieve data file.

End_Btrieve Terminates the memory-resident Btrieve record manager.

Get_Record Retrieves a data record from a Btrieve data file.

Highest_Record Retrieves the last data record in a Btrieve data file based on the index path specified.

Lowest_Record Retrieves the first data record in a Btrieve data file based on the index path specified.

Make_File Creates a new Btrieve data file from a structure defined in a data file created by the utility Make Definition. (See Sample Applications and Utilities, Chapter 5.)

Mode_Select Controls selection of the standard file maintenance options menu.

Mode_Update Redisplays the current file maintenance mode as selected during Mode_Select.

Next_Key Returns the next consecutive index key from a Btrieve data file.

Next_Record Returns the next consecutive record from a Btrieve data file.

Open_File Opens an existing Btrieve data file.

Prev_Key Returns the preceding index key from a Btrieve data file.

Prev_Record Returns the preceding data record from a Btrieve data file.

Record_Entry_Control Controls forward and backward record movement while using data entry screens.

RMake_File Creates a new Btrieve data file from a structure defined in the application.

Search_Record Locates the record equal to or greater than the specified key value using the indicated index path in a Btrieve data file.

Used_Recs Returns the number of active records in a Btrieve data file.

Btrieve is a software package designed to provide high-performance file management in several environments. The package can be used in PC/MS-DOS environments in single- or multiuser operations and with the OS/2 and Xenix operating systems. With the multiple environments supported by Btrieve, it can also be used by almost any programming language available for those environments. The manufacturer provides an interface routine, Btrv, for a wide variety of languages. Listing 3-1 is a modified version, designed to take advantage of the pseudovariables available in Turbo C for specifying memory models during compilation. This routine allows you to make calls to the memory-resident record manager that actually performs the file management operations.

The routines provided in this chapter are used for direct file management from within your application and for creating data entry screens using the associated routines from the main library's. Although the routines described in this section were written for use with Btrieve, the concepts and design relate to any file management system that provides similar operations. Btrieve provides excellent performance for file management and the flexibility to move an application from single- to multiuser without modification. However, because the record manager is loaded as a memory-resident facility, it does consume memory. If your application is memory-bound, you may need to be cautious when using Btrieve. Btrieve is now available under some networking environments (e.g., NetWare 2.1) as a server process (value-added process or VAP), however, which helps reduce the memory problem.

In addition to the memory consumption tendency, application developers should beware of what we call Btrieve's "King of the Hill" problem. There are many applications which use Btrieve. Some are well behaved; unfortunately, some are not. When Btrieve is loaded, processing and memory parameters are given from the command line, and they remain with the resident record manager until it is removed from memory. Btrieve does not allow you to load a new record manager with its different parameters until the present one is removed. Therefore, if a user runs an application that loads Btrieve but is not kind enough to unload it before exiting, when another application tries to load the record manager with different parameters or a different version, it can't. The user is stuck with the loaded version. We therefore recommend that you call the routine End_Btrieve to remove the resident record manager before your application exits.

For your own protection, you may also wish to call the Btrv function that returns the version number of the resident record manager (26 Version). Those applications using Btrieve are run through a batch file that loads the record manager first, then calls the program. (See BCust.bat in Chapter 5.) Developers should also note that these Btrieve routines were designed only for the large memory model of the Turbo C compiler. To ease the parameter burden normally associated with these types of operations, a global array structure was set up so that file numbers could be used to reference files. (See Cust.c in Chapter 5.)

Listing 3-1 is a modified version of Btrieve's Turbo C interface, changed slightly to compile properly with these routines.

Listing 3-1. *Btrv.c (modified)*

```
#include <stddef.h>
#include <math.h>
#include <dos.h>
#include <string.h>
#include <stdio.h>
#include <stdlib.h>
#include <ctype.h>
#include <plib.h>

/*
  Turbo C Version    interface to the
  Btrieve Record Manager, version 4
*/

#define BTR_ERR      20           /* record manager not started */
#define BTR_INT      0x7B         /* Btrieve interrupt vector */
#define BTR2_INT     0x2F         /* multiuser interrupt vector */
#define BTR_VECTOR   BTR_INT * 4  /* offset for interrupt */
#define BTR_OFFSET   0x33         /* Btrieve offset within segment */
#define VARIABLE_ID  0x6176       /* id for variable length records - 'va' */
#define _2FCODE      0xAB00       /* function code for int 2F to btrieve */

static unsigned
  ProcId = 0;  /* initialize to no process id */

static char
  MULTI = 0;   /* flag set to true if MultiUser */

static char
  VSet = 0;    /* flag set to true if checked version */

int BTrv (int OP,
```

Listing 3-1. Btrv.c (modified) (cont'd)

```
          char *POS_BLK,
          char *DATA_BUF,
          int *DATA_LEN,
          char *KEY_BUF,
          int KEY_NUM)
/*
  Turbo C Version of interface to the
  Btrieve Record Manager, version 4.xx.
  ProcId is used for communicating with the Multi Tasking Version of
  Btrieve. It contains the process id returned from BMulti and should
  not be changed once it has been set.
*/

{
  struct REGVAL
  {
    unsigned int
      AX,
      BX,
      CX,
      DX,
      SI,
      DI,
      CY,
      FLAGS;
  } REGS;

  struct SEGREG
  {
    unsigned int
      ES,
      CS,
      SS,
      DS;
  } SREGS;

  struct BTRIEVE_PARMS  /* structure passed to Btrieve Record Manager */
  {
   char
     *BUF_OFFSET;       /* caller's data buffer offset */
#ifndef __LARGE__
   int
     BUF_SEG;           /* caller's data buffer segment */
#endif
   int
     BUF_LEN;           /* length of data buffer */
```

Listing 3-1. Btrv.c (modified) (cont'd)

```
  char
    *CUR_OFFSET;          /* user position block offset */
#ifndef __LARGE__
  int
    CUR_SEG;              /* user position block segment */
#endif
  char
    *FCB_OFFSET;          /* offset of disk FCB */
#ifndef __LARGE__
  int
    FCB_SEG;              /* segment of disk FCB */
#endif
  int
    FUNCTION;             /* requested function */
  char
    *KEY_OFFSET;          /* offset of user's key buffer */
#ifndef __LARGE__
  int
    KEY_SEG;              /* segment of user's key buffer */
#endif
  char
    KEY_LENGTH,           /* length of user's key buffer */
    KEY_NUMBER;           /* key of reference for request */
  int
    *STAT_OFFSET;         /* offset of status word */
#ifndef __LARGE__
  int
    STAT_SEG;             /* segment of status word */
#endif
  int
    XFACE_ID;             /* language identifier */
  } XDATA;

  int
    STAT = 0;             /* status of Btrieve call */


  /*                                                                          */
  /*  Check to see that the Btrieve Record Manager has been started.     */
  /*                                                                          */
  if (!VSet)    /* if we don't know version of Btrieve yet */
  {
    VSet = 1;
    REGS.AX = 0x3000; /* check dos version */
    int86x (0x21, &REGS, &REGS, &SREGS);
    if ((REGS.AX & 0x00FF) >= 3)  /* if DOS version 3 or later */
```

Listing 3-1. Btrv.c (modified) (cont'd)

```
    {
      REGS.AX = _2FCODE;
      int86x (BTR2_INT, &REGS, &REGS, &SREGS);
      MULTI = ((REGS.AX & 0xFF) == 'M');  /* if al is M, bmulti is loaded */
    }
  }

  if (!MULTI)
  { /* if bmulti not loaded */
    REGS.AX = 0x3500 + BTR_INT;
    int86x (0x21, &REGS, &REGS, &SREGS);
    if (REGS.BX != BTR_OFFSET)
      return (BTR_ERR);
  }

/*  Read segment registers and initialize segment part of addresses to  */
/*  user's data segment.                                                 */
/*                                                                       */

  segread (&SREGS);
#ifndef __LARGE__
  XDATA.BUF_SEG = XDATA.CUR_SEG = XDATA.FCB_SEG =
  XDATA.KEY_SEG = XDATA.STAT_SEG = SREGS.SS;
#endif

  /*                                                                    */
  /*  Move user parameters to XDATA, the block where Btrieve expects them.*/
  /*                                                                    */

  XDATA.FUNCTION = OP;
  XDATA.STAT_OFFSET = &STAT;
  XDATA.FCB_OFFSET = POS_BLK;
  XDATA.CUR_OFFSET = POS_BLK + 38;
  XDATA.BUF_OFFSET = DATA_BUF;
  XDATA.BUF_LEN = *DATA_LEN;
  XDATA.KEY_OFFSET = KEY_BUF;
  XDATA.KEY_LENGTH = 255; /* use max since we don't know */
  XDATA.KEY_NUMBER = KEY_NUM;
  XDATA.XFACE_ID = VARIABLE_ID;

  /*                                                                  */
  /*  Make call to the Btrieve Record Manager.                        */
  /*                                                                  */

  REGS.DX = (int) &XDATA; /* parameter block is expected to be in DX */
  SREGS.DS = SREGS.SS;
```

Listing 3-1. Btrv.c (modified) (cont'd)

```
 if (!MULTI)
   int86x (BTR_INT, &REGS, &REGS, &SREGS);
 else
 {/* call bmulti */
   while (1)
   {
     REGS.AX = 1;  /*  assume no proc id obtained yet */
     if ((REGS.BX = ProcId) != 0) /* if we have a proc id */
       REGS.AX = 2; /* tell bmulti that */
     REGS.AX += _2FCODE;
     int86x (BTR2_INT, &REGS, &REGS, &SREGS);
     if ((REGS.AX & 0x00FF) == 0)
       break; /* if call was processed */
     REGS.AX = 0x0200; /* if multilink advanced is loaded, it will */
     int86x (0x7F, &REGS, &REGS, &SREGS); /* it will switch processes */
   }
   if (ProcId == 0)
     ProcId = REGS.BX;
 }
 *DATA_LEN = XDATA.BUF_LEN;
 return (STAT); /* return status */
}
```

XQL: Relational File Management for Btrieve

XQL is a relational database management system designed to be used in conjunction with Btrieve and most high-level programming languages such as C, Pascal, Basic, and Cobol. XQL allows developers to create relational databases using an extension of Structured Query Language (SQL).

Through the use of subroutine calls, XQL provides the capability to perform relational database operations from within a program on two different data access levels. These are done either by complete SQL commands passed to XQL or through relational primitives called from within the application. To perform SQL statements, the application stores each statement in a string variable passed to XQL for processing. XQL translates the statement, retrieves the requested data records, and returns the data sorted as specified. To perform relational primitives, the application performs function calls to the XQL interface routine, which bypasses the SQL interpreter. These commands are then processed directly by XQL.

XQL incorporates database manipulation features that allow the application to access data by field name, move forward or backward through the database, compute fields from other fields or constants, and even manipulate composite records built from multiple records or joined Btrieve files.

In general, XQL allows the application to query, update, and manage relational database files, dictionaries, and system security. In order to provide these capabilities, XQL uses special memory-resident programs that receive commands from your application. These programs are XQLP, The XQL Relational Primitives and XQLM, The XQL Manager.

XQLP provides the ability to create and manage relational database systems using highly efficient low-level primitives. With XQLP, developers can implement command- or menu-driven applications or a query language of their own design.

XQLP is the lowest level of the XQL interfaces and consists of over 35 relational primitive routines, any of which can be called directly by an application program. The primitives provide a relational link between the database application and the Btrieve record manager.

XQLM provides an SQL interface between an application and XQLP. XQLM consists of a group of functions that allow an application to directly utilize SQL statements. XQLM supports a subset of the ANSI standard SQL syntax and extensions providing more functionality at the natural language level.

Some XQLM functions receive SQL statements as part of their input, and parse the statements into the appropriate XQL primitive calls. The primitives perform the necessary low-level file and data management operations and return the results to the XQLM function. The XQLM function then passes the result of the SQL statement back to the application.

Other XQLM functions use the primitives to perform database administration and security operations. These operations include logging in and out of the system, specifying user rights, and closing files at the end of a session.

XQLI is an interactive query application that accepts SQL statements as input and then makes the appropriate function calls to XQLM. It is useful as a tutorial for SQL, and as a test program for SQL statements that will be used with an application.

Since XQL is a very sophisticated and complex development tool, we introduce it with the Btrieve section. However, because of its highly flexible nature, it would be very difficult to boil it down to just a select few routines, so none is included here. XQL can be a very useful tool to any developer for performing queries and managing large relational applications.

The only limitation with XQL is the amount of memory it requires to run. When using XQLP, you need between 110 and 150KB of RAM and the manager requires an additional 85KB. If you plan to use these packages on a Novell network, the memory constraints can be almost eliminated by using the VAP version of the packages. The VAP versions are run as a background process on the file server of the network through a memory-resident connection in the workstation that only requires 70KB of RAM. However, the VAP processes are only available with Advanced NetWare 2.1 and later.

Add_Record

Description ▼

Add_Record adds a new data record to a specified Btrieve data file. The routine returns the completion code set by the Btrieve record manager, with 0 indicating a successful operation and any other number indicating a Btrieve error code. This routine uses Btrieve operation 2 (Insert) to perform the addition of the new record. Listing 3-1, Btrv, used to interface Turbo C to Btrieve, is also discussed in the Btrieve reference manual.

Routine Declaration

▼

```
int Add_Record(int FileNum,
               char *DataRec,
               int  CurKeyNum)
```

Passed Variables

▼

FileNum integer This field contains the number of the file being manipulated (0-19). This number accesses the global array of structures that contain the file specifications.

***DataRec Pointer** This variable contains the address of the data record to be added by Btrieve.

CurKeyNum integer This field contains the key number (0-23) (Search Path) used by Btrieve to determine the order in which the records are processed. For a more detailed description of the key indexes available in Btrieve, consult the Btrieve manual.

Global Variables

▼

BTrvRecInfo This global array of structures contains the pointer (*RecPtr) to the record commonly used by the Btrieve routines, the Btrieve data file position information buffer (BTrvVar), which is similar in use to a FILE stream buffer, and the length of the data record (RecLen). This structure is initialized by the library routine Open_File().

Error Codes/ Messages

▼

The completion code returned from the Btrieve record manager is the only error indicator provided by this routine. For a complete list of the error codes, see your Btrieve reference manual.

Discussion

▼

Add_Record adds new data records to a Btrieve database. The record pointed to by *DataRec is added to the Btrieve data file indicated by FileNum. The function calls Btrieve operation 2 (Insert) through the function Btrv. Btrv is provided by the manufacturer of Btrieve to interface it to Turbo C. You should consult the version of that routine included with your Btrieve package for more information on its use. (See also Listing 3-1.)

Limitations and Modifications

▼

The Btrieve Record Manager must be loaded prior to calling any Btrieve operations. If the record manager is not loaded, an error results on any calls to Btrv.

Since there are numerous error codes that can be returned from Btrv, you may want to establish an error message routine for displaying the meaning of the error returned. This provides more information on the error without having to use your Btrieve reference manual to look up the error code's meaning.

Routine Source Code

▼

```
#include <math.h>
#include <dos.h>
#include <string.h>
#include <stdio.h>
#include <stdlib.h>
#include <ctype.h>
#include <plib.h>

extern struct
{
  char
    *RecPtr,
    BTrvVar[128],
    CurInd[256];

  int
    RecLen;
} BTrvRecInfo[20];

int Add_Record(int FileNum,
               char *DataRec,
               int CurKeyNum)
/*
  This routine will add the data pointed to by DataRec to the BTrieve file
  (FileNum). This function uses the global structure array
  BTrvRecInfo[FileNum] to handle the miscellaneous record information.
  It will then return the BTrv status code.
*/
{/*Add_Record*/

  return(BTrv(2,BTrvRecInfo[FileNum].BTrvVar,DataRec,
       &BTrvRecInfo[FileNum].RecLen, BTrvRecInfo[FileNum].CurInd,
       CurKeyNum));
}/*Add_Record*/
```

Sample Usage Source Code

▼

See the library routine Record_Entry_Control, in this chapter, for an example of using this routine.

Change_Record

Description

▼

Change_Record updates existing records in a Btrieve database. The routine uses Btrieve operation 3 (Update) to change the current data record. Listing 3-1, Btrv, used to interface Turbo C to Btrieve, is also discussed in the Btrieve reference manual.

Routine Declaration

▼

```
int Change_Record(int  FileNum,
                  char *DataRec,
                  int  CurKeyNum)
```

Passed Variables

▼

FileNum integer This field contains the number of the file being manipulated. This number accesses the global array of structures that contain the file specifications.

***DataRec Pointer** This variable contains the address of the data record to be used to update the Btrieve file.

CurKeyNum integer This field contains the key number (Search Path) used by Btrieve to determine the order in which the records are processed. For a more detailed description of the key indexes available in Btrieve, consult the Btrieve manual.

Global Variables

▼

BTrvRecInfo This global array of structures contains the pointer (*RecPtr) to the record commonly used by the Btrieve routines, the Btrieve data file position information buffer (BTrvVar), which is similar in use to a FILE stream buffer, and the length of the data record (RecLen). This structure is initialized by the library routine Open_File().

Error Codes/ Messages

▼

The completion code returned from the Btrieve record manager is the only error indicator provided by this routine. For a complete list of the error codes, see your Btrieve reference manual.

Discussion

▼

Change_Record updates existing data records in a Btrieve database. Change_Record updates the record located at the position in the file (FileNum) established by the last Get operation (e.g., Get_Record, Next_record, etc.). The function calls Btrieve operation 3 (Update) through the function Btrv to actually change the record. Upon return from the Btrieve record manager, Btrv returns the completion code and Change_Record returns that code. If the code is zero, the operation was successful. Any other code indicates an unsuccessful operation. Consult your Btrieve manual for a complete list of the error codes.

Limitations and Modifications

▼

The Btrieve Record Manager must be loaded prior to calling any Btrieve operations. If the record manager is not loaded, an error results on any calls to Btrv.

Since there are numerous error codes that can be returned from Btrv, you may want to establish an error message routine for displaying the meaning of the error returned. This provides more information on the error without having to use your Btrieve reference manual to look up the error code's meaning.

Routine Source Code

▼

```
#include <math.h>
#include <dos.h>
#include <string.h>
#include <stdio.h>
#include <stdlib.h>
#include <ctype.h>
#include <plib.h>

extern struct
{
  char
    *RecPtr,
    BTrvVar[128],
    CurInd[256];

  int
    RecLen;
} BTrvRecInfo[20];

int Change_Record(int FileNum,
                  char *DataRec,
                  int CurKeyNum)
/*
  This function will change the contents of the last record retrieved
  from FileNum to the contents of DataRec. If unsuccessful, a nonzero
```

```
  BTrv status code will be returned.
*/
{/*Change_Record*/

  return(BTrv(3,BTrvRecInfo[FileNum].BTrvVar,DataRec,
         &BTrvRecInfo[FileNum].RecLen, BTrvRecInfo[FileNum].CurInd,
            CurKeyNum));
}/*Change_Record*/
```

Sample Usage Source Code

▼

See the library routine Record_Entry_Control, in this chapter, for an example of using this routine.

Close_File

Description

▼

Close_File closes a Btrieve database file to further operations until it is reopened with a call to Open_File. The routine uses Btrieve operation 1 (Close) to perform the file closure. Listing 3-1, Btrv, used to interface Turbo C to Btrieve, is also discussed in the Btrieve reference manual.

Routine Declaration

▼

```
int Close_File(int FileNum)
```

Passed Variables

▼

FileNum int This field contains the number of the file to be closed. This number accesses the global array of structures that contain the file specifications.

Global Variables

▼

None

Error Codes/ Messages

▼

The completion code returned from the Btrieve record manager is the only error indicator provided by this routine. For a complete list of the error codes, see your Btrieve reference manual.

Discussion

▼

Close_File simply instructs the Btrieve record manager to close the file indicated by FileNum. All other variables passed to Btrv are temporary dummy variables that contain no meaningful information. The function calls Btrieve operation 1 (Close) through the function Btrv (Listing 3-1). When completed, Btrv returns the appropriate completion code from the Btrieve memory-resident record manager.

Limitations and Modifications

▼

The Btrieve Record Manager must be loaded prior to calling any Btrieve operations. If the record manager is not loaded, an error results on any calls to Btrv.

Since there are numerous error codes that can be returned from Btrv, you may want to establish an error message routine for displaying the meaning of the error returned. This provides more information on the error without having to use your Btrieve reference manual to look up the error code's meaning.

Routine Source Code

▼

```
#include <math.h>
#include <dos.h>
#include <string.h>
#include <stdio.h>
#include <stdlib.h>
#include <ctype.h>
#include <plib.h>

extern struct
{
  char
    *RecPtr,
    BTrvVar[128],
    CurInd[256];

  int
    RecLen;
} BTrvRecInfo[20];

int Close_File(int FileNum)
/*
  This function will close a Btrieve file and return the BTrv status
  code.
*/
{/*Close_File*/
  char
    DumRec;

  return(BTrv(1,BTrvRecInfo[FileNum].BTrvVar,&DumRec,&DumRec,&DumRec,0));
}/*Close_File*/
```

Sample Usage Source Code

▼

See the sample application Customer, in Chapter 5, for an example of using this routine.

Delete_Record

Description

▼

Delete_Record deletes existing records in a Btrieve database. The routine uses Btrieve operation 4 (Delete) to perform the record deletion. Listing 3-1, Btrv, used to interface Turbo C to Btrieve, is also discussed in the Btrieve reference manual.

Routine Declaration

▼

```
int Delete_Record(char FileNum,
                  int  CurKeyNum)
```

Passed Variables

▼

FileNum integer This field contains the number of the file that contains the record being deleted. This number accesses the global array of structures that contain the file specifications.

CurKeyNum integer This field contains the key number (Search Path) used by Btrieve to determine the order in which the records are processed. For a more detailed description of the key indexes available in Btrieve, consult the Btrieve manual.

Global Variables

▼

BTrvRecInfo This global array of structures contains the pointer (*RecPtr) to the record commonly used by the Btrieve routines, the Btrieve data file position information buffer (BTrvVar), which is similar in use to a FILE stream buffer, and the length of the data record (RecLen). This structure is initialized by the library routine Open_File().

Error Codes/ Messages

▼

The completion code returned from the Btrieve record manager is the only error indicator provided by this routine. For a complete list of the error codes, see your Btrieve reference manual.

Discussion

Delete_Record deletes existing data records in a Btrieve database. Delete-_Record deletes the record located at the position in the file (FileNum) established by the last Get operation (e.g., Get_Record, Next_record, etc.). The function calls Btrieve operation 4 (Delete), through the function Btrv (Listing 3-1) to delete the current data record.

Limitations and Modifications

The Btrieve Record Manager must be loaded prior to calling any Btrieve operations. If the record manager is not loaded, an error results on any calls to Btrv.

Since there are several error codes that can be returned from Btrv, you may want to establish an error message routine for displaying the meaning of the error returned. This provides more information on the error without having to use your Btrieve reference manual to look up the error code's meaning.

Routine Source Code

```
#include <math.h>
#include <dos.h>
#include <string.h>
#include <stdio.h>
#include <stdlib.h>
#include <ctype.h>
#include <plib.h>

extern struct
{
  char
    *RecPtr,
    BTrvVar[128],
    CurInd[256];

  int
    RecLen;
} BTrvRecInfo[20];

int Delete_Record(char FileNum,
                  int CurKeyNum)
/*
  This function will delete the last record (or key) retrieved, updating
  the necessary information in the global structure BTrvRecInfo[FileNum].
  It will then return the BTrv status code.
*/
{/*Delete_Record*/
  char
```

```
    DumRec;

  return(BTrv(4,BTrvRecInfo[FileNum].BTrvVar,&DumRec,&DumRec,
          &DumRec,CurKeyNum));
}/*Delete_Record*/
```

Sample Usage Source Code

▼

See the library routine Record_Entry_Control, in this chapter, for an example of using this routine.

End_Btrieve

Description

▼

End_Btrieve terminates the interface to Btrieve and removes the memory-resident record manager. Once this routine has been called, you cannot make any additional calls to Btrieve until the record manager is reloaded from the DOS prompt. Do not attempt to reload the record manager from inside an application, because the memory-resident manager will load above your application in memory and cause numerous memory usage problems. The routine uses Btrieve operation 25 (Stop) to perform the removal of the record manager. Listing 3-1, Btrv, used to interface Turbo C to Btrieve, is also discussed in the Btrieve reference manual.

Routine Declaration

▼

```
int End_BTrieve(void)
```

Passed Variables

▼

None

Global Variables

▼

None

Error Codes/ Messages

▼

The completion code returned from the Btrieve record manager is the only error indicator provided by this routine. For a complete list of the error codes, see your Btrieve reference manual.

Discussion

▼

End_Btrieve removes the record manager from memory and subsequently closes all files not closed prior to calling the function. The function calls Btrieve operation 25 (Stop). All variables in the call to Btrv are passed as dummy values, because operation 25 does not require any values other than the operation number. The call to Btrieve is accomplished through the function Btrv (Listing 3-1).

Limitations and Modifications

▼

The Btrieve Record Manager must be loaded prior to calling any Btrieve operations. If the record manager is not loaded, an error results on any calls to Btrv.

Since there are several error codes that can be returned from Btrv, you may want to establish an error message routine for displaying the meaning of the error returned. This provides more information on the error without having to use your Btrieve reference manual to look up the error code's meaning.

Routine Source Code

▼

```
#include <math.h>
#include <dos.h>
#include <string.h>
#include <stdio.h>
#include <stdlib.h>
#include <ctype.h>
#include <plib.h>

extern struct
{
  char
    *RecPtr,
    BTrvVar[128],
    CurInd[256];

  int
    RecLen;
} BTrvRecInfo[20];

int End_BTrieve(void)
/*
  This function will terminate BTrieve, removing the record manager and
  closing the BTR.TRN file. If unsuccessful, it will return a nonzero
  code indicating the reason.
*/
{/*End_BTrieve*/
  char
    DumRec;

  return(BTrv(25,&DumRec,&DumRec,&DumRec,&DumRec,1));
}/*End_BTrieve*/
```

Sample Usage Source Code

▼

See the sample application Customer, in Chapter 5, for an example of using this routine.

Get_Record

Description

▼

Get_Record retrieves a record, located by the key value passed, from the specified Btrieve database file. If the record cannot be located, an error code is returned. The routine uses Btrieve operation 5 (Get Equal) to retrieve the record. Listing 3-1, Btrv, used to interface Turbo C to Btrieve, is also discussed in the Btrieve reference manual.

Routine Declaration

▼

```
int Get_Record(int  FileNum,
               char *DataRec,
               int  CurKeyNum,
               char *Key)
```

Passed Variables

▼

FileNum integer This field contains the number of the file containing the record being retrieved. This number accesses the global array of structures that contain the file specifications.

***DataRec Pointer** This variable contains the address in which to store the record retrieved.

CurKeyNum integer This field contains the key number (Search Path) used by Btrieve to determine the order in which the records are processed. For a more detailed description of the key indexes available in Btrieve, consult the Btrieve manual.

***Key String Pointer** A pointer to the key value to be used to locate the desired record. The key passed should be completely padded with Nulls before being passed.

Global Variables

▼

BTrvRecInfo This global array of structures contains the pointer (*RecPtr) to the record commonly used by the Btrieve routines, the Btrieve data file position information buffer (BTrvVar), which is similar in use to a FILE stream buffer, and the length of the data record (RecLen). This structure is initialized by the library routine Open_File().

Error Codes/ Messages

▼

The completion code returned from the Btrieve record manager is the only error indicator provided by this routine. For a complete list of the error codes, see your Btrieve reference manual.

Discussion

▼

Get_Record retrieves the actual data record from a Btrieve database. Get-_Record retrieves the record from file FileNum in the key path CurKeyNum that has the same key value as Key, and places the record at the location pointed to by *DataRec. The function calls Btrieve operation 5 (Get Equal). The call to Btrieve is accomplished through the function Btrv (Listing 3-1).

Limitations and Modifications

▼

The Btrieve Record Manager must be loaded prior to calling any Btrieve operations. If the record manager is not loaded, an error results on any calls to Btrv.

Since there are several error codes that can be returned from Btrv, you may want to establish an error message routine for displaying the meaning of the error returned. This provides more information on the error without having to use your Btrieve reference manual to look up the error code's meaning.

Routine Source Code

▼

```
#include <math.h>
#include <mem.h>
#include <dos.h>
#include <string.h>
#include <stdio.h>
#include <stdlib.h>
#include <ctype.h>
#include <plib.h>

extern struct
{
  char
    *RecPtr,
    BTrvVar[128],
    CurInd[256];

  int
    RecLen;
} BTrvRecInfo[20];

int Get_Record(int FileNum,
               char *DataRec,
```

```
            int CurKeyNum,
            char *Key)
/*
  This function will put the specified record that matches the value in
  Key into DataRec, and will return a nonzero BTrv error code (the
  BTrv status code) if it cannot find it.
*/
{/*Get_Record*/
  setmem(BTrvRecInfo[FileNum].CurInd, sizeof(BTrvRecInfo[FileNum].CurInd), 0);
  strcpy(BTrvRecInfo[FileNum].CurInd, Key);
  return(BTrv(5, BTrvRecInfo[FileNum].BTrvVar, DataRec,
             &BTrvRecInfo[FileNum].RecLen,
           BTrvRecInfo[FileNum].CurInd, CurKeyNum));
}/*Get_Record*/
```

Sample Usage Source Code

▼

See the sample usage for the library routine Search_Record in the sample application Customer, in Chapter 5, for an example of using this routine. Get_Record is used in the same manner except it retrieves exact matches of key values.

Highest_Record

Description

▼

Highest_Record returns the record at the high end of the search path in the specified database. The routine uses Btrieve operation 13 (Get Highest) to retrieve the last record in the data file. Listing 3-1, Btrv, used to interface Turbo C to Btrieve, is also discussed in the Btrieve reference manual.

Routine Declaration

▼

```
int Highest_Record(int  FileNum,
                   char *DataRec,
                   int  CurKeyNum)
```

Passed Variables

▼

FileNum integer This field contains the number of the file containing the desired record. This number accesses the global array of structures that contain the file specifications.

***DataRec Pointer** This variable contains the address in which to store the retrieved record.

CurKeyNum integer This field contains the key number (Search Path) used by Btrieve to determine the order in which the records are processed. For a more detailed description of the key indexes available in Btrieve, consult the Btrieve manual.

Global Variables

▼

BTrvRecInfo This global array of structures contains the pointer (*RecPtr) to the record commonly used by the Btrieve routines, the Btrieve data file position information buffer (BTrvVar), which is similar in use to a FILE stream buffer, and the length of the data record (RecLen). This structure is initialized by the library routine Open_File().

Error Codes/ Messages

▼

The completion code returned from the Btrieve record manager is the only error indicator provided by this routine. For a complete list of the error codes, see your Btrieve reference manual.

Discussion

▼

Highest_Record retrieves the last record in the search path in a Btrieve database file. Highest_Record retrieves the last record from the file FileNum in the search path CurKeyNum and places the record in the location pointed to by *DataRec. The function calls Btrieve operation 13 (Get Highest). The call to Btrieve is accomplished through the function Btrv (Listing 3-1).

Limitations and Modifications

▼

The Btrieve Record Manager must be loaded prior to calling any Btrieve operations. If the record manager is not loaded, an error results on any calls to Btrv.

Since there are several error codes that can be returned from Btrv, you may want to establish an error message routine for displaying the meaning of the error returned. This provides more information on the error without having to use your Btrieve reference manual to look up the error code's meaning.

Routine Source Code

▼

```
#include <math.h>
#include <dos.h>
#include <string.h>
#include <stdio.h>
#include <stdlib.h>
#include <ctype.h>
#include <plib.h>

extern struct
{
```

```
  char
    *RecPtr,
    BTrvVar[128],
    CurInd[256];

  int
    RecLen;
} BTrvRecInfo[20];

int Highest_Record(int FileNum,
                   char *DataRec,
                   int CurKeyNum)
/*
  This function will place the highest record for FileNum in the index
  list (chosen by CurKeyNum) into DataRec. If unsuccessful for some reason,
  a nonzero status code from BTrv is returned.
*/
{/*Highest_Record*/

  return(BTrv(13,BTrvRecInfo[FileNum].BTrvVar,DataRec,
         &BTrvRecInfo[FileNum].RecLen,
       BTrvRecInfo[FileNum].CurInd,
       CurKeyNum));
}/*Highest_Record*/
```

Sample Usage Source Code

▼

See the library routine Record_Entry_Control, in this chapter, for an example of using this routine.

Lowest_Record

Description

▼

Lowest_Record retrieves the very first record in a database search path specified, using Btrieve operation 12 (Get Lowest). Listing 3-1, Btrv, used to interface Turbo C to Btrieve, is also discussed in the Btrieve reference manual.

Routine Declaration

▼

```
int Lowest_Record(int  FileNum,
                  char *DataRec,
                  int  CurKeyNum)
```

Passed Variables

▼

FileNum integer This field contains the number of the file containing the desired record. This number accesses the global array of structures that contain the file specifications.

***DataRec Pointer** This variable contains the address in which to store the retrieved record.

CurKeyNum integer This field contains the key number (Search Path) used by Btrieve to determine the order in which the records are processed. For a more detailed description of the key indexes available in Btrieve, consult the Btrieve manual.

Global Variables

▼

BTrvRecInfo This global array of structures contains the pointer (*RecPtr) to the record commonly used by the Btrieve routines, the Btrieve data file position information buffer (BTrvVar), which is similar in use to a FILE stream buffer, and the length of the data record (RecLen). This structure is initialized by the library routine Open_File().

Error Codes/ Messages

▼

The completion code returned from the Btrieve record manager is the only error indicator provided by this routine. For a complete list of the error codes, see your Btrieve reference manual.

Discussion

▼

Lowest_Record retrieves the very first record found in a specified index search path in a Btrieve database file. Lowest_Record retrieves the first record from the file FileNum in the search path CurKeyNum and places the record at the address pointed to by *DataRec. The function calls Btrieve operation 12 (Get Lowest) through the function Btrv (Listing 3-1).

Limitations and Modifications

▼

The Btrieve Record Manager must be loaded prior to calling any Btrieve operations. If the record manager is not loaded, an error results on any calls to Btrv.

Since there are several error codes that can be returned from Btrv, you may want to establish an error message routine for displaying the meaning of the error returned. This provides more information on the error without having to use your Btrieve reference manual to look up the error code's meaning.

Routine Source Code

▼

```
#include <math.h>
#include <dos.h>
#include <string.h>
#include <stdio.h>
```

```
#include <stdlib.h>
#include <ctype.h>
#include <plib.h>

extern struct
{
  char
    *RecPtr,
    BTrvVar[128],
    CurInd[256];

  int
    RecLen;
} BTrvRecInfo[20];

int Lowest_Record(int FileNum,
                  char *DataRec,
                  int CurKeyNum)
/*
  This function will place the lowest record for FileNum in the index
  list (chosen by CurKeyNum) into DataRec. If unsuccessful for some reason,
  a nonzero status code from BTrv is returned.
*/
{/*Lowest_Record*/

  return(BTrv(12,BTrvRecInfo[FileNum].BTrvVar,DataRec,
        &BTrvRecInfo[FileNum].RecLen, BTrvRecInfo[FileNum].CurInd,
      CurKeyNum));
}/*Lowest_Record*/
```

Sample Usage Source Code

▼

See the library routine Record_Entry_Control, in this chapter, for an example of using this routine.

Make_File

Description

▼

Make_File creates a new Btrieve database file from a predefined specification stored in a disk file, but does not open the file after completion. The disk file can be created using the utility Make Definition, shown in Chapter 5. You must call Open_File after the file has been created before you can perform any file operations for maintaining records. The routine uses Btrieve operation 14 (Create) to perform the actual creation of the new file. Listing 3-1, Btrv, used to interface Turbo C to Btrieve, is also discussed in the Btrieve reference manual.

Routine Declaration

▼

```
int Make_File(char *BtrvVar,
              char *FileName,
              char *FileDefName)
```

Passed Variables

▼

***BTrvVar Pointer** The address of the Btrieve file position information.

***FileName String Pointer** A pointer to the filename of the Btrieve data file to be created.

***FileDefName String Pointer** A pointer to the string that contains the name of the definition file.

Global Variables

▼

None

Error Codes/ Messages

▼

```
Error - not enough memory to load data base definition
```

This fatal error message appears if there is not enough available far heap memory to contain the definition information.

```
F.N.F. - Data base specification file FILENAME
```

This fatal error message appears if the specified definition file cannot be opened.

The completion code returned from the Btrieve record manager is the only error indicator provided by this routine. For a complete list of the error codes, see your Btrieve reference manual.

Discussion

▼

Make_File creates new Btrieve database files. The operation call creates the file, but does not open the file for use. You must call the related routine Open_File to actually open the file for updating.

Make_File begins by attempting to open the specified definition file. If the file cannot be opened or found, a fatal error occurs. After the file is opened, the first two bytes are read as an integer which indicates the number of bytes of specification data following. Then, Make_File attempts to allocate enough memory to store the specifications. If the allocation is unsuccessful, a fatal error occurs. Once the space is allocated, the remaining specification information is read from the file. The function calls Btrieve operation 14 (Create). A pointer to the allocated space containing the specification information is passed to the Btrieve operation. The call to Btrieve is accomplished through the function Btrv

(Listing 3-1). Finally, the memory is deallocated, the files are closed, and the status is returned.

Limitations and Modifications

▼

The Btrieve Record Manager must be loaded prior to calling any Btrieve operations. If the record manager is not loaded, an error results on any calls to Btrv.

Since there are several error codes that can be returned from Btrv, you may want to establish an error message routine for displaying the meaning of the error returned. This provides more information on the error without having to use your Btrieve reference manual to look up the error code's meaning.

Routine Source Code

▼

```
#include <math.h>
#include <mem.h>
#include <alloc.h>
#include <dos.h>
#include <string.h>
#include <stdio.h>
#include <stdlib.h>
#include <ctype.h>
#include <plib.h>

extern struct
{
  char
    *RecPtr,
    BTrvVar[128];

  int
    RecLen;
} BTrvRecInfo[20];

int Make_File(char *BtrvVar,
              char *FileName,
              char *FileDefName)
/*
  This function will create a BTRIEVE data file called FileName of the type
  specified by the file FileDefName (a file created by the utility MakDef).
  The first word in the file specified by FileDefName is the length of the
  definition record.  The remaining data is the definition record.
  Make_File will load this remaining data into a dynamic buffer if enough
  memory is left to do it, then make the BTrv call to create a file.
  When complete, the buffer space will be deallocated and Make_File will
  return with the status from the BTrv call.
*/
```

```
{/*Make_File*/
  char
    *Rec,
    TStr[128];

  int
    Stat,
    RecSize;

  FILE
    *DefFile;

  Stat=0;
  DefFile=fopen(FileDefName,"rb");
  if (DefFile!=NULL)
  {
    fread(&RecSize,2,1,DefFile);
    Rec=farmalloc(RecSize);
    if (Rec!=NULL)
    {
      fread(Rec,1,RecSize,DefFile);
      Stat=BTrv(14,BtrvVar,Rec,&RecSize,FileName,0);
      fclose(DefFile);
      farfree(Rec);
    }
    else
    {
      fclose(DefFile);
      Bomb_Mess("Error - not enough memory to load database definition");
    }
  }
  else
  {
    sprintf(TStr,"F.N.F. - Database specification file %s",FileDefName);
    Bomb_Mess(TStr);
  }
  return(Stat);
}/*Make_File*/
```

Sample Usage Source Code

▼

See the similar usage of RMake_file in the sample application Customer, in Chapter 5, for an example of using this routine.

Mode_Select

Description

▼

Mode_Select uses the library routine Menu to display a menu for selecting record updating options for data entry screens. The menu provides options for changing records, adding records, locating records by key index, and selecting help.

Routine Declaration

```
void Mode_Select(int  FileNum,
                 int  *Mode,
                 char *Title)
```

Passed Variables

FileNum integer This field contains the number of the file being manipulated. This number accesses the global array of structures that contain the file specifications.

***Mode integer Pointer** A pointer to the integer that contains the current mode and the selected mode from the menu upon exit.

***Title String Pointer** A pointer to the title string to be displayed on the top left side of the window displayed. The title string should not exceed 37 characters. If it is longer, it will be truncated to 37 characters before being displayed.

Global Variables

CurKey This global variable contains the value of the keyboard keystroke retrieved by Get_One_Char or Look_One_Char. If the keystroke is prefixed (a two-byte scan code), CurKey contains a negative value equal to the significant byte of the scan codes. For example, pressing A returns a 65 in CurKey and pressing F1 returns −59.

Error Codes/ Messages

```
This selection is not used
```

Option four of the menu is currently set to NotUsed. This was installed so you may implement your own additional option. With the code installed as shown in this text, this option displays the message shown above.

```
No records exist in this file, select "Add", "Help" or press Esc
```

This message is displayed on the 25th line of the display if Change, Locate, or NotUsed mode is selected and the file does not contain any records.

Discussion

Mode_Select provides an alternative to the usual menu used to select file maintenance options. Most software uses a vertical menu for selecting whether to add, modify, or locate a record in a data file. Mode_Select uses a horizontal menu that requires less space and is more interactive with the user.

Mode_Select begins by writing a double graphics line to the top line of the screen, assumes a Draw_Frame has been done, and displays the first 37 characters of the title. Then a do-while loop is entered, which uses Menu to present and select a menu option. The option is verified for the different modes and the loop exits if the mode is valid. Upon exiting the loop, Mode_select checks to see if the current file has valid records. If no records are present, an error message is displayed informing the user. Before completion, Mode_Select resets the top line of the window to a double graphics line.

Limitations and Modifications

▼

Mode_Select has several areas for potential modification. The current state shows the method we used to organize our applications. However, you may want to change the border control, currently hard set to double graphics lines, or the options designed for the menu. The option NotUsed was left open to accommodate record query capabilities like those provided with Novell's XQL product. XQL is an SQL-based (Structured Query Language) product used to create relational database applications.

Routine Source Code

▼

```
#include <math.h>
#include <dos.h>
#include <mem.h>
#include <string.h>
#include <stdio.h>
#include <stdlib.h>
#include <ctype.h>
#include <plib.h>

extern char
  Normal,
  Reverse,
  VidHigh,
  Background,
  RecChanged;

extern int
  CurKey;

extern struct
{
  char
    *RecPtr,
    BTrvVar[128],
    CurInd[256];

  int
```

```
    RecLen;
} BTrvRecInfo[20];

void Mode_Select(int FileNum,
                 int *Mode,
                 char *Title)
/*
  This function will allow the user to select the standard five record
  management options available for standard record entry screens.
  Title will be shown on the top left, *Mode will contain the user's
  choice.
*/
{ /*Mode_Select*/
  char
    NotPass,
    Tag[81];

  F_Write(2, 1, Blend(Normal), Rpt("=", Tag, 78));
  F_Write(2, 1, VidHigh, Copy(Title, 1,
          strlen(Title)+((strlen(Title) > 37) * (37-strlen(Title))),
          Tag));
  do
  {
    do
    {
      Menu(
      "/1/1/Change══/9/1/Add════/16/1/Locate══/24/1/NotUsed══/33/1/Help════/",
          Mode, Tag, 0, 39, 1, 40, 1, Background);
      if ((*Mode == 5) && (CurKey != 27))
      {
        Help_File("updt.hlp", "File Maintenance Options - Help");
        CurKey = 13;
      }
      /*Remove the following code block when installing NotUsed*/
      if (*Mode == 4)
      {
        Lo_Mess("This selection is not used.");
        *Mode = 5;
      }
    }while ((*Mode == 5) && (CurKey != 27));
    if (*Mode == 2)
      setmem(BTrvRecInfo[FileNum].RecPtr,
             BTrvRecInfo[FileNum].RecLen,0);
    NotPass = ((Used_Recs(BTrvRecInfo[FileNum].BTrvVar) < 1.0) &&
              ((*Mode == 1) || (*Mode ==3) || (*Mode == 4)) &&
              (CurKey != 27));
    if (NotPass)
    {
```

```
        Cnvg_Mess(
              "No records exist in this file, select 'Add', 'Help' or Press Esc"
                );
        Beep_Lo();
        *Mode = 2;
      }
    }while (NotPass);
    F_Write(2, 1 ,Blend(Normal), Rpt("=", Tag, 78));
} /*Mode_Select*/
```

Sample Usage Source Code

▼

See the sample application Customer, in Chapter 5, for an example of using this routine.

Mode_Update

Description

▼

Mode_Update displays the screen title, current number of records in the active file, and current mode name on the top line of the update screen. For more information on Mode and the different options, see Mode_Select.

Routine Declaration

▼

```
void Mode_Update(int  FileNum,
                 int  Mode,
                 char *Title)
```

Passed Variables

▼

FileNum integer   This field contains the number of the file being manipulated. This number accesses the global array of structures that contain the file specifications.

Integer Pointer   The integer that contains the current mode and the selected mode from the menu upon exit.

***Title String Pointer**   A pointer to the title to be displayed on the top left side of the window displayed. The title string should not exceed 37 characters. If it is longer, it will be truncated to 37 characters before being displayed.

Global Variables

▼

None

Error Codes/ Messages

▼

None

Discussion

▼

Mode_Update provides an easy way to inform the user of the current file maintenance mode being used. The routine is primarily a cosmetic enhancement to file maintenance routines. However, it does provide you with a route to performing specialized processing for different modes at specific points in the file maintenance cycle.

Mode_Update starts by displaying the title along the top line of the update window and then uses a switch statement with F_Writes writing the appropriate title for each mode.

Limitations and Modifications

▼

If you change the titles of the maintenance options in Mode_Select, you will also need to change the options here in Mode_Update. You can also use the switch statement in Mode_Update to perform other application-specific processing at the change of each mode.

Routine Source Code

▼

```
#include <math.h>
#include <dos.h>
#include <string.h>
#include <stdio.h>
#include <stdlib.h>
#include <ctype.h>
#include <plib.h>

extern char
  Normal,
  Reverse,
  VidHigh,
  BackGround,
  RecChanged;

extern int
  CurKey;

extern struct
{
  char
    *RecPtr,
    BTrvVar[128],
    CurInd[256];
```

```
  int
    RecLen;
} BTrvRecInfo[20];

void Mode_Update(int FileNum,
                 int Mode,
                 char *Title)
/*
  This procedure will redisplay the condition of Mode, based on the standard
  five options for it as it is currently set. (see Mode_Select).
*/
{ /*Mode_Update*/
  char
    TStr[81];

  int
    Loc = 70;

  F_Write(40-(strlen(Title) / 2), 1, Reverse, Copy(Title, 1,
          strlen(Title) + ((strlen(Title) > 37) * (37-strlen(Title))),
          TStr));
  sprintf(TStr, "Recs : %6.0f",Used_Recs(BTrvRecInfo[FileNum].BTrvVar));
  F_Write(3, 1, Reverse, TStr);
  switch (Mode)
  {
    case 1:
      F_Write(Loc, 1, Reverse, "=Change=");
    break;
    case 2:
      F_Write(Loc, 1, Reverse, "==Add==");
    break;
    case 3:
      F_Write(Loc, 1, Reverse, "=Locate=");
    break;
    case 4:
      F_Write(Loc, 1, Reverse, "=Qualify=");
    break;

    case 5:
      F_Write(Loc, 1, Reverse, "==Help==");
    break;
  }
} /*Mode_Update*/
```

Sample Usage Source Code

▼

See the sample application Customer, in Chapter 5, for an example of using this routine.

Next_Key

Description

▼

Next_Key returns the next index key, but not the data record, in the specified index search path. The routine uses Btrieve operations 50 (Get Key) and 6 (Get Next), added together, to perform the index key retrieval. Listing 3-1, Btrv, used to interface Turbo C to Btrieve, is also discussed in the Btrieve reference manual.

Routine Declaration

▼

```
int Next_Key(int  FileNum,
             char *Key,
             int  CurKeyNum)
```

Passed Variables

▼

FileNum integer This field contains the number of the file being manipulated. This number accesses the global array of structures that contain the file specifications.

***Key String Pointer** A pointer to the key value to be used to locate the desired record. It contains the key value located upon return. The key passed should be completely padded with Nulls before being passed.

CurKeyNum integer This field contains the key number (Search Path) used by Btrieve to determine the order in which the records are processed. For a more detailed description of the key indexes available in Btrieve, consult the Btrieve manual.

Global Variables

▼

BTrvRecInfo This global array of structures contains the pointer (*RecPtr) to the record commonly used by the Btrieve routines, the Btrieve data file position information buffer (BTrvVar), which is similar in use to a FILE stream buffer, and the length of the data record (RecLen). This structure is initialized by the library routine Open_File().

Error Codes/ Messages

▼

The completion code returned from the Btrieve record manager is the only error indicator provided by this routine. For a complete list of the error codes, see your Btrieve reference manual.

Discussion

▼

Next_Key searches the index search path specified by CurKeyNum for the next consecutive index key value. The operation does not retrieve the data record, only the index key. The function calls Btrieve operations 50 (Get Key) and 6 (Get Next). Adding these two values together retrieves the next records key and not the actual data record. This is often much faster then simply retrieving the entire data record. The call to Btrieve is accomplished through the function Btrv (Listing 3-1).

Limitations and Modifications

▼

The Btrieve Record Manager must be loaded prior to calling any Btrieve operations. If the record manager is not loaded, an error results on any calls to Btrv.

Since there are several error codes that can be returned from Btrv, you may want to establish an error message routine for displaying the meaning of the error returned. This provides more information on the error without having to use your Btrieve reference manual to look up the error code's meaning.

Routine Source Code

▼

```
#include <math.h>
#include <dos.h>
#include <string.h>
#include <stdio.h>
#include <stdlib.h>
#include <ctype.h>
#include <plib.h>

extern struct
{
  char
    *RecPtr,
    BTrvVar[128],
    CurInd[256];

  int
    RecLen;
} BTrvRecInfo[20];

int Next_Key(int FileNum,
             char *Key,
             int CurKeyNum)
/*
  This function will place the next key in path CurKeyNum
  from the last one (record or key) retrieved from FileNum into Key.
  If there are no more records in the search path (it's at the end of the file),
  a nonzero status code from the BTrv function will be returned.
*/
{/*Next_Key*/
  char
```

```
    DumRec;

  int
    Stat,
    DumRecLen;

  Stat = BTrv(56,BTrvRecInfo[FileNum].BTrvVar, &DumRec,
        &DumRecLen, BTrvRecInfo[FileNum].CurInd, CurKeyNum);
  strcpy(Key, BTrvRecInfo[FileNum].CurInd);
  return(Stat);
}/*Next_Key*/
```

Sample Usage Source Code

▼

See the usage of Next_Record in the library routine Record_Entry_Control, in this chapter. Next_Record works the same way except it retrieves a key instead of a data record.

Next_Record

Description

▼

Next_Record retrieves the next consecutive record from the Btrieve database file specified by FileNum. The index key search path specified (CurKeyNum) is used to determine the next record. The routine uses Btrieve operation 6 (Get Next) to perform the retrieval of the next record. Listing 3-1, Btrv, used to interface Turbo C to Btrieve, is also discussed in the Btrieve reference manual.

Routine Declaration

▼

```
int Next_Record(int  FileNum,
                char *DataRec,
                int  CurKeyNum)
```

Passed Variables

▼

FileNum integer This field contains the number of the file containing the desired next record. This number accesses the global array of structures that contain the file specifications.

***DataRec Pointer** This variable contains the address of the data structure to receive the retrieved record.

CurKeyNum integer This field contains the key number (Search Path) used by Btrieve to determine the order in which the records are processed. For a more detailed description of the key indexes available in Btrieve, consult the Btrieve manual.

Global Variables

▼

BTrvRecInfo This global array of structures contains the pointer (*RecPtr) to the record commonly used by the Btrieve routines, the Btrieve data file position information buffer (BTrvVar), which is similar in use to a FILE stream buffer, and the length of the data record (RecLen). This structure is initialized by the library routine Open_File().

Error Codes/ Messages

▼

The completion code returned from the Btrieve record manager is the only error indicator provided by this routine. For a complete list of the error codes, see your Btrieve reference manual.

Discussion

▼

Next_Record finds and retrieves the next record from the Btrieve file specified by FileNum. The order of retrieval is determined by the search path specified in CurKeyNum. The function calls Btrieve operation 6 (Get Next). The call to Btrieve is accomplished through the function Btrv (Listing 3-1).

Limitations and Modifications

▼

The Btrieve Record Manager must be loaded prior to calling any Btrieve operations. If the record manager is not loaded, an error results on any calls to Btrv.

Since there are several error codes that can be returned from Btrv, you may want to establish an error message routine for displaying the meaning of the error returned. This provides more information on the error without having to use your Btrieve reference manual to look up the error code's meaning.

Routine Source Code

▼

```
#include <math.h>
#include <dos.h>
#include <string.h>
#include <stdio.h>
#include <stdlib.h>
#include <ctype.h>
#include <plib.h>

extern struct
{
  char
    *RecPtr,
    BTrvVar[128],
    CurInd[256];
```

```
  int
    RecLen;
} BTrvRecInfo[20];

int Next_Record(int FileNum,
                char *DataRec,
                int CurKeyNum)
/*
  This function will place the next record in path CurKeyNum
  from the last one retrieved from FileNum into DataRec. If there
  are no more records in the search path (it's at the end of the file),
  a nonzero status code from the BTrv function will be returned.
*/
{/*Next_Record*/

  return(BTrv(6,BTrvRecInfo[FileNum].BTrvVar,DataRec,
         &BTrvRecInfo[FileNum].RecLen, BTrvRecInfo[FileNum].CurInd,
       CurKeyNum));

}/*Next_Record*/
```

Sample Usage Source Code

▼

See the library routine Record_Entry_Control, in this chapter, or the sample application Customer, in Chapter 5, for an example of using this routine.

Open_File

Description

▼

Open_File establishes a precreated Btrieve file for use in Btrieve input and output routines. Open_File does not create a new file. This must be accomplished with the library routine RMake_File or Make_File. Open_File allows four options for the method of file manipulation desires. Option 0 is for standard retrieval, −1 is for accelerated updating, −2 is for read-only, and −3 for automatic verification of all updates. The routine uses Btrieve operation 0 (Open) to perform the addition of the new record. Listing 3-1, Btrv, used to interface Turbo C to Btrieve, is also discussed in the Btrieve reference manual.

Routine Declaration

▼

```
int Open_File(int  FileNum,
              char *FileName,
              char *StandardRec,
              int  Mode)
```

Passed Variables

▼

FileNum integer This field contains the number to associate with the file being opened. This number accesses the global array of structures that contain the file specifications.

***FileName String Pointer** A pointer to the filename of the Btrieve data file to be opened.

***StandardRec Pointer** Address of the standard data structure used for record transmission and reception to the Btrieve record manager.

Mode integer This field contains the file opening options allowed by Btrieve. The options are 0 for standard retrieval, −1 for accelerated updating, −2 for read-only, and −3 for automatic verification of all updates. See your Btrieve manual for more information on using these modes.

Global Variables

▼

None

Error Codes/ Messages

▼

The completion code returned from the Btrieve record manager is the only error indicator provided by this routine. For a complete list of the error codes, see your Btrieve reference manual.

Discussion

▼

Btrieve allows you to open a file for a specific user by passing the owner's name to the operation for opening a file. Open_File does not specify a specific owner for any files. Instead, it passes the owner's name as a null string allowing anyone to have access to the file. The function calls Btrieve operation 0 (Open). The call to Btrieve is accomplished through the function Btrv (Listing 3-1).

To accomplish the opening, Open_File first initializes OwnerName and sets OwnerNameLen to 0. Then, Open_File opens the specified file and saves the return code in the variable Stat. If the operation is successful, a status call is made to Btrieve to determine the record length for that file so the global variable BTrvRecInfo[FileNum].RecLen can be set. Next, the global variable BTrvRecInfo[FileNum].RecPtr is set to the address of the StandardRec. Finally, Open_File returns the status of the file-open operation.

Limitations and Modifications

▼

The Btrieve Record Manager must be loaded prior to calling any Btrieve operations. If the record manager is not loaded, an error results on any calls to Btrv.

Because there are several error codes that can be returned from Btrv, you may want to establish an error message routine for displaying the meaning of the error returned. This provides more information on the error without having to use your Btrieve reference manual to look up the error code's meaning.

Routine Source Code

▼

```
#include <math.h>
#include <dos.h>
#include <string.h>
#include <stdio.h>
#include <stdlib.h>
#include <ctype.h>
#include <plib.h>

extern struct
{
  char
    *RecPtr,
    BTrvVar[128],
    CurInd[256];

  int
    RecLen;
} BTrvRecInfo[20];

int Open_File(int FileNum,
              char *FileName,
              char *StandardRec,
              int Mode)
/*
  This function opens a file under the BTrieve system and sets the global
  variable BTrvRecInfo[FileNum] up with all necessary information (one of
  which is the location of the data buffer to move information in and out
  of with the other calls). The routine then returns the code returned from
  the BTrv open file call.
*/
{/*Open_File*/
  char
    OwnerName[1],
    ExtendName[65], /*Name of extension file*/
    StatRec[400]; /*Maximum definition record size*/

  int
    StatRecLen = 400,
    Stat,
    OwnerNameLen;

  OwnerName[0]=0;
  OwnerNameLen=0;
```

```
  Stat=BTrv(0,BTrvRecInfo[FileNum].BTrvVar,OwnerName,
        &OwnerNameLen,FileName,Mode);
  if (Stat==0)
  {

    if (BTrv(15, BTrvRecInfo[FileNum].BTrvVar, StatRec, &StatRecLen,
        ExtendName, 0) == 0)
    {
      BTrvRecInfo[FileNum].RecLen = (int)(((unsigned char)StatRec[0]) +
                                   ((unsigned char)StatRec[1] << 8));
      BTrvRecInfo[FileNum].RecPtr=StandardRec;
    }
  }
  return(Stat);
}/*Open_File*/
```

Sample Usage Source Code

▼

See the sample application Customer, in Chapter 5, for an example of using this routine.

Prev_Key

Description

▼

Prev_Key returns the previous index key, but not the data record, in the specified index search path. The routine uses Btrieve operations 50 (Get Key) and 7 (Get Previous) added together, to perform the index key retrieval. Listing 3-1, Btrv, used to interface Turbo C to Btrieve, is also discussed in the Btrieve reference manual.

Routine Declaration

▼

```
int Prev_Key(int  FileNum,
             char *Key,
             int  CurKeyNum)
```

Passed Variables

▼

FileNum integer This field contains the number of the file that contains the key values being retrieved. This number accesses the global array of structures that contain the file specifications.

***Key String Pointer** A pointer to the string that will contain the retrieved key. The key passed should be completely padded with Nulls before being passed.

CurKeyNum integer This field contains the key number (Search Path) used by Btrieve to determine the order in which the records are processed. For a more detailed description of the key indexes available in Btrieve, consult the Btrieve manual.

Global Variables

▼

BTrvRecInfo This global array of structures contains the pointer (*RecPtr) to the record commonly used by the Btrieve routines, the Btrieve data file position information buffer (BTrvVar), which is similar in use to a FILE stream buffer, and the length of the data record (RecLen). This structure is initialized by the library routine Open_File().

Error Codes/ Messages

▼

The completion code returned from the Btrieve record manager is the only error indicator provided by this routine. For a complete list of the error codes, see your Btrieve reference manual.

Discussion

▼

Prev_Key searches the index search path specified by CurKeyNum for the previous consecutive index key value. The order of retrieval is determined by the search path specified in CurKeyNum. The operation does not retrieve the data record, only the index key. The function calls Btrieve operations 50 (Get Key) and 7 (Get Previous). Adding these two values together retrieves the previous records key and not the actual data record. This is often much faster then simply retrieving the entire data record. The call to Btrieve is accomplished through the function Btrv (Listing 3-1).

Limitations and Modifications

▼

The Btrieve Record Manager must be loaded prior to calling any Btrieve operations. If the record manager is not loaded, an error results on any calls to Btrv.

Since there are several error codes that can be returned from Btrv, you may want to establish an error message routine for displaying the meaning of the error returned. This provides more information on the error without having to use your Btrieve reference manual to look up the error code's meaning.

Routine Source Code

▼

```
#include <math.h>
#include <dos.h>
#include <string.h>
#include <stdio.h>
#include <stdlib.h>
#include <ctype.h>
#include <plib.h>
```

```
extern struct
{
  char
    *RecPtr,
    BTrvVar[128],
    CurInd[256];

  int
    RecLen;
} BTrvRecInfo[20];

int Prev_Key(int FileNum,
             char *Key,
             int CurKeyNum)
/*
  This function will place the previous key in path CurKeyNum
  from the last one (record or key) retrieved from FileNum into Key. If there
  are no more records in the search path (it's at the beginning of the file),
  a nonzero status code from the BTrv function will be returned.
  Key operations are generally faster than record operations.
*/
{/*Prev_Key*/
  char
    DumRec;

  int
    Stat,
    DumRecLen;

  Stat = BTrv(57,BTrvRecInfo[FileNum].BTrvVar, &DumRec,
              &DumRecLen, BTrvRecInfo[FileNum].CurInd, CurKeyNum);
  strcpy(Key, BTrvRecInfo[FileNum].CurInd);
  return(Stat);
}/*Prev_Key*/
```

Sample Usage Source Code

▼

See the routine Prev_Record, because Prev_Record operates the same way as Prev_Key, except this routine only retrieves the key value.

Prev_Record

Description

▼

Prev_Record retrieves the previous consecutive record from the Btrieve database file specified. The index key search path specified is used to determine the previous record. The routine uses Btrieve operation 7 (Get Previous) to perform the retrieval of the previous record. Listing 3-1, Btrv, used to interface Turbo C to Btrieve, is also discussed in the Btrieve reference manual.

Routine Declaration

▼

```
int Prev_Record(int  FileNum,
                char *DataRec,
                int  CurKeyNum)
```

Passed Variables

▼

FileNum integer This field contains the number of the file that contains the record to be retrieved. This number accesses the global array of structures that contain the file specifications.

***DataRec Pointer** This variable contains the address of the data structure to receive the retrieved record.

CurKeyNum integer This field contains the key number (Search Path) used by Btrieve to determine the order in which the records are processed. For a more detailed description of the key indexes available in Btrieve, consult the Btrieve manual.

Global Variables

▼

BTrvRecInfo This global array of structures contains the pointer (*RecPtr) to the record commonly used by the Btrieve routines, the Btrieve data file position information buffer (BTrvVar), which is similar in use to a FILE stream buffer, and the length of the data record (RecLen). This structure is initialized by the library routine Open_File().

Error Codes/ Messages

▼

The completion code returned from the Btrieve record manager is the only error indicator provided by this routine. For a complete list of the error codes, see your Btrieve reference manual.

Discussion

▼

Prev_Record finds and retrieves the previous record from the Btrieve file specified by FileNum and places the record in *DataRec. The order of retrieval is determined by the search path specified in CurKeyNum. The function calls Btrieve operation 7 (Get Previous). The call to Btrieve is accomplished through the function Btrv (Listing 3-1).

Limitations and Modifications

▼

The Btrieve Record Manager must be loaded prior to calling any Btrieve operations. If the record manager is not loaded, an error results on any calls to Btrv.

Since there are several error codes that can be returned from Btrv, you may want to establish an error message routine for displaying the meaning of the error returned. This provides more information on the error without having to use your Btrieve reference manual to look up the error code's meaning.

Routine Source Code

▼

```
#include <math.h>
#include <dos.h>
#include <string.h>
#include <stdio.h>
#include <stdlib.h>
#include <ctype.h>
#include <plib.h>

extern struct
{
  char
    *RecPtr,
    BTrvVar[128],
    CurInd[256];

  int
    RecLen;
} BTrvRecInfo[20];

int Prev_Record(int FileNum,
                char *DataRec,
                int CurKeyNum)
/*
  This function will place the previous record in path CurKeyNum
  from the last one retrieved from FileNum into DataRec. If there
  are no more records in the search path (it's at the beginning of the file),
  a nonzero status code from the BTrv function will be returned.
*/
{/*Prev_Record*/

  return(BTrv(7,BTrvRecInfo[FileNum].BTrvVar,DataRec,
        &BTrvRecInfo[FileNum].RecLen, BTrvRecInfo[FileNum].CurInd,
      CurKeyNum));
}/*Prev_Record*/
```

Sample Usage Source Code

▼

See the next routine, Record_Entry_Control, for an example of using this routine.

Record_Entry_Control

Description

▼

Record_Entry_Control manages the record movement and file manipulation for data entry screens. The routine accommodates the Modes described in the library routines Mode_Select and Mode_Update. Within the record management modes, Record_Entry_Control manages the forward (Tab) and backward (BackTab) record movements, changes, additions, and record deletion. In data entry screens designed with the libraries, Escape is used to exit the entry screen and has special processing in this routine.

Routine Declaration

▼

```
char Record_Entry_Control(char PassThru,
                          int  CurKeyNum,
                          int  FileNum,
                          int  *Mode)
```

Passed Variables

▼

PassThru char This field is used to indicate if function keys not used by the routine should have a message displayed or be passed back in CurKey to the calling section. If PassThru is true (1), any function or command key not used in Record_Entry_Control is left in CurKey and the routine returns. If PassThru is false, these keys result in a Bad Key Pressed message displayed for the user.

CurKeyNum integer This field specifies the index search path to use in the data file being manipulated.

FileNum integer This field contains the number of the file being manipulated. This number accesses the global array of structures that contain the file specifications.

***Mode integer Pointer** This field indicates the record manipulation mode currently active upon entering the routine and upon exit. The predefined Modes are 1 through 5 (Modify, Add, Locate, NotUsed, and Help, respectively.)

Global Variables

▼

CurKey This global variable contains the value of the keyboard keystroke retrieved by Get_One_Char or Look_One_Char. If the keystroke is prefixed (a two-byte scan code), CurKey contains a negative value equal to the significant byte of the scan codes. For example, pressing A returns a 65 in CurKey and pressing F1 returns −59.

RecChanged This global char variable informs Record_Entry_Control that the current record being manipulated has been modified by the data entry screen routines. This triggers the file update sections of Record_Entry_Control to perform an update to the file, instead of just moving to the next appropriate record or action.

Error Codes/ Messages

▼

```
Beginning of file
```

When in Modify mode and a BackTab has been pressed to move to the previous record, this message is displayed on the 25th line if the file pointer is already at the first record in the file.

```
Confirm: Delete this record (Y/N)?
```

This message appears on the 25th line of the screen when Function Key 5 has been pressed in the Modify Mode. Function Key 5 asks for a deletion of the current record. If you answer the question by pressing a Y or y, the record is deleted. Any other key cancels the deletion request. Note: a carriage return is not required after pressing the key.

```
Record on screen not found in data file to delete.
```

This message is displayed if the record on the screen is no longer in the data file open. This occurs in a multiuser environment when another user deletes the record while the current user is viewing the record.

```
Save this record (Y/N)?
```

This message is displayed on the 25th line of the screen when Escape has been pressed and the record displayed has been changed. A y or Y answer saves the changed record and any other key discard the changes.

```
Bad key pressed
```

This message is displayed on the 25th line of the screen if PassThru is set to false and a function or command key was pressed that is not supported by this routine.

Discussion

▼

Record_Entry_Control provides a single routine that handles all the file management required during entry or modification of records. The routine supports all five modes described in Mode_Select and Mode_Update, the command keys required to move forward and backward in data files, record deletion, and exiting the entry screen.

Record_Entry_Control is divided into the five main modes by a switch statement based on the Mode value passed. Within the Modify and Add modes, there is another switch statement used to interpret the value passed in CurKey for the last key pressed. Modes 3, 4, and 5 were primarily designed for application-specific use. Mode 3, Locate, was primarily designed for using indexes to locate a particular record. To implement this concept, prompt the user for the key and search path desired. Mode 4, NotUsed, is included for using a query facility such as XQL from Novell. Mode 5, Help, provides an interface to the help system made possible by Help_File. You can expand on this section by adding a menu for selecting different help topics.

Limitations and Modifications

▼

Record_Entry_Control has several predefined command keys for performing the record management. You may want to add additional command keys to the modes to accommodate functions required by your application. For example, you could add function keys for using the library routine Calculator or additional help systems. You can also perform special processing for pop-up displays by intercepting the function keys in this routine.

Routine Source Code

▼

```
#include <math.h>
#include <mem.h>
#include <dos.h>
#include <string.h>
#include <stdio.h>
#include <stdlib.h>
#include <ctype.h>
#include <plib.h>

extern char
  Normal,
  Reverse,
  VidHigh,
  Background,
  RecChanged;

extern int
  CurKey;

extern struct
{
  char
    *RecPtr,
    BTrvVar[128],
    CurInd[256];

  int
    RecLen;
} BTrvRecInfo[20];
```

```
int Record_Entry_Control(char PassThru,
                         int CurKeyNum,
                         int FileNum,
                         int *Mode)
/*
  This function handles forward (Tab) and backward (BackTab) record movement
  for entry screens. Also, the updating of records, addition of new
  records and deletion of records shown. If PassThru is true (1), this
  routine will not display a "Bad Key pressed" message for all unused command
  keys. If in add mode (2), the status of the Add_Record operations will
  be returned for option checking. If in modify mode (1), the status of the
  Change_Record of Delete_Record operations will be returned for optional
  checking.

  Example:
  while (CurKey != 27)
  {
    - Entry screen may go here
    Record_Entry_Control(., ., ., .);
  }

*/
{/*Record_Entry_Control*/
  char
    DontChange,
    Response[11];

  int
    Stat;

  DontChange = 0;
  Stat = 0;
  switch (*Mode)
  {
    case 1: /*Modify*/
      switch (CurKey)
      {
        case 9: /* Tab - Forward record*/
        case 13: /*Enter*/
          if (RecChanged)
            Stat = Change_Record(FileNum, BTrvRecInfo[FileNum].RecPtr,
                   CurKeyNum);
          if (Next_Record(FileNum, BTrvRecInfo[FileNum].RecPtr, CurKeyNum))
          { /*End of file clear record & goto Add mode*/
            *Mode=2;
            setmem(BTrvRecInfo[FileNum].RecPtr,
                   BTrvRecInfo[FileNum].RecLen,0);
          }
```

```
break;

case -15: /*BackTab - Back Record*/
  if (RecChanged)
    Stat = Change_Record(FileNum, BTrvRecInfo[FileNum].RecPtr,
                CurKeyNum);
  if (Prev_Record(FileNum, BTrvRecInfo[FileNum].RecPtr, CurKeyNum))
    Lo_Mess("Beginning of file");
break;

case -63: /*F5 - Delete Record*/
  Response[0]=0;
  Prompt(1, 25, Reverse, "Confirm: Delete this record (Y/N)? ",
       "A.,YN", Response);
  if (Response[0] == 'Y')
  {
    if (Stat = Delete_Record(FileNum, CurKeyNum))
      Lo_Mess("Record on screen not found in data file to delete.");
    else
    {
      if (Used_Recs(BTrvRecInfo[FileNum].BTrvVar) > 0.0)
      {
        Prev_Record(FileNum, BTrvRecInfo[FileNum].RecPtr, CurKeyNum);
        Next_Record(FileNum, BTrvRecInfo[FileNum].RecPtr, CurKeyNum);
      }
      else
        setmem(BTrvRecInfo[FileNum].RecPtr,
            BTrvRecInfo[FileNum].RecLen,0);
      Message("");
    }/*else*/
  }/* if Response */
  if (Used_Recs(BTrvRecInfo[FileNum].BTrvVar) < 1.0)
    *Mode=2; /*Set add mode*/
break;

case 27: /*Esc - exit */
  if (RecChanged)
  {
    Response[0]=0;
    Prompt(1, 25, Reverse, "Save this record (Y/N)? ",
         "A.,YN", Response);
    if (Response[0] == 'Y')
      Stat = Change_Record(FileNum, BTrvRecInfo[FileNum].RecPtr,
                CurKeyNum);
  }
  CurKey=27;
break;
```

```
      default:
        if (!(PassThru))
          Lo_Mess("Bad key pressed");
        DontChange = 1;
      break;
    } /*case CurKey of*/
  break;

  case 2: /*add*/
    switch (CurKey)
    {
      case -15: /*BackTab*/
        if (RecChanged)
          Stat = Add_Record(FileNum, BTrvRecInfo[FileNum].RecPtr,
                      CurKeyNum);
        if (Used_Recs(BTrvRecInfo[FileNum].BTrvVar) >= 1.0)
          *Mode = 1;
        if (Highest_Record(FileNum, BTrvRecInfo[FileNum].RecPtr, CurKeyNum))
          Lo_Mess("Beginning of file");
      break;

      case 13: /*Enter - Add record and prepare for new entry*/
      case 9:/*Tab*/
        if (RecChanged)
        {
          if (Stat = Add_Record(FileNum, BTrvRecInfo[FileNum].RecPtr,
                      CurKeyNum) == 5)
            Lo_Mess("Cannot enter a duplicate record.");
          else
            setmem(BTrvRecInfo[FileNum].RecPtr,
                  BTrvRecInfo[FileNum].RecLen,0);
        }
        else
          Lo_Mess("End of file");
      break;

      case -63: /*F5 - Delete Record*/
        Response[0] = 0;
        Prompt(1, 25, Reverse,
              "Confirm: Clear this record from screen (Y/N)? ",
              "A.,YN", Response);
        if (Response[0] == 'Y')
          setmem(BTrvRecInfo[FileNum].RecPtr,
                BTrvRecInfo[FileNum].RecLen,0);
        Message("");
      break;

      case 27: /*Esc - exit*/
```

```
        if (RecChanged)
        {
          Response[0] = 0;
          Prompt(1, 25, Reverse, "Save this record (Y/N)? ",
                 "A.,YN", Response);
          if (Response[0] == 'Y')
            Stat = Add_Record(FileNum, BTrvRecInfo[FileNum].RecPtr,
                       CurKeyNum);
          CurKey = 27;
        }
      break;

      default:
        if (!(PassThru))
          Lo_Mess("Bad key pressed");
        DontChange = 1;
      break;
    } /*case CurKey of*/
  break;

  case 3: /*Find*/
    /*Find_Record  Add code for record lookup or hooks to
                   XQL or other SQL package*/
  break;

  case 4: /*Query*/
    /*Query_Records   Add code for record lookup or hooks to
                      XQL or other SQL package*/
  break;

  case 5: /*Help*/
    /*Help('Mode.Hlp');*/
  break;
}
if (!DontChange)
  RecChanged = 0;
return(Stat);
} /*Record_Entry_Control*/
```

Sample Usage Source Code

▼

See the sample application Customer, in Chapter 5, for an example of using this routine.

RMake_File

Description

▼

RMake_File creates a new Btrieve database file from a predefined definition structure, but does not open the file after completion. You need to call Open_File after the file has been created before you can perform any file operations for maintaining records. The routine uses Btrieve operation 14 (Create) to perform the actual creation of the new file. Listing 3-1, Btrv, used to interface Turbo C to Btrieve, is also discussed in the Btrieve reference manual.

Routine Declaration

▼

```
int RMake_File(char *BTrvVar,
               char *FileName,
               char *FileDef,
               int DefRecLen)
```

Passed Variables

▼

***BTrvVar Pointer** The address of the Btrieve file position information.

***FileName String Pointer** A pointer to the filename of the Btrieve data file to be created.

***FileDef Pointer** A pointer to the data structure that contains the creation information structure.

DefRecLen integer The length of the data file creation information structure in bytes.

Global Variables

▼

None

Error Codes/ Messages

▼

The completion code returned from the Btrieve record manager is the only error indicator provided by this routine. For a complete list of the error codes, see your Btrieve reference manual.

Discussion

▼

RMake_File creates new Btrieve database files. The operation call creates the file, but does not open the file for use. You must call the related routine Open_File to actually open the file for updating. The function calls Btrieve operation 14 (Create) through the function Btrv (Listing 3-1).

Limitations and Modifications

▼

The Btrieve Record Manager must be loaded prior to calling any Btrieve operations. If the record manager is not loaded, an error results on any calls to Btrv.

Since there are several error codes that can be returned from Btrv, you may want to establish an error message routine for displaying the meaning of the error returned. This provides more information on the error without having to use your Btrieve reference manual to look up the error code's meaning.

Routine Source Code

▼

```
#include <math.h>
#include <dos.h>
#include <string.h>
#include <stdio.h>
#include <stdlib.h>
#include <ctype.h>
#include <plib.h>

extern struct
{
  char
    *RecPtr,
    BTrvVar[128],
    CurInd[256];

  int
    RecLen;
} BTrvRecInfo[20];

int RMake_File(char *BTrvVar,
               char *FileName,
               char *FileDef,
               int DefRecLen)
/*
  This function will create a Btrieve file from the definition at
  FileDef. The structure at FileDef should be layed out like this:
     (This is the structure to be used by Btrieve)
      struct
      {
        Name[31],
        Address[41],
        City[16],
        State[3],
        Zip[11],
        Phone[13];
      } Person;

      and the file creation structure would look like this for a
      key on the Name and Zip fields:
      (For the purpose of brevity, we will show this structure and
       its values as if autoinitialization of structure fields were
       possible. However, in practice, we must set these values in
       the executable portion of the code.)
```

```
     struct
     {
       int
         RecLen = 115,
         PageSize = 1024,
         NumIndex = 2;
       char
         Blank1[4] = {0,0,0,0};
       int
         Variable = 0;
       char
         Blank2[4] = {0,0,0,0};

         int
           KeyPos0 = 1,
           KeyLen1 = 30,
           KeyFlags1 = 3; (Add together 1  -  Duplicates, 2  -  Modifiable,
                                        4  -  Binary,     8  -  Null,
                                        16 -  Has Segment 32 -  Alt Col Seq)
         char
           NU1[10] = {0,0,0,0,0,0,0,0,0,0};

         int
           KeyPos2 = 92,
           KeyLen2 = 11,
           KeyFlags2 = 3;
         char
           NU2[10] = {0,0,0,0,0,0,0,0,0,0};
       } BPersonRecDef;
  To create and open the file as #0, the following
  calls would then be made:

  RMake_File(BTrvRecInfo[0].BTrvVar, "Example.Dat",
          BPersonRecDef, sizeof(BPersonRecDef));
  Open_File(0, "Example.Dat", &Person, 0);

  The alternative to creating Btrieve data files is to use the utility
  MakDef to create a definition file and the Routine Make_File instead of
  this routine to create the Btrieve data file.
*/
{/*Make_File*/
  int
    DumLen;

  return(BTrv(14, BTrvVar, FileDef, &DefRecLen, FileName, 0));
}
```

Sample Usage Source Code

▼

See the sample application Customer, in Chapter 5, for an example of using this routine.

Search_Record

Description

▼

Search_Record finds and retrieves a record whose key is equal to or greater than the key value specified for the index search path specified. If the exact index key is not found, the next consecutive larger key is used to retrieve the record. The routine uses Btrieve operation 9 (Get Greater or Equal) to perform the retrieval of the record. Listing 3-1, Btrv, used to interface Turbo C to Btrieve, is also discussed in the Btrieve reference manual.

Routine Declaration

▼

```
int Search_Record(int  FileNum,
                  char *DataRec,
                  int  CurKeyNum,
                  char *Key)
```

Passed Variables

▼

FileNum integer This field contains the number of the file being manipulated. This number accesses the global array of structures that contain the file specifications.

***DataRec Pointer** This variable contains the address of the data record retrieved by the search function.

CurKeyNum integer This field contains the key number (Search Path) used by Btrieve to determine the order in which the records are processed. For a more detailed description of the key indexes available in Btrieve, consult the Btrieve manual.

***Key String Pointer** A pointer to the key value to be used to locate the desired record. It will contain the key value located upon return. The key passed should be completely padded with Nulls before being passed.

Global Variables

▼

BTrvRecInfo This global array of structures contains the pointer (*RecPtr) to the record commonly used by the Btrieve routines, the Btrieve data file position information buffer (BTrvVar), which is similar in use to a FILE stream buffer, and the length of the data record (RecLen). This structure is initialized by the library routine Open_File().

Error Codes/ Messages

▼

The completion code returned from the Btrieve record manager is the only error indicator provided by this routine. For a complete list of the error codes, see your Btrieve reference manual.

Discussion

▼

Search_Record is useful in finding data records when you only know part of the actual key you want. The routine finds the key that is equal to the value you specify or the next larger index key in the list. The function calls Btrieve operation 9 (Get Greater or Equal). The call to Btrieve is accomplished through the function Btrv (Listing 3-1).

Limitations and Modifications

▼

The Btrieve Record Manager must be loaded prior to calling any Btrieve operations. If the record manager is not loaded, an error results on any calls to Btrv.

Because there are several error codes that can be returned from Btrv, you may want to establish an error message routine for displaying the meaning of the error returned. This provides more information on the error without having to use your Btrieve reference manual to look up the error code's meaning.

This routine goes through extra maneuvers to return a float, so returning an unsigned long would be more efficient. This is one of those oversights that is only realized after the fact.

Routine Source Code

▼

```
#include <math.h>
#include <mem.h>
#include <dos.h>
#include <string.h>
#include <stdio.h>
#include <stdlib.h>
#include <ctype.h>
#include <plib.h>

extern struct
{
  char
    *RecPtr,
    BTrvVar[128],
    CurInd[256];

  int
    RecLen;
} BTrvRecInfo[20];
```

```
int Search_Record(int FileNum,
                  char *DataRec,
                  int CurKeyNum,
                  char *Key)
/*
  This function will put the specified record that matches or is greater
  than Key in DataRec based on the path CurKeyNum. It will then return
  the BTrv status code.
*/
{/*Search_Record*/
  int
    Stat;
  setmem(BTrvRecInfo[FileNum].CurInd, sizeof(BTrvRecInfo[FileNum].CurInd), 0);
  strcpy(BTrvRecInfo[FileNum].CurInd, Key);
  Stat = BTrv(9,BTrvRecInfo[FileNum].BTrvVar,DataRec,
              &BTrvRecInfo[FileNum].RecLen,
              BTrvRecInfo[FileNum].CurInd, CurKeyNum);
  strcpy(Key, BTrvRecInfo[FileNum].CurInd);
  return(Stat);
}/*Search_Record*/
```

Sample Usage Source Code

▼

See the sample application Customer, in Chapter 5, for an example of using this routine.

Used_Recs

Description

▼

Used_Recs returns the number of active records in the specified Btrieve database file as a float number. The routine uses Btrieve operation 15 (Stat) to retrieve the status of the file. Listing 3-1, Btrv, used to interface Turbo C to Btrieve, is also discussed in the Btrieve reference manual.

Routine Declaration

▼

```
float Used_Recs(char *BTrvVar)
```

Passed Variables

▼

***BTrvVar Pointer** The address of the Btrieve data file positioning information.

Global Variables

▼

None

Error Codes/ Messages

▼

None

Discussion

▼

Used_Recs uses the status information returned from a call to the Btrieve operation 15 (Stat) to determine the number of records currently active in a database file. The call to Btrieve is accomplished through the function Btrv (Listing 3-1).

Limitations and Modifications

▼

The Btrieve Record Manager must be loaded prior to calling any Btrieve operations. If the record manager is not loaded, an error results on any calls to Btrv.

Since there are several error codes that can be returned from Btrv, you may want to establish an error message routine for displaying the meaning of the error returned. This would provide more information on the error without having to use your Btrieve reference manual to look up the error code's meaning.

Routine Source Code

▼

```
#include <math.h>
#include <dos.h>
#include <string.h>
#include <stdio.h>
#include <stdlib.h>
#include <ctype.h>
#include <plib.h>

extern struct
{
  char
    *RecPtr,
    BTrvVar[128],
    CurInd[256];

  int
    RecLen;
} BTrvRecInfo[20];

float Used_Recs(char *BTrvVar)
/*
  This function returns the number of active records in the file indicated
  by BTrvVar.
*/
{/*Used_Recs*/
```

```
  char
    TStr[50], /*Temporary string for conversion of long to float*/
    ExtendName[65], /*Name of extension file*/
    StatRec[400]; /*Maximum definition record size*/

  int
    StatRecLen = 400;

  BTrv(15, BTrvVar, StatRec, &StatRecLen, ExtendName, 0);
  ltoa(*(unsigned long *)(StatRec + 6), TStr, 10);
  return(atof(TStr));
}/*Used_Recs*/
```

Sample Usage Source Code

▼

See the routine Mode_Update used in the sample application Customer, in Chapter 5, for an example of using this routine.

4 Novell Networking Routines

Close_LST_Device Closes a spooled output device on a Novell Network file server.

Get_NTime Retrieves the current time maintained by the network.

Get_Station_Number Returns the Novell Network station number of the current user.

Global_Broadcast_Message Sends a specified message to all users on a Novell Network.

Modify_LST_Device Activates the Novell Network spooler based on the default spooler values established by Set_Spool_Flags.

Set_File_Attributes Sets or changes the attributes attached to a file on a Novell Network file server.

Set_Spool_Flags Sets the default spooler flags for a Novell Network printer.

This chapter provides selected routines for use on a Novell, Inc. NetWare local area networking (LAN) environment. We chose Novell because they are the leading manufacturer of network software. Novell's software works with a large number of hardware configurations, including Arcnet, OmniNet, IBM Token Ring, PCNet, G-Net, NESTAR, StarLan, and many others. Compatibility with the networking hardware allows NetWare to be used in almost any PC network environment. This portability and NetWare's ease of use prompted us to choose it for developing our multiuser network-based routines. The routines included in this section are only a small sampling of the functions available with NetWare. We chose several of the most useful to provide an example of how to use the functions.

For a complete list of operations available on NetWare, contact Novell and become a NetWare affiliate. This provides you with special technical support contacts and free periodic updates on what is occurring in Novell's world, as well as an extra edge in keeping your applications on the forefront of new technology. To become an affiliate, contact Novell, Inc., Mail Stop #BA2MS11, 122 E. 1700 Street, Provo, Utah 84601. When you have become an authorized affiliate, you can request the reference guide for the NetWare function Calls.

Close_LST_Device

Description

▼

Close_LST_Device terminates capture of printed output by the spooler, starts the printing of the data spooled, and resets the LST device to the local printer. The routine uses NetWare 4.0 function 0xDF, Modify LST Device, subfunction 0x01, End LST catch and queue for printing.

Routine Declaration

```
char Close_Lst_Device(void)
```

Passed Variables

None

Global Variables

None

Error Codes/ Messages

None

Discussion

Close_LST_Device stops NetWare from capturing any additional output to the DOS printer and inserts the information already captured into the queue list to be printed. Once the information has been placed in the queue, you can use the spooler support programs to remove the report or use NetWare function 0xE0, Print Spooling Functions, subfunction 0x05, Remove Entry from Spool Queue.

The logic used in Close_LST_Device is very simple. The routine sets the high-order byte of the AX register (AH) to the main function 0xDF and the low-order byte of the DX register to the subfunction 0x01. The Turbo C routine intr86 is used to call interrupt 0x21. The result of the call is returned in the low-order byte of the AX register (AL).

Limitations and Modifications

None

Routine Source Code

```
#include <dos.h>
#include <mem.h>

char Close_LST_Device(void)
/*
  This function will close the catch and queue for printing
  and return the byte 0x00 upon completion.
*/
{/* Close_LST_Device */
  union REGS
    Regs;
```

```
  /* Setup the call */
  Regs.h.ah = 0xDF; /* Network call function - Print Function */
  Regs.h.dl = 0x01; /* Network subfunction call - Start LST catch */

  /* Do It */
  int86(0x21, &Regs, &Regs);
  return(Regs.h.al);
}/* Close_LST_Device */
```

Sample Usage Source Code

▼

```
/*
  This program will output to the local printer, the network printer 0,
  and the network printer 1, using the Novelle spooling
  functions.
*/

extern unsigned _stklen=16384; /* Minimum recommend stack size */
#include <stdio.h>
#include <math.h>
#include <dos.h>
#include <mem.h>
#include <alloc.h>
#include <ctype.h>
#include <string.h>
#include <stdlib.h>
#include <plib.h>
#include <plib.glo>


/***************************************************************************/
main()
{

  Calibrate_Delay();            /* Calibrate delay factor */
  Get_Video_Mode("Video.CFG"); /* Get display adapter type */
  Install_Crit_Error();         /* Set up application critical error handler */
  InputAbsolute=AbortPrint=0;  /* Initialize global variables */

  /* Application code to follow */

  Clr_Scr () ;
  Close_LST_Device();
  Print ("Here I am on the local printer.", 1) ;
  if (Modify_LST_Device())
  {
    printf ("Couldn't Modify List device.") ;
    exit(0);
```

```
  }

  Set_Spool_Flags(0);
  Print ("Here I am on the network printer 0.", 1) ;

  Close_LST_Device();
  Print ("Here I am on the local printer again.", 1) ;

  if (Modify_LST_Device())
  {
    printf ("Couldn't Modify List device.") ;
    exit(0);
  }

  Set_Spool_Flags (1) ;
  Print ("Here I am on the network printer 1.", 1) ;

  Close_LST_Device();
  Print ("Here I am on the local printer yet again.", 1) ;

} /* main */
```

Sample Usage Output ▼

```
Here I am on the local printer.
Here I am on the network printer 0.
Here I am on the local printer again.
Here I am on the network printer 1.
Here I am on the local printer yet again.
```

Get_NTime

Description ▼

Get_NTime returns a string pointer (*Buffer) containing the current network server's time. The returned time can be in several formats. The formats are: 1 for HHMMSS, 2 for HH:MM:SS, 3 for HHMMa, and 4 for hH:MM am/pm.

Routine Declaration ▼

```
char *Get_NTime(int  TimeFormat,
                char *Buffer)
```

Passed Variables ▼

TimeFormat integer The format for the returned time string. Valid values for

TimeFormat are 1 through 4. Table 4-1 lists the abbreviations used in the format descriptions, and table 4-2 lists the formats for each value of TimeFormat. Time formats 1 and 2 are in 24-hour or military format. Time formats 3 and 4 are in 12-hour am/pm format.

Global Variables

▼

None

Error Codes/ Messages

▼

None

Discussion

▼

Get_NTime retrieves the current network server's time in several formats. The formats, shown in table 4-2, provide an excellent range of styles for the returned string. However, we realize that you will probably discover other formats that will meet the needs of particular applications. Keeping this in mind, we put the actual formats into a switch statement so you could add new formats or easily change the existing formats.

The Get_NTime routine is divided into three main areas: getting the time using a DOS interrupt 21 hex, service E7 hex, NetWare-Return Date/Time String, concatenating the registers into a standard time string, and formatting the time string as indicated by the format number selected.

Limitations and Modifications

▼

The only limitations to Get_NTime are the formats for the returned time. You can correct this limitation by adding any formats that you need.

Table 4-1. *Time Format Abbreviations*

Abbreviation	Meaning
HH	Two digits for the hours
hH	One or two digits for the hours
MM	Two digits for the minutes
SS	Two digits for the seconds
a	One character for a.m. or p.m.

Table 4-2. *TimeFormat Formats*

Format No.	General Format	Example
1	HHMMSS	093015
2	HH:MM:SS	09:30:15
3	HHMMa	0930a
4	hH:MM am/pm	9:30 am

Routine Source Code

▼

```
#include <mem.h>
#include <math.h>
#include <dos.h>
#include <string.h>
#include <stdio.h>
#include <stdlib.h>
#include <ctype.h>
#include <plib.h>

char *Get_NTime(int TimeFormat,
                char *Buffer)
/*
  This function gets the Novell Server's time and returns it in the
  format specified by TimeFormat:
    if TimeFormat =
      1:
        HHMMSS - where HH is 24 hour clocktime 00 to 23, MM is
                 minutes 00 to 59, SS is seconds 00 to 59.
      2:
        HH:MM:SS - same as 1 with colons.
      3:
        HHMMa - where HH is the 12 hr 1 to 12 and MM is minutes 00 to 59
                and a is am or pm indicator (a/p), e.g., 13:30 would
                be '0130p'.
      4:
        hH:MM am/pm - where H is the 12 hr 1 to 12, MM is minutes 00 to
                      59 and am/pm is the am or pm indicator, e.g., 13:30
                      would be '1:30 pm' - 11:45 would be '11:45 am'.
*/
{ /* Get_NTime */

  int
    I;

  char
    Buff1[16],
    Buff2[16],
    Buff3[16];

  union REGS
    Reg;

  struct SREGS
    SReg;

  segread(&SReg);
```

```
/* Retrieve Server Date & Time */
Reg.h.ah = 0xE7;
SReg.ds = FP_SEG(Buff1);
Reg.x.dx = FP_OFF(Buff1);
int86x(0x21, &Reg, &Reg, &SReg);

/* Set up initial time string of HHMMSS */
Buffer[0] = 0;
for (I = 3; I <= 5; I++)
{
  if (Buff1[I] <= 9)
    strcat(Buffer, "0");
  itoa(Buff1[I], Buff2, 10);
  strcat(Buffer, Buff2);
} /* for I */

switch (TimeFormat)
{
  case 1:/* HHMMSS */
  break;

  case 3: /* HHMMa/p */
    /* If time is in PM */
    if (strcmp(Copy(Buffer, 1, 2, Buff1), "12") > 0)
    {
      sprintf(Buff3, "%02d%sp", atoi(Copy(Buffer, 1, 2, Buff2)) - 12,
              Copy(Buffer, 3, 2, Buff1));
      strcpy(Buffer, Buff3);
    } /* if strcmp */
    else /* if time is in AM */
    {
      if (strcmp(Copy(Buffer, 1, 2, Buff1), "01") < 0)
      {
        sprintf(Buff3, "12%sa", Copy(Buffer, 3, 2, Buff2));
        strcpy(Buffer, Buff3);
      } /* if strcmp */
      else
      {
        sprintf(Buff3, "%sa", Copy(Buffer, 1, 4, Buff2));
        strcpy(Buffer, Buff3);
      } /* if strcmp else */
    } /* if strcmp else */
  break;

  case 2:
  case 4:/* HH:MM:SS or hH:MM am/pm */
    Insert(":", Buffer, 3);
    Insert(":", Buffer, 6);
```

```
      if (TimeFormat == 4)
      {
        if (strcmp(Copy(Buffer, 1, 2, Buff1), "12") > 0)
        {
          sprintf(Buff3, "%2d%s pm", atoi(Copy(Buffer, 1, 2, Buff2)) - 12,
                  Copy(Buffer, 3, 3, Buff1));
          strcpy(Buffer, Buff3);
        } /* if strcmp */
        else
        {
          if (strcmp(Copy(Buffer, 1, 2, Buff1), "01") < 0)
          {
            sprintf(Buff3, "12%s am", Copy(Buffer, 3, 3, Buff2));
            strcpy(Buffer, Buff3);
          } /* if strcmp */
          else
          {
            if (strcmp(Copy(Buffer, 1, 2, Buff1), "10") < 0)
            {
              sprintf(Buff3, "%s am", Copy(Buffer, 2, 4, Buff2));
              strcpy(Buffer, Buff3);
            } /* if strcmp */
            else
            {
              sprintf(Buff3, "%s am", Copy(Buffer, 1, 5, Buff2));
              strcpy(Buffer, Buff3);
            } /* if strcmp else */
          } /* if strcmp */
        } /* if strcmp else */
      } /* if TimeFormat */
    break; /* case 2, 4 */
  } /* switch TimeFormat */
  return(Buffer);
} /* Get_NTime */
```

Sample Usage Source Code

▼

```
/*
  This program will demonstrate the use of Get_NTime and the results of
  its various formats.
*/

extern unsigned _stklen=16384; /* Minimum recommend stack size */
#include <stdio.h>
#include <math.h>
#include <dos.h>
#include <mem.h>
#include <alloc.h>
```

```
#include <ctype.h>
#include <string.h>
#include <stdlib.h>
#include <plib.h>
#include <plib.glo>


/****************************************************************************/
main()
{
  int
    Formatloop = 0;

  char
    TimeBuffer[12] = "";

  Calibrate_Delay();             /* Calibrate delay factor */
  Get_Video_Mode("Video.CFG");   /* Get display adapter type */
  Install_Crit_Error();          /* Set up application critical error handler */
  InputAbsolute=AbortPrint=0;    /* Initialize global variables */

  /* Application code to follow */
  Clr_Scr();
  printf ("\n\nThe following are network time formats: \n\n");
  for (Formatloop = 1; Formatloop <= 4; Formatloop++)
    printf("%s\n", Get_NTime(Formatloop, TimeBuffer));
} /*main*/
```

Sample Usage Output

▼

```
The following are network time formats:

145946
14:59:46
0259p
2:59 pm
```

Get_Station_Number

Description

▼

Get_Station_Number returns a string containing the two-digit logical station number from the file server. The logical station number is the communication channel referenced by the file server when the server is in Monitor Mode. This number can vary each time a user logs into the server, because it is assigned on a first-come, first-assigned basis.

Routine Declaration

▼

```
char *Get_Station_Number(char *Buffer)
```

Passed Variables

▼

None

Global Variables

▼

None

Error Codes/ Messages

▼

None

Discussion

▼

Get_Station_Number retrieves the file server's station number assigned to the user for the current login. This number can be used in several of the other NetWare functions available on a Novell network. The number returned indicates the logical station number the user is logged into. When you use Monitor Mode on the server, the server displays that user's activity.

Get_Station_Number uses interrupt 0x21 and the Turbo C int86 to retrieve the station number. To set up the interrupt, the routine puts the function number 0xDC in the high-order byte of the AX register (AH). After the interrupt, the station number is returned in the CX register. The low-order byte of the CX register (CL) contains the second ASCII digit of the station number and the high-order byte of the CX register (CH) contains the first ASCII digit of the station number.

Limitations and Modifications

▼

None

Routine Source Code

▼

```
#include <stdio.h>
#include <mem.h>
#include <dos.h>
#include <string.h>

char *Get_Station_Number(char *Buffer)
/*
  This function will return the logical station number in string form.
*/
{ /* Get_Station_Number */
  union REGS
```

```
    Reg; /* 8086 type registers */

  /* Initialize Parameters */
  Reg.h.ah = 0xDC; /* Network environment function - Get station number */

  /* Do It */
  int86(0x21, &Reg, &Reg);

  /* Return station number */
  Buffer[0] = Reg.h.cl;
  Buffer[1] = Reg.h.ch;
  Buffer[2] = 0;
  return(Buffer);
} /* Get_Station_Number */
```

Sample Usage Source Code

▼

```
/*
  This program will use the function Get_Station_Number (for Novell)
  to show the user's station number.
*/

extern unsigned _stklen=16384; /* Minimum recommend stack size */
#include <stdio.h>
#include <math.h>
#include <dos.h>
#include <mem.h>
#include <alloc.h>
#include <ctype.h>
#include <string.h>
#include <stdlib.h>
#include <plib.h>
#include <plib.glo>


/******************************************************************************/
main()
{
  char
    Buffer[10] = "";

  Calibrate_Delay();            /* Calibrate delay factor */
  Get_Video_Mode("Video.CFG"); /* Get display adapter type */
  Install_Crit_Error();         /* Set up application critical error handler */
  InputAbsolute=AbortPrint=0;  /* Initialize global variables */

  /* Application code to follow */
```

```
  Clr_Scr();
  printf("User station # %s", Get_Station_Number(Buffer));

} /*  main  */
```

Sample Usage Output

```
User station # 02
```

Global_Broadcast_Message

Description

Global_Broadcast_Message sends a message to all users on the same file server. The message can be up to 60 characters in length and will be truncated if longer. A completion code of 0x00 will be returned for each station sent the message if the message was transmitted successfully. If the message transmission failed, 0xFF is returned.

Routine Declaration

```
char *Global_Broadcast_Message(char *SenMess)
```

Passed Variables

***SenMess String Pointer** A pointer to the message to be transmitted over the network. If the message exceeds 60 characters, it will be truncated. The message can be only 60 characters because Novell appends an additional message to the end of the string when it is transmitted.

Global Variables

None

Error Codes/ Messages

The error codes returned by the function indicate failure (0xFF) or successful completion (0x00) for each station in the send list. To review the values, you need to read the value of each character in the 100-byte list returned.

Discussion

Global_Broadcast_Message transmits a message to the first 100 users on the current file server. If less than 100 users are on the network, the extra stations listed in the broadcast request are ignored and 0xFF is returned for them in the completion code list.

Global_Broadcast_Message uses two structures in the setup of the call. The first, ReqBuff, sends the list of stations that are to receive the message broadcast and the message itself. The second structure, RepBuff, receives the completion list back from the file server after the messages have been sent. The request buffer's (ReqBuff) station list is comprised of a sequential list of bytes from 1 to 100, a limit set because NetWare can only accommodate 100 users per server.

Once ReqBuff is set up, the address for the request and reply buffers are loaded into CPU register structures and the interrupt is called. Upon completion, the RepBuff's completion list is transferred to the *Buffer parameter and the pointer to *Buffer is returned.

Limitations and Modifications

▼

You can easily create a single-user transmit routine from Global-_Broadcast_Message by changing the station list to contain a station number passed into the routine. This allows you to selectively send messages to particular users.

Routine Source Code

▼

```
#include <stdio.h>
#include <mem.h>
#include <dos.h>
#include <string.h>

char *Global_Broadcast_Message(char *SenMess,
                               char *Buffer)
/*
  This function will attempt to broadcast the *SenMess string to all users
  and return the completion list ($00 - means message sent, $FF means
  message not sent). The maximum length the message can be is 60
  characters. *Buffer must be at least 101 characters long!
*/
{ /* Global Broadcast Message */
  int
    I; /* General purpose counter */

  union REGS
    Reg;  /* 8088 registers */

  struct SREGS
    SReg;

  struct /* Broadcast buffer data */
  {
    int
      PacketLength;
```

```
    char
     ComFunction,
     StationList[101],
     Message[61];
  } ReqBuff;

  struct /* Reply buffer data */
  {
    int
      PacketLength;
    char
      CompList[101];
  } RepBuff;

  /* Initialize buffers */
  setmem(&ReqBuff, sizeof(ReqBuff), 0);
  setmem(&RepBuff, sizeof(RepBuff), 0);
  segread(&SReg);

  /* Initialize send stations list to all */
  ReqBuff.StationList[0] = 100;
  for (I = 1; I <= 100; I++)
    ReqBuff.StationList[I] = I;

  /* Initialize message to be sent */
  movmem(SenMess, ReqBuff.Message+1, strlen(SenMess));
  ReqBuff.Message[0] = strlen(SenMess);

  /* Set up the call */
  Reg.h.ah = 0xE1;                /* Function call */
  ReqBuff.ComFunction = 0x00;  /* SubFunction call */

  /* Initialize remaining parameters */
  ReqBuff.PacketLength = sizeof(ReqBuff);
  RepBuff.PacketLength = sizeof(RepBuff);
  SReg.ds = FP_SEG(&ReqBuff);
  Reg.x.si = FP_OFF(&ReqBuff);
  SReg.es = FP_SEG(&RepBuff);
  Reg.x.di = FP_OFF(&RepBuff);
  /* Do It */
  int86x(0x21, &Reg, &Reg, &SReg);
  /* Return completion list */
  movmem(RepBuff.CompList, Buffer, 101);
  return(Buffer);
} /* Global_Broadcast_Message */
```

Sample Usage Source Code

▼

```
/*
  This program will use the function Global_Broadcast_Message to
```

```
  send a message to every station logged on the server, then
  will display a list of the stations that received the message.
*/

extern unsigned _stklen=16384; /* Minimum recommend stack size */
#include <stdio.h>
#include <math.h>
#include <dos.h>
#include <mem.h>
#include <alloc.h>
#include <ctype.h>
#include <string.h>
#include <stdlib.h>
#include <plib.h>
#include <plib.glo>

/****************************************************************************/
main()
{
  int
    C = 0;

  char
    GBuff[101] = ""; /*Minimum length of completion list */

  Calibrate_Delay();            /* Calibrate delay factor */
  Get_Video_Mode("Video.CFG"); /* Get display adapter type */
  Install_Crit_Error();         /* Set up application critical error handler */
  InputAbsolute=AbortPrint=0;   /* Initialize global variables */

  /* Application code to follow */

  Clr_Scr () ;
  Global_Broadcast_Message ("Is anyone out there?", GBuff);
  for ( C=1 ; C<=100 ; C++)
  {
    if ( GBuff[C] == 0 )
      printf ("Message received by station %d\n", C) ;
  }

} /*  main  */
```

Sample Usage Output

▼

```
Message received by station 1
Message received by station 2
Message received by station 3
```

```
>> Is anyone out there?                                    (CTRL-ENTER to clear)
```

Modify_LST_Device

Description

▼

Modify_LST_Device disables the local LST (printer) output and enables the spooler based on the values currently set in the default spool flags. (See Set_Spool_Flags for setting the flags.) A returned completion code of 0x00 indicates successful completion and any other value indicates failure.

Routine Declaration

▼

```
char Modify_LST_Device(void)
```

Passed Variables

▼

None

Global Variables

▼

None

Error Codes/ Messages

▼

The value returned by the function indicates success (0x00) or failure (any other value) from the interrupt call.

Discussion

▼

Modify_LST_Device activates the spooler's capture of data output to a local printer. The spooler is configured based on the values in the default spooler settings. The defaults can be set with the library routine Set_Spool_Flags. The flags control several options, including number of copies, destination printer number, local printer to be diverted, banner setup, and several others.

Modify_LST_Device uses the Novell function 0xDF, Print Function, subfunction 0x00, Start LST catch. The primary function number is set in the high-order byte of the AX register (AH) and the subfunction is set in the low-order byte of the DX register (DL). Once the registers are set, interrupt 0x21 is called and the completion code is returned in the low-order byte of the AX register (AL).

Limitations and Modifications

▼

None

Routine Source Code

```
#include <dos.h>
#include <mem.h>

char Modify_LST_Device(void)
/*
  This function will set the LST device to the network printer
  and return the byte 0x00 on completion.
*/
{ /* Modify_LST_Device */
  union REGS
    Regs;

  /* Set up the call */
  Regs.h.ah = 0xDF; /* Network call function - Print Function */
  Regs.h.dl = 0x00; /* Network subfunction call - Start LST catch */

  /* do it */
  int86(0x21, &Regs, &Regs);
  return(Regs.h.al);
} /* Modify_LST_Device */
```

Sample Usage Source Code

See the sample program for Close_LST_Device for example usage of this routine.

Set_File_Attributes

Description

Set_File_Attributes is used to change the network status of a particular file. The file can have a status of hidden, read-only, read/write, system, sharable, or nonsharable. You should use this routine when you create new files on Novell and need to change the default settings. Novell defaults all new files to non-sharable read/write.

Routine Declaration

```
char Set_File_Attributes(char *FileName,
                         int  Attribute)
```

Passed Variables

***FileName string pointer** A pointer to the filename that will have its attributes changed.

Attribute integer The file attributes to be established for the file named in *FileName.

Global Variables

▼

None

Error Codes/ Messages

▼

The value returned by Set_File_Attributes can have four error meanings. The return codes are listed in table 4-3.

Discussion

▼

Set_File_Attributes changes new files from single-user to multiuser from within an application. The routine changes several other attributes on files residing on the network server. Your applications may use these other attributes.

The routine's parameters and the memory location for the filename are set into registers. The interrupt is then called and the return value is evaluated and returned by the function.

Limitations and Modifications

▼

None

Table 4-3. *Set_File_Attributes Return Codes*

Code	Meaning
0x00	No error in attribute change
0x01	Invalid attribute value
0x03	Path not found for the indicated file
0x05	Access denied to the user attempting the change

Routine Source Code

▼

```
#include <stdio.h>
#include <mem.h>
#include <dos.h>
#include <string.h>

char Set_File_Attributes(char *FileName,
                         int Attribute)
/*
  This function will set *FileName files attributes, where
  if Attribute = 0x01 - Read Only, 0x02 Hidden, 0x04 System, 0x80 Sharable.
  Upon completion, this function will return a completion code
  (0x00 - No error, 0x01 - Invalid Function, 0x03 - Path not found,
```

```
  0x05h Access Denied).
*/
{/* Set_File_Attributes */
  union REGS
    Reg;

  struct SREGS
    SReg;

  segread(&SReg);
  /* Initialize parameters */
  Reg.h.ah = 0x43; /* NetWork Environment Function - Get or set file
                      attributes */
  Reg.h.al = 0x01; /* Set Attribute */
  Reg.x.cx = Attribute;
  SReg.ds = FP_SEG(FileName);
  Reg.x.dx = FP_OFF(FileName);

  /* Do It */
  int86x(0x21, &Reg, &Reg, &SReg);

  /* Return Completion Code */
  if (Reg.x.flags & 0x0001)
    return(Reg.h.al);
  else
    return(0);
} /* Set_File_Attibutes */
```

Sample Usage Source Code

▼

```
/*
  This program will use the function Set_File_Attributes to
  set the file flags for the file EX_121.C to sharable, read/write.
*/

extern unsigned _stklen=16384; /* Minimum recommend stack size */
#include <stdio.h>
#include <math.h>
#include <dos.h>
#include <mem.h>
#include <alloc.h>
#include <ctype.h>
#include <string.h>
#include <stdlib.h>
#include <plib.h>
#include <plib.glo>

/****************************************************************************/
```

```
main()
{
  Calibrate_Delay();             /* Calibrate delay factor */
  Get_Video_Mode("Video.CFG"); /* Get display adapter type */
  Install_Crit_Error();          /* Set up application critical error handler */
  InputAbsolute=AbortPrint=0;  /* Initialize global variables */

  /* Application code to follow */

  Clr_Scr () ;
  if ( Set_File_Attributes ("tc.exe", 0x80) == 0 )
    printf ("TC.EXE has been set to S/R/W.\n") ;
  else
    printf ("Error - Access denied or file not found.") ;

} /*  main  */
```

Sample Usage Output

```
What file do you wish to flag SRW? bp_bomb.exe


bp_bomb.exe has been set to S/R/W.
```

Set_Spool_Flags

Description

Set_Spool_Flags sets the indicator flags and values used by NetWare's spooler. These flags are then used when a call to Modify_LST_Device, which starts the spooler capture process, is made. The parameters and options available with this routine are described in the Discussion section of this routine. For more information on using the spooler, see Modify_LST_Device.

Routine Declaration

```
void Set_Spool_Flags(char PrntNo)
```

Passed Variables

PrntNo char The network printer number to which the output is to be directed.

Global Variables

None

Error Codes/ Messages

▼

None

Discussion

▼

Set_Spool_Flags uses the Advanced NetWare 2.0 function call 0xB8, Get/Set Default Spool Flags. These flags must be set prior to calling Modify_LST_Device in order to actually execute the default values set. The following options are available with this network function:

Print Flags This field sets up suppression of the automatic form feed at the end of the print job, deletion of the spool file after the print job, enabling of the tab expansion, and printing of the the banner page. Each of these options has an associated value that you add together to enable the desired options. The values are listed in table 4-4.

Tabsize This field specifies the number of spaces to be used for expansion of detected tab characters. If you don't select tab expansion in the print flags, this field does not have any affect.

Target Printer This field specifies the network printer that receives the spooled output.

Number of copies This field specifies the number of copies of the spooled file that are to be printed.

Form Type This field specifies the form type reference for the file to be printed.

Banner text This field contains the banner text to be printed on the first page of the capture files output, if banner printing was selected in the Print Flags.

Local Printer Number This field specifies which local printer (LPT1-3) is to be diverted to the spooler.

Printer Timeout Count This field specifies the number of clock ticks (1/18th of a second) the spooler should wait from the last output before automatically closing the capture file. If you specify zero, the timeout is ignored.

Table 4-4. *Print Flags Options*

Option	Value
Suppress auto form feed	0x08
Delete Spool file after print	0x20
Enable tab expansion	0x40
Print banner page	0x80

Device Close This field specifies if the device should have an automatic EndSpool (NetWare command) performed at the timeout. Zero enables the auto EndSpool and any other value disables the auto Endspool. This option is only effective with DOS 3.0, 3.1, and 3.2.

The routine included with the library is only set up for making a network printer (selectable) to appear and be controlled as a local printer would be. To accomplish this, it first initializes the variables required to set the defaults. The routine sets the auto form feed off, enables deletion of the spool file, sets the timeout to 10 ticks, and sets the tab expansion to one character. After initializing the variables, the registers are set with the buffer's memory address and the function numbers, and the interrupt is performed.

Limitations and Modifications

▼

Set_Spool_Flags initiates a specific set of spooler conditions. The Novell function the routine uses has a much wider scope and the routine can be modified to provide greater flexibility for your particular applications.

Routine Source Code

▼

```
#include <mem.h>
#include <dos.h>

void Set_Spool_Flags(char PrntNo)
/*
 This is a NetWare 4.0 function call and will set the spool flags.
 Process for outputting:
   start with LST device closed (local)

   Modify_LST_Device
   Set_Spool_Flags(N)
     Perform output
   Close_LST_Device
   repeat for new output
*/
{/* Set_Spool_Flags */

  typedef struct
  {
    int
      PacketLength;
    char
      SetFlags,
      PrntFlags,
      TabSize,
      TargetPrinter,
```

```
    NumCopies,
    FormType,
    BannerTxt[13],
    Terminator;
  } ReqBuffType;

  ReqBuffType
    ReqBuff;

  union REGS
    Regs;

  struct SREGS
    SReg;

  setmem(&ReqBuff, sizeof(ReqBuff), 0);
  segread(&SReg);
  ReqBuff.PacketLength = 0x0006;
  ReqBuff.SetFlags = 0x02;
  ReqBuff.PrntFlags = 0x28;
  ReqBuff.TabSize = 1;
  ReqBuff.TargetPrinter = PrntNo;
  ReqBuff.NumCopies = 1;

  Regs.h.ah = 0xE0;
  SReg.es = SReg.ds = FP_SEG(&ReqBuff);
  Regs.x.di = Regs.x.si = FP_OFF(&ReqBuff);
  int86x(0x21, &Regs, &Regs, &SReg);
}/* Set_Spool_Flags */
```

Sample Usage Source Code

▼

See the sample program for Close_LST_Device for example usage of this routine.

5 Sample Applications and Utilities

Customer—a customer tracking system

Make Menu—a menu layout file utility

VideoCFG—a video configuration utility

Make Definition—a file definition management utility

Shell—a sample template for starting an application

Getting to know someone else's programming methods and techniques is never an easy task. That is why we have included this chapter of sample applications. We feel that by providing actual applications that use the library routines, you will be able to reduce the time required to begin integrating the libraries into your projects.

Even though the following sample applications are included to provide examples of how to use the libraries, you will find that several can be very useful as they stand or when included in your applications.

The samples include: Customer, a customer inquiry tracking system; VideoCFG, a utility for configuring the video attributes used in the library; Make Menu, a utility for creating menu definition files; Make Definition, a utility for creating and managing Btrieve data file definition files; and Shell, a sample template for starting an application with the libraries.

Customer

Customer uses many of the main library routines, including the Btrieve routines. You must have Btrieve to use the application as it is presented here. If you don't have Btrieve, you can rewrite Btrieve routines to use your record management system, but be careful of multiuser accessing if you are using it on a network.

Customer was created as a means of tracking the inquiries we receive from our national advertising campaigns. The application provides a multiuser method of entering our inquiries and tracking information needed to produce mailout listings. The data records have numerous fields for tracking different forms of information. You can change the names for these fields to match your tracking requirements.

The main menu provides three primary options: Customer Information Maintenance, Information Sheet Printing, and Mailing Label Printing. Customer

Information Maintenance is used to add, delete, update, and locate inquiry records in the database. Information Sheet Printing creates a single-page form for each record selected for printing. Mailing Label Printing creates mailing labels for inquiry records in the database. Even though Customer was developed for our specific environment, you can easily adapt the application to fit your own needs for a mailing list system.

Cust.c is divided into four routines: Maint_Screen, Print_Info_Sheets, Print_Labels, and main. Maint_Screen is used to control the data entry screen for the customer information files. It also provides an excellent example for using the library routine Ent_Scr and Ent_Control. Print_Info_Sheets uses the library printing routines to create individual information sheets for each customer in the data file. Print_Labels is used to create mailing labels for the customers listed in the database. The primary routine, main, controls the operation of the other routines and the menuing capabilities of the application. Customer uses a batch file that first loads the Btrieve record manager and then calls the application. The file Bcust.bat shows the commands for this batch file. The source code listing for Bcust.bat is

```
Btrieve /P:1024 /T:Btr.trn
Cust
```

Cust.c Source Code

▼

```
extern unsigned _stklen=65536; /* Recommend stack size */
#include <stdio.h>
#include <math.h>
#include <dos.h>
#include <mem.h>
#include <alloc.h>
#include <ctype.h>
#include <string.h>
#include <stdlib.h>
#include <plib.h>
#include <plib.glo>
#include <plib.btv>  /*Global variables for Btrieve routines*/

struct
{
  char
    CoName[31],  /*Key 0 - 1*/
    Contact[31], /*Key 1 - 32*/
    Addr1[31],
    Addr2[31],
    City[16],    /*KeySeg 2b - 125*/
    State[3],    /*Key 2a - 141*/
    Zip[11],     /*Key 3 - 144*/
    Phone[15],
    DLCont[9],
```

```
    NCont[9],
    Notes[4][71];
} CustRec;

/****************************************************************************/
void Maint_Screen()
/*
  This routine is the file maintenance screen for the customer's information
  records. It will use full entry screen and record control facilities +
  has key locations system.
*/
{/*Maint_Screen*/
  char
    Done,
    TStr[81],
    TStr1[81];

  int
    Page,
    Mode,
    KeyNum;

  Draw_Frame(1, 1, 80, 24, 2, "NR", "", Blue);
  F_Write(3, 24, VidHigh, " <F5> : Delete Record - <ESC> : Return to menu ");
  KeyNum = 1; /*Starts at one for menu reasons, is decremented in use*/
  Mode = 1;
  Done = 0;
  do
  {
    Clear_Frame(Blue, 2, 2, 78, 22);
    Lowest_Record(0, &CustRec, 0);
    Mode_Select(0, &Mode, "Customer Information Maintenance");
    if (CurKey != 27)
    {
      switch (Mode)
      {
        case 3:/* Key find */
          Draw_Frame(5, 5, 60, 10, 1, "NR", "Specify Key", Green);
          Menu("/1/1/Company/1/2/Name/1/3/State + City/1/4/Zip/",
               &KeyNum, TStr, 0, 6, 6, 58, 8, Green);
          if (CurKey != 27)
          {
            Clear_Frame(Green, 6, 6, 58, 8);
            TStr[0] = TStr1[0] = 0;
            switch (KeyNum)
            {
              case 1:
                Prompt(7, 10, Normal, "Company : ", "A30,", TStr);
```

```
            break;
            case 2:
              Prompt(7, 10, Normal, "Name  : ", "A30,", TStr);
            break;
            case 3:
              Prompt(7, 10, Normal, "State : ", "A2,", TStr);
              Prompt(7, 11, Normal, "City  : ", "A15,", TStr1);
              strcat(TStr, TStr1);
            break;
            case 4:
              Prompt(7, 10, Normal, "Zip   : ", "A10,", TStr);
            break;
          }/*switch KeyNum*/
          Lowest_Record(0, &CustRec, KeyNum - 1);
          if (Search_Record(0, &CustRec, KeyNum - 1, TStr))
            Lo_Mess("No Match found - closest record");
        Mode = 1;
        }/*if CurKey*/
      break;
      case 4:/* Query */
      break;
    }/*switch Mode*/
    Clear_Frame(Blue, 2, 2, 78, 22);
    while (CurKey != 27)
    {
      Mode_Update(0, Mode, "Customer Information Maintenance");
      F_Write(3, 15, Reverse, "Notes:");
      FieldLineNum = 0;
      do
      {
        Ent_Scr( 1, 3, 3, "Company   : ", "A30,", CustRec.CoName);
        Ent_Scr( 2, 3, 4, "Contact   : ", "A30,", CustRec.Contact);
        Ent_Scr( 3, 3, 5, "Address 1: ", "A30,", CustRec.Addr1);
        Ent_Scr( 4, 3, 6, "Address 2: ", "A30,", CustRec.Addr2);
        Ent_Scr( 5, 3, 7, "City      : ", "A15,", CustRec.City);
        Ent_Scr( 6, 3, 8, "State     : ", "A2," , CustRec.State);
        Ent_Scr( 7, 3, 9, "Zip       : ", "A10,", CustRec.Zip);
        Ent_Scr( 8, 3, 10, "Phone     : ", "A14,", CustRec.Phone);
        Ent_Scr( 9, 3, 12, "Last Contacted: ", "C", CustRec.DLCont);
        Ent_Scr(10, 3, 13, "Next Contact  : ", "C", CustRec.NCont);
        Ent_Scr(12, 3, 16, "1) ", "A70,", CustRec.Notes[0]);
        Ent_Scr(13, 3, 17, "2) ", "A70,", CustRec.Notes[1]);
        Ent_Scr(14, 3, 18, "3) ", "A70,", CustRec.Notes[2]);
        Ent_Scr(15, 3, 19, "4) ", "A70,", CustRec.Notes[3]);
      } while (Ent_Control(15, 1, 0, &Page));
      Record_Entry_Control(0, KeyNum - 1, 0, &Mode);
    }/*while CurKey*/
  }/* if CurKey*/
```

```
    else
      Done = 1;
  } while (!Done);
  CurKey = 13;
}/*Maint_Screen*/


/******************************************************************************/
void Print_Info_Sheets()
/*
  This routine will list all the customers, or those within a given
  state or city.
*/
{/*Print_Info_Sheets*/
  char
    Stop[18],
    TStr1[81],
    TStr[81];

  int
    Option;

  Option = 1;
  Draw_Frame(1, 1, 80, 24, 1,"NR",
           "Customer Information Sheet Printing", Blue);
  Menu("/5/5/All Customers/5/7/State wide/5/9/City wide/",
       &Option, TStr, 0, 2, 2, 78, 22, Blue);
  if (CurKey != 27)
  {
    Lowest_Record(0, &CustRec, 2);
    setmem(TStr, sizeof(TStr), 0);
    switch(Option)
    {
      case 1:/*All*/
        strcpy(Stop, "zzzzzzzzzzzzzzzzz");
      break;
      case 2:/*State wide*/
        TStr[0] = 0;
        Prompt(6, 15, Normal, "State : ", "A2,", TStr);
        if (Search_Record(0, &CustRec, 2, TStr))
          Lo_Mess("No Match found");
        sprintf(Stop, "%szzzzzzzzzzzzzzzz", TStr);
      break;
      case 3:/*City wide*/
        TStr[0] = TStr1[0] = 0;
        Prompt(6, 15, Normal, "State : ", "A2,", TStr);
        Prompt(6, 17, Normal, "City  : ", "A2,", TStr1);
        strcat(TStr, TStr1);
```

```
        strcpy(Stop,TStr);
        if (Search_Record(0, &CustRec, 2, TStr))
          Lo_Mess("No Match found");
      break;
    }/*switch(Option)*/
   Message("Press <Esc> to abort printing");
   while ((strcmp(TStr, Stop) <= 0) && (CurKey != 27))
   {
     Print_At(0, 0, "");
     Print_At(5, 2, "Customer Information Sheet");
     Print_At(5, 0, "Company  :");
     Print_At(15, 1, CustRec.CoName);
     Print_At(5, 0, "Contact  :");
     Print_At(15, 1, CustRec.Contact);
     Print_At(5, 0, "Address 1:");
     Print_At(15, 1, CustRec.Addr1);
     Print_At(5, 0, "Address 2:");
     Print_At(15, 1, CustRec.Addr2);
     Print_At(5, 0, "City     :");
     Print_At(15, 1, CustRec.City);
     Print_At(5, 0, "State    :");
     Print_At(15, 1, CustRec.State);
     Print_At(5, 0, "Zip      :");
     Print_At(15, 1, CustRec.Zip);
     Print_At(5, 0, "Phone    :");
     Print_At(15, 2, CustRec.Phone);
     Print_At(5, 0, "Last Contacted:");
     Print_At(21, 1, CustRec.DLCont);
     Print_At(5, 0, "Next Contact  :");
     Print_At(21, 2, CustRec.NCont);
     Print_At(5, 1, "Notes:");
     Print_At(5, 0, "1)");
     Print_At(9, 1, CustRec.Notes[0]);
     Print_At(5, 0, "2)");
     Print_At(9, 1, CustRec.Notes[1]);
     Print_At(5, 0, "3)");
     Print_At(9, 1, CustRec.Notes[2]);
     Print_At(5, 0, "4)");
     Print_At(9, 1, CustRec.Notes[3]);
     Print_At(1, 0, "\f"); /*Eject a page */

     if (Next_Record(0, &CustRec, 2))
       CurKey = 27; /*End of file */
     if (Look_One_Char())
       Get_One_Char();
     sprintf(TStr,"%s%s", CustRec.State, CustRec.City);
   }/*while ((strcmp(TStr, Stop) <= 0) && (CurKey != 27))*/
  }/*if (CurKey != 27)*/
```

```
  Message("");
  CurKey = 13;
}/*Print_Info_Sheets*/

/******************************************************************************/
void Print_Labels()
/*
  This routine will print the mailing labels
*/
{/* Print_Labels */
  char
    Done,
    Response[2];

  Done = 0;
  while (!Done)
  {
    Response[0] = 0;
    Prompt(2, 23, Normal, "Print Alignment Test (Y/N)? ", "YN", Response);
    if ((CurKey != 27) && (Response[0] == 'Y'))
    {
      /* Mailing Label Alignment Layout */
      Print("123456789012345678901234567890", 1);
      Print("123456789012345678901234567890", 1);
      Print("123456789012345678901234567890", 1);
      Print("123456789012345678901234567890", 1);
      Print("123456789012345, 12 1234567890", 2);
    }
    else
      Done = 1;
  }/*while (!Done)*/
  /* Customer Mailing Label Format */
  Done = Lowest_Record(0, &CustRec, 2);
  Message("Press <ESC> to abort print");
  while ((!Done) && (CurKey != 27))
  {
    Print(CustRec.CoName, 1);
    Print(CustRec.Contact, 1);
    Print(CustRec.Addr1, 1);
    Print(CustRec.Addr2, 1);
    Print(CustRec.City, 0);
    Print(", ", 0);
    Print(CustRec.State, 0);
    Print(" ", 0);
    Print(CustRec.Zip, 2);
    Done = Next_Record(0, &CustRec, 2);
    if (Look_One_Char())
      Get_One_Char();
```

```
  }
  Message("");
  CurKey = 13;
}/* Print_Labels */

/****************************************************************************/
main()
{
  char
    TStr1[81];

  int
    Stat,
    MenuOption;

  struct
  {
    int
      RecLen,
      PageSize,
      NumIndex;
    char
      Blank1[4];
    int
      Variable;
    char
      Blank2[4];
      /*Keys:*/
      int  /*Key 0 - CoName*/
        KeyPos0,
        KeyLen0,
        KeyFlags0;
      char
        NU0[10];
      int  /*Key 1 - Contact*/
        KeyPos1,
        KeyLen1,
        KeyFlags1;
      char
        NU1[10];
      int  /*Key 2a State/City*/
        KeyPos2a,
        KeyLen2a,
        KeyFlags2a;
      char
        NU2a[10];
      int  /*Key 2b Zip*/
        KeyPos2b,
```

```
      KeyLen2b,
      KeyFlags2b;
    char
      NU2b[10];
    int  /*Key 3 */
      KeyPos3,
      KeyLen3,
      KeyFlags3;
    char
      NU3[10];
}BCustRecFileDef;

/* Standard PLib Initialization Routines */
Calibrate_Delay();            /* Calibrate delay factor */
Get_Video_Mode("Video.CFG");  /* Get display adapter type */
Install_Crit_Error();         /* Set up application critical error handler */
InputAbsolute=AbortPrint=0;   /* Initialize global variables */

Clr_Scr();
/* Application code to follow */
/*Initialize BCustRecFileDef for creating Btrieve file if
  necessary.*/

setmem(&BCustRecFileDef, sizeof(BCustRecFileDef), 0);
BCustRecFileDef.RecLen = sizeof(CustRec);
BCustRecFileDef.PageSize = 1024;
BCustRecFileDef.NumIndex = 4;
BCustRecFileDef.Variable = 0;
/*For Key flags :
  Add together 1  -  Duplicates, 2  -  Modifiable,
               4  -  Binary,     8  -  Null,
               16 - Has Segment  32 -  Alt Col Seq
*/

BCustRecFileDef.KeyPos0 = 1;
BCustRecFileDef.KeyLen0 = 30;
BCustRecFileDef.KeyFlags0 = 3;
BCustRecFileDef.KeyPos1 = 32;
BCustRecFileDef.KeyLen1 = 30;
BCustRecFileDef.KeyFlags1 = 3;
BCustRecFileDef.KeyPos2a = 141;
BCustRecFileDef.KeyLen2a = 2;
BCustRecFileDef.KeyFlags2a = 19;
BCustRecFileDef.KeyPos2b = 125;
BCustRecFileDef.KeyLen2b = 15;
BCustRecFileDef.KeyFlags2b = 3;
BCustRecFileDef.KeyPos3 = 144;
BCustRecFileDef.KeyLen3 = 10;
```

```
BCustRecFileDef.KeyFlags3 = 3;

if (Open_File(0, "TCust.Dat", &CustRec, 0))
{
  if (Stat=RMake_File(BTrvRecInfo[0].BTrvVar, "TCust.Dat", &BCustRecFileDef,
      sizeof(BCustRecFileDef)))
  {
    sprintf(TStr1, "Error - Could not create TCust.Dat (%d)", Stat);
    Bomb_Mess(TStr1);
  }
  Open_File(0, "TCust.Dat", &CustRec, 0);
}

MenuOption = 1;
while (CurKey != 27)
{
  Draw_Frame(1, 1, 80, 24, 2, "NR", "Customer Tracking System - Main Menu",
           Blue);

  /* This is a hard code method of making menus rather than
     using a menu definition file */
  F_Write(22, 8, Normal, "Customer Information Maintenance");
  F_Write(22, 10, Normal, "Information Sheet Printing");
  F_Write(22, 12, Normal, "Mailing Label Printing");
  F_Write(22, 16, Normal, "Pop-up Calculator");
  F_Write(22, 17, Normal, "Help for using this system");
  F_Write(22, 19, Normal, "Exit system");

  Menu(
  "/1/1/1    /1/3/2    /1/5/3    /1/9/Calc /1/10/Help /1/12/Exit /",
  &MenuOption, TStr1, 0, 17, 8, 5, 12, Blue);

  if (CurKey != 27)
  {
    switch(MenuOption)
    {
      case 1:/*Maintenance*/
        Maint_Screen();
      break;
      case 2:/*Information sheet printing*/
        Print_Info_Sheets();
      break;
      case 3:/*Mailing label printing*/
      Print_Labels();
      break;
      case 4:/*Pop-up calculator*/
        Calculator();
      CurKey = 13;
```

```
        break;
        case 5:/*System help*/
          Help_File("Cust.Hlp", "Customer Tracking System Help");
        CurKey = 13;
        break;
      case 6:/*Exit*/
        CurKey = 27;
      break;
      }/*switch CurKey*/
    }/*if CurKey*/
  }/*while CurKey */
  Close_File(0);
  End_BTrieve();
  Clr_Scr();
} /*main*/
```

Make Menu

Make Menu is a utility used to create menu record files that can be called by the library routine Menu. This allows you to create menus for an application by using Make Menu as a menu editor. Make Menu allows you to add, modify, and delete menu options and display only information that is to be displayed on the menu.

When you run Make Menu, you are prompted to enter the name of the menu file to be edited. If the file exists, it is loaded and you can edit the existing menu layout. If the file does not exist, it is created. Once the menu layout has been retrieved, if it is an existing menu, the main editing screen is displayed. The screen shows the current menu tag number, the total number of tags entered, the X position for the current tag, the Y position for the current tag, and the tag's text to be displayed. At startup, Make Menu defaults to look at the Selectable Tags, the tags the user can actually select, first. The message Selectable Tag appears near the center of the screen above the line that contains the tag itself. To switch between selectable and display only, press the <F1> key and the tag type will toggle to the other type. To move forward and backward through the tags, use <Tab> to move forward and <Shift> <Tab> (BackTab) to move backward. At any point during the editing process, you can view the current layout by pressing <F10>. To exit the view and return to editing, press <F10> a second time or press <Escape>. When you have completed your entry screen, press <Escape> to exit the menu editor. Make Menu will then create your menu record file, and create MENU.LST, which contains a textual list of the menu options you entered. The menu options are sorted by X position, sorted by Y position, and stored.

The actual operation of Make Menu is fairly simple. The utility has several subsidiary routines: Valid_Tag—check for valid entered text; Delete_Tag—remove a tag from the list; Sort_Tags—sort the tags for output; Save_Menu—save the current menu and create MENU.LST; and Load_Menu—load the defined menu if it exists. These subsidiary routines are called as needed by the processing performed in the main() loop of Make Menu.

For an example of the menu structure output into MENU.LST, see the Sample Usage for the library routine Menu.

Make Menu Source Code

▼

```
extern unsigned _stklen=64000; /* Minimum recommend stack size */
#include <stdio.h>
#include <math.h>
#include <dos.h>
#include <mem.h>
#include <alloc.h>
#include <ctype.h>
#include <string.h>
#include <stdlib.h>
#include <plib.h>
#include <plib.glo>

typedef struct /*Structure used by Menu*/
{
  char
    X1;
  int
    Y1;
  char
    Str[81];
} TagDef;

#define MaxTags 200 /*Maximum # text tags and Maximum # selectable*/

int
  MSTags, /*Highest Tags*/
  MTTags;

TagDef
  STags[MaxTags], /* Selectable tags */
  TTags[MaxTags]; /* Text tags */

/****************************************************************************/
char Valid_Tag(TagDef *Tag)
/*
  This routine will return a 1 if the tag is complete and a zero if
  not.
*/
{/*Valid_Tag*/
  return((Is_Text(Tag -> Str)) && (Tag -> X1 > 0) && (Tag -> Y1 > 0));
}/*Valid_Tag*/
```

```
/***************************************************************************/
void Delete_Tag(TagDef *Tag,
                int TagNum)
/*
  This routine will delete a tag from a tag list.
*/
{ /*Delete_Tag*/
  movmem(Tag + TagNum + 1, Tag + TagNum,
         (MaxTags - TagNum) * sizeof(TagDef));
} /*Delete_Tag*/

/***************************************************************************/
void Sort_Tags(TagDef *TagAr,
               int *MaxEl)
/*
  This routine will sort the TagAr first by Y order (ascending), then
  by X order ascending, (e.g., result would be:
                    (1,1), (10,1), (25,1),
                    (1,2), (30,2), (45,2),
                    (5,3), (19,3), (26,3)...)
*/
{/*Sort_Tags*/
  int
    C;

  TagDef
    *TagP,
    *NTagP,
    HTag;

  *MaxEl -= (Valid_Tag(TagAr + *MaxEl) == 0);
  if (*MaxEl < 0)
    *MaxEl = 0;
  /* Sort by Y first */
  TagP = TagAr;
  C = 0;
  while (C < *MaxEl) /* Bubble sort */
  {
    NTagP = TagP + 1;
    if (TagP -> Y1 > NTagP -> Y1)
    {
      movmem(TagP, &HTag, sizeof(TagDef));
      movmem(NTagP, TagP, sizeof(TagDef));
      movmem(&HTag, NTagP, sizeof(TagDef));
      if (C>0)
      {
        C--;
        TagP--;
```

```
      }
    }
    else
    {
      C++;
      TagP++;
    }
  }
  /*TagP is pointing to last element*/
  NTagP = TagAr;
  while (NTagP != TagP)
  {
    /*Sort till last common Y element*/
    NTagP += (NTagP -> Y1 != (NTagP + 1) -> Y1);
    while (NTagP -> Y1 == (NTagP + 1) -> Y1) /* Bubble sort */
    {
      if (NTagP -> X1 > (NTagP + 1) -> X1)
      {
        movmem(NTagP, &HTag, sizeof(TagDef));
        movmem(NTagP + 1, NTagP, sizeof(TagDef));
        movmem(&HTag, NTagP + 1, sizeof(TagDef));
        if (NTagP != TagAr)
          NTagP--;
      }
      else
        NTagP++;
    }/* while NTagP */
    TagAr = NTagP; /*Set marker at net Y*/
  }/* while NTagP */
}/*Sort_Tags*/

/****************************************************************************/
char Save_Menu(char *FName)
/*

  This routine will sort the STags and the TTags, then write out the STags
  separated by a blank record and the TTags ended by a blank record,
  then create a file called "Menu.Lst," which will contain a textual list
  of all the tags.
*/
{/*Save_Menu*/
  char
    TStr[256];

  int
    C;

  FILE
```

```
    *MnFile;

  Sort_Tags(&STags[0], &MSTags);
  Sort_Tags(&TTags[0], &MTTags);
  MnFile = fopen(FName, "wb");
  if (MnFile != NULL)
  {
    fwrite(&STags, sizeof(TagDef), MSTags + 1, MnFile);
    setmem(TStr, sizeof(TagDef), 0);
    fwrite(TStr, 1, sizeof(TagDef), MnFile);
    fwrite(&TTags, sizeof(TagDef), MTTags + 1, MnFile);
    fwrite(TStr, 1, sizeof(TagDef), MnFile);
    fclose(MnFile);
    MnFile = fopen("Menu.lst", "wb");
    if (MnFile !=NULL)
    {
      sprintf(TStr," Tag definitions for file %s:",FName);
      Write_Line(MnFile, TStr);
      Write_Line(MnFile, "");
      Write_Line(MnFile,"Selectable Tags:");
      Write_Line(MnFile,"  #  Coords    Tag");
      for (C = 0; C <= MSTags; C++)
      {
        sprintf(TStr," %3d (%d,%d) - ", C + 1, STags[C].X1, STags[C].Y1);
        Replace(STags[C].Str, TStr, 16);
        Write_Line(MnFile,TStr);
      }
      Write_Line(MnFile, "");
      Write_Line(MnFile,"Display only Tags:");
      Write_Line(MnFile,"Coords        Tag");
      for (C = 0; C <= MTTags; C++)
      {
        sprintf(TStr,"(%d,%d) - ", TTags[C].X1, TTags[C].Y1);
        Replace(TTags[C].Str, TStr, 15);
        Write_Line(MnFile,TStr);
      }
      putc(26, MnFile);
      fclose(MnFile);
    }
    else
      Bomb_Mess("Could not create Menu.lst");
    return(1);
  }
  else
    return(0);
}/*Save_Menu*/

/***************************************************************************/
```

```
char Load_Menu(char *FName)
/*
  This function will load and try to read FName into STag and TTag, setting
  MSTags and MTTags then returning 1. If the file is not present or cannot
  be opened, it will return 0.
*/
{/*Load_Menu*/
  char
    RR;

  FILE
    *MnFile;

  MnFile = fopen(FName, "rb");
  if (MnFile != NULL)
  {
    MSTags = MTTags = 0;
    /*Read until blank tag*/
    RR = fread(&STags[MSTags], sizeof(TagDef), 1, MnFile);
    while (Is_Text(STags[MSTags].Str))
    {
      MSTags++;
      RR = fread(&STags[MSTags], sizeof(TagDef), 1, MnFile);
    }
    if (RR)
    {
      /*Read until Blank tag*/
      fread(&TTags[MTTags], sizeof(TagDef), 1, MnFile);
      while (Is_Text(TTags[MTTags].Str))
      {
        MTTags++;
        fread(&TTags[MTTags], sizeof(TagDef), 1, MnFile);
      }
    }/*if RR */
    fclose(MnFile);
    return(1);
  }
  else
    return(0);
}/*Load_Menu*/

/****************************************************************************/
main()
{
  char
    TagType,
    FName[51] = "",
    TStr1[81],
```

```
  ScreenBuff[4000];

int
  C,
  TopPage = 0,
  Page,
  TagNum,
  TTagNum;

Calibrate_Delay();             /* Calibrate delay factor */
Get_Video_Mode("Video.CFG"); /* Get display adapter type */
Install_Crit_Error();         /* Set up application critical error handler */
InputAbsolute=AbortPrint=0;  /* Initialize global variables */

/* Application code to follow */
Clear_Frame(Blue, 1, 1, 80, 25);
Prompt(1, 1, Blend(Normal), "File : ", "A50,", FName);
if (CurKey != 27)
{
  setmem(&STags, sizeof(STags), 0);
  setmem(&TTags, sizeof(TTags), 0);
  if (!Load_Menu(FName))
    MSTags = MTTags = 0;

  Draw_Frame(1, 1, 80, 20, 2, "NR", "Menu Data File Maker", Blue);
  F_Write(2, 15, VidHigh, Cen("Press <Tab> or <BackTab> to scan tags",
          TStr1, 78));
  F_Write(2, 16, VidHigh,
       Cen("Press <F1> to toggle Tag type, <F5> to delete", TStr1, 78));
  F_Write(2, 17, VidHigh,
       Cen("<F10> to show, and <Esc> to exit save", TStr1, 78));
  F_Write(2, 18, VidHigh,
       Cen("File Menu.Lst will be created as a reference text",
         TStr1, 78));
  TTagNum = TagType = TagNum = 0;
  CurKey = 0;
  while (CurKey != 27)
  {
    FieldLineNum = 0;
    if (!TagType)
    { /* Entry screen for selectable tags*/
      F_Write(2, 8, Normal, Cen("Selectable Tag :", TStr1, 78));
      sprintf(TStr1, "Tag # %3d of %3d", TagNum, MSTags);
      F_Write(5, 3, VidHigh, TStr1);
      do
      {
        itoa(STags[TagNum].X1, TStr1, 10);
        Ent_Scr(1, 5, 5, "X Position :   ", "2I,0 80", TStr1);
```

```
      STags[TagNum].X1 = atoi(TStr1);
      itoa(STags[TagNum].Y1, TStr1, 10);
      Ent_Scr(2, 5, 7, "Y Position : ", "4I,0 2000", TStr1);
      STags[TagNum].Y1 = atoi(TStr1);
      InputAbsolute = 1;
      Ent_Scr(3, 2, 9, "", "A78,", STags[TagNum].Str);
      InputAbsolute = 0;
    } while (Ent_Control(3, 1, 0, &Page));
  }
  else
  {/* Entry screen for display only tags*/
    F_Write(2, 8, Normal, Cen("Display only Tag :", TStr1, 78));
    sprintf(TStr1, "Tag # %3d of %3d", TTagNum, MTTags);
    F_Write(5, 3, VidHigh, TStr1);
    do
    {
      itoa(TTags[TTagNum].X1, TStr1, 10);
      Ent_Scr(1, 5, 5, "X Position :   ", "2I,0 80", TStr1);
      TTags[TTagNum].X1 = atoi(TStr1);
      itoa(TTags[TTagNum].Y1, TStr1, 10);
      Ent_Scr(2, 5, 7, "Y Position : ", "4I,0 2000", TStr1);
      TTags[TTagNum].Y1 = atoi(TStr1);
      InputAbsolute = 1;
      Ent_Scr(3, 2, 9, "", "A78,", TTags[TTagNum].Str);
      InputAbsolute = 0;
      } while (Ent_Control(3, 1, 0, &Page));
  }
  switch (CurKey)
  {/* Handle command selection*/
    case -59: /*F1 - toggle selectable*/
      TagType = !TagType;
    break;

    case -63: /*F5 - delete tag*/
      if (TagType)
      {
        if (MTTags > 0)
        {
          if (TTagNum == MTTags)
          TTagNum--;
          MTTags--;
            Delete_Tag(&TTags[0], TTagNum);
        }
      }
      else
      {
        if (MSTags > 0)
        {
```

```
      if (MSTags == TagNum)
      TagNum--;
      MSTags--;
        Delete_Tag(&STags[0], TagNum);
    }
  }
break;

case 9: /*Tab - Next Tag*/
case 13:/*Enter*/
  if (TagType)
  {
    if (Valid_Tag(&TTags[TTagNum]))
    {
      MTTags += (TTagNum == MTTags);
        TTagNum += (TTagNum < MaxTags);
    }
    else
      Lo_Mess("New Tag");
  }
  else
  {
    if (Valid_Tag(&STags[TagNum]))
    {
      MSTags += (TagNum == MSTags);
        TagNum += (TagNum < MaxTags);
    }
    else
      Lo_Mess("New Tag");
  }
break;

case -15: /*BackTab - Previous Tag*/
  if (TagType)
  {
    if (TTagNum)
        TTagNum--;
    else
      Lo_Mess("First Tag");
  }
  else
  {
    if (TagNum)
        TagNum--;
    else
      Lo_Mess("First Tag");
  }
break;
```

```
        case -68: /*F10 - show Menu facsimile*/
          Save_Screen(ScreenBuff);
          CurKey = 0;
          while ((CurKey != 27) && (CurKey != -68))
          {
            Clr_Scr();
            F_Write(1, 1 , Reverse, Cen(
                "<Up> & <Down> to scroll, <Esc> or <F10> to return",
                TStr1, 80));
            for(C = 0; C < MSTags; C++)
            {
              if ((TopPage < STags[C].Y1) && (TopPage + 22 >STags[C].Y1) &&
                (Valid_Tag(&STags[C])))
              F_Write(STags[C].X1, STags[C].Y1 - TopPage + 2, Reverse,
                    STags[C].Str);
            }
            for(C = 0; C < MTTags; C++)
            {
              if ((TopPage < TTags[C].Y1) && (TopPage + 22 >TTags[C].Y1) &&
                (Valid_Tag(&TTags[C])))
              F_Write(TTags[C].X1, TTags[C].Y1 - TopPage + 2, Normal,
                    TTags[C].Str);
            }
            Get_One_Char();
            switch(CurKey)
            {
              case -72: /*Up*/
                TopPage += (TopPage < 2000);
              break;
              case -80: /*Down*/
                TopPage -= (TopPage > 0);
              break;
            }
          }
          Restore_Screen(ScreenBuff);
          CurKey = 0;
        break;

        case 27: /*Esc - exit*/
        break;
      }
    } /* while CurKey */
    if (!Save_Menu(FName))
      Bomb_Mess("Could not save file.");
  }/* if CurKey */
  Clr_Scr();
}/* main */
```

VideoCFG

VideoCFG.c provides a means for the end user to set the video attributes used in an application at run-time by defining the foreground and background attributes for the global library variables Normal, Reverse, and VidHigh, and the colors used by the global color variables (see the Global Variables section in Chapter 1). This utility is very useful with off-brand video adapters or monochrome monitors with a color video adapter. The results from the application are stored in the file specified as the command-line parameter following the call to VideoCFG. For example, if the user starts the utility with the command VIDEOCFG VIDEO.CFG, the attributes are stored in the file VIDEO.CFG. The library routine Get_Video_Mode looks for this file (if specified) and, if it exists on the default drive, the values are used to initialize the video attribute variables used by the library routines in the running application.

The application uses a single entry screen to allow the user to enter the values for the video attributes. If the file already exists when the routine is started, Get_Video_Mode initializes with the current values in the file, so users can change the values to meet their needs. When the user presses <ESC> to exit the entry screen, the defined attributes are saved to the file specified when VideoCFG was called.

VideoCFG.c Source Code

▼

```
/*                    Program VideoCFG.c
    This program will allow the user to change or set up a video
    configuration file for use with programs that use the Development C
    library.
*/

extern unsigned _stklen=48000;
#include <stdio.h>
#include <math.h>
#include <dos.h>
#include <mem.h>
#include <alloc.h>
#include <ctype.h>
#include <string.h>
#include <stdlib.h>
#include <Plib.h>
#include <plib.glo>

typedef struct
{
  char
    Normal,
    VidHigh,
    Reverse,
```

```
    Black,
    Blue,
    Green,
    Cyan,
    Red,
    Magenta,
    Brown,
    White,
    BWhite,
    Background;
}VidCfgType;

VidCfgType
  CfgVidRec;

/****************************************************************************/
void Init_Video_Record(char *FName)
/*
  This routine will attempt to read the file FName into the video
  configuration record VidCfgRec.  If the file is not present, it will set
  the record to the default values specified within this routine.
*/
{/*Init_Video_Record*/
  FILE
    *Cfg;

  Cfg=fopen(FName,"rb");
  if (Cfg!=NULL)
  {
    fread(&CfgVidRec,1,sizeof(CfgVidRec),Cfg);
    Background=CfgVidRec.Background;
    Normal=CfgVidRec.Normal;
    VidHigh=CfgVidRec.VidHigh;
    Reverse=CfgVidRec.Reverse;
    Black=CfgVidRec.Black;
    Blue=CfgVidRec.Blue;
    Green=CfgVidRec.Green;
    Cyan=CfgVidRec.Cyan;
    Red=CfgVidRec.Red;
    Magenta=CfgVidRec.Magenta;
    Brown=CfgVidRec.Brown;
    White=CfgVidRec.White;
    BWhite=CfgVidRec.BWhite;
    fclose(Cfg);
  }
  /* else - leave all values set to defaults by Get_Video_Mode */
}/*Init_Video_Record*/
```

```
/*****************************************************************************/
void Show_BSample(int X,
                  int Y,
                  char Attr,
                  char *VType)
/*
  This routine will write a sample of Attr's foreground at X,Y and write
  VType at 67,Y, if VType is not null.
*/
{/*Show_BSample*/
  if ((Attr & 0x80)==0x80)
    F_Write(X, Y, (Attr & 0xF0)|0x0F, "[ Blink  ]");
  else
    F_Write(X, Y, (Attr & 0xF0)|0x0F, "[        ]");
  if (VType[0])
    F_Write(67,Y, Attr, VType);
}/*Show_BSample*/

/*****************************************************************************/
void Show_FSample(int X,
                  int Y,
                  char Attr,
                  char *VType)
/*
  This routine will write a sample of Attr's background at X,Y and write
  VType at 67,Y, if VType is not null.
*/
{/*Show_FSample*/
  if ((Attr&0x08)==0x08)
    F_Write(X, Y,((Attr&0x0F)<<4)|0x0F, "[ High   ]");
  else
    F_Write(X, Y,((Attr&0x0F)<<4)|0x0F, "[        ]");
  if (VType[0])
    F_Write(67,Y, Attr, VType);
}/*Show_FSample*/

/*****************************************************************************/
void Edit_Attr(int X,
               int Y,
               char *Attr,
               char Fore,
               int *C)
/*
  This routine will allow the user to change the foreground or background
  of Attr. If Fore==1 then it will change the foreground, else the background.
*/
{/*Edit_Attr*/
  char
```

```
  TStr[81];

unsigned char
  Ch;

F_Write(X-1,Y,Blend(Normal),"->");
Get_One_Char();
switch(CurKey)
{
  case -75: /*Left*/
    if ((*C<=6) && (*C>=4))
     (*C)-=3;
  break;
  case -77: /*Right*/
    if (*C<=3)
     (*C)+=3;
  break;
  case -80: /*Down*/
    if ((*C==3) || (*C==6))
      (*C)=7;
    else
      (*C)+=(*C<14);
  break;
  case -72: /*Up*/
    (*C)-=(*C>1);
  break;
  case 43:/*+ - increment color pointer*/
    if (Fore)
    {
      Ch=(*Attr)&0x0F;
      F_Write(17,23,Blend(Normal),Rpt(" ",TStr,34));
      Ch++;
      Ch=Ch&0x0F;
      (*Attr)=(*Attr)&0xF0;
      (*Attr)=(Ch | (*Attr));
      F_Write((Ch*2)+17,23,Blend(0x07),"*");
    }
    else
    {
      Ch=((*Attr)>>4);
      F_Write(62,23,Blend(Normal),Rpt(" ",TStr,17));
      Ch++;
      Ch=Ch&0x0F;
      (*Attr)=(*Attr)&0x0F;
      (*Attr)=((Ch<<4) | (*Attr));
      F_Write(((Ch&0x07)*2)+62,23,Blend(0x07),"*");
    }
  break;
```

```
    case 45: /* - decrement color pointer*/
      if (Fore)
      {
        Ch=(*Attr)&0x0F;
        F_Write(17,23,Blend(Normal),Rpt(" ",TStr,34));
        Ch--;
        Ch=Ch&0x0F;
        (*Attr)=(*Attr)&0xF0;
        (*Attr)=(Ch | (*Attr));
        F_Write((Ch*2)+17,23,Blend(0x07),"*");
      }
      else
      {
        Ch=((*Attr)>>4);
        F_Write(62,23,Blend(Normal),Rpt(" ",TStr,17));
        Ch--;
        Ch=Ch&0x0F;
        (*Attr)=(*Attr)&0x0F;
        (*Attr)=((Ch<<4) | (*Attr));
        F_Write(((Ch&0x07)*2)+62,23,Blend(0x07),"*");
      }
    break;
  }/*switch*/
  F_Write(X-1,Y,Blend(Normal),"  ");

}/*Edit_Attr*/


/*****************************************************************************/
void Edit_Video_Vars(char *FName)
/*
  This routine will allow users to modify the video variables and see
  the changes they make to them.
*/
{/*Edit_Video_Vars*/
  char
    TStr[80];

  int
    C;

  Clear_Frame(Blue,1,1,80,25);
  sprintf(TStr,"Editing video file %s",FName);
  Draw_Frame(1,1,80,24,2,"NR",TStr,Blue);
  Draw_Frame(42,10,35,11,1,"NR","Commands",Green);
  F_Write(45,12,Blend(Normal),"(->) is the Attribute selector");
  F_Write(45,13,Blend(Normal),"<Up>   - Attribute selector");
  F_Write(45,14,Blend(Normal),"<Down> - Attribute selector");
```

```
F_Write(45,15,Blend(Normal),"<Right>- Attribute selector");
F_Write(45,16,Blend(Normal),"<Left> - Attribute selector");
F_Write(45,17,Blend(Normal),"<+>    - Increment Color");
F_Write(45,18,Blend(Normal),"<->    - Decrement color");
F_Write(45,19,Blend(Normal),"<Esc>  - Save changes & Exit");
Background=Blue;
F_Write(3,2,VidHigh,"Text Attributes");
F_Write(7,3,Reverse,"Reference Name");
F_Write(30,3,Reverse,"Foreground");
F_Write(49,3,Reverse,"Background");
F_Write(67,3,Reverse,"Sample");
F_Write(9,5,Normal,"Normal");
F_Write(9,6,Normal,"VidHigh");
F_Write(9,7,Normal,"Reverse");
F_Write(3,10,VidHigh,"Background Attributes");
F_Write(7,11,Reverse,"Reference Name");
F_Write(30,11,Reverse,"Background");
F_Write(9,13,Normal,"Black");
F_Write(9,14,Normal,"Blue");
F_Write(9,15,Normal,"Green");
F_Write(9,16,Normal,"Cyan");
F_Write(9,17,Normal,"Red");
F_Write(9,18,Normal,"Magenta");
F_Write(9,19,Normal,"Brown");
F_Write(9,20,Normal,"White");
F_Write(27,22,Reverse,"Foreground");
F_Write(66,22,Reverse,"Background");
for (C=0; C<=15; C++)
  F_Write((C*2)+17,24,(char)(C<<4)," ");
for (C=0; C<=7; C++)
  F_Write((C*2)+62,24,(char)C," ");
C=1;
do
{
  Show_FSample(30,5,Normal,"NORMAL");
  Show_FSample(30,6,VidHigh,"VIDHIGH");
  Show_FSample(30,7,Reverse,"REVERSE");
  Show_BSample(49,5,Normal,"NORMAL");
  Show_BSample(49,6,VidHigh,"VIDHIGH");
  Show_BSample(49,7,Reverse,"REVERSE");
  Show_BSample(30,13,Black,"");
  Show_BSample(30,14,Blue,"");
  Show_BSample(30,15,Green,"");
  Show_BSample(30,16,Cyan,"");
  Show_BSample(30,17,Red,"");
  Show_BSample(30,18,Magenta,"");
  Show_BSample(30,19,Brown,"");
  Show_BSample(30,20,White,"");
```

```
    switch(C)
    {
      case 1: /*Normal Foreground*/
        Edit_Attr(28,5,&Normal,1,&C);
      break;
      case 2: /*VidHigh Foreground*/
        Edit_Attr(28,6,&VidHigh,1,&C);
      break;
      case 3: /*Reverse Foreground*/
        Edit_Attr(28,7,&Reverse,1,&C);
      break;
      case 4: /*Normal Background*/
        Edit_Attr(47,5,&Normal,0,&C);
      break;
      case 5: /*VidHigh Background*/
        Edit_Attr(47,6,&VidHigh,0,&C);
      break;
      case 6: /*Reverse Background*/
        Edit_Attr(47,7,&Reverse,0,&C);
      break;
      case 7: /*Black*/
        Edit_Attr(28,13,&Black,0,&C);
      break;
      case 8: /*Blue*/
        Edit_Attr(28,14,&Blue,0,&C);
      break;
      case 9: /*Green*/
        Edit_Attr(28,15,&Green,0,&C);
      break;
      case 10: /*Cyan*/
        Edit_Attr(28,16,&Cyan,0,&C);
      break;
      case 11: /*Red*/
        Edit_Attr(28,17,&Red,0,&C);
      break;
      case 12:/*Magenta*/
        Edit_Attr(28,18,&Magenta,0,&C);
      break;
      case 13: /*Brown*/
        Edit_Attr(28,19,&Brown,0,&C);
      break;
      case 14:  /*White*/
        Edit_Attr(28,20,&White,0,&C);
      break;
    }
  }while (CurKey!=27);
}/*Edit_Video_Vars*/
```

```
/****************************************************************************/
void Save_Video_Vars(char *FName)
/*
*/
{
  FILE
    *EFile;

  EFile=fopen(FName,"wb");
  if (EFile!=NULL)
  {
    CfgVidRec.Normal=Normal;
    CfgVidRec.VidHigh=VidHigh;
    CfgVidRec.Reverse=Reverse;
    CfgVidRec.Black=Black;
    CfgVidRec.Blue=Blue;
    CfgVidRec.Green=Green;
    CfgVidRec.Cyan=Cyan;
    CfgVidRec.Red=Red;
    CfgVidRec.Magenta=Magenta;
    CfgVidRec.Brown=Brown;
    CfgVidRec.White=White;
    CfgVidRec.BWhite=BWhite;
    fwrite(&CfgVidRec,sizeof(CfgVidRec),1,EFile);
    fclose(EFile);
  }
  else
    Bomb_Mess("Could not create Video File.");
}/*Save_Video_Vars*/

/****************************************************************************/
main(int argc, char *argv[], char *env[])
{
  char
    FName[80] = {""};

  int
    OldCursor;

  FILE
    *EFile;

  Calibrate_Delay();
  Install_Crit_Error();
  InputAbsolute=AbortPrint=0;


  if (argc==2)
```

```
  {
    strcpy(FName,argv[1]);
    EFile=fopen(FName,"rb");
    if (EFile!=NULL)
      fclose(EFile);
    Get_Video_Mode(FName);
    Message("");
    OldCursor=Cursor_Off();
    Help_File("CFGVIDEO.HLP","Using CFGVIDEO");
    Init_Video_Record(FName);
    Edit_Video_Vars(FName);
    Save_Video_Vars(FName);
    Clear_Frame(0x07,1,1,80,25);
    Cursor_On(OldCursor);
  }
  else
    printf("\nMissing video file specification\n");
} /*main*/
```

```
VideoCFG Help File - for use with the library routine Help_File


- Page  1 -

VIDEOCFG is a generic utility used to set up color video
configuration files for Perpetual Data Systems (PDS) applications.
PDS applications will generally use the attributes NORMAL, REVERSE
and VIDHIGH. These three attributes each have their own foreground
and background settings, which can be configured by VIDEOCFG.
Normally PDS applications, such as FreeForm, will use the
attribute NORMAL to color a frame, REVERSE for entering prompted
text, and VIDHIGH for displaying entered text and prompt messages.

By using the VIDEOCFG utility, you can change the foreground
and background colors of NORMAL, REVERSE, and VIDHIGH. When this
is done, you will notice that when you run a PDS application on a
color system, there will be changes in the color in various parts
of the application. Additionally, the background colors, Black,
Red, Green, etc., may be changed. If you see a background color in
a PDS application you would like to change, try changing the
reference of that background color through VIDEOCFG. A little
tinkering may be necessary to satisfy your eye.
- Page  2 -

In order to use VIDEOCFG, you must know the name of the video
configuration file your PDS program uses. This is noted in all
```

PDS manuals for the particular application you're using.

Make Definition

Make Definition enters and edits a definition file for Btrieve data files. This utility provides the capabilities for setting up the data record length, page size, number of indexes, variable, length record flag, and key value specifications. These values are required to create any Btrieve file and this utility provides an easy means of creating and managing your file definitions. The files created by this utility are used by the library routine Make_File to create Btrieve database files.

Make Definition begins by attempting to open and read the specified file. If the file is found, the file is read into the structures FileInfo and KeySpec. If the file is not found, these structures are initialized to nulls.

Next, the main editing routine, Record_Info is called for updating the data structures. The FileInfo structure is updated through calls to the library routine Ent_Scr. Then, if PgDown is pressed, a second entry screen is displayed for entry of the KeySpec structures. These entry screens provide examples of using the multipage entry screen facility of Ent_Control and using entry screen routines for nonstring data.

When Escape is pressed, the user is prompted for the file name to save the structures to; if Escape is not pressed for the filename, the file is written.

Make Definition Source Code

▼

```
extern unsigned _stklen=16384; /* Minimum recommend stack size 32768 minimum
                                  recommended for use with Btrieve */
#include <stdio.h>
#include <stdarg.h>
#include <math.h>
#include <dos.h>
#include <mem.h>
#include <alloc.h>
#include <ctype.h>
#include <string.h>
#include <stdlib.h>
#include <plib.h>
#include <plib.glo>
/* #include <plib.btv>  - remove comment for Btrieve usage*/
int
  HiKey,
  KeyNum;

struct
{
  int
```

```
    RecLen,
    PageSize,
    NumIndex;
  char
    Blank1[4];
  int
    Variable;
  char
    Blank2[4];
} FileInfo;

struct
{
  int
    KeyPos,
    KeyLen,
    KeyFlags;
  char
    NU[10];
} KeySpec[24];

/****************************************************************************/
void Record_Info(void)
/*
  This routine will acquire the main file information.
*/
{/*Record_Info*/
  char
    TStr[81];

  int
    KeyNum,
    Page;

  KeyNum = 0;
  Page = 1;
  while (CurKey != 27)
  {
    switch (Page)
    {
      case 1: /*Main file info*/
        Draw_Frame(1, 1, 80, 24, 2, "NR", "File Information Entry", Blue);
        F_Write(3, 24, VidHigh, " <PgDown> for Key Specs ");
        F_Write(40, 24, VidHigh, " <Esc> to exit ");
        FieldLineNum = 0;
        do
        {
          itoa(FileInfo.RecLen, TStr, 10);
```

```
        Ent_Scr(1, 5, 5, "Data Record Length : ", "5I,0 99999", TStr);
        FileInfo.RecLen = atoi(TStr);
        itoa(FileInfo.PageSize, TStr, 10);
        Ent_Scr(2, 5, 6, "Page Size          : ", "4I,0 92160", TStr);
        FileInfo.PageSize = atoi(TStr);
        itoa(FileInfo.NumIndex, TStr, 10);
        Ent_Scr(3, 5, 7, "Number of Indexes  : ", "2I,1 24", TStr);
        FileInfo.NumIndex = atoi(TStr);
        if (FileInfo.Variable)
          strcpy(TStr,"Y");
        else
          strcpy(TStr,"N");
        Ent_Scr(4, 5, 8, "Variable length    : ", "A1,YN", TStr);
        FileInfo.Variable = (TStr[0] == 'Y');
      }while (Ent_Control(4, 0, 1, &Page));
      Page += (Page == 0);
    break;

    case 2:
      Draw_Frame(1, 1, 80, 24, 2, "NR", "Key Information Entry", Blue);
      F_Write(3, 24, VidHigh, " <PgUp> for File Info ");
      F_Write(40, 24, VidHigh, " <Esc> to exit ");
      do
      {
        FieldLineNum = 0;
        sprintf(TStr, "Key Spec Number : %d", KeyNum);
        F_Write(3, 3, VidHigh, TStr);
        F_Write(5, 12, VidHigh, "1  - Duplicate");
        F_Write(5, 13, VidHigh, "2  - Modifiable");
        F_Write(5, 14, VidHigh, "4  - Binary");
        F_Write(5, 15, VidHigh, "8  - NULL");
        F_Write(5, 16, VidHigh, "16 - Segmented");
        F_Write(5, 17, VidHigh, "32 - Alt Col Seq");
        do
        {
          itoa(KeySpec[KeyNum].KeyPos, TStr, 10);
          Ent_Scr(1, 5, 5, "Key Position : ", "4I,0 9999", TStr);
          KeySpec[KeyNum].KeyPos = atoi(TStr);
          itoa(KeySpec[KeyNum].KeyLen, TStr, 10);
          Ent_Scr(2, 5, 7, "Key Length   : ", "4I,0 9999", TStr);
          KeySpec[KeyNum].KeyLen = atoi(TStr);
          itoa(KeySpec]KeyNum].KeyFlags, TStr, 10);
          Ent_Scr(3, 5, 9, "Key Flags    : ", "4I,0 9999", TStr);
          KeySpec[KeyNum].KeyFlags = atoi(TStr);
        }while (Ent_Control(3, 1, 1, &Page));
        switch (CurKey)
        {
          case 9: /*Tab*/
```

```
            KeyNum += ((KeyNum < 24) && (KeySpec[KeyNum].KeyPos != 0));
          break;
          case -15: /*Backtab*/
            KeyNum -= (KeyNum > 0);
          break;
        }
      } while ((CurKey != -73 ) && (CurKey != 27));
      Page -= (Page == 3);
    break;
  }/* switch*/
  for (HiKey = 0; (KeySpec[HiKey].KeyPos > 0); HiKey++);
  if ((HiKey == 0) && (CurKey == 27))
  {
    Hi_Mess("Error - No keys defined or Key position less than 1.");
    CurKey = 13;
  }
 }/* while CurKey != 27*/
}/*Record_Info*/


/****************************************************************************/
main()
{
 int
   RecLen;

 char
   FName[81];

 FILE
   *DefFile;

 Calibrate_Delay();           /* Calibrate delay factor */
 Get_Video_Mode("Video.CFG"); /* Get display adapter type */
 Install_Crit_Error();        /* Set up application critical error handler */
 InputAbsolute=AbortPrint=0;  /* Initialize global variables */
 Clr_Scr();
 /* Application code to follow */
 FName[0] = 0;
 Prompt(1, 1, Normal, "BTrieve Definition File : ", "A40,", FName);
 if (CurKey != 27)
 {
   DefFile = fopen(FName, "rb");
   if (DefFile != NULL)
   {
     fread(&RecLen, 1, 2, DefFile);
     fread(&FileInfo, 1, sizeof(FileInfo), DefFile);
     fread(&KeySpec[0], 1, RecLen - sizeof(FileInfo), DefFile);
```

```
      fclose(DefFile);
    }
    else
    {
      Lo_Mess("New File");
      setmem(&FileInfo, sizeof(FileInfo), 0);
      setmem(&KeySpec[0], sizeof(KeySpec[0]), 0);
      Delay(1500);
    }
    Record_Info();
    Clr_Scr();
    Prompt(1, 1, Normal, "Save to file : ", "A40,", FName);
    if (CurKey != 27)
    {
      DefFile = fopen(FName, "wb");
      RecLen = sizeof(FileInfo) + (sizeof(KeySpec[0]) * HiKey);
      fwrite(&RecLen, 2, 1, DefFile);
      fwrite(&FileInfo, sizeof(FileInfo), 1, DefFile);
      fwrite(&KeySpec[0], sizeof(KeySpec[0]), HiKey, DefFile);
      fclose(DefFile);
    }
  }
  Clr_Scr();
} /*main*/
```

Shell

Shell demonstrates how to start a new application using the *Developer's Library*. Shell includes the header include statements required for compilation and the initialization operations required for the library.

We recommend that you use Shell as a template and add on to it to construct an application. Comments indicate where you should begin placement of your application's code.

```
extern unsigned _stklen=16384; /* Minimum recommend stack size,
                                  32768 minimum recommended for
                                  use with Btrieve */
#include <stdio.h>
#include <math.h>
#include <dos.h>
#include <mem.h>
#include <alloc.h>
#include <ctype.h>
#include <string.h>
#include <stdlib.h>
#include <plib.h>
```

```
#include <plib.glo>
/* #include <plib.btv> */ /* - remove comment for Btrieve usage*/

/*****************************************************************************/
main()
{
  /* Initialize library values */
  Calibrate_Delay();            /* Calibrate delay factor */
  Get_Video_Mode("Video.CFG"); /* Get display adapter type */
  Install_Crit_Error();         /* Set up application critical error handler */
  InputAbsolute=AbortPrint=0;  /* Initialize global variables */
  Clr_Scr();
  /* Application code to follow */

  /* End of application code */
  Clr_Scr();
} /*main*/
```

A Cross-Reference Guides

Cross-Reference by Category

This section categorizes the library to provide you with an easy method for finding a routine by the type of function it performs. The categories, and the routines within each category, are listed alphabetically.

Btrieve File Management Routines

Add_Record	Adds a new record to a Btrieve data file.
BTrv	Interfaces with the Btrieve record manager.
Change_Record	Updates a data record in a Btrieve data file.
Close_File	Closes a Btrieve data file.
Delete_Record	Deletes a data record from a Btrieve data file.
End_Btrieve	Terminates the memory-resident Btrieve record manager.
Get_Record	Retrieves a data record from a Btrieve data file.
Highest_Record	Retrieves the last data record in a Btrieve data file, based on the index path specified.
Lowest_Record	Retrieves the first data record in a Btrieve data file, based on the index path specified.
Make_File	Creates a Btrieve database file from a definition file.
Mode_Select	Controls selection of the standard file maintenance options menu.
Mode_Update	Redisplays the current file maintenance mode as selected during Mode_Select.

Next_Key	Returns the next consecutive index key from a Btrieve data file.
Next_Record	Returns the next consecutive record from a Btrieve data file.
Open_File	Opens an existing Btrieve data file.
Prev_Key	Returns the preceding index key from a Btrieve data file.
Prev_Record	Returns the preceding data record from a Btrieve data file.
Record_Entry_Control	Controls forward and backward record movement while using data entry screens.
RMake_File	Creates a new Btrieve data file.
Search_Record	Locates the record equal to or greater than the specified key value using the indicated index path in a Btrieve data file.
Used_Recs	Returns the number of active records in a Btrieve data file.

Data Entry and Menu Routines

Ent_Control	Manages the looping structure for data entry screens using Ent_Scr.
Ent_Scr	Provides the capability for user-defined data entry screens.
Get_One_Char	Reads a character from the keyboard buffer, accommodates standard characters and command keys.
Input_Alpha	Allows formatted entry of alphanumeric data.
Input_Date	Allows validated entry of calendar dates.
Input_Num	Allows formatted entry for string representations of numeric values, with specified minimum/maximum values and in a specified format.
Menu	Allows multiple screen capacity for cursor-selectable menus or option listings.
Prompt	Gets the user's response to a specified message with entry formatting.

Show_Dir	Shows directory and allows selection of file for path and wildcards passed.

DOS Error Control and Printer Output

Install_Crit_Error	Installs the library error handling of DOS errors.
Print	Outputs the passed string to a printer followed by the specified number of line feeds.
Print_At	Outputs the passed string to a printer at the specified column followed by the indicated number of line feeds.
Print_Char	Outputs the passed character to the current printer.
Print_Codes	Prints the ASCII value of a textual representation of numeric values.

File Manipulation Routines

Copy_File	Creates a duplicate copy of a disk file.
Created	Determines if the specified disk file has been created.
Help_File	Provides an interactive on-screen help system based on a specified text file.
Read_Line	Reads a line of text from an ASCII file with a specified maximum line size.
Write_Line	Writes a line of text to an ASCII file and appends a carriage return and line feed after the string.
Write_String	Writes a line of text to an ASCII file without appending a line terminator (carriage return, line feed).

Keyboard Routines

Flush_KB_Buffer	Removes all characters remaining in the keyboard buffer.
Look_One_Char	Reads the next key from the keyboard buffer without removing the character from the buffer.

Math Routines

Calculator	Produces a pop-up numeric and date calculator for use in applications.
Range_Max	Retrieves the maximum value of a number to be updated by Input_Num or Prompt.

Range_Min	Retrieves the minimum value of a number to be updated by Input_Num or Prompt.

Novell Network Routines

Close_LST_Device	Closes a spooled output device on a Novell Network file server.
Get_Station_Number	Returns the Novell Network station number of the current user.
Get_NTime	Retrieves the current time maintained by the network.
Global_Broadcast_Message	Sends a specified message to all users on a Novell Network.
Modify_LST_Device	Activates the Novell network spooler based on the default spooler values established by Set_Spool_Flags.
Set_File_Attributes	Sets or changes the attributes attached to a file on a Novell Network file server.
Set_Spool_Flags	Sets the default spooler flags for a Novell Network Printer.

Screen and Sound Routines

Beep_Bomb	Produces a distinctive sound used by library routines to indicate fatal errors.
Beep_Hi	Produces a short high-pitch tone used to indicate general errors during the execution of library routines.
Beep_Lo	Produces a short low-pitch tone used to indicate data or entry errors during the execution of library routines.
Blend	Provides integration of the specified video attribute on a string written to the screen with the attributes set for the current window.
Bomb_Mess	Used for fatal error handling, executes a Beep_Bomb with a message on the 25th line and then halts the program.
Clear_Frame	Clears all text in a portion of the display screen.
Clr_Scr	Clears all text from the video display.
Cnvg_Mess	Divides a string into two equal portions and converges the strings from the outer edges of the screen until they meet in the center of the screen.

Cursor_Off	Disables the display of the video cursor block.
Cursor_On	Enables the display of the video cursor block.
Draw_Frame	Displays a window of a specified size with the designated title and border format.
F_Write	Displays the passed string on the video screen using the specified attributes at the indicated column and row. This routine is written in machine language and displays text very rapidly without flicker or snow.
F_WriteXY	Displays the string in the same manner as F_Write, except the cursor is placed at the end of the displayed string.
Get_Video_Mode	Initializes the global video control variables for the library display routines.
GotoXY	Sets the current video position to the row and column positions passed.
Hi_Mess	Displays the passed string message and produces a Beep_Hi.
Lo_Mess	Displays the passed string message and produces a Beep_Lo.
Message	Displays the passed message on the 25th line of the video display.
Move_Scrn_Mem	Copies a specified number of bytes to or from screen memory and a specified memory buffer.
No_Sound	Turns off any sound being generated through the computer's speaker.
Restore_Screen	Restores the contents of a global buffer to the video display.
Save_Screen	Stores the current video display memory into a global variable.
Scroll_Mess	Scrolls a line of text from right to left in a specified window.
Set_Window_Attr	Changes the video attributes of a specified window.
Sound	Produces a tone on the computer's speaker at a specified frequency until a No_Sound operation is called.
WhereX	Returns the current column position of the video cursor.

WhereY	Returns the current row position of the video cursor.

String Manipulation Routines

Cen	Centers the passed string in a specified length of spaces.
Common_Chars	Indicates if all the characters in a specified string are in common with the second specified string.
Copy	Copies a selected portion of a string into another string.
Delete	Deletes a specified portion of the indicated string value.
Erase_White	Removes all spaces from the passed string.
Erase_White_Begin	Removes all leading spaces from the passed string.
Erase_White_End	Removes all ending spaces from the passed string.
Insert	Inserts a substring into a string at a specific starting position.
Is_Text	Determines if the string passed contains characters in the ASCII range of 33 to 255.
LJ	Left justifies the indicated string in the specified number of spaces.
Num_Chars	Returns the number of occurrences of a specified character in a string.
Num_Decs	Returns the number of decimal digits in a floating point number.
Num_Ints	Returns the number of integer digits in an integer or floating point number.
Num_Pattern_Size	Returns the maximum field length for a data entry field based on the pattern string indicated.
Num_To_Word	Converts a real number to its textual representation.
Pattern	Formats the passed string number to the specified length and number of decimal places.
Pos	Locates the position of the first occurrence of a character in a string.
Replace	Overwrites a section of a specified string with a second string.

RJ	Right justifies the passed string in the specified number of spaces.
Rpt	Repeats the specified string the indicated number of times.
Str_IsInt	Checks to determine if a string is an integer value representation.
Str_Pos	Locates the first occurrence of a string or character in another string.

Time and Date Manipulation Routines

Calibrate_Delay	Determines the proper number of looping cycles to use to create an exact delay-time value for the library routine Delay.
Cal_Julian	Calculates the Julian number of days since year 0 of the date passed.
Check_Date	Verifies that the date passed is a valid calendar date.
Date_Add	Calculates the date resulting from the addition of a specified number of days to a specified date.
Date_Comp	Returns a string date in the form YY/MM/DD from a string date passed in the form MM/DD/YY.
Date_Diff	Calculates the number of days between two dates.
Date_Sub	Calculates the date resulting from the subtraction of a specified number of days from a specified date.
Day_Of_Week	Returns the textual name for the day of the week indicated by the specified date.
Delay	Causes a delay in program processing for the number of milliseconds specified.
Get_Time	Returns the current system time in one of several formats.
Julian_Cal	Calculates the calendar date for the Julian date passed.
Month_Of_Year	Returns the month of the year in a specified format for the passed date.
M_D_Y	Returns the textual representation in a specified format of the passed date.

Time_Add	Adds a specified number of hours to the indicated time.
Time_Diff	Determines the number of hours between two specified times.
Time_Sub	Subtracts a specified number of hours from the indicated time.
Today	Returns the system date in the form MM/DD/YY.
Undate_Comp	Returns a string date in the form MM/DD/YY from a string date in the form YY/MM/DD.

Cross-Reference of Routines Used by Other Routines

The following cross-reference lists what library routines call each routine. This will aid you in determining which are the key library routines. Also, you can use the listed routines to find additional examples of how to use a particular procedure or function.

Main Library Routines

Routine	Used by
Beep_Bomb	Bomb_Mess Menu Print_Codes
Beep_Hi	Help_File Hi_Mess Install_Crit_Error
Beep_Lo	Help_File Install_Crit_Error Lo_Mess Mode_Select
Blend	Ent_Scr Help_File Menu Mode_Select
Bomb_Mess	Make_File
Calculator	None
Calibrate_Delay	None
Cal_Julian	Date_Add Date_Diff Date_Sub

Routine	Used by
	Day_Of_Week
Cen	Calculator Cnvg_Mess Draw_Frame Help_File Message Num_To_Word
Check_Date	Input_Date
Clear_Frame	Blend Clr_Scr Draw_Frame Help_File Menu
Clr_Scr	None
Cnvg_Mess	Help_File Mode_Select
Common_Chars	Print_Codes
Copy	Cal_Julian Check_Date Cnvg_Mess Date_Comp Ent_Scr Get_NTime Get_Time Input_Date Mode_Select Mode_Update Month_Of_Year M_D_Y Num_To_Word Print_Codes Prompt Range_Max Range_Min Scroll_Mess Time_Add Time_Diff Time_Sub Undate_Comp
Copy_File	None
Created	None
Cursor_Off	Calculator

Routine	Used by
	Help_File Install_Crit_Error Menu
Cursor_On	Calculator Help_File Install_Crit_Error Menu
Date_Add	Calculator
Date_Comp	None
Date_Diff	Calculator
Date_Sub	Calculator
Day_Of_Week	M_D_Y
Delay	Beep_Bomb Beep_Hi Beep_Lo Cnvg_Mess Get_Video_Mode Prompt Scroll_Mess
Delete	Calculator Check_Date Num_To_Word Print_Codes
Draw_Frame	Help_File
Ent_Control	None
Ent_Scr	None
Erase_White	Calculator Check_Date Draw_Frame Input_Alpha Input_Date Num_To_Word Print_Codes
Erase_White_Begin	Draw_Frame Num_To_Word
Erase_White_End	Draw_Frame Input_Alpha
Flush_KB_Buffer	None
F_Write	Blend

Routine	Used by
	Calculator
	Clear_Frame
	Cnvg_Mess
	Draw_Frame
	Ent_Scr
	F_WriteXY
	Get_Video_Mode
	Help_File
	Input_Alpha
	Input_Date
	Input_Num
	Install_Crit_Error
	Menu
	Message
	Mode_Select
	Mode_Update
	Prompt
	Scroll_Mess
F_WriteXY	Calculator
	Ent_Scr
	Prompt
Get_One_Char	Calculator
	Flush_KB_Buffer
	Help_File
	Input_Alpha
	Install_Crit_Error
	Menu
	Prompt
Get_Time	None
Get_Video_Mode	None
Goto_XY	Calculator
	Clr_Scr
	F_WriteXY
	Input_Alpha
	Input_Date
	Input_Num
Help_File	Mode_Select
Hi_Mess	Calculator
	Input_Num
Input_Alpha	Ent_Scr
	Input_Date
	Input_Num

Routine	Used by
	Prompt
Input_Date	Ent_Scr Prompt
Input_Num	Ent_Scr Num_Pattern_Size Prompt
Insert	Get_NTime Get_Time
Install_Crit_Error	None
Is_Text	Calculator Date_Comp Input_Num Undate_Comp
Julian_Cal	Date_Add Date_Sub
LJ	Calculator Ent_Scr Input_Alpha Prompt Scroll_Mess
Look_One_Char	Flush_KB_Buffer
Lo_Mess	Calculator Ent_Control Help_File Input_Alpha Input_Date Input_Num Menu Mode_Select Prompt Record_Entry_Control
Menu	Mode_Select
Message	Bomb_Mess Calculator Cnvg_Mess Global_Broadcast_Message Help_File Hi_Mess Input_Alpha Input_Num Install_Crit_Error

Routine	Used by
	Lo_Mess Menu Print_Codes Record_Entry_Control
Month_Of_Year	M_D_Y
Move_Scrn_Mem	Restore_Screen Save_Screen Set_Window_Attr
M_D_Y	None
No_Sound	Beep_Bomb Beep_Hi Beep_Lo
Num_Chars	Input_Num
Num_Decs	Input_Num
Num_Ints	Input_Num
Num_Pattern_Size	Ent_Scr Input_Num
Num_To_Word	None
Pattern	Ent_Scr Input_Num
Pos	Calculator Check_Date Copy Ent_Scr Input_Alpha Input_Date Input_Num Insert Num_To_Word Print_Codes Prompt Range_Max Range_Min Replace RMake_File
Print	Print_At
Print_At	None
Print_Char	Print Print_Codes

Routine	Used by
Print_Codes	None
Prompt	Calculator Record_Entry_Control
Range_Max	None
Range_Min	None
Read_Line	Help_File
Replace	Input_Alpha
Restore_Screen	Calculator Help_File Install_Crit_Error
RJ	Calculator Ent_Scr Input_Num Scroll_Mess
Rpt	Calculator Message Mode_Select Print_At Scroll_Mess
Save_Screen	Calculator Help_File Install_Crit_Error
Scroll_Mess	None
Set_Window_Attr	None
Show_Dir	None
Sound	Beep_Bomb Beep_Hi Beep_Lo
Str_IsInt	Check_Date In_Date
Str_Pos	None
Time_Add	None
Time_Diff	None
Time_Sub	None
Today	Calculator
Undate_Comp	None

Routine	Used by
WhereX	Calculator Input_Alpha Input_Date Input_Num Prompt
WhereY	Calculator Input_Alpha I

Btrieve Routines

Routine	Used by
Add_Record	Record_Entry_Control
BTrv	Add_Record Change_Record Close_File Delete_Record End_Btrieve Get_Record Highest_Record Lowest_Record Make_File Next_Key Next_Record Open_File Prev_Key Prev_Record RMake_File Search_Record Used_Recs
Change_Record	Record_Entry_Control
Close_File	None
Delete_Record	Record_Entry_Control
End_Btrieve	None
Get_Record	None
Highest_Record	Record_Entry_Control
Lowest_Record	None
Mode_Select	None
Mode_Update	None
Next_Key	None
Next_Record	Record_Entry_Control
Open_File	None

Routine	Used by
Prev_Key	None
Prev_Record	Record_Entry_Control
Record_Entry_Control	None
RMake_File	None
Search_Record	None
Used_Recs	Mode_Select Mode_Update Record_Entry_Control

Novell Routines

Routine	Used by
Close_LST_Device	None
Get_NPrinter_Status	None
Get_NTime	None
Get_Station_Number	None
Global_Broadcast_Message	None
Modify_LST_Device	None
Set_File_Attributes	None
Set_Spool_Flags	None

Cross-Reference of Required Routines

The following cross-reference provides a list of the routines required to execute each routine in the library. The cross-reference provides an easy means of determining what you need to use for any routine. This makes using only one routine from the library much easier because you will know what you must include prior to calling the routine.

Under each routine is a list of the routines that particular library operation uses. The list only includes the first level of requirements. It does not list the calls that the listed routines require. If a routine does not have any required library procedures, it is listed as requiring none. This means that the routine can be used as is without having to enter any other procedures or functions from the library.

Main Library Routines

Routine	Uses
Beep_Bomb	Delay No_Sound Sound
Beep_Hi	Delay

Routine	Uses
	No_Sound Sound
Beep_Lo	Delay No_Sound Sound
Blend	None
Bomb_Mess	Beep_Bomb Message
Calculator	Cen Cursor_Off Cursor_On Date_Add Date_Diff Date_Sub Delete Erase_White F_Write F_WriteXY Get_One_Char Goto_XY Hi_Mess Is_Text LJ Lo_Mess Message Pos Prompt Restore_Screen RJ Rpt Save_Screen Today WhereX WhereY
Calibrate_Delay	None
Cal_Julian	Copy
Cen	None
Check_Date	Copy Delete Erase_White Pos Str_IsInt

Routine	Uses
Clear_Frame	F_Write
Clr_Scr	Clear_Frame Goto_XY
Cnvg_Mess	Cen Copy Delay F_Write Message
Common_Chars	None
Copy	None
Copy_File	None
Created	None
Cursor_Off	None
Cursor_On	None
Date_Add	Cal_Julian Julian_Cal
Date_Comp	Copy Is_Text
Date_Diff	Cal_Julian
Date_Sub	Cal_Julian Julian_Cal
Day_Of_Week	Cal_Julian
Delay	None
Delete	None
Draw_Frame	Cen Clear_Frame Erase_White Erase_White_Begin Erase_White_End F_Write
Ent_Control	Lo_Mess
Ent_Scr	Blend Copy F_Write F_WriteXY Input_Alpha Input_Date

Routine	Uses
	Input_Num LJ Num_Pattern_Size Pos RJ
Erase_White	None
Erase_White_Begin	None
Erase_White_End	None
Flush_KB_Buffer	Get_One_Char Look_One_Char
F_Write	None
F_WriteXY	F_Write Goto_XY
Get_One_Char	None
Get_Time	Copy Insert
Get_Video_Mode	Delay F_Write
Global_Broadcast_Message	None
Goto_XY	None
Help_File	Beep_Hi Beep_Lo Blend Cen Clear_Frame Cnvg_Mess Cursor_Off Cursor_On Draw_Frame F_Write Get_One_Char Lo_Mess Message Read_Line Restore_Screen Save_Screen
Hi_Mess	Beep_Hi Message
Input_Alpha	Erase_White

Routine	Uses
	Erase_White_End
	F_Write
	Get_One_Char
	Goto_XY
	LJ
	Lo_Mess
	Message
	Pos
	Replace
	WhereX
	WhereY
Input_Date	Check_Date
	Copy
	Erase_White
	F_Write
	Goto_XY
	Input_Alpha
	Lo_Mess
	Str_IsInt
	WhereX
	WhereY
Input_Num	F_Write
	Goto_XY
	Hi_Mess
	Input_Alpha
	Is_Text
	Lo_Mess
	Message
	Num_Chars
	Num_Decs
	Num_Ints
	Num_Pattern_Size
	Pos
	RJ
	WhereX
	WhereY
Insert	None
Install_Crit_Error	Beep_Hi
	Beep_Lo
	Cursor_Off
	Cursor_On
	F_Write
	Get_One_Char
	Message
	Restore_Screen

Routine	Uses
	Save_Screen
Is_Text	None
Julian_Cal	None
LJ	None
Look_One_Char	None
Lo_Mess	Beep_Lo Message
Menu	Beep_Bomb Blend Clear_Frame Cursor_Off Cursor_On F_Write Get_One_Char Lo_Mess Message
Message	Cen F_Write Rpt
Month_Of_Year	Copy
Move_Scrn_Mem	None
M_D_Y	Copy Day_Of_Week Month_Of_Year
No_Sound	None
Num_Chars	None
Num_Decs	None
Num_Ints	None
Num_Pattern_Size	None
Num_To_Word	Cen Copy Delete Erase_White Erase_White_Begin Pos
Pattern	None
Pos	None

Routine	Uses
Print	Print_Char
Print_At	Print Rpt
Print_Char	None
Print_Codes	Beep_Bomb Common_Chars Copy Delete Erase_White Message Pos Print_Char
Prompt	Copy Delay F_Write F_WriteXY Get_One_Char Input_Alpha Input_Date Input_Num LJ Lo_Mess Pos WhereX WhereY
Range_Max	Copy Pos
Range_Min	Copy Pos
Read_Line	None
Replace	Pos
Restore_Screen	Move_Scrn_Mem
RJ	None
Rpt	None
Save_Screen	Move_Scrn_Mem
Scroll_Mess	Copy Delay F_Write LJ RJ

Routine	Uses
	Rpt
Set_Window_Attr	Move_Scrn_Mem
Show_Dir	Blend Clear_Frame Copy Cursor_Off Cursor_On Delay Draw_Frame F_Write Get_One_Char Hi_Mess Lo_Mess Message Pos Restore_Screen Save_Screen
Sound	None
Str_IsInt	None
Str_Pos	None
Time_Add	Copy
Time_Diff	Copy
Time_Sub	Copy
Today	None
Undate_Comp	Copy Is_Text
WhereX	None
WhereY	None
Write_Line	None
Write_String	None

Btrieve Routines

Routine	Uses
Add_Record	BTrv
BTrv	None
Change_Record	BTrv
Close_File	BTrv
Delete_Record	BTrv

Routine	Uses
End_Btrieve	BTrv
Get_Record	BTrv
Highest_Record	BTrv
Lowest_Record	BTrv
Make_File	Bomb_Mess BTrv
Mode_Select	Beep_Lo Blend BTrv Cnvg_Mess Copy F_Write Help_File Lo_Mess Menu Rpt Used_Recs
Mode_Update	Copy F_Write Used_Recs
Next_Key	BTrv
Next_Record	BTrv
Open_File	BTrv
Prev_Key	BTrv
Prev_Record	BTrv
Record_Entry_Control	Add_Record BTrv Change_Record Delete_Record Highest_Record Lo_Mess Message Next_Record Prev_Record Prompt Used_Recs
RMake_File	BTrv Pos
Search_Record	BTrv
Used_Recs	BTrv

Novell Routines

Routine	Uses
Close_LST_Device	None
Get_NPrinter_Status	None
Get_NTime	Copy Insert
Get_Station_Number	None
Modify_LST_Device	None
Set_File_Attributes	None
Set_Spool_Flags	None

B Keyboard Scan Code Table

The following table provides the scan codes returned from the keyboard handling routines in the library.

Key	Unshifted	Shift	Ctrl	Alt
[	91	123	27	
\	92	124	28	
]	93	125	29	
`	96	126		
0	48	41		- 129
1	49	33		- 120
2	50	64	- 3	- 121
3	51	35		- 122
4	52	36		- 123
5	53	37		- 124
6	54	94	30	- 125
7	55	38		- 126
8	56	42		- 127
9	57	40		- 128
*	42		- 114	
+	43	43		
-	45	95	31	- 130
=	61	43		- 131
,	44	60		
/	47	63		
;	59	58		
F1	- 59	- 84	- 94	- 104
F2	- 60	- 85	- 95	- 105
F3	- 61	- 86	- 96	- 106
F4	- 62	- 87	- 97	- 107
F5	- 63	- 88	- 98	- 108
F6	- 64	- 89	- 99	- 109

Key	Unshifted	Shift	Ctrl	Alt
F7	- 65	- 90	- 100	- 110
F8	- 66	- 91	- 101	- 111
F9	- 67	- 92	- 102	- 112
F10	- 68	- 93	- 103	- 113
LArr	- 75	52	- 115	- 178
RArr	- 77	54	- 116	- 180
UArr	- 72	56	- 160	- 175
DArr	- 80	50	- 164	- 183
Home	- 71	55	- 119	- 174
End	- 79	49	- 117	- 182
PgUp	- 73	57	- 132	- 176
PgDn	- 81	51	- 118	- 184
Ins	- 82	48	- 165	- 185
Del	- 83	46	- 166	- 186
Esc	27	27	27	
BackSp	8	8	127	
Tab	9	- 15		
RETURN	13	13	10	
A	97	65	1	- 30
B	98	66	2	- 48
C	99	67	3	- 46
D	100	68	4	- 32
E	101	69	5	- 18
F	102	70	6	- 33
G	103	71	7	- 34
H	104	72	8	- 35
I	105	73	9	- 23
J	106	74	10	- 36
K	107	75	11	- 37
L	108	76	12	- 38
M	109	77	13	- 50
N	110	78	14	- 49
O	111	79	15	- 24
P	112	80	16	- 25
Q	113	81	17	- 16
R	114	82	18	- 19
S	115	83	19	- 31
T	116	84	20	- 20
U	117	85	21	- 22
V	118	86	22	- 47
W	119	87	23	- 17
X	120	88	24	- 45
Y	121	89	25	- 21
Z	122	90	26	- 44

Reader Feedback

Although the routines in this library have been thoroughly tested, we acknowledge the possibility for errors in the listings or discussions. If you have a problem using a routine from the library, here are some suggestions that may help.

First, check all library routines that are called by the routine you are having a problem with. We strongly recommend that you thoroughly test each routine you enter before moving on to another. Testing the lower level routines will save time when testing the more sophisticated upper level routines.

If the lower level routines check out, have someone else read the code for the routine you are having difficulty with. Often, a different perspective of the situation can help spot a problem that you have overlooked. We often call on each other to look at a routine. Frequently, the solution materializes during the explanation of the design to the other person.

We cannot emphasize enough the importance of proofreading the routines. We have found that most errors in any program come from typographical errors by the person creating the file. Before concluding that the routine doesn't work, check your code three or more times, read the entire section again to ensure that you understand the actual operation of the routine, and check your lower level routines.

If after careful review, you are sure that the routine does not work, please contact us at the address at the end of this section. We need specific information from you about the problem. Don't say, "this thing doesn't work." When sending us a problem, include the following:

A self-addressed stamped envelope large enough to hold the listings for the routines you are having difficulty with.

A printed listing of the problem routine and all lower level routines it uses.

A detailed explanation of the problem, including exactly what went wrong, error codes and their source (e.g., compiler, run-time, etc.), and, if possible, screen dumps of the error as it occurred.

We also need detailed information about your computer system. Include computer manufacturer, memory capacities, drive types and sizes, video display type and manufacturer, printer type and manufacturer, DOS version, ROM BIOS manufacturer, the version of Turbo C you are using, compiler directives you are using, and anything else specific to your situation.

If you assemble all the information we require, it indicates to us that you have made an honest effort to find the problem yourself. Without the information requested, we would not be able to find the problem without tremendous difficulty. If you send in a problem not properly documented, we will return a listing of the current errata without attempting to find your specific problem.

Please don't send us a customized version of a routine and ask us to debug it for you. This is far from the scope of the service we want to provide. We will return such a request to you.

If you want a copy of the errata sheet, send a self-addressed stamped envelope to the address at the end of this section. Mark the envelope "C-DL Errata." The errata sheet will contain any program corrections and notes on documentation changes.

If you want to save the trouble of having to enter the code and debug the routines, you can order the library, sample application, example programs, and some added goodies on disk from the same address. An order form for the disk versions of the library is located at the end of the book. Since the library is an integrated environment, we strongly recommend ordering the disks to eliminate the time required to enter the routines.

C-DL
P.O. Box 6780
Reno, Nevada 89513

Bibliography

Borland International, Inc. 1985. *Turbo C Version 1.0, 1.5 Reference Manual.* Scotts Valley, California.

Hyman, Michael. 1986. *Memory Resident Utilities, Interrupts, and Disk Management with MS and PC DOS.* Portland, Oregon: Management Information Source, Inc.

IBM. 1983. *Personal Computer Disk Operating System (2.1).* Boca Raton, Florida.

Jourdain, Robert. 1986. *Programmer's Problem Solver for the IBM PC, XT & AT.* New York: Brady Books.

Lafore, Robert. 1986. *Turbo C Programming for the IBM.* First Edition. Indianapolis: Hayden Books.

Lemone, Karen. 1985. *Assembly Language and Systems Programming for the IBM PC and Compatibles.* Boston: Little, Brown and Company.

MicroSoft Corporation. 1985. *MicroSoft Macro Assembler Version 4.0 Reference Manual.* Bellevue, Washington: Microsoft Press.

Norton, Peter. 1985. *The Peter Norton Programmer's Guide to the IBM PC.* Bellevue, Washington: Microsoft Press.

Novell, Inc. 1986. *NetWare Function Call Reference Manual.* Orem, Utah.

———. 1987. *XQL Reference Manual.* Austin, Texas.

SoftCraft, Inc. 1982. *Btrieve Reference Manual Version 3.1N.* Austin, Texas.

Index

The Waite Group's Advanced C Primer+ +

Stephen Prata, The Waite Group

›grammers, students, managers, and ːkers alike, will learn to master the programming language. Anyone who ows the basics of C will learn prac- ıl C tips never before published. This depth coverage gives you rare and nplete examination of video access rts, segmented memory, and registers.

vanced C Primer+ + takes the der further than most C books on market, showing how to manipulate hardware of the IBM PC family of nputers directly from C. Readers rn how to access routines in the ıd Only Memory (ROM) of an IBM , how to use system calls in PC S from C and i/o ports, how to con- the video screen, and to integrate embly routines into C programs.

pics covered include:

- Advanced C Programming
- Register and Bit Level System Control
- Hardware Operation for Beginners and Experienced Users
- Advanced Use of Pointers, Functions, Storage Classes, Arrays and Structures
- C Library Access
- Use of Assembly Language Modules
- Binary and Text File Input and Output

ludes chapter questions and answers.

: Pages, 7½ x 9¾, Softbound
N: 0-672-22486-0
. 22486, $24.95

The Waite Group's C Primer Plus, Revised Edition

Mitchell Waite, Stephen Prata, and Donald Martin, The Waite Group

This revised and expanded edition of a best-seller presents everything you should know to begin programming in the exciting C language, now used by over 80 percent of the software community. The book is organized for quick learning and encourages problem solving through questions and exercises.

Topics covered include:

- Structure of a Simple C Program
- Variables, Constants, and Data Types
- Character Strings, *#define, print( ), and scanf( )*
- Operators, Expressions, and Statements
- Input/Output Functions and Redirection
- Choosing Alternatives: *if, else,* Relational and Conditional Operators
- Loops and Other Control Aids
- How to "Function" Properly
- Storage Classes and Program Development
- The C Preprocessor
- Arrays and Pointers
- Character Strings and String Functions
- Structures and Other Data Delights
- The C Library and File I/O
- Bit Fiddling, Keywords, Binary Numbers, IBM® PC Music, and More

576 Pages, 7½ x 9¾, Softbound
ISBN: 0-672-22582-4
No. 22582, $24.95

The Waite Group's Microsoft® C Programming for the IBM®

Robert Lafore, The Waite Group

Programmers using the Microsoft C compiler can learn to write useful and marketable programs with this entry level book on Microsoft C programming.

This title is a tutorial geared specifically to the IBM PC family of computers. Unlike other introductory C titles, it is written for the Microsoft C compiler. It provides special coverage of IBM features such as sound, color graphics including CGA and EGA, keyboard, variable storage, and character graphics.

Topics covered include:

- Getting Started
- Building Blocks
- Loops
- Decisions
- Functions
- Arrays and Strings
- Pointers
- Keyboard and Cursor
- Structures, Unions, and ROM Bios
- Memory and the Monochrome Display
- CGA and EGA Color Graphics
- Files Preprocessor
- Serial Ports and Telecommunications
- Larger Programs
- Advanced Variables
- Appendices Include: Supplemental Programs, Hexadecimal Numbering, IBM Character Codes, and a Bibliography

640 Pages, 7½ x 9¾, Softbound
ISBN: 0-672-22515-8
No. 22515, $24.95

The Waite Group's Turbo C® Programming for the IBM®

Robert Lafore, The Waite Group

This entry-level text teaches readers the C language while also helping them write useful and marketable programs for the IBM PC, XT, AT, and PC/2.

This tutorial is based on Borland's new Turbo C compiler with its powerful integrated environment that makes it easy to edit, compile, and run C programs. The author's proven hands-on intensive approach includes example programs, exercises, and questions and answers and covers CGA and EGA graphic modes.

Topics covered include:

- C Building Blocks
- Loops
- Decisions
- Functions
- Arrays and Strings
- Pointers
- Keyboard and Cursor
- Structures, Unions, and ROM BIOS
- Memory and the Character Display
- CGA and EGA Color Graphics
- Files
- Larger Programs
- Advanced Variables
- Appendices Include: References, Hexadecimal Numbering, Bibliography, ASCII Chart, and Answers to Questions and Exercises

608 Pages, 7½ x 9¾, Softbound
ISBN: 0-672-22614-6
No. 22614, $22.95

Visit your local book retailer, use the order form provided, or call 800-428-SAMS.

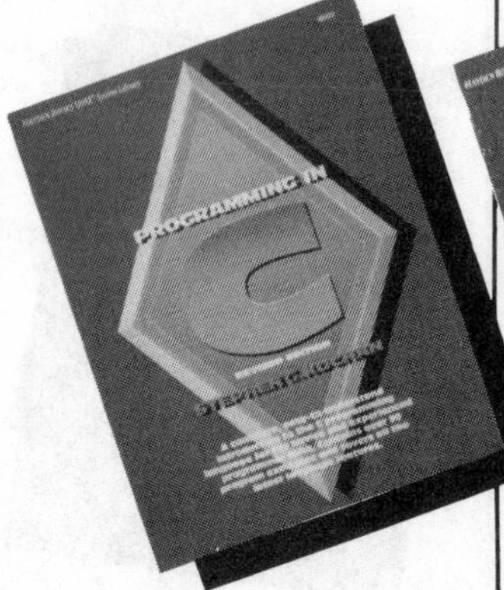

Programming in C, Revised Edition

Stephen G. Kochan

This timely revision provides complete coverage of the C language, including all language features and over 90 program examples. The comprehensive tutorial approach teaches the beginner how to write, compile, and execute programs and teaches the experienced programmer how to write applications using features unique to C. It is written in a clear instructive style and is ideally suited for classroom use or as a self-study guide.

Topics covered include:

- Introduction and Fundamentals
- Writing a Program in C
- Variables, Constants, Data Types, and Arithmetic Expressions
- Program Looping
- Making Decisions
- Arrays
- Functions
- Structures
- Character Strings
- Pointers
- Operations on Bits
- The Preprocessor
- Working with Larger Programs
- Input and Output
- Miscellaneous and Advanced Features
- Appendices: Language Summary, ANSI Standard C, Common Programming Mistakes, The UNIX C Library, Compiling Programs under UNIX, The Program LINT, The ASCII Character Set

464 Pages, 7½ x 9¾, Softbound
ISBN: 0-672-48420-X
No. 48420, $24.95

Programming in ANSI C

Stephen G. Kochan

This comprehensive programming guide is the newest title in the Hayden Books C Library, written by the series editor Stephen G. Kochan. A tutorial in nature, the book teaches the beginner how to write, compile and execute programs even with no previous experience with C.

The book details such C essentials as program looping, decision making, arrays, functions, structures, character strings, bit operations, and enumerated data types. Examples are complete with step-by-step explanations of each procedure and routine involved as well as end-of-chapter exercises, making it ideally suited for classroom use.

Topics covered include:

- Introduction and Fundamentals
- Writing a Program in ANSI C
- Variables, Data Types, and Arithmetic Expressions
- Program Looping
- Making Decisions
- Arrays, Functions, Structures
- Character Strings, Pointers
- Operations on Bits
- The Preprocessor
- More on Data Types
- Working with Larger Programs
- Input and Output
- Miscellaneous Features and Topics
- Appendices: ANSI C Language Summary, The UNIX C Library, Compiling Programs Under UNIX, The Program LINT, The ASCII Character Set

450 Pages, 7½ x 9¾, Softbound
ISBN: 0-672-48408-0
No. 48408, $24.95

Advanced C: Tips and Techniques

Paul L. Anderson and Gail C. Anderson

If you have a working knowledge of the C language and want to enhance your programming skills, the examples and techniques found in this new book are just what you need. It is an in-depth look at the C programming language with special emphasis on portability, execution efficiency, and application techniques.

With entire chapters devoted to special areas of C such as debugging techniques, C's run-time environment, and a memory object allocator, the book contains detailed explanations and examples that will show you how to speed up your C programs. Techniques for creating and deciphering expressions, moving data, and coding expressions that execute predictably are included as well as end-of-chapter exercises that help you learn what has been explained.

Topics covered include:

- C Refresher
- The Run-Time Environment
- Bits of C
- There's No Such Thing as an Array
- A Closer Look at C
- C Debugging Techniques
- A Memory Object Allocator
- Appendices: Portable C Under UNIX System V, Microsoft C Under XENIX, Microsoft C Under DOS, Turbo C Under DOS

325 Pages, 7½ x 9¾, Softbound
ISBN: 0-672-48417-X
No. 48417, $24.95

Topics in C Programming

Stephen G. Kochan and Patrick H. W

Here is the most advanced and com prehensive coverage of the maturing market. This sequel to *Programmin C* describes in detail some of the m difficult concepts in the C language- structures and pointers. It also explc the standard C library and standard library, dynamic memory allocation, linked lists, tree structures, and disp tables.

Experienced C programmers can examine the UNIX System Interface through discussions on controlling p cesses, pipes, and terminal I/O. *To in C Programming* also explains hc to write terminal-independent progra how to debug C programs and analy their performance, and how to use "make" for automatic generation of programming system.

Topics covered include:

- Structures and Pointers
- The Standard C Library
- The Standard I/O Library
- UNIX System Interface
- Writing Terminal-Independent Pr grams with the "curses" Library
- Debug and Performance Analysis C Programs
- Generating Program Systems wit "make"

528 Pages, 7½ x 9¾, Softbound
ISBN: 0-672-46290-7
No. 46290, $24.95

Visit your local book retailer, use the order form provided, or call 800-428-SAMS.

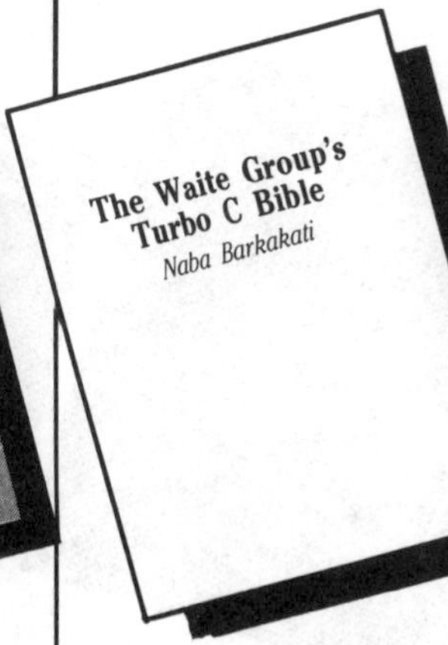

C Programmer's Guide to Serial Communications

Joe Campbell

book offers a comprehensive ination and unprecedented ction of asynchronous serial munications. Written for C pro- mers and technically advanced s, it contains both theoretical ission of communications con- s and a practical approach to ram design for the IBM® PC Kaypro environments.

author introduces a startling nce in the art of pro- mming—the "virtual" UART— h he uses to develop a highly able C programming library outperforms costly commercial ucts; provides functions for fast calculation, XMODEM file sfer, XON/XOFF control, and h more.

ics covered include:

- The ASCII Character Set
- Fundamentals of Asynchronous Technology
- Errors and Error Detection
- Information Transfer
- Modems and Modem Control
- The UART—A Conceptual Model
- Real-World Hardware: Two UARTs
- The Hayes Smartmodem
- Designing a Basic Serial I/O Library
- Portability Considerations
- Timing Functions
- Functions for Baud Rate and Data Format
- RS-232 Control
- Formatted Input and Output
- Smartmodem Programming
- XMODEM File Transfers
- CRC Calculations
- Interrupts

Pages, 7½ x 9¾, Softbound
N: 0-672-22584-0
22584, $26.95

Portability and the C Language

Rex Jaeschke

Portability, the feature that distinguishes C from other programming languages, is thoroughly defined and explained in this definitive reference work. The book primarily addresses the technical issues of designing and writing C programs that are to be compiled across a diverse number of hardware and operating system environments.

Organized around the ANSI C Standard, it explains the C preprocessor and the run-time library and tackles portability from a C language perspective, discussing implementation-specific issues as they arise.

Topics covered include:

- Introduction and Overview
- The Environment
- Conversions, Expressions, Declarations, and Statements
- The Preprocessor
- Diagnostics, Character Handling, Errors
- Numerical Limits and Localization
- Mathematics, Non-Local Jumps, Signal Handling
- Variable Arguments and Common Definitions
- Input/Output, General Utilities, String Handling
- Date and Time
- Appendix: Keywords and Reserved Identifiers

400 Pages, 7½ x 9¾, Softbound
ISBN: 0-672-48428-5
No. 48428, $24.95

The Waite Group's Turbo C Bible

Naba Barkakati

Clear and well-written tutorials point out the different purposes and appropriate uses of each Turbo C function to make programming more organized, complete, and powerful. The library routines are organized into functional categories with explanations that include the purpose, syntax, example call, includes, common uses, returns, comments, cautions and pitfalls, and cross-reference for that function. Unique compatibility check boxes show portability with Microsoft C versions 3.0, 4.0, and 5.0; Microsoft QuickC, and the UNIX System V compilers.

Topics covered include:

- Overview of the C Language
- Turbo C 1.0 Compiler Features and Options
- Process Control
- Variable-Length Argument Lists
- Memory Allocation and Management
- Buffer Manipulation
- Data Conversion Routines
- Math Routines
- Character Classification and Conversion
- String Comparison and Manipulation
- Searching and Sorting
- Time Routines
- File and Directory Manipulation
- Input and Output Routines
- System Calls
- Graphics Modes
- Drawing and Animation
- Combining Graphics and Text

950 Pages, 7½ x 9¾, Softbound
ISBN: 0-672-22631-6
No. 22631, $24.95

QuickC™ Programming for the IBM

Carl Townsend

This book is an entry-level tutorial for the beginning C programmer who desires to develop programs using the Microsoft® QuickC compiler. It will also acquaint the business professional or serious user with the basic aspects of programming in C.

The book includes hands-on interaction between the high-speed, low-cost compiler and the IBM® PC.

Topics covered include:

- Getting Started
- Representing Data
- Basic Input and Output
- Arithmetic Operations
- Program Control: IF, CASE, and Iteration Structures
- Using Functions and Macros
- Managing the Storage of Variables
- Arrays and Pointers
- Using Character Strings, Data Structures, Files and Other I/O, and Graphics
- Introduction to Structured Programming
- Developing Programs with QuickC
- Managing Databases with QuickC
- High-level Design: Menus
- Adding Database Records
- Editing and Deleting Records
- Reporting and Processing Programs

400 Pages, 7½ x 9¾, Softbound
ISBN: 0-672-22622-7
No. 22622, $22.95

Visit your local book retailer, use the order form provided, or call 800-428-SAMS.

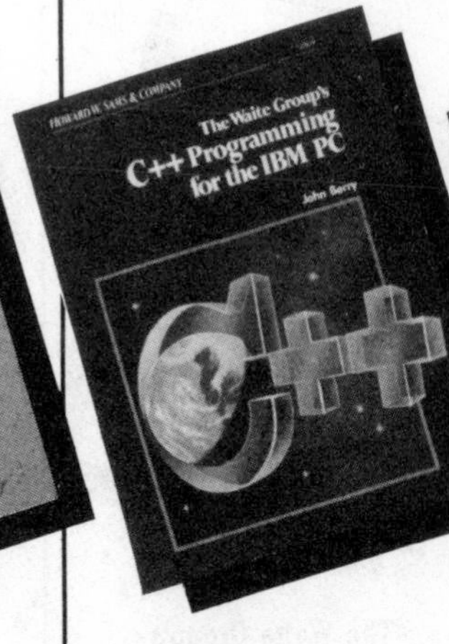

Understanding C

Carl Townsend

This is an entry-level tutorial providing the novice C programmer with a complete overview of the language in the MS-DOS® environment. Using the successful Understanding Series format which features key terms, marginal notes, and end-of-chapter questions and answers, the book can be used with the Turbo C or QuickC compilers as well as with other ANSI C compilers on the market.

Beginning with an overview of the language itself, the book then discusses file input and output, the basic concepts of program design, strategies for debugging a program, and preprocessor directives.

Topics covered include:

- The C Language
- C Data Types
- Arithmetic Operations and Expressions
- The User Interface: Input and Output
- Program Control: Conditional and Loop Structures
- Using Pointers
- Using Functions and Macros
- Managing Variable Storage
- Building Arrays
- Using Data Structure
- Files and Other Inputs and Outputs
- Using Graphics
- Using BIOS Services
- Structured Programming
- Appendices: Turbo C/QuickC Comparison, Glossary, ASCII Character Set, C Operators, C Data Types, C Keywords, Tips

288 Pages, 7 x 9, Softbound
ISBN: 0-672-27278-4
No. 27278, $17.95

C++ Programming Guide for the IBM®

John Berry and Mitchell Waite, The Waite Group

C++ Programming Guide for the IBM is a complete guide and tutorial to the C++ language specifically adapted to the IBM PC family.

Aimed at developers and students, it teaches the use of object-oriented programming skills and introduces the major features of the language with explanations followed by practical examples. It builds three professional libraries—cEntry, cGraphics, and cWindows—which enable programmers and developers to find shortcuts to the often cumbersome programming process.

Topics covered include:

- How the C++ Translator Works
- New C++ Syntax
- The C++ Stream h. Library
- The Inline Functions
- What the New C++ Pointers Offer
- Memory Allocation Functions
- Void Type Pointer to Generic Object
- New C++ Structured Data Type Versus the Old
- Private and Public Structures
- Hiding the Implementation
- Access by Non-member Functions
- Constructors and Destructors
- Overloading Functions and Operators

400 Pages, 7½ x 9¾, Softbound
ISBN: 0-672-22619-7
No. 22619, $24.95

Microsoft® C Bible

Nabajyoti Barkakati, The Waite Group

Microsoft C Bible provides a thorough description of the 370 functions of the Microsoft C library, complete with practical, real-world MS-DOS-based examples for each function. Library routines are broken down into functional categories with an intermediate-level tutorial followed by the functions and examples.

Included are two "quick-start" tutorials, complete ANSI prototypes for each function, extensive program examples, and handy jump tables to help enhance learning.

Topics covered include:

- Overview of the C Language
- Microsoft C 5.0 Compiler Features and Options
- Process Control
- Variable Length Argument Lists
- Memory Allocation and Management
- Buffer Manipulation
- Data Conversion Routines
- Math Routines
- Character Classification and Conversion
- String Comparison and Manipulation
- Searching and Sorting
- Time Routines
- File and Directory Manipulation
- Input and Output Routines
- System Calls
- Graphics Modes, Coordinates, and Attributes
- Drawing and Animation
- Combining Graphics and Text

824 Pages, 7½ x 9¾, Softbound
ISBN: 0-672-22620-0
No. 22620, $24.95

C Programmer's Guide to Microsoft® Windows 2.0

Carl Townsend

This intermediate-level programming guide shows the C programmer how t create applications under the Windows environment. Emphasizing the Microsc C compiler, a sample application is presented along with the rationale behind its development.

Written as a tutorial, the book shows the experienced programmer how to e ploit the extended features of Windows providing an alphabetical list of functions and an easy-to-use guide to thos extended features including printing, accelerators, and the GDI interface.

Topics covered include:

- Windows Overview
- The User Interface
- The Role of Messages
- The WinMain Program
- Managing Text with Windows
- Creating Menus and Using Dialog Boxes
- The Graphic Interface
- Windows, I/O, and Memory Management
- Creating and Managing Libraries
- Data Transfer
- Debugging Strategies
- Appendices: Installation, Message Boxes, Keyboard Interface, Functior Summary, Using Windows with Pa cal or Assembly Languages, Glossa

440 Pages, 7½ x 9¾, Softbound
ISBN: 0-672-22621-9
No. 22621, $24.95

Visit your local book retailer, use the order form provided, or call 800-428-SAMS.

Use this form to order sets of companion diskettes containing all the code in the *Turbo C Developer's Library*. The diskettes are 5¼″ floppies prepared for IBM-compatible personal computers running under DOS 2.0 or higher. The diskettes are formatted to 360KB per diskette.

The set of diskettes sells for $40 (U.S.), including shipping and handling, and may be purchased with check, money order, or credit card (Visa or MasterCard only). Checks and money orders should be made out to "Perpetual Data Systems." If you are using a credit card, be sure to include the account number, expiration date, and your signature.

Send this form with your payment to:

CDL Diskettes—Rought/Hoops
c/o Howard W. Sams & Company
Public Relations Department
4300 West 62nd Street
Indianapolis, IN 46268

Howard W. Sams & Company assumes no liability with respect to the use or accuracy of the information contained in these diskettes.

Diskette Order Form

Rought/Hoops, *Turbo C Developer's Library*, 22642

Name ______________________ Company ______________________

Address ____

City ______________________ State ________ Zip ________

Phone (______) ______-________ Date ______________

Place of Book Purchase ______________________________________

Number of sets ordered __________ @ $40 Order Total Amount: $__________

Check #__________ M.O. #__________ Visa __________ M/C __________

Credit Card Account # ______________________________________

Expiration Date ______________________________________

Signature ______________________________________

All orders will be shipped U.S. Postal Service First Class.